ENGLISH STUDIES ONLINE

ENGLISH STUDIES ONLINE

Programs, Practices, Possibilities

Edited by
William P. Banks and Susan Spangler

Parlor Press
Anderson, South Carolina
www.parlorpress.com

Parlor Press LLC, Anderson, South Carolina, USA

© 2021 by Parlor Press
All rights reserved.

Printed in the United States of America
S A N: 2 5 4 - 8 8 7 9

Library of Congress Cataloging-in-Publication Data on File

978-1-64317-261-3 (paperback)
978-1-64317-262-0 (hardcover)
978-1-64317-263-7 (pdf)
978-1-64317-264-4 (epub)

1 2 3 4 5

Book design by David Blakesley.
Cover photo by Thomas Charters on Unsplash.

Printed on acid-free paper.

Parlor Press, LLC is an independent publisher of scholarly and trade titles in print and multimedia formats. This book is available in paperback, hardcover, and eBook formats from Parlor Press on the World Wide Web at http://www.parlorpress.com or through online and brick-and-mortar bookstores. For submission information or to find out about Parlor Press publications, write to Parlor Press, 3015 Brackenberry Drive, Anderson, South Carolina, 29621, or email editor@parlorpress.com.

Contents

Acknowledgments   *vii*

1 Introduction: Moving English Studies Online   *1*
    William P. Banks and Susan Spangler

I Programs

2 Designing Online Programs for Student Engagement and Community Building: Three Programs at the University of Arkansas at Little Rock   *24*
    Heidi Skurat Harris, George Jensen, and Karen Kuralt

3 Lessons Learned: Navigating Online Teaching and Learning in English Studies   *40*
    Michele Griegel-McCord, Cynthia Nitz Ris, and Lisa Beckelhimer

4 Making Pedagogically Responsible Decisions in Online Course Programming   *60*
    John C. Havard, Lilian W. Mina, and Eric Sterling

5 It Takes a Village to Create Successful Online Composition Courses   *84*
    Elizabeth Burrows, Samantha McNeilly, and Matthew Kemp

II Practices

6 Teaching "Teaching Technologies in English Studies": Training a New Generation of Teachers   *106*
    Stephanie Hedge

7 Virtual Literature Circles: Re-Embodying Discussion in Online Literature Courses   *128*
    William P. Banks

8 Redesigning Assignment Sheets for Online Teaching: A Case Study in Universal Design and Multimodality   *142*
    Ashley J. Holmes

9 Experimental Research and Reflective Teaching Practice in Online Writing Instruction   *167*
    Joanne Addison

10 More Than Replication: Online Pedagogy Informing Face-to-Face Writing Instruction   *182*
    Michael Neal, Amy Cicchino, and Katelyn Stark

11 A Tale of Two Courses: Class Discussion Issues in English Studies Online   *201*
    Susan Spangler

III Possibilities

12 It's on the Syllabus: Notes from a Black Professor Teaching English Studies Online   *221*
    Cecilia D. Shelton

13 Expanding Instructional Contexts: Why Student Backgrounds Matter to Online Teaching and Learning   *232*
    Catrina Mitchum, Marcela Hebbard, and Janine Morris

14 Teaching Ethically Online: Using Universal Design for Learning and Predesigned Courses to Increase Accessibility   *258*
    Dev K. Bose and Rochelle Rodrigo

15 Performing Identities in Cyberspace: Imagining the Online Multicultural Learning Community   *282*
    Richard C. Taylor

16 Lessons from Journalism: Developing Online Programs for the Public Good   *304*
    Erin A. Frost

Contributors   *319*

Index   *327*

Acknowledgments

One of the joys of the edited collection is the opportunity that the editors and contributors have to collaborate with so many talented writers, teachers, and scholars whose expertise and experiences cross different institutional contexts and missions. This collection is no different, and we are grateful first of all to the wonderful contributors who trusted us as editors to understand, respect, and value their work. We hope that the finished versions of each chapter–and the manuscript as a whole–honors the commitments each contributor made to the overall project.

We came to the idea of this collection through our shared passion for teaching in online contexts, a passion that we have maintained through a friendship that began twenty years ago in graduate school. We were each drawn to Illinois State University's English department in large part because of its focus on English studies at the doctoral level, a recognition that the many disciplines that make up English studies can function to interanimate each other, and through doing so, provide a powerful way of understanding the impact that the humanities can continue to have in our world. What was harder to imagine then was just how much change the still emerging World Wide Web would have on teaching the different disciplines in our field. As English departments continue to redefine themselves, often as a result of external pressures around funding, student credit hour production, and career preparation, online education has emerged as a key vector around which so many of these conversations are happening. As teachers, we often still find ourselves in conversations with colleagues who do not believe that online spaces can be "real" learning spaces, and yet just as often, we hear of colleagues who are doing truly innovative and engaging things in their online classes. We felt it was time to collect some of those voices and to share their experiences building online programs and exploring new ways to teach English studies.

As we sent the resulting manuscript off to be considered for publication, the world began moving into a global lockdown because of COVID-19. By the time we heard from Parlor Press that they were interested in publishing the collection, it was clear that most of us would spend at least a year in our homes, teaching and learning online. For us, this is not an opportunistic collection; we did not rush to publish it because of the pandemic. But this past year has certainly reminded us that effective online instruction doesn't occur without careful planning and thought, without time and inquiry into high-impact teaching and learning practices. We are grateful that the authors who contributed to this collection showcase how difficult it can be to provide online students with a truly engaging educational experience, and we hope that the stories and examples they provide can be useful to readers as we emerge into "what's next" after COVID-19.

We are also extremely grateful to David Blakesley and the brilliant staff at Parlor Press for their encouragement and support for *English Studies Online*. Seeing the COVID-19 pandemic as a tipping point in online education, David embraced the opportunity to publish an entire collection devoted to teaching English studies in fully online and hybrid contexts, and he challenged us to make sure that the chapters we selected for inclusion represented a diverse and engaged set of writers, teaching contexts, and institutions. We are also thankful to Jared Jameson for his excellent work editing and indexing the manuscript, and to Matt Blakesley for creating the EPUB version of our manuscript.

WILL

In addition to those mentioned above, I first have to thank my co-editor and closest friend, Susan Spangler, who has been the driving force behind this collection. Susan's work ethic is unmatched, and whenever my administrator duties began to take over my life, Susan helped to ground me again with the parts of this project that also needed our attention. I am primarily a social/extroverted person, and I'm grateful for any chance to work closely with a collaborator who can help me to focus on the tasks at hand without making me feel bad for being distracted. Likewise, I'm grateful for the support of my department chair, Marianne Montgomery; for wonderful colleagues in the University Writing Program–Nikki Caswell, Kerri Flinchbaugh, Rebecca

Johnson, Rachel Winn, and Claudia Sadowski–who support and challenge me in equal measure; for great colleagues who care deeply about teaching and who are always eager to brainstorm and explore new ideas–Michelle Eble, Erin Frost, and Stephanie West-Puckett; and for dear and supportive friends like Shane Ernst and James Coker, who tolerate far more "work talk" at dinner parties and other get togethers than they should have to.

I am particularly grateful to my colleague, friend, co-teacher, and fellow thespian Rick Taylor. Rick has been one of my most constant teaching friends since I joined the faculty of ECU's English department in 2003, and I knew almost from the first day I met him that we shared a love of teaching and a commitment to students that would make us close. Early in my career, Rick welcomed me as a co-teacher in the London Study Abroad program he had developed, and that experience with a different type of "distance learning" has been one of the most sustaining of my career. But beyond that, Rick took to online teaching with a gusto when he first began to discover it in the early 2000s, and while I may have had more technological know-how under my belt as an online teacher, Rick reminded me that after all the bells and whistles, it is our compassion and care that makes online teaching, just like more traditional campus-based teaching, a meaningful experience for students. Rick remains one of my true pedagogical idols, and his chapter in our collection represents his swan song, his final piece of scholarly writing before retiring in summer 2021. I will miss our regular talks about teaching, books, theater, and family, but I remain grateful that his impact on my teaching, my scholarship, my career, and my life will continue across the miles that will soon separate us.

I remain equally grateful and humbled by the love and support of my family. Throughout the writing and editing process, Jackson provided more hugs and cuddles than I deserved. I'm also so thankful to Rey, who always found the space, despite their own grueling time commitments involved in writing novels, to help me and Susan plan our writing and editing days, organize our time, and stay on task when our teaching and administrative work tried to take over. And, finally, I'm especially thankful that so many hours of writing and editing at home are accompanied by—and sometimes appropriately interrupted by—the calming and supportive snoozles of great dogs.

Susan

I am grateful for the mentorship and support of my co-editor and closest friend, Will Banks, without whom this collection would not have been completed. His expertise in English studies, online teaching, and publishing allowed the process to run smoothly from the call for proposals to the final proofing, and I appreciate the patience he showed and the guidance he gave at every stage of writing and production. I value his counsel, whether about the profession or life in general, and I could not ask for a better colleague and fellow-traveler for this journey.

I also want to thank the people at Fredonia who have been supportive of online learning and teaching from the start: Barb Mallette, who took time out of her summer to tutor me on designing my first online course many years ago; and Lisa Melohusky, whose steady leadership at the helm of the Committee of Online Learning (COOL) made me want to continue teaching online. I am also grateful to Dawn Eckenrode in the Professional Development Center for giving me space to share my expertise with others and validating my efforts in online teaching. My friend and mentor, KimMarie Cole, has also been instrumental throughout my career at Fredonia; her support and advice on my teaching and scholarship has been invaluable through the years.

And of course my success is also due to the support of my family: Rey, Jackson, and Will. Each offered gentle prodding, cuddles, and good-natured ribbing in turn, with the firm foundation of unconditional love underneath. I could not have written these pages of my life without them.

1 Introduction: Moving English Studies Online

William P. Banks and Susan Spangler

In an age of ubiquitous computing and internet access, colleges and universities have been called upon to reimagine the work of teaching and learning. Where they once moved among small dormitory rooms, stuffy classrooms, and cold libraries on walking campuses, students now learn across all disciplines from a variety of locations. These online learning spaces, while often welcomed by administrators who wonder where to house or teach the ever-increasing numbers of students enrolled in community colleges and four-year schools, are sometimes met by faculty with suspicion, asking questions like, how can we replicate what we do in face-to-face environments on digital platforms? Will going online with our courses or programs mean the end of face-to-face (F2F) teaching and learning? How do we balance the need for both F2F and online learning spaces? In conversations with colleagues, we often hear these questions as laments for what feels to them like a real loss of something, perhaps the very reason some of them went into teaching as a profession. Yet for most of us who teach online with any regularity, these sorts of questions serve as distractions from the more interesting questions we might ask, questions focused on the types of unique educational experiences that digital spaces afford students and teachers alike, as well as questions focused on how online learning spaces might serve to open up and democratize higher education—or at the very least provide access to many students whose lives have prevented them from matriculating on a brick-and-mortar campus for four years.

While many of us who teach online have done so with open arms, excited to explore new ways of teaching and reaching students, we also recognize that for just as many faculty in English studies departments, the shift to online teaching has been a difficult one, with faculty and department-level administrators trying to imagine how they could replicate their in-person discussions of various texts in digital environments where attention may be fragmented and asynchronous. The face-to-face model that many of us carry in our heads features a dynamic, back-and-forth conversation among students and teachers. Sure, some of us complain about the occasional quiet classroom or the lack of engagement from particular students, but the overriding image we still think of as "teaching" is often one replete with robust conversation and a free-flowing exchange of ideas. Yet even a casual discussion with college faculty throughout the humanities will typically reveal that these imagined discussions are rare; too often, faculty find themselves engaging the same small subset of vocally participating students, while others listen and engage in far more silent ways.

Even for those teachers who do not practice the Socratic seminar style of discussion, there may still be an alluring image of meaning-making activity: students acting out scenes from a Shakespeare play, for example, or chattering away during peer review about the strengths and weaknesses of a paper. Then there are the important informal conversations that happen before or after class that seem to build connections among students and perhaps aid in developing trust that can be essential to sharing and discussing difficult ideas. In these moments, it can be easy for us as teachers to see the forest and not the trees: to see the presumed success of the large group, fully engaged, and miss all the students who sit quietly around the edges, or who participate in peer review but do not say anything beyond what they write in the margins of their peers' papers. And it can be easy not to realize that some students are always ill or called in to work on days when we have planned performances or other activities that require them to be "on stage" in the classroom. Stock images of deeply engaged learners is one that we have heard invoked repeatedly by our colleagues who resist movement into online spaces. Yet, despite what many have seen—and still see—as significant challenges posed by online/web-based coursework, large numbers of faculty in the humanities are moving their courses and degree programs into online spaces to engage the diverse audiences that have always found it difficult to take four to six years out of their lives to be full-time college students.

This collection seeks to intervene in current conversations around online pedagogy and teaching by asking how English studies practitioners are rethinking their teaching practices, course designs, and degree programs in ways that can deepen our understanding of what we may already know about online learning and effective digital pedagogies. In this introduction to the collection, we seek to highlight some of what we have already discovered and to demonstrate why the large-scale, theoretical visions that have often permeated early work in this field require more sustained attention at the local level of the classroom, assignment, and individual program.

What We Talk about When We Talk about Online Learning

To date, the vast majority of scholarship related to teaching English studies in online and/or digital environments has emerged in two areas, namely studies of digital learning in K–12 environments and studies of writing courses/online writing instruction in higher education settings. This phenomenon is not necessarily surprising to us as a number of forces beyond teachers themselves worked throughout the end of the twentieth century to make computers ubiquitous in both K–12 and higher education, while similar forces worked to fund and support the expansion of networked and globally connected computers for learners across their academic lifespans (Selfe 1999; Hawisher et al. 1996). Having ourselves taught in high schools, community colleges, and four-year universities starting in the 1980s, we have watched this shift occur and were generally persuaded by the pragmatic arguments being made at the time. If the future of writing were going to happen on computers, first through word processing programs and more recently through various networked platforms, it made sense to us that so many schools were transforming their typing courses into keyboarding courses and their first-year writing courses at college into computer-mediated writing classrooms. In fact, many of us who were early adopters of networked computer technologies were eager to try our hand at teaching writing in connected classrooms. As such, for those who taught primarily writing courses in higher education, as well as those teachers who early on saw digital literacies as key twenty-first-century skills, early adoption led to a host of research around key issues in teaching English studies in digital environments. In fact, this over-representation in writing studies is visible in our collection, though the writers here also make connections between their writing classrooms and other areas of English studies.

Writing studies, in particular, often led this charge. Major figures like Charles Moran, Hugh Burns, Cynthia Selfe, Gail Hawisher, Richard Lanham, and Anne Herrington wrote compellingly about the changes that computers were and still could bring to Writing studies and to literacy more generally, and their work established a subfield in the 1980s that would simultaneously produce a major research journal, *Computers and Composition*, and a major conference, Computers and Writing. That journal and conference became the core spaces for studying the interconnectedness of writing and digital tools, so when networked computers and computer labs on college campuses became increasingly common in the 1990s and early 2000s, there were already scholar-teachers hard at work trying to understand how writing happened in these contexts and, then, how to teach writing in these contexts. These same scholar-teachers were also prepared as the World Wide Web and other digital networks became commonplace in the early twenty-first century to carry their study of digital writing practices into this emerging context, whether they did so by studying hybrid courses that met face-to-face and supplemented instruction through online activities, or whether they were innovating higher education by promoting some of the earliest fully online courses.

Therefore, it is no surprise that this group has led scholarly efforts both to study online teaching and learning in English studies and to engage that work. Key to this effort, as several contributors to this collection note, has been the development of "A Position Statement of Principles and Best Practices for Online Writing Instruction (OWI)" by the Conference on College Composition and Communication. Begun in 2007 and finalized in 2013, this set of fifteen principles and practices "reveals a blueprint for further investigation into OWI"; the authors of the document also note that

> Addressing OWI is complex and challenging, particularly given the vast array of learner settings, needs, circumstances, contexts, and other factors. Fundamentally, however, educators must acknowledge that OWI is not a panacea for any failures in writing instruction more generally. Rather, OWI provides an opportunity for teaching various student populations in a distinctive instructional setting. As educators, it is our responsibility to be frank in our discussions about the realistic limitations of our work with students, and this doc-

ument is designed to provide a clear entry point into those types of conversations about OWI.

Many of these fifteen principles show up either directly or indirectly referenced in the chapters in this collection as they name key values and/or outcomes that those of us teaching in online environments have come to embrace:

- OWI Principle 1: Online writing instruction should be universally inclusive and accessible.
- OWI Principle 2: An online writing course should focus on writing and not on technology orientation or teaching students how to use learning and other technologies.
- OWI Principle 3: Appropriate composition teaching/learning strategies should be developed for the unique features of the online instructional environment.
- OWI Principle 4: Appropriate onsite composition theories, pedagogies, and strategies should be migrated and adapted to the online instructional environment.
- OWI Principle 5: Online writing teachers should retain reasonable control over their own content and/or techniques for conveying, teaching, and assessing their students' writing in their OWCs.
- OWI Principle 6: Alternative, self-paced, or experimental OWI models should be subject to the same principles of pedagogical soundness, teacher/designer preparation, and oversight detailed in this document.
- OWI Principle 7: Writing Program Administrators (WPAs) for OWI programs and their online writing teachers should receive appropriate OWI-focused training, professional development, and assessment for evaluation and promotion purposes.
- OWI Principle 8: Online writing teachers should receive fair and equitable compensation for their work.
- OWI Principle 9: OWCs should be capped responsibly at 20 students per course with 15 being a preferable number.
- OWI Principle 10: Students should be prepared by the institution and their teachers for the unique technological and pedagogical components of OWI.

- OWI Principle 11: Online writing teachers and their institutions should develop personalized and interpersonal online communities to foster student success.
- OWI Principle 12: Institutions should foster teacher satisfaction in online writing courses as rigorously as they do for student and programmatic success.
- OWI Principle 13: OWI students should be provided support components through online/digital media as a primary resource; they should have access to onsite support
- OWI Principle 14: Online writing lab administrators and tutors should undergo selection, training, and ongoing professional development activities that match the environment in which they will work.
- OWI Principle 15: OWI/OWL administrators and teachers/tutors should be committed to ongoing research into their programs and courses as well as the very principles in this document. (OWI)

CCCC also provides extensive justification for each of these principles, as well as examples of these principles in action on their website. More recently, Beth L. Hewett and Kevin Eric DePew (2015) published *Foundational Practices of Online Writing Instruction*, which serves as a key text for unpacking the OWI principles and demonstrating how they work in the contexts of specific classrooms and teacher experiences. However, despite the recentness of its publication, Hewett and Scott Warnock note in their concluding chapter to *Foundational Practices* that these principles as they have been enacted and represented throughout that collection and elsewhere still address primarily writing instruction in hybrid environments, not in fully online courses and programs (547–48). Many of the writers included in *English Studies Online* seek to address this gap in current scholarship by demonstrating where our current OWI principles do and do not work in the fully online writing course, while others seek to connect the OWI principles to other areas of English studies.

A similar conundrum exists throughout most of the work that has been generated from and for our English studies colleagues in K–12 contexts. While a number of fully online K–12 schools have emerged in the last decade, these schools are more often specialized in some way, typically by the population they serve or by the supplementary function they serve: to offer additional coursework for Advanced

Placement or to offer remediation to students who are struggling in face-to-face settings or perhaps to provide courses that might not be offered at smaller public schools in remote areas. For example, North Carolina offers the North Carolina Virtual Public School (https://ncvps.org) as an online supplement to students enrolled in traditional public schools throughout NC, although the state now also offers a couple of fully online public charter academies that have been authorized by the North Carolina Department of Public Instruction.

While these sorts of online K–12 options have proliferated across the country, the vast majority of scholarship related to K–12 English studies in digital environments remains focused on a hybrid model where face-to-face teachers supplement their instruction with various online platforms and projects. And even that work remains primarily focused on writing instruction rather than on the full breadth of English studies. For example, one of the most prominent voices in both K–12 and college-level digital pedagogies is Troy Hicks, who to date has authored or co-authored around ten books on teaching writing in online environments. Hicks is often a speaker at state and national English teacher conferences, and perhaps because of his work with the National Writing Project, K–12 teachers are particularly fond of his books. But from *The Digital Writing Workshop* (2009) to *Crafting Digital Writing* (2013) to *From Texting to Teaching* (2017), the majority of this work has been about technologies for writing, many of which become dated with the technologies themselves. Despite its being a revolutionary text for K–12 teachers, *The Digital Writing Workshop* already needs a major overhaul in terms of the technologies and tools that Hicks discusses—the speed of digital tool development and change naturally requires constant revision. Of note, in *Argument in the Real World: Teaching Adolescents to Read and Write Digital Texts*, Kristen Hawley Turner and Troy Hicks (2016) focus on the reading-writing connection, although they do so, again, primarily in the context of a hybrid pedagogy. Similarly, important texts like Serafini's *Reading Workshop 2.0* (2015) and Ziemke and Muhtaris's *Read the World: Rethinking Literacy for Empathy and Action in a Digital World* (2019) take up online/digital contexts only as spaces for understanding how society has changed, not as spaces for teaching and learning as such.

So beyond a wealth of ideas on how to teach writing, there remains very little to be found for the English studies teacher when it comes time to figure out how to design an online course, how to connect with and engage students in online environments, or how to develop a whole program for an exclusively online context. Certainly, there is a wealth of general how-to books on teaching online (Ko and Rossen 2017; Vai and Sosulski 2011; Nilsen and Ludwika 2019; Collison 2000), and some even from reputable scholarly publishers, but none of these engage an English studies context specifically. With this book, we hope to initiate a conversation that has been lacking for some time, in higher education in particular. To our minds, online contexts are often the perfect spaces to engage students in deep and thoughtful reading, thinking, and composing practices, and as such, we're surprised that more of our colleagues are not making the shift to teaching in online spaces beyond first-year writing courses. Or rather, if they have, they are not yet being encouraged to write about, theorize, and research those experiences.

What Still Needs Our (Pedagogical) Attention?

Despite the significant work noted above, what we often find while working with our own colleagues—and what several of the contributors this collection note as well—is that the more abstract or large-picture work on digital contexts and pedagogies have not always engaged an English studies context specifically, where faculty who teach literature, writing, and language can see demonstrated the connections that are important for making the humanities, and especially the digital humanities, a pedagogically sophisticated project. What might such a move look like, and why might college and university English departments benefit from engaging in a more critical digital pedagogy? In addition to the models and frameworks that the contributors to this collection provide, we would like to suggest a number of critical interventions that English studies can make by engaging more fully with teaching in online spaces.

First, the focus across English studies on the intersections of language and culture seems particularly important as higher education institutions move courses and programs into online spaces. For example, despite early assumptions that online spaces could "free" us from our bodies and remove issues of race, gender, sexuality, and class (Turkle 1995), research in computers and writing has continually demonstrated that online spaces can be just as violent or uncomfortable for marked bodies as face-to-face spaces (Benjamin 2019; Gonzales 2018; Noble 2018; Medina and Pimentel 2018; Wernimont and Losh 2018; O'Neil 2017). We would argue that we need continually to be engaged in research into how a diverse student body is shaping and is shaped by language and texts. One space for better understanding these issues is by studying the work we do in online learning environments and letting that work challenge assumptions that have become tacit in our face-to-face pedagogies. We see promising work emerging to address this sort of backward-facing critique, like Neal et al.'s recognition in this collection that online pedagogy can critically inform face-to-face pedagogy. Likewise, with the proliferation of low-residency creative writing programs, which often involve hybrid approaches that use online spaces for continuity between residency sessions, we have space to investigate what happens when the traditional writing workshop, popularized by the Iowa Writers Workshop, goes online.

Similarly, because we know that English studies pedagogies tend to value writing and discussion and a host of other interactive practices, we believe that scholar-teachers across our disciplines are poised to rethink what online learning spaces can do and how they can function. Many students can sit quietly in face-to-face classrooms without seeming to demonstrate active engagement in discussions, and while sometimes this silence indicates thoughtful and engaged processing of new information, for many teachers, when students do not jump in and contribute to a conversation that is moving quickly, it can seem as though students are not paying attention. Other times, we may accuse them of not reading the assigned material. In online contexts, it is more difficult for students to get through without producing texts—discussion board posts, peer reviews, blog posts, or other forums that show evidence of student engagement. These texts make visible how and where students are contributing, and they allow teachers to connect with each student. As such, they may offer a more detailed and nuanced understanding of what types of learning are and are not happening in our courses. Similarly, while being called on by a teacher in a seated classroom can feel like being "called out" to some students, who are then put on the spot to perform in that moment, those of us who teach online tend to value these primarily asynchronous spaces for how they allow students to join the conversation when they are ready. Perhaps students get time to rehearse their thoughts and revise what they wanted to contribute, where the seated classroom can sometimes move on from a topic before all students have formulated their ideas to contribute. Similarly, as we often talk about difficult subjects and ideas that are brought up in the texts we read together, students in seated classrooms can worry that if they contribute their first thoughts, they will misspeak and say something they did not necessarily intend, which may lead them to choose not to speak at all. For so many students, impromptu classroom performances feel forced and inauthentic, or rushed and anxiety-producing, and they tend to favor more extroverted styles of engagement. While there is much to be said for learning to "think on our feet," students may benefit just as much from learning in contexts where they have time to think carefully and clearly.

At the more local level of individual courses and activities, where English studies faculty study texts and composing processes, we are poised to consider how these objects and activities change in online spaces and with different digital tools. Numerous online composing platforms, from open-source Wikis and blogging technologies to Google Docs, provide easy access to drafts through versioning. As each new draft is auto-saved, many of these platforms maintain a history of document revisions and changes so that students and teachers can track the compositional processes more carefully than they can in face-to-face classes, where often all we see are one or two drafts and a final product for evaluation. Rather than study writing practices exclusively in the first-year writing classroom, online contexts make similar study a viable opportunity for faculty across English studies. Given the current promotion across many campuses to engage in the Scholarship of Teaching and Learning (SoTL), online courses provide a rich context for us to contribute to that larger educational project. Similarly, when we look for and teach with technologies that match and/or amplify our pedagogies, we position ourselves to disrupt the "training" models that can too often permeate online learning across our campuses. To us, this is a contribution that English studies faculty can make to the larger project of online learning design.

To this end, we believe that English studies faculty are also positioned effectively to critique the types of digital tools that currently dominate online learning in higher education. As for-profit educational retailers like University of Phoenix and Walden University were often some of the first accredited programs to go fully online, the needs and interest of these groups have often dominated learning management system (LMS) development. Similarly, on many of our own campuses, some of the first programs to move into online spaces have been those in pre-professional schools (e.g., education, social work) or those that are attractive to large numbers of already-employed students (e.g., business, nursing). Across these spaces, corporatized models of "training" often dominate as a key educational goal, which involves mastering discrete concepts or legal/professional policies that impact work on a daily basis. Training toward specific tasks or projects often asks not for a critical pedagogy centered on exploration, but for a model where mastery is the overriding outcome. As such, while many of the ideas central to online learning pedagogies involve modular frameworks for moving students through predetermined pathways—a useful security blanket of sorts in a context where the teacher is not physically present and available for quick follow-up questions—teachers in English studies tend to value frameworks based less around training than those based around pedagogical models that engage open inquiry and discussion, as well as synthesis of concepts across texts, in order to build sophisticated arguments in writing. Yet the digital learning platforms that we most often encounter on our campuses, secured by six- and seven-figure contracts, tend toward quickly-graded tools like quizzes and tests, and on the uploading of discrete projects read and evaluated only by the instructor. Even more nefarious, they often come bundled with ethically dubious tools like plagiarism detection services (e.g., TurnItIn, SafeAssign) and "grammar" checkers. While these grammar checkers have gotten more sophisticated over time, they are still as often wrong as they are right when they mark more sophisticated sentences and paragraph structures as incorrect or questionable, which, as April Baker-Bell (2020) has noted in *Linguistic Justice: Black Language, Literacy, Identity, and Pedagogy,* can enact racist language practices that can seriously harm Black students (21). As language scholars, we are prepared to help our campuses to think through purchasing these tools, and once purchased, to help our colleagues in other departments not to misuse or abuse them (Donnelly et al. 2013).

Beginning the Conversation: An Overview

English Studies Online: Programs, Practices, Possibilities brings together contributions from college and university faculty across many of the different disciplines in English who have transitioned from the brick-and-mortar classroom to web-based instructional experiences. As a collection of essays by established teacher-scholars in English studies, this book offers critical commentary on the programs (majors, minors, certificates) that have been developed in English studies, as well as the creation of individual courses within online programs or as an element of a more traditional face-to-face program of study. Ultimately, these chapters explore the programs and classroom practices that can help faculty across English studies to think carefully and critically about the changes that online education affords us, the rich possibilities that such courses and programs afford, and the potential challenges they can introduce into our department and college ecologies. By highlighting both innovative pedagogies and hybrid methods, the authors in our collection demonstrate how we might engage these changes more productively.

Divided into three interrelated conversations—practices, programs, and possibilities—the essays in this collection demonstrate some of the innovative pedagogical work going on in English departments around the United States to highlight how both hybrid and fully online programs in English studies can help us to more meaningfully and purposefully enact the values of a liberal arts education. We see this collection as both a cautionary history of teaching practices and programs that have developed in English studies, and a space to support faculty and administrators in making the case for why and how humanities disciplines like English can be important contributors to digital teaching and learning.

In the Programs section, our authors discuss how their online English studies programs were created and the changes they have undergone since implementation. They reflect on what programmatic assessments have revealed about their programs and the evolving needs of students, faculty, and disciplines. These chapters offer ideas that faculty and administrators should consider in developing online programs and they explore the elements that may need to be put in place before designing such programs.

In "Designing Online Programs for Student Engagement and Community Building: Three Programs at the University of Arkansas at Little Rock," Heidi Skurat Harris, George Jensen, and Karen Kuralt recount how their department built their online programs in multiple ways: UALR's online BA and MA degree programs in professional and technical writing evolved over time, but its graduate certificate program in online writing instruction was designed and launched as a fully online program, which allowed them to create from scratch rather than trying to replicate an existing program in an online context. Drawing on the experiences of growing, building, teaching in, assessing, and revising these programs, the authors discuss what their experience and funded research has shown them about creating successful online programs, from the institutional conditions to the student experience. This chapter shares insights that may help program administrators prepare for moving courses and programs online, as well as to help departments develop robust online English studies programs, whether they evolve over time or are intentionally created as online programs from the start.

The idea of evolution factors into "Lessons Learned: Navigating Online Teaching and Learning in English Studies," by Michele Griegel-McCord, Cynthia Nitz Ris, and Lisa Beckelhimer, three early adopters who were compelled to find their own way in the world of online learning, seek out professional development and guidance from a variety of sources, develop their own community of practice, and advocate for changes in practices and policies surrounding online learning. Since beginning to teach online, these authors' roles as teachers have evolved into administrative ones that have provided them with multiple perspectives on and approaches to creating, teaching, and supporting online courses in English studies. The authors identify the lessons that emerged from those disparate perspectives and describe a combination of familiar and reconceptualized expectations, supports, and resources they have curated. This "familiar and reconceptualized" concept explains how some approach online teaching, as a way to replicate what happens in face-to-face courses, but these authors (as well as Neal et al. in section 2) reveal that online teaching requires innovations and making connections within the department and college as well as the university in order to move the academic culture and discipline forward.

Similarly, in "Making Pedagogically Responsible Decision in Online Course Programming," John Havard, Lilian Mina, and Eric Sterling discuss their roles from their various administrative positions at Auburn University at Montgomery (AUM). As department chair, composition director, and director of the Master of Liberal Arts program, they each have unique opportunities to influence online programming offered at AUM. Here, the authors discuss department-level initiatives in online learning, professional development for faculty teaching online in first-year composition, and online programming efforts in a graduate program. While each administrative position caters to specific program needs, the authors have united to discover an effective pattern to the decision-making process for creating pedagogically responsible programs.

Section 1 ends with "It Takes a Village to Create Successful Online Composition Classes," where authors Elizabeth Burrows, Samantha McNeilly, and Matthew Kemp advocate replicating face-to-face pedagogy, but only through intentionally reconceptualizing highly authentic, interactive, and collaborative spaces that mimic the best interaction and communication patterns of face-to-face courses in digital spaces. The chapter recounts the collaboration across multiple units on campus and the rich, multi-layered communication among students, instructors, librarians, tutors, and other campus parties necessary to design and deliver an online composition course that capitalized on online formats. Enhancing the connection between writing in digital environments and writing in the academy, students learn skills that transfer to the university at large as well as the workplace. This chapter complicates Ris et al.'s "Lessons Learned" and provides an alternative viewpoint to Neal et al.'s "More Than Replication" in the next section.

The chapters in the Practices section offer specific teaching strategies for maximizing the online learning environment in English studies courses. Here, the writers focus on effectively adjusting our teaching practices from face-to-face environments and on developing new pedagogical practices specifically for fully online courses, as well as on mentoring and modeling for students' current best practices in teaching online.

In "Teaching 'Teaching Technologies in English Studies': Training a New Generation of Teachers," Stephanie Hedge describes a unique course in the digital pedagogy track for the English studies MA at the University of Illinois Springfield. The course prepares graduates to teach in both fully online spaces and face-to-face courses supported with technology, providing both theoretical grounding and practical experiences in teaching online. Hedge also demonstrates how we can better support future English studies teachers in considering the complexities of student/teacher bodies and identities that are mediated by technologies, testing the boundaries of traditional literacies and pedagogical strategies in emergent digital spaces, and grappling with the challenges of adhering to traditional expectations of literacy in a increasingly digital and connected world. In the academic reality that many graduates face today—that of teaching online—this course adds to their ability to do so effectively and to talk about it in applications and interviews effectively, adding to their employability as teachers.

Ashley Holmes examines the disconnect between what many teachers ask of students in their writing and what they model as writers themselves in "Redesigning Assignment Sheets for Online Teaching: A Case Study in Universal Design and Multimodality." Holmes discusses the evolution of an assignment sheet from a course she taught as it transitioned from face-to-face to hybrid to a fully online mode of instruction. Using herself and her teaching as a case example, she analyzes the revisions she made to reconceptualize a traditional, text-heavy assignment sheet to formats more conducive to online instruction and more reflective of the kinds of texts she asked students to write. The revision process compelled Holmes to consider audience needs in terms of multimodality and interactivity as well as accessibility. Holmes highlights best practices in designing assignment sheets for online courses while also considering the responsibilities we have to model and the kinds of texts we expect from students in the rhetorical design and genre performance of our assignment sheets.

Several authors (Addison, and Neal et al. among them) in this collection discuss the reluctance among some colleagues and administrators to accept the legitimacy and value of online education. Susan Spangler responds to this skepticism about the effectiveness of teaching online in "A Tale of Two Courses: Class Discussion Issues in English Studies Online." Using examples from a graphic literature course and a rhetoric course, Spangler dispels the pervasive myth of democratic and dynamic classroom discussion in face-to-face classrooms and demonstrates how engagement and interaction between students can be intentionally fostered even more dynamically in digital platforms. Exploring similar issues in "Virtual Literature Circles: Re-Embodying Discussion in Online Literature Courses," William P. Banks explores a model for engaging with synchronous discussion in online classes while avoiding some of the problems that live, whole class discussions can create. Through his reimagination of the traditional "lit circle," Banks finds a middle ground with synchronous discussions that feature student choice and flexibility as key leverage points for student interactivity and learning.

Joanne Addison takes a broader approach to effective online teaching practices in "Experimental Research and Reflective Teaching Practice in Online Writing Instruction." Drawing inspiration from George Hillocks's caution to teachers of English that "[s]ome practices and approaches [to teaching] are clearly better than others and we had better not ignore the differences," Addison argues that English studies needs to articulate what counts as effective teaching in digital environments so we can better convey the value of online education to others. To do so, Addison reviews research in the practices of teaching English online and ultimately maintains that without empirical data, we are more likely to make decisions about what classes move online out of economic necessity than out of pedagogical or ethical choices that benefit students and faculty, as well as our academic disciplines.

Michael Neal, Amy Cicchino, and Katelyn Stark also question the definition of effective teaching in online courses, but rather than argue for a particular kind of practice, these authors challenge the assumption that ideal standards for English course pedagogies simply mirror face-to-face practices and standards for teaching. In "More Than Replication: Online Pedagogy Informing Face-to-Face Writing Instruction," the authors reimagine three face-to-face practices (homespaces, class discussions, and workshopping) in light of their online writing instruction experiences, and they discuss how their online instruction at first moved starkly away from but then later informed their face-to-face instructional strategies.

In the final section, Possibilities, contributors reflect on critical theories that inform online teaching and learning in English studies courses at the programmatic, departmental, or college level. They explore key issues related to designing and implementing sustainable and scalable programs, courses, and pedagogical practices.

The first chapter in this section asks us to reconsider how we understand the most ubiquitous of pedagogical genres: the syllabus. In "It's on the Syllabus: Notes from a Black Professor Teaching English Studies Online," Cecilia Shelton reflects on how the course syllabus works to frame the course to students, and as such, it should be "oriented to inclusion, equity, and justice." When we move our courses online, it is particularly important that we reconsider just how we frame the course and our bodies as teachers. Turning our attention back to students, Catrina Mitchum, Marcela Hebbard, and Janine Morris discuss the results from a two-year, cross-institutional investigation in "Expanding Instructional Contexts: Why Student Backgrounds Matter to Online Teaching and Learning." The authors reveal why understanding four key dimensions of student backgrounds and expectations for online education in the early stages of planning online curriculum can broaden the potential for online program success.

Attempting to meet students' expectations and needs in online learning can be challenging, and in "Teaching Ethically Online: Using Universal Design for Learning and Predesigned Courses to Increase Accessibility," Dev K. Bose and Rochelle Rodrigo offer the use of predesigned courses (PDCs) and universal design as possibilities for meeting those expectations. They highlight the ethics of designing and teaching accessible courses while also emphasizing fairness and equity in labor issues, a balance that is easily upset because of the typically high number of contingent faculty teaching in first-year writing courses. The authors discuss theories and practices of universal design and how predesigned courses can capitalize on them, and they acknowledge the concerns institutions and programs may have with using PDCs. Their experiences will help administrators and faculty in other programs understand how institutions can advance social justice issues by implementing ethically developed online education for all students.

Erin Frost is also invested in social justice issues, and she discusses how journalism can inform the relationship between English studies and online learning. In "Lessons from Journalism: Developing Online Programs for the Public Good," Frost draws on feminist, decolonial, and queer frameworks to analyze how online English studies programs can support marginalized and underrepresented groups and foster situations in which these students can better their lives. This responsible model of education for which Frost advocates can be innovative and progressive, but only if teachers commit to looking beyond the tools and technologies that bombard them in typical discussions of online education; they must engage in examining deeper pedagogical theories that underpin teaching for social justice.

In the final chapter of the collection, "Performing Identities in Cyberspace: Imagining the Online Multicultural Learning Community," Richard Taylor approaches the building of fully online English studies programs from a different stance. Instead of speaking specifically to various technical tools/platforms or different practices for engaging students and managing the nuts and bolts of online course loads,

Taylor examines the important "turns of identity" that are necessary for faculty, particularly literature faculty, to make in order to imagine themselves into an online program. Taylor discusses the process through which he formed the foundational belief that the fusion of multiethnic literatures as a subject and distance education as a primary means of disseminating that subject represent the important and justice-oriented possibilities for the immediate future of English studies.

What will be clear to readers of this collection as they move through the various chapters is the deep commitments that many English studies scholar-teachers have to a democratic and engaged model of education, one that increasingly embraces online contexts where ubiquitous computer technologies are opening avenues for students who would have been unable to participate in higher education in previous decades. While digital contexts do not provide a panacea for addressing all the problems of higher education, and while these spaces do not necessarily provide fully equitable access to all learners, we have seen a dramatic increase in the types of students for whom online education becomes a genuine opportunity for growth and advancement. From the older student returning to college to prepare for a different career to the student who cannot afford to leave home at eighteen to be resident on a college campuses, from the high school teacher who continues to teach while earning a master's degree to the stay-at-home parent who plans to return to the workforce after rearing children—across a broad range of demographics and experiences, students are turning to our online programs for personal growth and career development. The writers in this collection showcase how our developing programs and practices are working to support different types of learners in unique and exciting learning environments, and they remind us of how important the humanities are to better understanding the work of digital learning spaces. In moving English studies online, we are excited to explore the innovative impact that the study of language, literature, and writing will continue to have in the twenty-first century.

Coda: English studies Online after COVID-19

We could not end this introduction to the collection at this particular moment in time without recognizing the significant impact that the COVID-19 pandemic has had on college campuses and particularly on online teaching and learning. The authors in this collection all drafted and revised their chapters before the United States went on lockdown in March 2020, and despite the havoc that quarantine visited on us all, they generously returned to their chapters in the summer of 2020 and revised to highlight moments where online teaching and learning in their departments had changed as a result of the pandemic. In some instances, the revisions to their chapters have been minor, while in others, the writers have noted significant take-aways from their experiences of the pandemic. This is not a collection focused on the pandemic and its impact—no doubt, many of those will appear soon—but what has become clear to us as the editors in reading and re-reading the chapters in this collection is that the teacher-scholars we include here make a fundamental distinction between online learning and what might more accurately be called "emergency remote teaching" (Hodge et al. 2020). The former, focused on learning and student engagement, names the sort of practices that effective online educators have been using for decades; as many of the writers in this collection note, effective online learning involves planning and careful consideration; it is not simply a speedy replication of what may be done as part of in-person classroom settings. Emergency remote teaching, on the other hand, is what many of us found ourselves neck-deep in toward the spring of 2020: courses that had begun on campus in traditional classrooms, taught in most cases by teachers with extensive teaching experience, suddenly pivoted to fully online environments. In this context, many otherwise effective teachers struggled to focus on learning and student experience; they were doing their best just to get materials online, often in a campus LMS they had never used, or only rarely as a supplement to their F2F instruction. Often, they were so busy trying to create documents from lecture notes and then to upload materials, they couldn't even begin to think about what access would look like for students who had been suddenly scattered to the winds. In such a context, *learning* became the hoped-for by-product of frenzied teaching.

While many faculty were frustrated and anxious, journalists were quick to pounce on the moment and offer their own hasty analyses of the situation; this was true of both the popular press and professional academic venues like InsideHigherEd.com and *The Chronicle*. Writing for the *New York Times* in May 2020, Hans Taparia declared that "COVID-19 is about to ravage [the] business model" common to contemporary higher education: "if universities embrace this moment strategically, online education could expand access exponentially and drop its cost by magnitudes—all while shoring up revenues for universities in a way that is more recession-proof, policy-proof and pandemic-proof." Certainly, one of the responses to the pandemic will be a rehashing of the once hoped-for MOOC-revolution, an uber-economical model where thousands of students are taught by one professor, and the money comes rolling in. When we read Taparia's framework, we see similar neoliberal notions of more-for-less in higher education, which sees online learning as somehow disembodied and mechanical. Sure, colleges need fewer residence halls if students are online, but that doesn't make classes "pandemic-proof": students still get sick during a pandemic, and what most teachers have found over the summer and fall months of 2020 is that students invariable are getting sick and then needing significant time off from school to recover; this problem has been made worse by students also needing to support their family members who may get ill, often taking on low-paying, at-risk jobs to help pay bills, all while still in school. Under these conditions, it's hard to develop effective teaching and learning situations. Higher ed, even online, is not "pandemic proof." The authors in this collection write generously about how much emotional, mental, and physical effort is required to support students both during a pandemic and before; this sort of humane labor is not something we can off-load or outsource when teaching moves online.

More critical of the whole experience have been writers like Peter Herman, professor of English literature at San Diego State University, whose "Online Learning Is Not the Future" article from InsideHigherEd.com ends with the declarative statement, "But online learning is not the future. Never was. Never will be. It's just not what students want." Herman's jeremiad throws darts at all the regular enemies of higher education—governors like former Florida governor Jeb Bush and New York's Andrew Cuomo, who called for a reimagining of higher education; billionaire philanthropists like Bill and Melinda Gates; and the obvious problem, neoliberalism—before focusing on all the things his students hated about the spring 2020 transition to emergency remote teaching: students were distracted, they felt like they were "teaching themselves," they missed the in-person conviviality of classrooms and the teachers' personalities, and ultimately, they found their days unstructured and unfocused. But of course, we would argue that what Herman is describing is not "online learning" at all, and certainly not the sort of online teaching and learning experiences that the writers in this collection value and enact through their online courses and programs. Ultimately, Herman frames his critique through a straw-person Student, unwilling or unable to recognize how many students value online learning over traditional campus-based settings for the myriad reasons that writers in this collection elucidate.

Pundits like Taparia and Herman sound similar to many of the colleagues we've interacted with over the majority of 2020 on our own campuses, and what we have learned is that most faculty in English studies seem to fall into one of three categories. One group has been legitimately traumatized by emergency remote teaching; having never given it much thought, they were simply unprepared for what it would be like, and they struggled to make the shift. This group may never again teach in an online context, and if we're fair, they probably have good reasons not to, though it will certainly fall on those of us who value online teaching and learning to help these colleagues see that their experience was not at all what English studies online can be under the right circumstances and for the right students. The second group didn't seem to find the shift all that difficult, perhaps because they already had some online teaching experiences, and they were encouraged by all the possibilities that teaching online could offer, particularly by fall 2020 when they had had some time to plan more effectively. The third group—and the set that this collection is most likely to speak to—are those who had been apprehensive before and who have not necessarily been reassured over the course of 2020, but who can see in their online courses new ways of doing things that simply had not occurred to them before or that they didn't have the time to experiment with.

We believe that readers who fall into this group will find kindred spirits among the writers included in *English Studies Online*, and we, too, are eager to welcome these colleagues to the difficult, complex, nuanced, and exciting work of online teaching and learning. This collection presents a host of innovative and exciting ideas for how to engage students across English studies in meaningful online learning experiences, and we hope that readers will find both reassurance that effective teaching practices can work across contexts and also gentle nudging to not simply try to transpose from one key to another, but to really dig into online contexts and explore their various affordances and constraints.

References

Arola, Kristin L. 2017. "Indigenous Interfaces" In *Social Writing/Social Media: Publics, Presentations, and Pedagogies*, edited by Douglas M. Walls and Stephanie Vie. *Perspectives on Writing.* Fort Collins, CO: The WAC Clearinghouse; Louisville, CO: University Press of Colorado. https://wac.colostate.edu/books/perspectives/social/.

Baker-Bell, April. 2020. *Linguistic Justice: Black Language, Literacy, Identity, and Pedagogy.* NCTE-Routledge Research Series. New York: Routledge.

Benjamin, Ruha. 2019. *Race After Technology: Abolitionist Tools for the New Jim Code.* Cambridge, UK; Medford, MA: Polity Press.

Boettcher, Judith V., and Rita-Marie Conrad. 2016. *The Online Teaching Survival Guide: Simple and Practical Pedagogical Tips.* 2nd edition. San Francisco: Jossey-Bass.

Collison, George, Bonnie Elbaum, Sarah Haavind, and Robert Tinker. 2000. *Facilitating Online Learning: Effective Strategies for Moderators.* Madison, WI: Atwood Publishing.

Conference on College Composition and Communication. 2020. "Establishing a Statement of Principles for Online Writing Instruction (OWI)." Accessed February 29, 2021. https://cccc.ncte.org/cccc/resources/positions/owiprinciples/establishing.

Deane, Mary, and Teresa Guasch. 2015. *Learning and Teaching Writing Online: Strategies for Success.* Leiden; Boston: Brill.

Donnelley, Michael, Rebecca Ingalls, Tracy Ann Morse, Joanna Castner Post, and Anne Meade Stockwell-Giesler, eds. 2013. *Critical Conversations about Plagiarism.* Anderson, SC: Parlor Press.

Goodwyn, Andrew, ed. 2000. *English in the Digital Age: Information and Communications Technology (ICT) and the Teaching of English.* London: Cassell.

Gonzales, Laura. 2018. *Sites of Translation: What Multilinguals can Teach Us about Digital Writing and Rhetoric.* Ann Arbor: University of Michigan Press.

Haas, Angela. 2018. "Toward a Digital Cultural Rhetoric." In *Routledge Handbook of Digital Writing & Rhetoric,* edited by Jonathan Alexander and Jaqueline Rhodes, 412–22. London: Routledge.

Hawisher, Gail E., Paul LeBlank, Charles Moran, and Cynthia L. Selfe. 1996. *Computers and the Teaching of Writing in American Higher Education, 1979–1994: A History.* Norwood, NJ: Ablex.

Hewett, Beth L., and Kevin E. DePew, eds. 2015. *Foundational Practices of Online Writing Instruction.* Anderson, SC: Parlor Press.

Hewett, Beth. L., and Scott Warnock. 2015. "The Future of OWI." In *Foundational Practices of Online Writing Instruction,* edited by Beth L. Hewett and Kevin E. DePew, 547–63. Anderson, SC: Parlor Press.

Hicks, Troy. 2009. *The Digital Writing Workshop.* Portsmouth, NH: Heinemann.

Hicks, Troy, and Christopher Lehman. 2013. *Crafting Digital Writing: Composing Texts across Media and Genres.* Portsmouth, NH: Heinemann.

Hodges, Charles, Stephanie Moore, Barb Lockee, Torrey Trust and Aaron Bond. 2020. "The Difference Between Emergency Remote Teaching and Online Learning." *Educause Review*. Accessed October 1, 2020. https://er.educause.edu/articles/2020/3/the-difference-between-emergency-remote-teaching-and-online-learning.

Hyler, Jeremy, and Troy Hicks. 2017. *From Texting to Teaching: Grammar Instruction in a Digital Age*. New York: Routledge.

Jody, Marilyn, and Marianne Saccardi. 1996. *Computer Conversations: Readers and Books Online*. Urbana, IL: National Council of Teachers of English.

Kayalis, Takis, and Anastasia Natsina, eds. 2010. *Teaching Literature at a Distance: Open, Online and Blended Learning*. London; New York: Continuum.

Ko, Susan, and Steve Rossen. 2017. *Teaching Online: A Practical Guide*. 4th Edition. New York: Routledge.

Medina, Cruz, and Octavio Pimentel, eds. 2018. *Racial Shorthand: Coded Discrimination Contested in Social Media*. Logan: Computers and Composition Digital Press; Utah State University Press.

Nilsen, Linda B., and Ludwika A. Goodson. 2019. *Online Teaching at Its Best: Merging Instructional Design with Teaching and Learning Research*. 1st edition. San Francisco: Jossey-Bass.

Noble, Safiya Umoja. 2018. *Algorithms of Oppression: How Search Engines Reinforce Racism*. New York: New York University Press.

O'Neil, Cathy. 2017. *Weapons of Math Destruction: How Big Data Increases Inequality and Threatens Democracy*. New York: Broadway Books.

Selfe, Cynthia L. 1999. *Technology and Literacy in the 21st Century: The Importance of Paying Attention*. Studies in Writing and Rhetoric. Carbondale, IL: Southern Illinois University Press.

Serafini, Frank. 2015. *Reading Workshop 2.0: Supporting Readers in the Digital Age*. Portsmouth, NH: Heinemann.

Turkle, Sherry. 1995. *Life on the Screen: Identity in the Age of the Internet*. New York: Touchstone.

Turney, Kristen Hawley, and Troy Hicks. 2016. *Argument in the Real World: Teaching Adolescents to Read and Write Digital Texts*. Portsmouth, NH: Heinemann.

Vai, Marjorie, and Kristen Sosulski. 2016. *Essentials of Online Course Design: A Standards-Based Guide*. 2nd edition. New York: Routledge.

Wernimont, Jacqueline, and Elizabeth Losh, eds. 2018. *Bodies of Information: Intersectional Feminism and Digital Humanities*. Debates in the Digital Humanities Series. Minneapolis: University of Minnesota Press.

Ziemke, Kristen, and Katie Muhtaris. 2019. *Read the World: Rethinking Literacy for Empathy and Action in a Digital World*. Portsmouth, NH: Heinemann.

2 Designing Online Programs for Student Engagement and Community Building: Three Programs at the University of Arkansas at Little Rock

Heidi Skurat Harris, George Jensen, and Karen Kuralt

Building effective online writing programs requires constant assessment and revision, regardless of whether programs develop gradually over time or are carefully and intentionally designed before they are launched. In the Department of Rhetoric and Writing at the University of Arkansas at Little Rock (UALR), we've developed programs both ways. Our online BA and MA programs in professional and technical writing evolved one course at a time with no overarching vision for online program design other than to preserve the qualities we valued in our already-existing face-to-face programs. In 2015, we launched a graduate certificate program in online writing instruction (GCOWI) that was designed to be online-only. The GCOWI began with intentional grounding in the Conference on College Composition and Communication's "A Position Statement of Principles and Effective Practices for Online Writing Instruction" (CCCC 2013). Even with that grounding, within two years of implementing the OWI certificate, we realized we needed to completely overhaul the curriculum to better meet the needs of students in the program.

In 2017, we received a College Conference on Composition and Communication Research Grant to collect longitudinal data that would help us evaluate how our online programs have evolved and how students were reacting to them. As part of this research, we collected survey data from current students and alumni, interviewed campus administrators and online faculty, and conducted focus groups with students and alumni. In this chapter, we discuss what this research has shown us about creating successful online programs, from the institutional conditions to the student experience. In the process, we share insights that may help other programs starting down this path, whether their circumstances lead them to build their programs one course at a time or fully online from the start.

"TRANSLATING" PROGRAMS FROM ON-CAMPUS TO ONLINE: THE BA AND MA PROGRAMS

Both the BA and the MA programs in professional and technical writing (PTW) were first on-campus programs. They were designed to provide in-depth instruction in a wide range of specialties, including academic writing, persuasive writing, technical writing, business communication, editing and publishing, and creative nonfiction.

THE MA IN PROFESSIONAL AND TECHNICAL WRITING

The MA program was actually created before the BA program while many of our department's faculty were still part of the English department. Originally called the MA in technical and expository writing (TEW), this program became part of the Department of Rhetoric and Writing in 1993 when UALR established one of the first independent writing programs in the country (Maid 2002). The name was eventually changed to the MA in professional and technical writing, partly for consistency with the later-established BA, and partly because "professional writing" was seen as more relatable for prospective students than "expository writing."

The initial focus of the program included preparing graduate students to teach college writing and pursue doctoral work, and consequently the curriculum featured a theory-heavy core, including Composition Theory, Rhetorical Theory, and Language Theory first, with Theory of Technical Communication added later. The program offered two concentrations: one in nonfiction (which included both creative nonfiction and the teaching of writing) and one in technical writing. The concentrations were supported through rotating topics courses until the faculty grew large enough to support regularly offered specialized courses in memoir writing, travel writing, writing healing narratives, writing for children and families, document design, software documentation, grant writing, writing on the web, and more. As the program grew, a third concentration in editing and publishing was added.

Over time, the department began to see a shift in the graduate student population from students who wanted to pursue doctoral work to students who wanted to pursue the MA as a means to change careers or to gain promotions in their current workplaces. This shift paralleled growing opportunities for writing careers outside of academia in Arkansas, a state evolving from an agricultural and manufacturing-based economy to an information-based economy. In addition to the increase in workplace-oriented students, we also noticed that we had increasing numbers of talented writers who did not complete their degrees because they became mired in the thesis writing process. In response to the needs of these two populations, we added a portfolio option to the degree in 2011.

The BA in Professional and Technical Writing

The BA program was established after the Department of Rhetoric and Writing split from the Department of English. Recognizing that not all workplace writers necessarily needed an MA, the BA program was designed to prepare students for writing careers after completing a bachelor's degree, as well as giving them a strong grounding to go on to pursue graduate degrees and law school. The BA degree was originally shared between Rhetoric and Journalism, with one track emphasizing journalism coursework and the other track emphasizing rhetoric coursework. When Journalism became part of the School of Mass Communication in 2008, Mass Communication and Rhetoric decided to collapse the two tracks of the professional and technical writing major into a single track. Since then, the BA in PTW has belonged to rhetoric and writing alone.

The BA in PTW is comprised of a core of 3000-level classes in editing, persuasive writing, technical writing, nonfiction writing, document design, and theories of rhetoric and writing. The BA core also includes an introductory course that orients majors to careers in the field and a capstone course in which students prepare their assessment portfolios. Upper-division electives are shared partly with the graduate program in a series of 4000- and 5000-level courses that meet concurrently. The full design of the program is extensively discussed in L'Eplattenier & Jensen (2015) and Skurat Harris and Jensen (2019).

"We Might As Well Do It": The Challenge of Moving the BA and MA Online

Far from being planned in advance, the online versions of our BA and MA programs were half-grown before we realized it. We did not start with the goal of putting either program fully online. Rather, the process began with our dean (then in the College of Arts, Humanities, and Social Sciences, or CAHSS) encouraging us to contribute courses to a new online initiative she was spearheading: the interdisciplinary online Bachelor of Arts in Liberal Arts (BALA). In the early 2000s at UALR, online education was still relatively new, and few departments had the critical mass of courses needed to offer an entire degree on their own. The creation of the BALA degree meant that students could combine courses from three different departments to form an online interdisciplinary bachelor's degree—one of the first available in Arkansas.

Demand was brisk because of the program's uniqueness, and similar online programs were strongly encouraged across the university. The university incentivized online course development by offering pedagogical training, technology workshops, money to purchase needed hardware and software, funding for graduate assistant support, and stipends to develop online courses. No faculty were *required* to create online courses, but those with an entrepreneurial spirit about creating such courses were rewarded. Within our department, undergrad core courses in editing, creative nonfiction, and technical writing were among the first to move online. Upper-division electives shared between the BA and MA programs soon followed, particularly courses offered in the summer, as it quickly became apparent that online courses drew stronger enrollment numbers than on-campus courses during summer semesters. Around 2013, we reached a point where we offered enough online courses that we needed just a few more to offer both degrees entirely online. After multiple discussions with the faculty, and based partly on the steadily growing online demand, the decision felt almost inevitable: we might as well just do it. We then needed to figure out how to evolve from a department that offered a sampling of online courses to a department that offers fully online programs.

Two barriers stood in the way of adding the missing courses. For the BA program, the issue was primarily technological, and it concerned two courses in particular: the introductory orientation course for the major and a course in document design. The introductory orientation course heavily features guest speakers and real-time discussion, a course design that was not easy to bring into an asynchronous format using the technologies that were available when we first started moving courses online. Document Design is a technology-heavy course that requires navigating multiple types of design software to produce the end products; much of this software was not available online and was prohibitively expensive for students to purchase. In both cases, time and progress brought the technology solutions we needed. The development of higher-quality video conferencing and recording software allowed us to preserve the guest speaker and discussion format that we valued in the introductory course. The expansion of Microsoft Office in 2007 to include better image editing and graphics creation options was a major boon to Document Design, as were the proliferation of YouTube technology tutorials, the addition of a robust version of Microsoft Publisher in 2010, and the explosion of free web-based design technologies such as Canva, Vectr, Crello, and others.

The second barrier was pedagogical and philosophical, and it affected both the BA and the MA programs. Part of the issue was that some faculty who normally taught certain required courses (such as the upper-division Theories of Rhetoric and Writing in the BA, or Language Theory in the MA) were slower to take the leap to teaching online. Our faculty felt it was counterproductive to force colleagues to teach online who specifically disliked that modality. The fact that theory courses were involved in this debate was not coincidental; these courses involve the heaviest reading and academic writing load that students in both programs face. With respect to the MA program, faculty and students alike were concerned that moving the theory courses online would reduce the sense of community that often helped students survive their initial sense of being overwhelmed and disoriented by the heavier content. Given that four theory courses were then required for the MA program, faculty worried that students might not learn as effectively, or that they might become discouraged and leave the program. Interviews with past students indicated that while many valued their experience in the theory courses, others found them too difficult or irrelevant to their goals. Several students complained that these courses were taking up space in their degree plans that they would rather spend on more "practical" courses. In 2014, the department reached a compromise, changing the MA core theory requirements to require just two specific theory courses (Rhetorical Theory and Research Methods) plus a third theory course selected by the student from a menu of four options. This change allowed for the MA program to go fully online in 2015, and the BA followed later that same year.

CHANGES OVER TIME: MORE INTERACTION, MORE COMMUNITY

During the fourteen years that our BA and MA programs moved slowly online, innovations in technology introduced major changes to the program, ultimately making the courses in the program and the program itself much more interactive and community-based. In the early years (2001–2009), online courses were primarily print- or text-based; students had a heavy reading/writing load, which could be cognitively challenging (see Hewett 2015 for more about cognitive load in online courses). Our focus group research with alumni who took online courses during these early years shows that many students strongly preferred their on-campus courses to the online courses, in part because they missed directly interacting with their professors and classmates. Several noted that during these years, their comfort with online classes grew as different classes exposed them to different technologies; the more comfortable they felt navigating the technologies, the more they enjoyed taking classes online. Others remarked that they felt the quality of the program improved over time because the *professors* became more willing to experiment with audio and video technologies that made the professor feel more present in the course and helped the students feel more connected with their professor and classmates.

As Voice over Internet Protocol (VOIP) and broadband access improved in the late 2000s, online MA and BA classes could more easily implement interactive and multimedia components (e.g., video chat, instructional video, etc.). In Fall 2018, our Research in Nonfiction course brought in guest speakers to classes through Zoom, and faculty in the course gave public lectures that online students could attend remotely. New majors in the BA program participate in weekly Zoom synchronous chats with program faculty, students, and alumni. In addition, UALR became a Google campus in 2010, allowing students and faculty to use Google Apps to store, share, and collaborate on written and visual documents.

Once the programs were both fully online, interaction and community building became particularly important. Students in our on-campus programs frequently cited their connection to specific professors and their sense of belonging in the department as reasons that they both chose our BA and MA programs and persisted in them. Up until 2015, even if students took some (or many) of their courses online, their experience in the program was grounded in at least a few face-to-face classes and face-to-face advising sessions where they met their professors and classmates. Others may have gathered to work and study together in the Writing Center, and occasionally attended departmental events. For the MA program in particular, we worried that fully online students, especially those who were geographically far away, might feel isolated and disconnected during early courses when grad students are evaluating whether the program is a good fit. We wondered whether they would be able to connect to professors enough to receive the kind of mentoring and professional advice that we often share outside of class, and we wondered whether they would have difficulties finding a thesis or portfolio chair and committee members to guide them through the end stages of the degree.

The fully online BA also posed challenges in advising online students. Our online faculty advisor encountered roadblocks with admissions (students had to apply to a separate UALR Online program to receive tuition discounts), financial aid, registration, and with getting sufficient technical support at a distance. Many of the campus services were designed for students on-campus or students taking a few online courses. While UALR has a Scholarly Technology and Resources department that provides support with our LMS, Blackboard, students were not always able to receive sufficient technical support for Google Apps. As is the case with many online programs, the programs developed before the infrastructure to support them was in place.

We are now graduating students from our online BA and MA each term, including some of our first students who have taken all of their program-level requirements online. Online-only enrollment makes up 40 percent of our undergraduate program and 60 percent of our graduate program. In addition to fully online students, most of our on-campus majors and graduate students also take several online courses.

Our initial program assessment results and our focus group research shows promising trends. First, we have seen no significant difference in our MA portfolio scores on any of the program's eight learning outcomes when we compare the performance of students taking courses entirely or partly on campus compared to students who are fully online. Second, our fully online students in both the BA and MA programs report that they do feel connected to the community of the department. Students point to their advisors' use of video advising and phone calls when they first join the program and at each subsequent advising session as part of what helps them feel connected, as well as extracurricular conversations in the department's informal Facebook group. One student noted that the kindness of other students in the program has made him feel that he fits in when he works in online groups. Another noted that one of her online professors has continued to check up on her progress in the program, even after the class with that professor ended. Several students reported that they feel online professors may spend more time working on their online courses than their on-campus courses and are easier to reach when students have questions than they would be on campus. This ease of access encourages some students to interact more with their professors, leading them to feel they are seen and valued. One of our first fully online MA students was recently accepted into a high-quality doctoral program, and she credits her success in part to the mentoring she received during her online graduate work and the training she received in our program's courses.

Comments from students suggest there is also still room for growth and improvement. While some students felt comfortable interacting with professors online, others said that they found it harder to read social cues. They were initially reluctant to approach their professors, concerned that they might be bothering them. Students also noted that sometimes there is a mismatch between the student's pace or schedule of communication and the professor's, leaving them waiting for uncertain periods of time for the professor to respond, or receiving replies late at night or on weekends. These students suggested that they may need tips for having effective online discussions and more direction on social norms for interacting with instructors. And while most of the students valued interactivity and the use of multiple technologies, some also pointed out that the downside of multiple technologies is that courses can become confusing to navigate. Some said that they felt overwhelmed trying to remember where they needed to click to access which parts of the course, and that they sometimes lost track of parts of the lesson materials or assignments as a result. These comments are a good reminder that while we are designing for interactivity, we also need to keep usability and accessibility in mind.

Designing the Fully Online Graduate Certificate in OWI

Unlike the online BA and MA in PTW, both of which developed over an eight-year period, the Graduate Certificate in OWI (GCOWI) was intentionally designed over about a year. The program exemplifies the CCCC's "A Position Statement of Principles and Example Effective Practices" (2013). Having over two decades of combined experience in OWI, Heidi Skurat Harris and Michael Greer designed the fifteen-hour program to include five classes: Introduction to OWI, Multimedia in OWI, Special Topics in OWI, Composition Theory, and a practicum in course design. The OWI-specific courses (which were all eight-week classes) were first taught in Fall 2016 with the program going fully online in Spring 2017. We anticipated that the certificate would enroll ten students within three years. In the first two years, we had over twenty-five students enroll in the program. In 2017, the program won the College for Social Sciences and Communication Curricular Innovation Award for being the first program dedicated to online writing instruction in the nation.

Unlike the BA and MA, the GCOWI was developed to be an online-only program and has gone through two complete revision cycles in the last four years (for a more complete description of how the program incorporates the CCCC OWI Principles and how the curriculum has been revised, see Greer and Skurat Harris 2018). This program is designed around three overarching principles: course design, presence and interaction, and accessibility. Students are assessed in each OWI-specific class by writing reflections that indicate where their coursework meets the course outcomes. At the end of the program (during the practicum), students create a fully online course and write a reflective description of where they met each of the overarching principles and sub-principles in their course.

In the first iteration of the program (2017–2018), students created the outline for their course and then used the remainder of the program to build the course (culminating in the final practicum). After the first year, Skurat Harris and Greer analyzed student feedback from these classes, including the reflective descriptions and discussions with the first group of students to finish the program, and reorganized the curriculum to become an eighteen-hour program (by adding an extra departmental elective), by opening the theory component to any theory course in the MA program or adult learning theory from our education program, and by more explicitly implementing user-centered design as a fundamental core of the certificate. Thus, the focus moved away from designing an online course and toward designing smaller units of a fully online course, user-testing those sections, and then using user-feedback to revise those units. The program still culminates in a practicum in which students put together a fully online writing course. However, the individual classes focus much more on modeling user-centered design and providing students with practice in the more interactive components of online instruction (e.g., giving student feedback in text and via video and chat, working in discussion boards, creating effective course instructions, pacing the course to work best for student and teacher demands).

Our iterative design model based on student feedback is the key to the success of the program. Because the program is developed, assessed, and revised collaboratively, course and program revisions are not left to the whim of faculty. Students exiting the final practicum course provide exit interviews, and faculty collect reflections from students in each class to identify ways that the classes are and are not meeting student needs. While this practice is obviously simpler with an eighteen-hour certificate than with a thirty-six-hour graduate program, we believe this model will be scalable as the program grows.

In 2018–2019, the program went through its first full cycle of assessment using faculty in the department to review the final student portfolios. Three factors have helped us create a tightly focused, fully online certificate program: user-centered design, basing design in OWI best practices, and collaboratively designing and teaching the courses.

User-centered design requires that the two primary program faculty (Skurat Harris and Greer) continually monitor student progress in the courses to see areas where many students struggle. They then discuss with students what elements of the course did and did not work well (usually through synchronous small group meetings or individual conferences). This user-centered focus allows the program to adapt quickly to the needs of the students in the program.

Because the entire program is based on the CCCC's "A Position Statement of Principles and Example Effective Practices," Skurat Harris and Greer had research-based principles on which to design each course and the entire program. The course outcomes for each course indicate which principles and effective practices those outcomes are drawn from. The final course not only requires students to demonstrate the principles in their course design, presence and interaction, and accessibility, but requires that students be cognizant of HOW they have based their course on those principles. Because each OWI-specific course has similar design, pacing, and outcomes, students can easily see how the courses build on each other.

Finally, the collaborative design and iteration of the courses and program allow Skurat Harris and Greer to ensure that changes to one course are reflected in all of the courses in the program. Skurat Harris and Greer alternate teaching the OWI-specific courses, and they meet at the end of every course and term as well as several times during the term to discuss how students are progressing and make notes about how classes will need to be tweaked to better serve student needs. For example, the Introduction to OWI class is taught the first half of each term, and Skurat Harris and Greer utilize what they learn from this course each term to adjust to student needs in the second course of the term (either Multimedia in Online Writing Instruction or Special Topics in Online Writing). This iterative process ensures that each cohort of students moves through a certificate program that adjusts to their particular experiences, skills, and needs.

Creating the GCOWI as a user-designed, principle-centered program has helped OWI certificate students build communities and interact more frequently with other students and with the program faculty. Current grant-funded studies of the relationship between online course retention rates and instructor rapport show that having a high-rapport class (defined as being led by an instructor who frequently communicates with students, provides clear and relevant course instructions, and is prompt in responding to students' questions) can increase course retention by 30 percent (Glazier and Harris 2020). While retention is not necessarily an issue with the GCOWI because most students who began the program matriculate, the rapport-based nature and interactive, community-focused activities and structure of the classes both model effective instructor presence and help online students not only create bonds in the classroom but after they complete the program as well.

Lessons Learned from Our Online Programs

Our data from the CCCC Research Initiative Grant suggests how program administrators can prepare for moving courses and programs online and what they should avoid. In particular, our research provides insights into how to pivot from a fully- or mostly-on-campus program to a hyflex or online one.

About 70 percent of our students are nontraditional. In the early days of moving courses online, students with dial-up access struggled to stay active in online courses. Data from the focus groups indicated that changes in broadband access and interactive technology between 2003 and 2018 have made a difference in how students respond to online courses and what they think about their connection to the program as a result. Early online courses effectively helped students achieve the programs' learning outcomes, but because we put them together on a trial-and-error basis, they were not as enjoyable or engaging as our current crop of courses. We learned a lot about effective online course structure in those years, and the improving technologies made it easier for us to execute more engaging designs.

Over that same period, we've seen an influx of students who are more comfortable communicating online, which has affected how students perceive the ease of use in the online courses. Our assessment data so far shows that a program's learning outcomes need not suffer when moving online and that there are a few common features of good program development that are not very hard to implement but that make a big difference in students' perceptions of quality.

Data from faculty and administrator interviews indicates that a key component to successful online course and program design is faculty buy-in. As described earlier, our development of online courses was gradual: incentivized by the university in terms of providing support, but not forced upon us from the top down. As a result, faculty members who contributed to the program did so by their own choice, for their own reasons, which made them feel personally invested in the courses they developed. We realize that such slow program development and faculty buy-in might not be an option for programs called to quickly move online. However, working within departments to build online courses and programs can help pivot and sustain those programs regardless of the speed they move online.

To move our programs online, we needed support within the department. This buy-in would need to come with dialogue and time;

it would not come from top-down initiatives from the chair or from administrators outside the department. During the eight years that our department was developing online courses, the chancellor's office decided to hire a private company to accelerate the development of online programs across campus, promote them, and recruit students. This plan was "sold" primarily top-down, through deans to department chairs. Faculty were never convinced that the plan would work, and it ultimately failed. Our department, in contrast, had frequent discussions at faculty meetings to develop general buy-in for the goal of moving the programs online. Once the basic goal was widely accepted, the department chair encouraged individual faculty members to develop online versions of specific required courses. We also made willingness to teach online a priority in hiring new faculty.

Our department was fortunate that most tenured and tenure-track faculty, all our full-time instructors, and many of our adjuncts were already teaching online in March 2020 when we moved our entire campus to emergency remote teaching (Hodges et al. 2020). Many of our graduate teaching assistants and adjuncts have taken courses in the Graduate Certificate for Online Writing Instruction, and several of our full-time faculty were already teaching hyflex courses. Our faculty prepared students in face-to-face classes to move online weeks before the university made the decision. Except for a few adjuncts who had never taught online, most classes moved online quickly and seamlessly.

A key component in our quick pivot to online courses was our pre-existing hyflex course options. Six of our full-time faculty already taught hyflex classes with positive feedback from both online and on-campus students. Our hyflex classes allow students to select (1) attending on-campus during class time, (2) attending synchronously via Zoom during class time, or (3) watching a recording of the class session and completing a follow-up activity. We implemented this model initially to address two issues: the need for some technology-heavy courses to have more synchronous instruction and our commitment to forming communities of students regardless of modality.

As we move into an uncertain future, the Department of Rhetoric and Writing has created hybrid/hyflex models for all on-campus courses. Traditional online sections (for both on-campus and fully online students) remain unchanged. Courses originally scheduled for F2F delivery are now listed as hybrid, allowing faculty to begin courses on campus and then move to online or a hyflex model based on student needs and the trajectory of the pandemic. In hindsight, our movement from on-campus to online prepared us for teaching during the pandemic, and we continue to plan our curriculum for an increasingly online educational future.

Conclusion

Some elements of online program development take time. In 2020, educators did not have the luxury of time to develop their emergency remote courses. However, we can make recommendations based on our program development and research.

Institutional support is crucial. This includes not only a general commitment from administrators to building quality programs but also an openness to learn about online education. Online instruction, if done well, is more time-consuming than F2F instruction and, thus, the need to limit class-size must be appreciated.

Individual courses can be developed based on faculty willingness and student need, but program development is best approached slowly at the department or program level. It is difficult to develop faculty buy-in by directives from upper administration, and administrators should not expect faculty buy-in to emerge quickly. At the same time, a program cannot be successful without faculty buy-in. Programs can move more quickly online by focusing first on individual course, student, and instructor needs.

Training should be developed within programs. Several initial issues with delivering our online content resolved themselves as synchronous technologies became more ubiquitous. However, we also conducted in-department training where faculty in rhetoric and writing could share their best practices in OWI. A number of us had already taken or coordinated LMS training at the college or university level, but periodic in-department training sessions helped to maintain enthusiasm for the online program and made our program more cohesive. When we were called to move online during the pandemic, Dr. Melvin Beavers, our director of composition, ran a workshop for adjuncts who had never taught online, and he and other members of the department have monitored adjuncts and graduate students as they adapt to online instruction.

Instructor presence dramatically improves student persistence. While this might seem obvious, too many online instructors think that online classes run on autopilot. Simple methods of creating faculty presence (weekly videos, online conferencing, engagement on discussion boards, addressing students by name) do not necessarily take a great deal of time, but they can improve student retention, commitment to the course, and attitude toward the program. In particular, instructors need to monitor course metrics and contact students who have been absent from the course in the first few weeks. Developing an engaging class takes time, but selecting one or two elements of a class (discussion board, peer reviews, synchronous meetings) that build instructor presence can serve as the center of a quickly developed online class.

Community is important for both students and faculty. Students want to interact with their classmates. Faculty want to interact with their colleagues. Advances in technology have allowed us to build a better community, even among students in ten different states and a foreign country. During the pandemic, we continued to have departmental meetings; thesis and portfolio defenses for graduate students; and smaller, less formal meetings of instructors and students to check in with each other and problem-solve the move to emergency remote learning. In some ways, the need for the whole department to respond to the crisis brought us together in ways that wouldn't have been possible in the F2F setting.

Assessment should begin early in the semester and/or cover longer time frames than a semester. Just as Skurat Harris and Greer do with the GCOWI program, online course and program assessments should begin during each semester and be used for iterative revisions to curriculum. Assessments done only at the end of the semester will not include students who have not persisted, thus reinforcing that classes are working for all students because they worked for the students being assessed. Assessment restricted to a single course for a single semester rarely evaluates more than the performance of a single instructor. But methodically reviewing program and course content in light of frequent assessment helps programs not just move online but stay online.

The development of our online programs demonstrates that online programs can be more than big-box LMS-driven courses. Our courses and programs are dynamic—as the students change and the technologies change, the course design and the faculty have to change as well. As we continue to collect and evaluate data from these programs, our focus remains on ensuring the best possible experience to our on-campus and online professional and technical writing students.

References

Conference on College Composition and Communication. 2013. *Position Statement of Principles and Example Effective Practices for Online Writing Instruction*. https://ncte.org/statement/owiprinciples/.

Glazier, Rebecca, and Heidi Skurat Harris. 2020. "How Teaching with Rapport Can Improve Online Student Success and Retention: Data from Two Empirical Studies." *Quarterly Review of Distance Education*, 21 (4): 1–17.

Greer, Michael, and Heidi Skurat Harris. 2018. "User-Centered Design as a Foundation for Effective Online Writing Instruction." *Computers and Composition* 49: 14–24.

Hewett, Beth. 2015. *Reading to Learn, Writing to Teach*. Boston: Bedford/St. Martin's.

Hodges, Charles, Stephanie Moore, Barb Lockee, Torrey Trust, and Aaron Bond. 2020. "The Difference Between Emergency Remote Teaching and Online Learning." *Educause Review*, March 27.

L'Eplattenier, Barbara, and George H. Jensen. 2015. "Reshaping the BA in Professional and Technical Writing at the University of Arkansas at Little Rock." In *Writing Majors: Eighteen Program Profiles*, edited by Gregory A. Giberson, Jim Nugent, and Lori Ostergaard, 22–35. Logan: Utah State University Press.

Maid, Barry M. 2002. "Creating Two Departments of Writing: One Past and One Future." In *A Field of Dreams: Independent Writing Programs and the Future of Composition Studies*, edited by Peggy O'Neil, Angela Crow, and Larry W. Burton, 130–52. Logan: Utah State University Press.

Skurat Harris, Heidi, and George H. Jensen. 2019. "The Future of Independent Online Writing Programs: The Department of Rhetoric and Writing at the University of Arkansas at Little Rock." In *Weathering the Storm: Independent Writing Programs in the Age of Fiscal Austerity*, edited by Richard N. Matzen, Jr. and Matthew Abraham, 118–27. Logan: Utah State University Press.

3 Lessons Learned: Navigating Online Teaching and Learning in English Studies

Michele Griegel-McCord, Cynthia Nitz Ris, and Lisa Beckelhimer

Recently stricken with a medical condition that immobilized her, one of our students said online courses "empowered" her and lifted her from a depression when she thought she would never be able to graduate college. Another student explained that he took online classes to continue working two hours north of our university on his family farm that, in turn, was the sole financial support enabling him to complete his degree. As classes moved online at the onset of the coronavirus pandemic in March 2020, a third student explained that she was able to continue her courses even though she was now back at her family home and helping to take care of two younger siblings on behalf of her parents, both essential workers. The positive experiences of our students, as well as the challenges they and we as faculty faced when we first moved to an online environment, encouraged us to consider how to cultivate an online teaching and learning experience that would not only rival the best face-to-face English classes but would also capitalize on this online modality. As the three of us moved from teaching full-time into various administrative roles within the university (undergraduate director, departmental coordinator of online instruction, faculty senate chair), these combined and shared experiences have convinced us that faculty and those making important curricular and programmatic decisions regarding online education need to adopt a proactive stance to the development of online learning. The recent pandemic confirmed our assumptions that online teaching is both a critical component of higher education, and one that requires all constituents to understand its important role and be prepared to use and support it.

Initially, online teaching raised questions for some faculty about its ability to truly engage students and provide a robust learning experience, particularly in reading and writing. It seemed to some like just another trend that would go the way of many MOOCs, which in their heyday, fostered hopes that these multi-user systems could bring educational resources to unlimited audiences. However, as online courses have become more manageable and recognition of their advantages as well as limitations have taken hold, we hear less skepticism of online education's staying power, and more questions about how we can enlarge its presence to meet expectations of increasing enrollment and shrinking budgets, while also fostering instructional integrity, maintaining fair working practices, and promoting the goals of sustaining and enriching English studies. We argue here that, in order to achieve this balance—so that any English studies faculty can have the knowledge and support to move easily from face-to-face to online environments in the future—faculty should critically analyze the needs of their students and departments, consider how changes to courses and faculty development can address these needs, and advocate for support throughout the university. In particular, we explore the following three main lessons in this chapter:

- enhancing transferability and relevance of online English courses through implementation of targeted student learning objectives;
- improving faculty engagement and development in online teaching through communities of practice; and
- becoming strong advocates for relevant changes to practices and policies that enhance the online education experience.

Through careful reflection on how to capitalize on the online environment by reviewing and rethinking current policies and practices and by creating alliances between faculty and across the institution, we can ensure that online modalities can both enhance the experience of our students and enrich and sustain English studies.

Emphasis on Student Learning Outcomes

Data suggests that many institutions are struggling to convince students of the value of English studies and the humanities. According to the National Center of Education Statistics, the number of humanities majors has declined since 2012 as have English majors across the country (ADE 2018, 49). Our university offers a diverse selection of programs in English studies, including majors and certificates in creative writing, literature, technical and professional writing, education, and copyediting and publishing. A survey of our own students confirmed national data, finding that while English majors generally ranked their English courses among "the best" (20%) or "better than most" (60%) of all of their courses, just 7% of non-majors ranked English courses as "the best," followed by 39% as "better than most" and 40% as "average." When focused on online instruction, only 29% of all students taking English classes online called our courses "better than most" (compared with 60% in face-to-face courses), and a disconcerting 30% called these courses less effective than most (Resly 2017, slides 13, 14, 17). This data seems to reinforce the importance of considering methods to improve the quality and support for online courses in all the areas in which we teach, ranging from general education courses such as composition and literature, to service courses such as technical writing for engineering majors and business writing for business majors, to courses required only of English majors. The pandemic served to highlight this data, increasing the sense of urgency that we must ensure the quality of online instruction in English studies.

One method of improving courses is through a thorough examination of student learning outcomes (SLOs), particularly as they are implemented in online and hybrid classes. SLOs describe the skills and knowledge that we value in English studies and want our students to gain, and those don't change depending on whether a course is offered in the classroom or online. Instead of seeing SLOs as challenges or obstacles that stand in the way of teaching a course as it has always been taught, we should view SLOs as opportunities to engage students in English studies. Instead of focusing on perceived hindrances of online instruction, faculty need to draw upon the unique strengths of online and hybrid formats to help us satisfy SLOs. In Lisa's administrative role as Director of Undergraduate Studies for our department, she has learned how a focus on SLOs can help us to showcase the relevance of our courses and major, and to deliver more effective English courses that can improve the potential for non-majors to explore English studies more fully through additional coursework and even by declaring an English major.

Applying the Lessons

Part of assessing SLOs also means considering how they can be implemented and highlighted to improve the transferability of skills. Today's English departments must examine how well we prepare students—both English majors and students who take our courses as part of other majors—to graduate with transferable skills, "[s]ometimes called 'soft skills' such as written and verbal communication, organizational skills, and problem solving" (LiveCareer n.d.). Transferable skills related to English studies include speaking effectively, writing concisely, listening attentively, expressing ideas, providing appropriate feedback, analyzing information, and editing (LiveCareer n.d.). While faculty may see these as inherent in our courses, it is up to us to purposefully showcase what we teach and what our students learn.

Here are four ways that we have drawn on the strengths of our discipline through our learning objectives in especially robust ways in online classes:

Recognize an online class as its own rhetorical situation. When developing an online version of a course, the first inclination is often to simply adjust a learning outcome from a face-to-face course to an online format. Of course, we all learned in March 2020 that this is easier said than done. Instead, we need to flip that thinking, and consider how to take advantage of the online environment to teach the SLOs as effectively, or perhaps even more effectively, than they are employed in the classroom. For example, an SLO for one of Lisa's courses stated that students will be able to: "demonstrate refined rhetorical awareness, including the ability to analyze, compare, and evaluate how rhetorical strategies function . . . [and] how meaning is made, communicated, and debated in various contexts" (Malek 2017, 6). Rather than asking herself, "how am I going to explain 'rhetorical situation' to students online?" and then creating a video to explain the concept, Lisa has learned to see the online community as a specific rhetorical situation that demands awareness of audience and purpose. She then helps students navigate the differences in writing for a cyber-audience versus a classroom of peers. Faculty can purposefully focus on language, tone, and genre of the online modality itself to emphasize our rhetorical strategies for online or face-to-face audiences. Students' skills in recognizing the differences and strengths in rhetorical situations can then transfer into the workplace, so that when something like the pandemic upends how they must communicate, they are prepared.

Address both traditional and digital reading outcomes. We need to recognize that students in online literature courses experience the same challenges as face-to-face students in learning how to read and analyze literary texts, plus the "additional challenge of learning and applying digital literacies before they can concentrate on the texts" (Lucas 2009, 373). English departments most often discuss reading as "'close' and 'critical,' without any explanation of these reading practices" (ADE 2018, 4). However, online literature courses give us the opportunity to examine what is meant by close or critical reading, and how those practices might be enhanced in a digital environment.

Case in point: Some of the SLOs in our department's literature courses ask students to analyze and interpret a variety of texts critically and closely, and to apply literary theory in the interpretation of texts ("Literary and Cultural Studies" 2014, 4). There is no reason why these outcomes cannot be taught effectively in an online or hybrid version of a literature course. Recognizing the value of digital reading skills doesn't diminish the importance of what we refer to as "close reading," and it doesn't mean that literature professors can no longer assign reading from thick, print versions of anthologies. It does mean that we have the opportunity to supplement reading with online resources such as video lectures, student discussion boards and blogs, digital archives, and author interviews that provide more modalities for comparison and study. Kristine Blair further suggests considering digital tools such as "YouTube for storing or accessing relevant video footage that can include dramatic adaptations, and image storing services such as Flickr . . . that can be useful when making connections between literature and art" (Blair 2010, 73). Such resources complement traditional strategies for teaching close reading. Literature faculty in our department who were already implementing digital tools and reading strategies found the transition to remote instruction in spring of 2020 to be far less stressful than faculty who had relied solely on in-person lecture and discussion.

Exploit technology-based outcomes that flourish in online classes. Students studying professional and technical writing are often preparing for careers in writing digital content such as website text and social media campaigns, but the pandemic showed us that all of our students need to become adept at reading and writing in online contexts. SLOs for those courses naturally address digital writing expectations. Unlike face-to-face courses, online classes function in the very environment where these students may eventually work. Some of the SLOs in professional and technical writing courses are well-suited for online instruction and can be more clearly identified to students and marketed as part of the online course experience. For example, our SLO that reads, "Demonstrate an ability to write in multiple genres (using conventions and formats) appropriate to the situation" ("Rhetoric and Professional Writing" 2014, 2) encourages professors to design assignments that allow students to examine or practice writing in online genres. Likewise, "Demonstrate appropriate technologies and software to write, design, organize, present, and communicate information to address a range of audiences and purposes" ("Rhetoric and Professional Writing" 2014, 2) has a built-in connection to online classes, which tend to rely on technology far more than do face-to-face classes. Outside of the classroom, many other learning experiences went remote during spring 2020, including internships, observations, and service learning. Students who were already comfortable with technology were better able to adapt to the sudden shift to online experiences and work.

Take advantage of writing process outcomes and transferable skills. One of the hallmarks of a creative writing course is teaching students how to give and receive constructive criticism, and yet that is sometimes difficult when students in a small classroom feel awkward offering criticism while sitting directly across the table from a classmate. One of our department's creative writing SLOs requires students to, "Construct and deliver useful criticism of others' work, demonstrated by thoughtful, diplomatic assessments of effective and ineffective technical elements" ("Creative Writing" 2014, 3). This criticism can easily be achieved via venues such as discussion boards and video conferences. In fact, when classes went remote in March 2020, our creative writing professors taught students how to form small critique groups—and pragmatically speaking how to use the video and mute functions of platforms such as Webex and Zoom—in order to continue the feedback process online. While an online class can't and shouldn't provide complete anonymity, the format does provide an environment where students can practice the transferable skills inherent in creative writing—carefully drafting and revising prior to posting, offering thoughtful and diplomatic feedback to classmates, and digesting peer feedback—before applying it to one's own work.

Online courses are well-situated to help English studies promote, meet, and strengthen productive SLOs. In turn, strengthening SLOs improves the online learning experience for students and can provide a positive experience comparable to that of a face-to-face course. In this way, online English courses provide us with opportunities to attract more non-majors and to show the value of the transferable skills offered through English studies that will directly apply to the "new normal" of the workplace.

Importance of Communities of Practice

Responding to institutional pressure and student demand, many English departments now offer a growing number of online and hybrid courses across all English studies subdisciplines, and that number might grow even further post-pandemic. An increasing number of contingent faculty (including graduate students and adjuncts), who now make up 70 percent of the academic workforce (AAUP 2017), are being assigned to teach these courses. English departments are particularly heavy users of adjunct labor, ranking second among all disciplines with 29 percent of all institutions relying on adjuncts to teach online courses (Magda, Poulin, and Clinefelter 2015, 7). These faculty may or may not have online teaching experience, and often do not have access to professional development or cohesive support groups. Unfortunately, this lack of support can make the challenging transition to online teaching even more difficult.

So how can individual units effectively address the lack of viable resources for faculty who may be willing but inexperienced online teachers? When she reflected on her own development as an online instructor, Michele saw her most salient positive experiences were gained through participation in a faculty group that began as an informal support system for new online teachers and evolved into what Lave and Wenger conceptualized as a "community of practice" or CoP (Wenger 2000, 229). The CoP she participated in focused on exploring new methodologies and tools to improve instruction in multiple modalities, including online and hybrid learning environments. A collective sense of "joint enterprise" allowed members to actively contribute to larger goals, while group interactions established "norms and relational expectations," and created a "shared repertoire of communal resources—languages, routines, sensibilities, artifacts, tools, stories, [and] styles, etc." (Wenger 2000, 229).

This formative experience helped Michele, newly appointed as her department's Coordinator of Online Instruction, integrate a CoP component into an online training program required of graduate students and adjuncts interested in teaching any online or hybrid English course. Such CoPs can establish an engaging environment that offers a "safe space for academics to get creative, test ideas, [and] innovate, on their own terms" (Green et al. 2017, 177). A robust CoP can allow members to grow individually and collectively as online teachers, respond to the needs of online students, and help initiate much needed departmental conversations about how English studies can embrace online teaching to help make the discipline more responsive to and relevant in the contemporary university landscape.

Supporting Faculty Through Communities of Practice

Communities of practice are noted for being driven by the needs of its members and can evolve as the concerns and experiences of its members change, making them useful models for faculty development (Vangieken et al. 2017, 49). Existing research shows that CoPs have successfully promoted changes in teaching practice, retained novice teachers, increased teacher satisfaction, and helped teachers navigate challenging pedagogical circumstances (Green et al. 2017, 160; Cuddapah and Clayton 2011, 70–71; Heath and Leiman 2017, 202). These benefits were realized when our department's existing graduate student CoP enlarged its scope at the beginning of the pandemic and became an important tool that helped English studies faculty from all ranks and sub-disciplines effectively transition to the online environment. Those new to online teaching were able to learn from and receive support from more experienced online instructors, and the CoP became an indispensable resource for our department during those chaotic early days of lockdown and emergency remote instruction. Several aspects that make CoPs a supportive and flexible infrastructure to help faculty learn about, experiment with, and reflect on online instruction are discussed below.

Cultivate meaningful social interaction. Because graduate students and adjunct faculty who are teaching online are already at risk of disconnection for a variety of reasons (comprehensive exams, dissertations, multiple teaching jobs), the isolating nature of online teaching can exacerbate that disconnect. Impromptu conversations about classes that result in important knowledge-sharing or problem-solving become less likely.

Communities of practice can provide emotional and professional support for those struggling with the growing pains of online teaching (Lu, Todd, and Miller 2011). The organic collegiality of CoPs fights against the frustration and fatigue that can come along with online teaching, especially for those new to the field (Green, Alejandro, and Brown 2009). During the initial weeks of the pandemic, for example, the weekly video calls of our department's online teaching CoP helped instructors stay connected and establish new faculty networks that transcended traditional departmental silos.

Communities of practice focused on online teaching can also open new professional avenues for faculty by enlarging the scholarly conversation beyond just English studies within which they can situate their teaching. Their experiences as online teachers can become productive fodder for research and scholarship individually or with others in their community.

Promote experimentation. Research shows that novice teachers thrive when they can develop their skills in the kind of low-stakes, non-threatening environment a CoP can provide (Einbinder 2018, 50; Cuddapah and Clayton 2011, 72–73). Teaching online situates even the most experienced English studies faculty as novices and requires a significant reorientation of our in-person pedagogies. Good online teaching praxis results from experimentation and pushing the boundaries of our comfort levels as we learn from both successes and failures. Technology changes quickly and can radically alter the experience of an online or hybrid course. CoPs are particularly effective at supporting faculty who explore new technological tools to enrich online courses (Lu, Todd, and Miller 2011). Furthermore, sharing this newly earned knowledge with CoP colleagues can motivate others, as research shows that faculty are more likely to adopt new technologies on a peer's recommendation (Jaschik and Lederman 2017, 27). Such sharing helps create more flexible professors who can adapt as technologies continue to evolve. This pedagogical agility will be even more necessary as online and hybrid learning become even more prominent in university culture post-pandemic.

Develop a disciplinary identity. Online teaching workshops offered institutionally or through professional organizations typically focus on generic best practices or technical skills applicable to any discipline. Being an effective online English studies instructor, however, means more than simply knowing how to set up a discussion board or upload an instructional video. As already stated, the online environment presents rich opportunities for achieving the unique learning outcomes that define English studies courses. However, skepticism among faculty new to teaching online remains. In recent discussions with diverse faculty stakeholders new to online instruction, many expressed fears shared by others that online courses will not allow them to create personalized and supportive course environments grounded in robust discussion and experimentation. One graduate student remarked, "What concerns me about online teaching is that my favorite parts of teaching are those personal interactions with students when you're leading a great discussion and the students are really getting a concept or they're using language you've taught them, and I'm afraid that I won't like teaching as much or be as excited about my work without the personal interactions." A CoP allows online teachers to collectively work through reservations like these, which can ultimately help cultivate a disciplinary identity that is responsive to new modalities and educational innovations at a time when English studies is increasingly characterized as a relic of the past.

Sustain productive conversations about teaching. Participating in a CoP addresses two problems faculty often face when transitioning to the online environment. First, faculty development sessions for online teaching typically follow a one-shot workshop model, focus on designing and building an online course, and occur before students even enroll in the course. However, these training sessions represent only one phase of online teaching. A CoP provides an outlet for faculty to collectively process the experience of teaching an online class while it is happening so they can immediately address issues that arise and experiment with modifications to improve online learning. This proved extremely helpful when faculty had to quickly transition to online teaching because of the pandemic and faced challenges navigating unfamiliar learning management system (LMS) features and video conferencing tools for which they were not adequately prepared.

Secondly, while individual departments often provide pedagogical instruction for graduate students new to a program, it does not typically extend beyond their first semester. Online and hybrid courses are typically assigned to more advanced graduate students who are far removed from those early pedagogical discussions. Adjunct faculty may find there are barriers preventing them from fully engaging in professional development opportunities with their departmental colleagues. Membership in a CoP for online teachers can help graduate students and adjuncts sustain a robust conversation about teaching praxis over several semesters. Research indicates that "when teams of instructors sustained a partnership over time, instructors were able to develop trust and rapport, which likely supported question-asking and critical self-reflection" (Bickerstaff and Cormier 2015, 6). This ongoing connection keeps online faculty invested in and engaged with the department.

Hope for the Future

As our discipline grapples with how best to integrate online learning more fully into English studies and to more effectively prepare all faculty to meet the challenges of these new environments, we should heed Glenn Blalock's call for prioritizing faculty development that creates and maintains engaged communities of practice: "our English Department, as a community, achieves its goals to the extent that all of its members contribute to that effort" (2008, 579). It is essential that we invite all department stakeholders—graduate students, adjuncts, full-time faculty, and administrators—to participate in this community of practice so that discussions of online teaching and pedagogy in general become more fully rooted in English studies culture.

Cross-University Coordination

When we identify elements in English studies that adapt especially well to the online environment such as student learning objectives, or determine crucial reasons why communities of practice are so important for those beginning to teach online, we are noting how established practices in one modality can be modified or enhanced in a different modality to significantly impact success. However, it is just as crucial to recognize that certain distinctions set online education apart and require us to consider the different kinds of support, practices, or policies that are either underemphasized or rarely considered in face-to-face delivery. Even with the electricity off, for example, give the classroom teacher in English studies a little natural lighting, and she can easily work with students. However, replace the classroom with an online environment, and many faculty and students are in unfamiliar territory; even for those adept at online teaching and learning, flood the eLearning system with users, as happened with the onslaught of the pandemic, and the system may not be able to adequately support the increased demand. It is imperative, therefore, to recognize the crucial components required to support online education and to engage in purposeful planning within our English studies departments, in our colleges, and at the institutional level. Attention to policies, personnel, support services, and priorities can improve the likelihood of successful online education, whether we are merely growing our programs or are subject to sudden and unexpected demands on them. Through Cynthia's engagement with colleagues within her department, on various IT committees and a university task force on online learning, and as Faculty Senate Chair, she learned the benefits of identifying crucial distinctions between modalities and moving the conversation outward from the English department to include the support and engagement from important affiliate groups. Such support can increase the likelihood that growth in online teaching and learning matches disciplinary needs and is sustainable.

Promoting Systemic Change

Promote policies and practices that support excellence. Unit and university practices and policies typically address issues such as workload, intellectual property, and student prerequisites. Faculty and administrators may not recognize the need to review these and other policies in light of relevant differences between face-to-face and online teaching. When the authors started teaching online, and for a significant period of time afterward, few program and unit heads in our department and across our institution had experience in online education, so it was only as faculty began teaching online that policy gaps became noticeable. For example, faculty raised issues concerning workload given the extra time demands of new online course preparations. When faculty were encouraged by program leaders to develop instructional units that could potentially be swapped into any online course, the question of intellectual property—to whom did this work now belong—was raised. On behalf of our students, we wondered how departments and the university as a whole could better prepare students to move from face-to-face courses to online environments in relation to technological requirements, accessibility needs, and demands on time management and other soft skills.

Just as communities of practice are valuable to share pedagogical ideas, so, too, is it important for faculty to meet to compare ideas about how to facilitate a cultural shift and how that might suggest changes to long-held policies. The authors chose to respond to the challenges that we began to experience and that other faculty began identifying by developing a white paper that situated such challenges in the course data and the literature. This helped us crystallize the need for change while helping to educate others who were not yet riding on the online bandwagon. The white paper was easily shared both within and outside our program and department, and it became a crucial component to emphasize to administrators that they should not underestimate the cultural and cognitive shift required in moving from teaching face-to-face to an online environment (Griegel-McCord, Ris, and Beckelhimer 2013, 2). For example, we were able to better argue that in order to provide the foundation for future growth, it would be imperative to encourage all faculty attempts to teach online, as departments dependent only on their technophiles, as ours was at the time, would soon find that sabbaticals or retirements can leave them critically short-handed (Griegel-McCord, Ris, and Beckelhimer 2013, 2). Moreover, to sustain quality courses, we needed to provide faculty with relevant training experiences, as well as the time to engage with such professional development. Faculty also needed access to qualified instructional designers and information technologists familiar with the demands of teaching English studies and writing-intensive courses online.

The white paper also created a useful record of the concerns and recommendations that we had at the time, providing a useful comparison to note the progress we have made since then—or lack thereof. While we were not able to bring about all the changes we recommended, continued experiences with online learning have helped reinforce the importance of creating a culture that recognizes and accepts the benefits offered by an online modality. For example, in helping faculty move courses online quickly as the pandemic began, it became clear that some faculty were not using even basic technology tools in the LMS such as the online gradebook—a function that can also improve face-to-face pedagogy as it provides students with more ready access to their progress and current standing in the class. Similarly, if faculty do not know how to utilize discussion boards, online journals, or quizzes, they may be missing useful methods to engage students in advance preparation for flipped classrooms and increased face-to-face engagement. In addition to improving the flexibility of moving between modalities, therefore, ensuring basic knowledge of and preparation for an online environment can improve overall pedagogy no matter what modality is utilized.

Identify and establish university-wide guidelines. As indicated, noting the need for policy changes doesn't automatically bring such changes about, but concerted effort across departments and colleges can make improvements more likely to happen. Sharing concerns with governance units such as a union chapter or faculty senate can help to identify issues that are significant, persistent, and widespread enough within a college or across an institution to warrant a more comprehensive—and united—response. At our university, this resulted in identifying pervasive concerns such as faculty being asked to teach online courses that doubled or tripled their face-to-face course caps; work with instructional designers that was claimed by both faculty and the designers as their own intellectual property; courses in which faculty were not compensated for creating course materials intended to be taught by others; and a lack of clarity as to how decisions were made about what courses should be taught online and who should teach them.

Once the extent of these concerns was identified, our university faculty senate created a task force to better understand and provide recommendations to address them. The task force provided a review of academic literature and of prior, and surprisingly consistent, institutional reports that had already addressed similar concerns; conducted interviews of key personnel, including department and decanal administrators and leaders of support units such as Instructional Technology (IT); and surveyed faculty to obtain not just experiential information but also perceptions of online teaching. What one dean called our "Wild West" of online education was confirmed as myriad practices and policies that, at times, undermined faculty engagement in online teaching. Revealed also, however, was a thread of interest and excitement about online education by those immersed in and experimenting with that modality—an interest that could be built on. Recommendations by the task force included the development of reappointment, tenure, and promotion (RPT) guidelines and workload policies appropriate to and encouraging of online teaching; requisite and appropriate faculty development opportunities and university-level support for that; transparency of practices and policies to promote equitable opportunities for all faculty to teach online; and the expectation that faculty familiar with online learning be an integral component in decision making related to the development of online courses (Ris et al. 2015).

Such foundational information and a united means of presenting recommendations can help promote a cultural shift toward acceptance of and improvements in online teaching as opposed to maintaining oppositional or status quo thinking. A crucial element in our case was also gaining the support of our provost at the time to share the document with college units to consider our recommendations. Such proactive steps are vital to informing college leaders who, like program and department heads, may not teach online and may not be aware of critical differences between online and face-to-face teaching and the need for a comprehensive approach toward solutions. The pandemic inadvertently resulted in this sudden realization for some and was instrumental at our institution in the creation of more online teaching workshops at the unit and university level and more robust IT infrastructure being put into place. Being aware of the needs across the university and planning for them are useful steps whether faculty must move online, are choosing to do so, or merely want to be prepared to do so.

Engage the mutual support of university-level support services. Faculty often benefit by asking for technological assistance, but it is equally important that those providing such support to faculty obtain input *from* faculty as well. This is evident in those decisions relating to the LMS and eLearning tools that are such important components in education in general, but especially in fully online teaching. If such advice is not routinely sought—and at our university, there are a number of IT-related committees on which faculty can serve as representatives—faculty should consider initiating such a connection through a request for such representation. Faculty can also ask IT representatives to attend unit or university-level forums to allow faculty to share ideas and needs and to request that pending decisions relating to technology tools be considered by faculty for review and input.

The advantages to such engagement for IT units include learning more specifically what technology tools are working well, which need adjustment by discipline, and what is either too difficult to understand or insufficiently explained so as to be of little use to faculty. IT units, like most units on campus, have to justify their existence and their expenditures, and feedback from faculty can help them do so. In the same way, however, such feedback can help faculty receive the tools that can best benefit them and their students in an online environment. Modification to an existing LMS, for example, can improve the method instructors use to provide formative feedback to students. If users in the humanities either make light use of the system and its tools, or do not express their needs, then the needs of robust users who are often not in the humanities, such as business or nursing, are more likely to be represented in the options that are made available. Both faculty and IT, therefore, should work together as allies in promoting to upper administration the need for support and sustainability of eLearning workshops, technology, and personnel that are able to not only enhance all existing courses, but provide a foundation for future enlargement of opportunities for online teaching and learning.

Bring long-term planning into university-level discussions. Where faculty serve on various cross-university committees—whether related to academic, budgetary, or student enrollment matters—these venues can provide the perfect opportunity for faculty to advocate for themselves and their students in promoting the benefits of online learning and the support required to maintain and grow excellence. Faculty can also help to explain the limitations of using online learning as a panacea for current budgetary or personnel concerns faced by institutions. A misconception, for example, that may be held by those who do not engage in online teaching, is that a "value added" benefit to online teaching is an almost limitless ability to increase class size. Those who teach online can offer important caveats to that perspective. We can identify research that shows how online courses can help fill gaps to retain students and provide higher graduation rates with less time to degree (Bailey et al. 2018, 20–23) but only where online courses are as good as, or better than, effective face-to-face courses. This means that online programming can help with crowded classrooms and budget deficits, but only with shared decision-making based on intentional, careful, and ongoing planning, taking into account faculty and student needs for online learning, incorporating disciplinary best practices, and planning ahead for increased faculty development opportunities and robust IT support.

Toward Sustainable Practices

Faculty, therefore, must work both within English studies and outside of it to develop allies in supporting online learning and in promoting best practices, and must also be attentive to possible university-wide changes that can impact the quality of online education. The enthusiasm for and budgetary reality of support for online teaching can ebb and flow, especially with changeovers in faculty and upper administration. Until better practices and policies are fully in place and habitualized, and until support is continuous and robust, diligence is necessary to continue to advocate for excellence in online education and for a strong faculty role in that progression. Attention both to improving our own courses and to the practices and policies surrounding online education is needed for the further development and delivery of quality online courses and programs in English studies that meet evolving needs.

Lessons Learned

We have learned through trial and error that, in order to effectively meet the needs of students who desire and benefit from online courses in English studies, faculty need to make ongoing and proactive efforts toward purposefully improving online English instruction and the support for that instruction. Reconceptualizing current practices within, and reaching out beyond, our own departments can be the first steps in improvements that will benefit students and faculty while also increasing the sustainability of English studies. To do that, we need to:

- Rethink the ways in which we can take advantage of the online environment. Rather than see student learning outcomes as hurdles to online development, we can identify how this modality can enhance those outcomes to better prepare students for other academic challenges and professional goals, while also providing faculty with flexibility in meeting course outcomes, whether the course is face-to-face or online.
- Proactively create opportunities for faculty development through communities of practice. Such groups provide the necessary safe space in which to share ideas and support faculty when making such major pedagogical shifts. Used in advance of the necessity of teaching online, CoPs can be spaces in which faculty can develop foundational knowledge to make later transitions more effective and efficient.
- Engage in advocacy for necessary changes in practices and policies at the program, department, college, and university levels. Voicing not only the benefits of, but also the necessary support for, best practices can promote online education that sustainably meets the ever-changing needs not only of higher education but of the society in which we operate.

Through such concerted efforts, students will benefit by online English courses that are carefully planned and robustly supported, and that inherently cultivate important transferable skills in which technology strengthens key academic goals. Effective online learning will provide students with positive experiences with technology through modeling for them how learning can continue to take place in that modality and encouraging facility in digital reading and composing skills. Faculty will have the chance to acclimatize to online teaching so that when moving fully into that modality, they do so with a better understanding of best practices to enhance the likelihood that students will successfully meet and exceed set learning objectives. By enhancing twenty-first century skill sets for teachers and students, these efforts collectively highlight the value and necessity of English studies as a vibrant and evolving discipline.

References

ADE (Association of Departments of English). 2018. "A Changing Major: The Report of the 2016–17 ADE Ad Hoc Committee on the English Major." *Association of Departments of English. July 2018.* https://www.ade.mla.org/content/download/98513/2276619/A-Changing-Major.pdf.

AAUP (American Association of University Professors). 2017. "Trends in the Academic Labor Force, 1975–2015." AAUP, March 2017. https://www.aaup.org/issues/contingent-faculty-positions/resources-contingent-positions.

Bailey, Allison, Nithya Vaduganathan, Tyce Henry, Renee Laverdiere, and Lou Pugliese. 2018. *Making Digital Learning Work: Success Strategies from Six Leading Universities and Community Colleges.* The Boston Consulting Group, March 2018. PDF file. https://edplus.asu.edu/what-we-do/making-digital-learning-work.

Bickerstaff, Susan, and Maria S. Cormier. 2015. "Examining Faculty Questions to Facilitate Instructional Improvement in Higher Education." *Studies in Educational Evaluation 46: 74–80.* https://dx.doi.org/10.1016/j.stueduc.2014.11.004.

Blair, Kristine L. 2010. "Delivering Literary Studies in the Twenty-First Century: The Relevance of Online Pedagogies." In *Teaching Literature at a Distance: Open, Online and Blended Learning,* edited by Takis Kayalis and Anastasia Natsina, 67–78. New York: Continuum.

Blalock, Glenn. 2008. "Faculty Development in English Studies." *Pedagogy: Critical Approaches to Teaching Literature, Language, Composition, and Culture* 8 (3): 555–86. https://doi.org/10.1215/15314200-2008-012.

"Creative Writing Assessment Plan." 2014. Department of English, College of Arts & Sciences, University of Cincinnati. PDF.

Cuddapah, Jennifer L., and Christine D. Clayton. 2011. "Using Wenger's Communities of Practice to Explore a New Teacher Cohort." *Journal of Teacher Education* 62 (1): 62–75. https://doi.org/10.1177/0022487110377507.

Einbinder, Susan D. 2018. "A Process and Outcome Evaluation of a One-Semester Faculty Learning Community: How Universities Can Help Faculty

Implement High Impact Practices." *Insight: A Journal of Scholarly Teaching* 13: 40–58.

Green, Tim, Jeffery Alejandro, and Abbie H. Brown. 2009. "The Retention of Experienced Faculty in Online Distance Education Programs: Understanding Factors that Impact their Involvement." *The International Review of Research in Open and Distributed Learning* 10 (3). http://www.irrodl.org/index.php/irrodl/article/view/683/1279.

Green, Wendy, Aaron Runtz, Luke Houghton, and Raymond Hibbins. 2017. "Enabling Stories: Narrative, Leadership, Learning, and Identity in Faculty-Based Teaching Community of Practice." In *Implementing Communities of Practice in Higher Education*, edited by J. McDonald and A. Cater-Steel 159–81. Springer Singapore. https://doi.org/10.1007/978-981-10-2866-3_28.

Griegel-McCord, Michele, Cynthia Nitz Ris, and Lisa Beckelhimer. 2013. "Online Writing Instruction Report and Recommendations." Advisories & Reviews, American Association of University Professors University of Cincinnati, April 2013. https://aaupuc.org/resources/advisories-reviews/.

Heath, Mary and Tania Leiman. 2017. "Choosing Change: Using a Community of Practice Model to Support Curriculum Reform and Improve Teaching Quality in the First Year." In *Implementing Communities of Practice in Higher Education,* edited by J. McDonald and A. Cater-Steel, 183–204. Springer Singapore. https://doi-org.proxy.ohiolink.edu:9100/10.1007/978-981-10-2866-3_9.

Jaschik, S., and D. Lederman, eds. 2017. *2017 Survey of Faculty Attitudes on Technology.* Washington, DC: Gallup. PDF File. https://www.insidehighered.com/booklet/2017-survey-faculty-attitudes-technology.

"Literary and Cultural Studies Assessment Plan." 2014. Department of English, College of Arts & Science, University of Cincinnati. PDF.

LiveCareer. n.d. "The Ultimate Transferable Skills List: 50+ Transferable Skills for Your Resume." *LiveCareer.* Accessed October 25, 2018. https://www.livecareer.com/career/advice/jobs/transferable-skills-set.

Lu, Mei-Yan, Ann Marie Todd, and Michael T. Miller. 2011. "Creating a Supportive Culture for Online Teaching: A Case Study of a Faculty Learning Community." *Online Journal of Distance Learning Administration* 14 (3). Accessed November 3, 2017. https://www.westga.edu/~distance/ojdla/fall143/lu_todd_miller143.html.

Lucas, Gerald. 2009. "World Literature: Envisioning Literary Education Online." In *Teaching Literature and Language Online,* edited by Ian Lancashire, 372–83. New York: Modern Language Association of America.

Magda, A. J., R. Poulin, and D. L. Clinefelter. 2015. *Recruiting, Orienting, & Supporting Online Adjunct Faculty: A Survey of Practices.* Accessed October 25, 2017. https://eric.ed.gov/?id=ED570518.

Malek, Joyce, Christopher Carter, Rich Shivener, and Kelly Blewett, eds. 2017. *Student Guide to English Composition 1001, 2016–2018*. Plymouth, MI: Hayden-McNeil/Macmillan Learning.

Resly, Alex. 2017. "English Student Survey." For University of Cincinnati Department of English. Results compiled January 2017. PowerPoint.

Rhetoric and Professional Writing Assessment Plan. 2014. Department of English, College of Arts & Sciences, University of Cincinnati. https://www.uc.edu/content/dam/uc/provost/docs/committees/Program%20Assessment/A&S/15BA-ENGL-RP%20—-%2015BA-ENGL-RPProgram_Assmt_PlanRevised.pdf.

Ris, Cynthia Nitz, Sharon Burns, Melody Clark, Nikole Hicks, Deborah Page, Kevin Raleigh, Eugene Rutz, and Alan W. Vespie. 2015. "Task Force Report on Online Teaching: Best Practices in Distance Delivered and Hybrid Courses." Faculty Senate, Governance, University of Cincinnati. March 2, 2015. PDF.

Vangrieken, Katrien, Chloe Meredith, Tlatit Packer, and Eva Kyndt. 2017. "Teacher Communities as a Context for Professional Development: A Systematic Review." *Teaching and Teacher Education* 61: 47–59. https://dx.doi.org/10.1016/j.tate.2016.10.001.

Wenger, Etienne. 2000. "Communities of Practice and Social Learning Systems." *Organization* 7 (2): 225–46. https://doi.org/10.1177/135050840072002.

4 Making Pedagogically Responsible Decisions in Online Course Programming

John C. Havard, Lilian W. Mina, and Eric Sterling

This essay describes the implementation of online course programming in the Department of English and Philosophy at Auburn University at Montgomery (AUM). The authors each play a role in administering this programming. John Havard is department chair, Lilian Mina the composition director, and Eric Sterling the director of the Master of Liberal Arts (MLA) program. From their administrative vantages, they describe their efforts: Havard describes broad department-level initiatives, Mina covers pedagogy and faculty professional development in first-year composition, and Sterling elaborates on the creation of such programming in the graduate program he directs. Uniting these efforts is the goal of responsible decision-making as we create online programming. While each unit of our department has specific needs, we observed a series of patterns as we made these decisions: concerns about retention in online courses; the need to advocate to senior administrators regarding appropriate advising, class sizes, and other issues related to online courses; and the need to select appropriate faculty and to provide them with suitable professional development for teaching online. Attentiveness to these contexts has allowed us to create our programming in a purposeful, pedagogically responsible manner. We here share and reflect on our experiences as well as ponder future possibilities for online courses. Included is discussion of our decision-making during the pivot to online instruction in Spring 2020 due to COVID-19.

Implementing online courses in a purposeful manner is necessary because in recent years department-level administrators at universities of all sorts have been increasingly asked by senior leadership to create such programming. This trend has been pronounced at regional institutions such as AUM, where upper administration is responding to nontraditional—such as first-generation, working, and adult—students' desire for the flexibility of distance courses when the scheduling challenges of a traditional college experience are insurmountable (Bednar 2018, 33). These factors have resulted across the country in the rapid expansion of online course offerings at such institutions over the past decade (Bednar 33). Our institutions' experience reflects broader national trends. National online enrollments have grown steadily each year from 2002 to the present. Between 2002 and 2012, that growth was concurrent with overall enrollment increases. However, between 2012 and 2016, online enrollments continued to increase despite overall enrollment decreases and even sharper declines in enrollments at online for-profit institutions that once served the majority of online learners (Seaman, Allen, and Seaman 2018, 3). Whereas online enrollments were once concentrated among the nontraditional students for whom for-profit colleges were appealing, and although such students certainly still gravitate toward online courses, more and more traditional students who also take courses face-to-face are taking some online classes (Seaman, Allen, and Seaman 16–17). These trends encapsulate the overall patterns regarding online enrollment. The pressure to create online programming quickly poses the risk of haphazard implementation, requiring administrative decisions that are equally responsive to institutional needs but also pedagogically responsible and that ensure student success.

DEPARTMENT-LEVEL DECISIONS

AUM's Department of English and Philosophy has undergone changes similar to those described above. My experience as department chair illustrates the need for department administrators and faculty to be attentive to concerns about retention, the need for faculty professional development, and the need to advocate on behalf of students, faculty, and programs to the upper administration as online programming is instituted quickly. In Fall 2012, nine of the department's 112 classes (8 percent) were offered online. Staffing decisions were made based on which specific faculty members were willing to experiment with online teaching. In Fall 2018, the department was offering roughly twice as many of these courses, with 19 of its 122 classes (16 percent) online. Moreover, online courses are now being scheduled in a more purposeful manner. Rather than being offered randomly across the department's curricula based on the expertise of the faculty willing to teach online, there has been an effort to make sure that it is possible to complete the department's three areas of the university core—first-year composition, sophomore literature surveys, and philosophy—online for students who wish to do so. A similar effort is being made to offer more upper-level courses for the English major become available online so that the degree is accessible to students needing scheduling flexibility. Lastly, with all required courses and sufficient electives offered regularly online, the department's two graduate programs, the Master of Liberal Arts and the Master of Teaching Writing, are now advertised as being possible to complete wholly online.

While some faculty have embraced the challenge to create online programming, others fear that the courses they create might be inferior in quality to those offered in traditional, face-to-face format. In many cases faculty being asked to create online courses have long histories of teaching in the classroom; accustomed to this format, they find online delivery foreign and alienating. These faculty may feel unprepared to create online courses quickly. Institutional support and training might be helpful, but the support available may be insufficient. AUM faculty who wish to teach online are required to complete a brief certification module, but this module is focused almost completely on the logistics of using AUM's learning management system (LMS), Blackboard, for presentation of course content. Deeper pedagogical concerns, such as whether online students will be sufficiently motivated to succeed in the course without the instructor's face-to-face social presence, remain unanswered by this training.

Compounding these anxieties, our experience is also consistent with national trends in that the pressure to create online courses at AUM is occurring concurrently with an institutional mandate to improve retention by decreasing D, F, or Withdrawal (DFW), or failure rates. In recent decades, higher-education administrators across the nation have increased focus on retention, and one strategy has been to identify courses with high DFW rates and to seek strategies for alleviating them. While some of those strategies pertain to non-pedagogical matters such as advising or cultivating an attractive campus culture and amenities, in others they pertain to pedagogy and course design (Bloemer, Day, and Swan 2017, 5–6). AUM, which serves a large number of at-risk students and has a lower retention rate (as of 2018, 66% freshman retention, 28% actual graduation rates) than state peer institutions such as Samford University (88% and 76%, respectively), University of Montevallo (77% and 50%, respectively), and University of North Alabama (75% and 44%, respectively), has followed suit with the focus on decreasing DFWs. This objective is at odds with the drive to create more online courses, as many studies reveal elevated online failure rates, a result attributed to factors ranging from the at-risk demographics who are drawn to online courses to the lack of instructor and student social presence in these courses (e.g., Angelino, Williams, and Natvig 2007; Brown 2011; Fetzner 2013; Jenkins 2011; Nora and Snyder 2009; Park and Choi 2009; Patterson and McFadden 2009; Russo-Gleicher 2014). Results in the AUM Department of English and Philosophy are consistent with this national pattern. For instance, our Spring 2018 DFW rates in core composition, literature, and philosophy courses were 24.3%, 30.3%, and 17%, respectively. In online delivery, they were 32.8%, 44.2%, and 23.9%. This is compared to 22.4%, 25.4%, and 11.9% for traditional delivery.

Given these factors, as department chair, I have initiated two broad, department- and university-level undertakings to improve retention in online courses. First of all, coordinating with a department colleague, Seth Reno, who is an experienced online instructor, I created a department teaching roundtable devoted to online pedagogy. After soliciting feedback from colleagues, we determined that many faculty desired to better understand the specific challenges struggling online students face and how to address those challenges pedagogically. Therefore, Seth distributed two articles to the department: Marie Fetzner's "What Do Unsuccessful Online Students Want Us to Know?" (2013) and Cynthia Clark, Neal Strudler, and Karen Grove's "Comparing Asynchronous and Synchronous Video vs. Text Based Discussions in an Online Teacher Education Course" (2015). The former was a study of students' perceptions of why they failed online courses that revealed misperceptions that students may bring to our courses. For instance, Fetzner reported that many students seem to believe that online courses are self-paced; she found that as few as 56.8 percent of failing students at her institution understood that they were expected to begin the course on a specific date (17). The latter article describes how faculty may use video-conferencing to enhance their social presence in online classes, build community, and encourage student persistence in their courses. Seth also reported on his initial queries to the department by compiling a list of common challenges and best practices from faculty that he then distributed to the department. After having been given time to read the materials, interested faculty met and discussed what they learned. The discussion covered a variety of topics, for instance how to use technological applications to achieve the kinds of video conferences advocated by Clark, Strudler, and Grove. (Lilian discusses the role of technology in online courses in more detail later.) Faculty left with a broader understanding of the challenges pertaining to online teaching as well as concrete ideas that they could put into practice. Nine of our twenty-three faculty attended this voluntary event, revealing a high level of interest.

I am also engaged in broader university-level initiatives to address online retention in English courses. Representing the department to other offices, I advocate for online instructors and students with other units on campus. My advocacy has been based on research pertaining to best practices in online education. For instance, Ellen Flynn (2016) and Michael Gos (2015) argue that institutions should carefully consider the dangers of online learning for at-risk students. These students may perceive failure in an early semester to indicate that they are unable to succeed in college. Therefore, enrolling in online courses that have higher DFW rates than traditional courses is a decision they should not take lightly (Flynn 131). Flynn thus advocates that institutions collect admissions data that helps identify at-risk students; pairing such students with a trained advocate/counselor; and tasking the counselors with assessing factors such as "study habits, time management strategies, written and reading proficiencies and most importantly, their psychosocial communication style" before allowing them to enroll in online courses (131). Flynn even goes so far as to suggest prohibiting self-registration for first-year at-risk students in online classes, instead requiring that such students demonstrate the academic skills to succeed in face-to-face courses first (Flynn 133). Such policies may not be feasible at all campuses. However, they should be part of the conversation, and if they are not being pursued by one's institution, the chair may be in a position to advocate for them. For instance, I informed AUM's central advising office of problems with online retention in our department. I urged Advising to explore options for identifying at-risk students; explaining to students the nature of work in online classes to correct any misconceptions about them being less rigorous than face-to-face ones; and providing students with counsel that sets them up for success by placing them in courses that are appropriate for their preparation level.

Even though working with various university units can be time-intensive, it may not always yield instant results due to many factors that remain out of our control. Meanwhile, working at the smaller scale of the department and the multiple programs under its umbrella can be more productive.

COMPOSITION PROGRAM-LEVEL DECISIONS

The steady growth and program expansion AUM has been undergoing over the past two years has meant serving a more diverse population of students and increasing demand for online courses. As part of the university core curriculum, first-year composition (FYC) courses were inevitably affected by these sweeping changes across our university. Our composition online course offerings grew from one class in Fall 2017 to five in Fall 2018 and seven in Spring and Fall 2019. Although the number is small in the larger scheme of composition courses (less than 1 percent in Fall 2018), as a program director, I had to take the time to consider the administrative decisions I need to make regarding pedagogy, instruction, and faculty professional development. Although these decisions take their particular shape in response to the specific needs of the composition program, they share with the broader, department-level initiatives a concern with ensuring student success in new, online educational environments. Like John, I found it necessary to be mindful of faculty selection, faculty development, and the necessity of advocating with the administration regarding class size.

My goal in this section is to discuss how the online composition classes at AUM respond to the *CCCC Position Statement of Principles and Example Effective Practices for OWI* (2013, hereafter *CCCC OWI Statement*) while remaining pedagogically responsible and appropriate for the local context and needs of AUM students. While the fourteen principles of the *CCCC OWI Statement* address all aspects of OWI, the principles relevant to the institution are beyond the scope of our chapter as well as my responsibilities as Writing Program Administrator (WPA). Therefore, I will address Instruction Principles 3 and 4 and Faculty Principles 7 and 9. Weaving these principles together allows me to discuss my decisions and practices about class size, course offerings, faculty selection, and faculty development.

Administrative Decisions

It is worth mentioning at the outset of this section that even though I work as part of a network of campus units (the department leadership, enrollment management, the dean's office, and the provost's office), all scheduling decisions remain my responsibility. John's and my approach has been to schedule proactively and to take decisions about our courses in our own hands before being forced to make unfavorable ones that may result in ineffective pedagogical models in our writing courses, especially online ones that have claimed a prominent position on the current administration's agenda. This approach has largely shaped my decisions regarding OWI.

Principle 9 of the *CCCC OWI Statement* stipulates that "OWCs should be capped responsibly at 20 students per course with 15 being a preferable number" (20). Not only do we cap our online composition classes at twenty students, similar to face-to-face ones, we also do not offer online sections of our Introduction to Composition (Basic Writing) course. This course has been traditionally populated by underprepared domestic and international multilingual students. As John noted above, there are reasoned concerns regarding inexperienced at-risk students in online courses; moreover, the *CCCC OWI Statement* offers a cautionary note regarding the "literacy load" (21) in online writing courses because of the heavy reliance on reading and writing by both the teacher and students, and June Griffin and Deborah Minter (2013) warn that this load may disadvantage "academically underserved and ELL students" (G153). They calculate that reading in online courses is "2.75 times greater than the face-to-face classes" (153). Similarly, John Barber (2000) argues that reading assignments "may balloon in size and complexity in the online classroom," and he cautions against the "information overload" that may overwhelm and dishearten some students to the point of "unproductive resistance" (254). Given this "literacy overload" that students in introduction to composition courses may struggle with, my decision was to limit the offerings of this course to face-to-face classes only. My belief is that students in these classes would benefit significantly from direct interaction with their instructors and peers without having to experience the frustration of handling an exponentially greater reading and writing load that does not match their literacy readiness.

Faculty Selection

Unlike most postsecondary institutions, teaching online composition classes at AUM is exclusive to full-time faculty, both tenure-line and contract lecturers, who "self-select or otherwise express willingness to teach in an OWI setting" (*CCCC OWI Statement* 18). Contingent faculty and graduate teaching assistants (GTAs) do not teach online classes even when they have completed the online teaching certification mandated by the university. Echoing Debbie Minter (2015), my rationale has been that contingent faculty may not have the time, technology, or pedagogical resources that enable them to properly plan, design, or teach an online class. On the contrary, full-time faculty have more resources available, as they regularly attend technology training workshops offered on campus, consult and share resources with each other (as in the teaching roundtable John discussed earlier), and have ongoing communication with campus offices and personnel responsible for technology. Moreover, because of their varied academic training, a majority of contingent faculty and GTAs may not have the intensive or current knowledge of writing theories and pedagogies required to engage in developing materials for online classes. Thus, restricting online teaching to full-time faculty comes in response to Principle 3 of the *CCCC OWI Statement* that "Appropriate composition teaching/learning strategies should be developed for the unique features of the online instructional environment" (12). It is also an embodiment of the department's philosophy of instituting and ensuring pedagogically responsible teaching practices in online classes.

Faculty Development

The Office of Online and Digital Learning at AUM offers a semester-long course to instructors interested in teaching online. As John mentioned, the course primarily focuses on efficiently using Blackboard while suggesting some basic pedagogical ideas for instructors to consider in their course design and implementation. I agree with John that this training is far from sufficient and does not guarantee successful instruction or learning in online writing classes. Scott Warnock (2015) repeatedly advocates for migrating on-site composition pedagogies and strategies to online classes. Like Lee-Ann Kastman Breuch (2015), I have reservations about the term *migration* because migrating a writing course online does not necessarily mean it was adapted for the electronic environment or the digital technologies available in these environments. Transforming and adapting these courses is a laborious and time-intensive job that requires a great deal of careful and reflective design of all course materials and work to remain grounded in the field's theories and best pedagogical practices. This transformation requires "planning, preparation, and practice" that is profoundly different from what is required for the "traditional classroom" (Barber 245). With this understanding in mind, I make informed decisions about selecting and training faculty to teach online composition classes. My decisions are guided by Principle 4, "Appropriate onsite composition theories, pedagogies, and strategies should be migrated and adapted to the online instructional environment" (14), and Principle 7, "Writing Program Administrators (WPAs) for OWI programs and their online writing teachers should receive appropriate OWI-focused training, professional development, and assessment for evaluation and promotion purposes" (17).

I extend Rich Rice's (2015) claim that faculty teaching online need training and continuing professional development to argue that training grounded in composition theories and research benefits all writing faculty. My goal is for students to have comparable learning experiences in both F2F and online sections of the same course without advantaging or disadvantaging any group because of their choice of instruction mode. Towards that end, we offer professional development sessions on using multiple digital spaces beyond the university's LMS, using audio-visual materials, and effective communication with students.

Grounding online work in composition theories, Kevin DePew (2015) argues that we should train teachers to develop critical use of the online writing space to achieve the course learning objectives. In our professional development meetings, experienced instructors share their observations about using social media, blogging, and interactive collaborative writing sites. They discuss the underpinning theories informing their choices and encourage other instructors, including contingent faculty and graduate teaching assistants (GTAs), to incorporate these and other digital spaces in their writing classes if doing so would help achieve instructional goals more efficiently. As Minter argues, moving the class discussions or mini-assignments outside the LMS may be rhetorically and pedagogically needed when the confinement of the LMS interferes with engaging all students or achieving the learning goals of the course. This move necessitates providing more scaffolding to students through introducing the rationale of moving some course components outside of the LMS, how to navigate that space, and how to stay engaged with content and conversations on both the LMS and that outside space. Although they do not teach online courses in our program, I believe contingent faculty and GTAs can greatly benefit from these discussions if they are asked to teach online in the future, either as full-time faculty at our department or elsewhere. Indeed, this proved to be true when they were forced to teach online during Spring 2020.

For students to stay informed and engaged in an online course, Scott Warnock (2015) emphasizes that teacher presence and engagement with students through different communication modes in the online writing course is essential. Teacher presence models communication expectations and practices to students who are new to online courses. In our online composition classes, we take Breuch's (2015) cautionary note about over-reliance on text-centric materials and communication seriously, and we incorporate multimedia instructional materials that capitalize on the affordances of the LMS and other digital technologies. Through short video lectures, PowerPoint presentations, audio feedback, and video-conference office hours and student conferences, instructors have been able to reach the majority of students and engage them in meaningful and effective practices that aim to achieve higher student success in online courses. We have also adopted the workshop model Breuch describes. While she mentions peer review activities as one example of that model, students in our online classes participate in weekly discussions on the LMS discussion board or in an external digital space that is conducive to discussions, such as Padlet and Slack. Students also complete peer review activities on the LMS or in Google Docs.

Furthermore, Warnock (2015) argues that leveraging time is crucial for teachers so that they do not get overworked in designing and delivering an OWC. He advocates for using "audio/video technologies to enhance communications" (158). Moving away from the text-centric model in OWC facilitates communication and engagement while reducing stress, confusion, and time on task for both teachers and students. For example, video conferencing on assignment drafts may replace instructor written feedback while opening for more interaction and better explanation of revision needs for the students. I video-conferenced with students in their out-of-town homes, while they were attending to their young children, and when they were coming home from their full-time jobs. In a university where adult, working-class, and nontraditional students are the majority, using these technologies in OWC works as a communication enhancer as well as a means of inclusivity by accommodating nontraditional students' varied life circumstances (Gos 340).

Communication changes to two-way rather than the traditional one-way written feedback; students develop agency as they actively engage in the conversation, ask questions, respond to clarity and comprehension check questions, and verbally articulate their revision plans. They also become more accountable for their learning because they have had the opportunity to interact and understand. The whole feedback process becomes more dialogic and allows for elevated understanding.

Not only has using the *CCCC OWI Statement* as a reference point enabled me to make informed decisions about online course programming and the parallel faculty development in the composition program, it also gave me the opportunity to share these decisions with colleagues in our department. Engaging in productive discussions at the department level opens the door for faculty to review their stance on online courses and their pedagogical choices in teaching these courses.

MLA Program-Level Decisions

The Master of Liberal Arts (MLA) program, the only interdisciplinary (literature, history, art history, philosophy, theatre, communications, and sociology) master's program in the state of Alabama, began in 1985, with all the courses being brick-and-mortar classes. In 2011, the provost requested that the degree program, particularly the three required core classes, be fully available online by 2012, with electives to follow. This ambitious plan was designed to increase enrollment by attracting students from all over the state as well as other parts of the country. The challenges I have faced as director of the program are similar to those described by John and Lilian: the need to staff courses appropriately in the face of faculty skepticism regarding online learning; to ensure the academic quality of the courses for AUM's local population of oftentimes nontraditional students; and to provide appropriate professional development to faculty who prefer the face-to-face environment for graduate courses.

My first step was to find faculty members willing to teach the three required core classes online: Research and Writing (a research class that teaches students how to write research papers and prepares them for their thesis) and the interdisciplinary, two-part Themes in Culture and Society: from the ancient Greeks and the Bible through 1700 and—part two—from the French Revolution to the present. One problem was that although the faculty greatly enjoyed teaching these courses in the evenings, they felt that the stimulating and thought-provoking discussions would be lost if the classes were taught online. Faculty members would agree to teach the course only if the online discussions could, to some extent, replicate the vibrant and stimulating in-class conversations.

Our university's request for online classes has led our faculty to re-evaluate their teaching methods and learning objectives for their students while exploring methods of creating online classes that can offer the same quality education that currently exists in traditional classes. Because of the need for online classes, resulting from the administration's mandate, and because of faculty members' reluctance to teach graduate courses online because of the extra work involved and the concern about replicating the quality of traditional classes, the dean offered professors a course release or a $2,500 stipend to create and teach online graduate classes, with the understanding that the teacher would receive the reward only for the first time the course was offered. This offer enticed several faculty members to agree to create new online graduate courses. Aside from myself, the professors who teach the required online courses are young and adept (much more so than I am) at using technology in the classroom. The problem is that in regard to distance education, some of the more experienced faculty members "lack a model or benchmark for online teaching because many of them have not taken online courses as students" (Schmidt, Tschida, and Hodge 2016).

Student reactions were—and still are—mixed. Because many of our MLA students work from 8:00 a.m. to 5:00 p.m. and have families, they were greatly encouraged by the creation of an online option. Initially, this option increased enrollment. Unfortunately, because a significant percentage of the MLA students are in their thirties, forties, fifties, and even sixties, some prefer brick-and-mortar classes and are resistant to online. They claim that they do not get to know their professors and classmates, and they believe that learning is inhibited when students and the professor are not in the room together and the communication is often asynchronous. However, most MLA students are content with our online offerings and mention that without distance learning, they would not be able to pursue their master's degree because of work and family obligations.

Some challenges that we have faced include attracting students who greatly prefer face-to-face learning and are thus resistant to online classes, helping students who do not log in to Blackboard on a regular or even periodic basis and thus do not succeed in the class, and finding ways for online instruction to replicate the learning process (such as discussion) and the bond between faculty and students that currently exists in the traditional classroom. Fortunately, the Information Technology Service (ITS) employees at our university offer training sessions at the beginning of the semester for those students who are unfamiliar or uncomfortable with using Blackboard or taking an online course. I always encourage nontraditional students to attend if they are apprehensive about taking online classes and have been out of college for years. I also encourage some younger students to attend because they often struggle with using Blackboard, such as when uploading documents. There is a popular misconception that because young college students grew up using digital technologies, they are adept at college learning management systems. Many millennials are adept at using smartphones, but may struggle with college software systems that are still modeled on older, office-based frameworks. This is problematic because smartphones, which many young students love to use, are not recommended for an LMS like Blackboard because the connection is often unstable and easily broken. Attending these Blackboard workshops at the beginning of the semester makes our nontraditional graduate students feel more confident about taking online courses. I also send emails to all the MLA students reminding them to log on to Blackboard at least several times per week and let them know when classes begin. Students who take only online classes and those who live out of town can easily forget when classes begin and thus get off to a rocky start. Some students even check Blackboard a day or several days before the semester begins and think that the course is not ready for a while because they cannot access the Blackboard shell, which becomes available only on the day the semester begins. I ask those faculty members who teach the core classes to send emails to their students, welcoming them to the class and informing them when classes begin. Furthermore, I ask those faculty members to use Blackboard Retention, which notifies them when students have not logged in to the course for a week or more. It is so easy to discern when a student stops attending a face-to-face class because instructors see the empty seat, but without checking student logins, a student can miss a month or so before the instructor notices, and by that time, it could be too late to help the at-risk student succeed.

From the faculty perspective, it was a great deal of work to redesign courses as online offerings because the professor would have to create and post new lectures (which take more time than preparing for in-class discussions or group work in a flipped classroom), grading would be done online, and there would be considerable time spent reading and commenting on Blackboard discussion boards. Unlike in traditional classes, in which the class ends at a certain time of day, in an online course, the faculty member can always be checking discussion board posts or interacting with students through video conferencing or another online platform. Teaching an online class can become a twenty-four-hour experience because the class never closes, so it involves more work. Faculty members need to use the discussion boards because student engagement and student interaction are essential to the success of online courses.

Furthermore, lectures would have to be videotaped rather than be presented live in class. Some faculty members greatly enjoyed teaching and interacting with students in the classroom but had trouble lecturing to a camera in an empty room. They could not gauge student reactions to their ideas and received no feedback, and they felt that the students' energy and attention in class, which inspired the faculty members' enthusiasm when they lectured to a class, would be lost.

Although Blackboard discussion boards were a step in the right direction, some faculty members and students wanted synchronous discussions so that they would resemble conversations rather than disconnected responses. One way to create smooth, synchronous online classroom discussions is with Blackboard Collaborate. This Blackboard program enables online teachers to facilitate group work and actively engage students so that they do not feel ignored by the professor or other students or generally feel disenfranchised in the course. Instructors can readily discern when their students wish to contribute to the class discussion because the students can virtually raise their hands. Instructors can employ Collaborate to conduct live polls on issues relating to the class's theme and conduct video chats in groups or between the professor and individual students. With Collaborate, teachers can do web conferencing by opening virtual chat rooms, allowing students to share the information and images on their computer screens, and implementing closed captioning for deaf students and color schemes for students with poor vision so that the class complies with American Disability Act regulations. All this leads to more active student engagement. It is also helpful that in the discussions, the students can physically see the other students, so they can put a face with the name and subsequently stop and chat with their classmates if they see them on campus. In "Asynchronous and Synchronous Modalities," Connie Snyder Mick and Geoffrey Middlebrook (2015) note that academic research indicates "that successful online teaching and learning are facilitated by 'high authenticity . . . high interactivity, and high collaboration,' [particularly] . . . in OWI, where vibrant virtual writing communities must thrive in order to meet the requirements of all students for timely and effective feedback together with a sense of real audience" (130; D'Augustino 2012, 148). Synchronous learning in online writing courses improves student enjoyment, learning, and retention, for it is "interpersonal rather than cognitive, ostensibly owing to participants' feeling of intimacy and real-time engagement, which tend to be associated with student satisfaction, student learning, and lower rates of attrition" (131).

Students may also interact with one another visually through asynchronous videoconferencing technologies. For instance, using Flipgrid, online students can make comments and provide feedback to their peers by making and sharing ninety-second videos on Blackboard or other sites. During a professional development presentation at AUM, composition specialist K. Shannon Howard (2018), who studies digital and material modes of writing and communication, distributed a handout in which she wrote, "Flipgrid allows students who have been raised primarily in an oral culture to capitalize on their strengths. This is particularly helpful with first-generation students raised in rural communities. . . . Flipgrid allows for a more casual 'third space' that exists between the formal online community and the home life of the student." Flipgrid is a free platform that helps students feel a stronger bond in an online class when they can see each other's face and hear them talk. This stronger bond allows students to feel more comfortable around one another online and to be more likely to share ideas and participate in online discussions.

The only other member of my department who I know uses Flipgrid is K. Shannon Howard. I intend to suggest that the faculty members who teach MLA core classes and electives try it and other such technologies that enable the benefits it facilitates. Faculty can instead ask their students to post three- to four-minute videos about themselves during the first week of classes, introducing themselves to their classmates as an icebreaker. They can talk about their jobs, academic and career goals, families, pets, hobbies, favorite musicians, etc. They can get to know a bit about each other, just as they do in the classroom; the result will be a stronger sense of community in the classroom, possible friendships, less reticence when making comments on the discussion boards, and more of a sense of belonging to the online course. Faculty can also assign three- to five-minute oral video presentations on assigned readings or share their ideas on topics that interest them so that the students can periodically see each other, aside from formal Zoom or Blackboard Collaborate sessions. Professors can also break the class into small groups and have Skype conferences, changing the groups each time so that all the students can become familiar with a large majority of their classmates. These visual experiences are essential, particularly now when students feel isolated during the learning process and in their everyday lives because of the unfortunate COVID-19 pandemic. Creating a communal feeling amongst the students in an online environment "plays an essential role in the effectiveness of the course in producing learning" (Darby and Lang 77). Anything that faculty can do online to replicate the face-to-face learning experience would benefit the students by creating a more communal and less stressful learning experience.

I have already encouraged those teaching the core classes to use the Discussion Boards and Skype (for individual and group conferences). My colleague Aaron Cobb breaks his students into groups and does group projects through Blackboard. As the administrator of the MLA program, I collect the syllabi of the online classes and read them before the semester begins to ensure that they adhere to the "Specific Review Standards from the Quality Matters (QM) Higher Education Rubric, Sixth Edition." I do this for quality control. In particular, I want to make sure that instructions on how students can get started are clear, that the methods of communication between the faculty member and students are indicated, that the learning objectives and assessment and measurements are specified, that the activities and due dates for assignments are spelled out in advance, and that methods of finding technical support are clarified. I serve as the liaison between the faculty member and students in case there are problems. If I can make sure that the syllabus is comprehensive and clear, I can help the instructor significantly limit any potential misunderstandings with students in the online classes. That is why John checks literature class syllabi and Lilian checks composition syllabi. There is a greater potential for confusion in online classes because of the lack of face-to-face interaction in the classroom and far fewer visits from online students during office hours. Anything that administrators can do to eliminate confusion and miscommunication in online classes helps the faculty and students have a more enjoyable and less stressful semester.

CROSS-DEPARTMENT PATTERNS

The common denominator among our experiences as administrators in our department involves retention: we are in an institutional climate where the senior administration is very concerned about DFW rates as part of an effort to improve AUM's overall retention rates, which are lower than those of peer institutions. Indeed, our recently adopted new strategic plan (2019) prioritizes attention to all courses with greater than 25 percent DFW. A wealth of studies demonstrates that DFW rates in online courses are higher than those in traditional delivery. Therefore, it is incumbent upon academic administrators to carefully select faculty who have the experience and talent necessary to teach effectively online, to persuade otherwise qualified faculty who fear being singled out by the administration for high DFW rates that they can teach online effectively, and to facilitate effective professional development to support those faculty members' efforts. We have described our efforts to do so in this essay.

Have our efforts been successful? The limited data we have available since we began focusing on these matters suggests mixed conclusions. Our Spring 2018 DFW rates in core composition, literature, and philosophy courses were 24.3%, 30.3%, and 17%, respectively, while in online courses, they were 32.8%, 44.2%, and 23.9% compared to 22.4%, 25.4%, and 11.9% for F2F courses. These results are consistent with national trends in which DFW rates are higher in online than in face-to-face courses. (We do not include data here for MLA Program courses because the smaller sample sizes make the data less meaningful and, in any event, DFWs are much rarer in graduate courses. However, our higher rate of As and Bs in face-to-face graduate courses, with more Cs in online courses, seems consistent with the pattern of greater student success in traditional courses.) In Fall 2018, although we were disappointed to see an uptick in DFW rates in philosophy, we were pleased to see that our overall retention rates in composition and literature courses were higher than in Spring: rates for composition, literature, and philosophy, respectively, were 19.2%, 29.3%, and 26.3%. However, the breakdown for traditional and online delivery presents a more complicated picture: rates in traditional delivery were 15.8% in composition, 27.8% in literature, and 19.4% in philosophy, whereas in online delivery they were, respectively, 46.2%, 32.4%, and 32.7%. Therefore, the improvements in overall success rates in composition were driven by improved outcomes in traditional delivery despite elevated DFW rates in online courses, whereas the opposite was true in literature courses.

Our interpretation is that overall improved success in literature courses and specifically improved success in online literature courses indicate that our efforts are paying off, particularly given that many of the attendees at our fall teaching roundtable were literature faculty, and much of the discussion pertained to teaching strategies for their courses. What was going on with those composition classes, though? Our online composition faculty reported elevated instances of students who withdrew or stopped submitting work despite the instructors' consistent efforts to design their courses to maximize engagement and to reach out to unengaged students to attempt to motivate them to refocus on their class. These problems are not peculiar to online composition courses in our department. Warnock and Gasiewski (2018) reported similar problems in the online course they discuss. They said that some students "simply vanish" while others communicate that these courses are "very difficult" and decide to withdraw even though the instructor has reached out to make sure they do not "feel socially isolated or out of touch with their instructor" (73). With only five composition classes offered online in spring 2019, an unusually high draw of such students in some of the classes would have a pronounced effect on the overall DFW rates in online courses. Online courses attract nontraditional students who, due to their work responsibilities, child-care responsibilities, lack of academic support systems, and other such factors, may be more likely to fail out of their courses than other students. The fact that AUM admission requirements did not change and there was no significant difference between average ACT scores in 2018 and those in previous years (Fall 2017 Report; Fall 2018 Report), we strongly believe that high DFW rates can be attributed to the nature and demographics of students in online classes. We did not perform a survey of this group to determine the exact explanation for the retention challenges we observed, but we would be surprised if these general patterns did not feature in the challenges our students faced. The faculty teaching these classes used what they learned about supporting students in online courses to attempt to help, but sometimes students face overwhelming challenges that they cannot overcome.

Such experiences illustrate that while department- and program-level administrators should put forth every effort to facilitate the professional development necessary to ensure effective teaching and to support university retention efforts, it is also necessary for them to help senior administrators understand that the retention challenges posed by online courses are not all the responsibility of faculty and are part of broader national trends that may reflect a combination of the limitations of the online medium and the experiences of the types of students drawn to distance courses. If senior administrators desire to expand online course offerings, they need to understand that collective efforts are required. On the faculty level, effective online course development requires support for professional development as well as time for faculty to develop and improve upon their courses. On the advising level, advisers must offer students interested in taking online courses accurate information about the workload and expectations in these courses to help students make informed decisions. Finally, on the student level, there must be robust tools that measure student preparedness for online courses to ensure student success. By orchestrating these efforts, senior administrators can minimize faculty frustrations with retention patterns in online courses as well as faculty fears that they might be targeted for reprisal in tenure-and-promotion and/or merit raise processes if their online classes have high DFW rates. Department- and program-level administrators have the responsibility of making those cases to senior administration.

RAPID TRANSITION TO ONLINE INSTRUCTION

Like other institutions, AUM underwent the transition to fully online instruction for Spring 2020 due to COVID-19. Over the span of several days, we moved through multiple planned transitions: we originally planned a two-day system test, then to switch to online instruction until April 10, to continuing online through the end of spring semester, to finally announcing that the summer term would be taught fully online.

That rapid transition was neither easy nor smooth for us as administrators. Although our department offers online courses at all levels and many of our faculty are trained to teach online, we faced a number of challenges. As we previously mentioned, we staff first-year composition online courses only with experienced full-time faculty, and the majority of composition courses are taught by adjunct faculty who had to be trained to teach online with short notice. Some senior faculty who teach literature surveys and upper-level literature courses have little or no experience teaching online, and they similarly needed support. Additionally, a philosophy faculty member who teaches a large proportion of courses in their area had no online teaching experience and needed support.

Lastly, faculty who are less experienced with teaching online wanted to continue to teach synchronously at regularly scheduled class times in an attempt to replicate their face-to-face pedagogy and classroom atmosphere in their new online classes.

As administrators in the department, we needed to face these challenges and to act swiftly but strategically while maintaining open channels of communication with all faculty in our respective programs and in the department at large. Our plan consisted of two parallel approaches: the first was to identify faculty "champions" with online teaching experience and leadership rapport to guide their colleagues through the transition, and the second to send consistent messages of support and calmness to our colleagues and our students.

John worked with two of our colleagues who have solid experience teaching online, Seth Reno and Aaron Cobb, to support literature and philosophy faculty, respectively. John was successful at convincing many faculty to either adopt asynchronous methods or to record their synchronous sessions for students with accessibility challenges and who could not participate in Collaborate Ultra and Zoom sessions because of their work or life conditions. For instance, one student who attended courses in the classroom could not attend synchronous online meetings during those times because the coronavirus emergency caused him to be labeled by the Air Force as essential personnel; thus, he was not available to participate in synchronous online meetings at times when he previously was free. Lilian worked with Elizabeth Burrows and Angela Fowler to support composition faculty. This latter effort proved particularly daunting due to the number of adjuncts and graduate students who needed support transitioning their composition courses online. Liz and Angela compiled a plethora of resources and tutorials that were made available via a Blackboard Community space for all instructors. Lilian continued to meet with adjunct and graduate student instructors to offer support, discuss pedagogical challenges, and suggest alternative plans to ease instructors' anxiety and apprehension. In any event, our approach was to assemble resources that instructors could use independently while making ourselves available to offer support, answer questions, offer advice, and discuss plans as needed. We were impressed by our faculty's dedication in using these resources to build courses that facilitated the unexpected transition to online instruction.

Simultaneously to these efforts, John and Lilian sent numerous emails to faculty in the department and instructors in the composition program, respectively, emphasizing that while we encouraged everyone to think carefully of their pedagogical choices as they transitioned to online instruction, perfection was not expected from anyone. Our message has been consistent: focus on large assignments that fulfill the major learning outcomes of the course, reduce coursework load and requirements, communicate regularly with students, be forgiving of yourselves and students, and reach out for help when needed. It was significant for us to send a message of kindness and support for everyone in the department at that time of personal and professional fear and panic. Fortunately, our university's Online Instructional Support staff held two sessions for those faculty members who were nervous or inexperienced in online teaching and disseminated video recordings of these meetings to the faculty. Faculty who had never used Collaborate Ultra, Zoom, or voice-over PowerPoints now had step-by-step instructions on how to use these programs. With only a week's notice because of spring break, we told our faculty to keep it simple and to focus on quality instruction, not attempting elaborate new methods. Having only one week was challenging for faculty who had never taught online before.

Conclusion

This discussion demonstrates the complexity of making pedagogically responsible decisions about online course programming in English studies. From core FYC, literature surveys, and philosophy courses to classes in the English major and at the graduate level, the three of us face challenges meeting the varying demands of students, faculty, advisers, and senior administration. Insisting on making the best decisions for student success is not always easy; it may require negotiations and research-supported argument to persuade others that such decisions are more fruitful and sustainable in the long run. As we reflect on our experiences and decisions and plan our future directions, especially with online and hybrid-flex models of instruction gaining attention in higher education, certain opportunities present themselves:

- We need to research the impact our decisions may have on student experience and success in online English courses, particularly success and DFW rates.
- We need to survey faculty in our department about the impact of initiatives, such as the roundtable discussion and faculty develop-

ment sessions, on their pedagogical practices in online courses. Such surveys would ideally point toward even more useful future undertakings.
- We need to have quality-material development that can be used consistently across online sections of the same course. Even though under normal circumstances our online courses are taught exclusively by self-selecting and qualified instructors, their ability to develop high quality and pedagogically suitable materials may vary. Therefore, we are considering a new initiative that aims to create a repertoire of digital materials to be piloted initially in online composition courses before they are shared at the department level. If successful, this undertaking might serve as a model for other core offerings.

Improving the quality of online learning in AUM's Department of English and Philosophy is an ongoing effort, and these three initiatives are our logical next steps.

References

Angelino, Lorraine M., Frankie Williams, and Deborah Natvig. 2007. "Strategies to Engage Online Students and Reduce Attrition Rates." *The Journal of Educators Online* 4 (2): 1–14.

Auburn University at Montgomery. 2017. "Fall 2017 New Student Report." http://www.aum.edu/sites/default/files/Fall_2017_New_student_report.pdf.

Auburn University at Montgomery. 2018. "Fall 2018 New Student Report." http://www.aum.edu/sites/default/files/Fall_2018_New_student_report.pdf.

Auburn University at Montgomery. 2019. "2019–2024 Strategic Plan." http://www.aum.edu/sites/default/files/AUM%20_Strategic_Plan_2019–2024.pdf.

Barber, John F. 2000. "Effective Teaching in the Online Classroom: Thoughts and Recommendations." In *The Online Writing Classroom*, edited by Susanmarie Harrington, Rebecca Rickly, and Michael Day, 243–64. Cresskill, N.J.: Hampton Press.

Bednar, Joseph. 2018. "Screen Test: Why Is Online Learning Seeing a Surge in Popularity?" *BusinessWest* 34 (26): 32–36.

Bloemer, William, Scott Day, and Karen Swan. 2017. "Gap Analysis: An Innovative Look at Gateway Courses and Student Retention." *Online Learning* 21 (3): 5–14.

Breuch, Lee-Ann Kastman. 2015. "Faculty Preparation for OWI." In *Foundational Practices of Online Writing Instruction*, edited by Beth L. Hewett and Kevin Eric DePew, 349–87. Fort Collins, CO: The WAC Clearinghouse.

Brown, Ryan. 2011. "Community-College Students Perform Worse Online than Face to Face." *The Chronicle of Higher Education*. https://www.chronicle.com/article/community-college-students-perform-worse-online-than-face-to-face/.

Conference on College Composition and Communication Committee for Best Practices in Online Writing Instruction. 2013. "A Position Statement of Principles and Example Effective Practices for Online Writing Instruction (OWI)." http://www.ncte.org/cccc/resources/93positions/owiprinciples.

Clark, Cynthia, Neal Strudler, and Karen Grove. 2015. "Comparing Asynchronous and Synchronous Video vs. Text Based Discussions in an Online Teacher Education Course." *Online Learning* 19 (3): 48–69.

Darby, Flower, and James M. Lang. 2019. *Small Teaching Online: Applying Learning Science in Online Classes*. San Francisco, CA: Jossey-Bass.

D'Augustino, Steven. 2012. "Toward a Course Conversion Model for Distance Learning." *Journal of International Education in Business* 5: 145–62.

DePew, Kevin Eric. 2015. "Preparing for the Rhetoricity of OWI." In *Foundational Practices of Online Writing Instruction*, edited by Beth L. Hewett and Kevin Eric DePew, 439–67. Fort Collins, CO: The WAC Clearinghouse.

Fetzner, Marie. 2013. "What Do Unsuccessful Online Students Want Us to Know?" *Journal of Asynchronous Learning Networks* 17 (1): 13–27.

Flynn, Ellen. 2016. "Should At-Risk Students Take Online Courses?" *College Student Journal* 50 (1): 130–34.

Gos, Michael W. 2015. "Nontraditional Student Access to OWI." In *Foundational Practices of Online Writing Instruction*, edited by Beth L. Hewett and Kevin Eric DePew, 309–46. Fort Collins, CO: The WAC Clearinghouse.

Griffin, June, and Deborah Minter. 2013. "The Rise of the Online Writing Classroom: Reflecting on the Material Conditions of College Composition Teaching." *College Composition and Communication* 65 (1): 140–61.

Hewett, Beth L. 2015. "Grounding Principles of OWI." In *Foundational Practices of Online Writing Instruction*, edited by Beth L. Hewett and Kevin Eric DePew, 33–92. Fort Collins, CO: The WAC Clearinghouse.

Howard, K. Shannon. "Eight Reasons for Flipgrid in Online Courses." Professional development lecture presented at Auburn University at Montgomery, Montgomery, AL, 2 Sept. 2018.

Jenkins, Rob. 2011. "Why Are So Many Students Still Failing Online?" *The Chronicle of Higher Education*. https://www.chronicle.com/article/why-are-so-many-students-still-failing-online/.

Mick, Connie Snyder, and Geoffrey Middlebrook. 2015. "Asynchronous and Synchronous Modalities." In *Foundational Practices in Online Writing In-*

struction, edited by Beth L. Hewett and Kevin Eric DePew, 129–48. Fort Collins, CO: The WAC Clearinghouse.

Minter, Deborah. 2015. "Administrative Decisions for OWI." In *Foundational Practices of Online Writing Instruction*, edited by Beth L. Hewett and Kevin Eric DePew, 211–25. Fort Collins, CO: The WAC Clearinghouse.

Nora, Amaury, and Blanco Plazas Snyder. 2009. "Technology and Higher Education: The Impact of E-Learning Approaches on Student Academic Achievement, Perceptions and Persistence." *Journal of College Student Retention: Research, Theory & Practice* 10 (1): 3–19.

Park, Ji-Hye, and Hee-Jun Choi. 2009. "Factors Influencing Adult Learners' Decision to Drop Out or Persist in Online Learning." *Educational Technology and Society* 12 (4): 207–17.

Patterson, Belinda, and Cheryl McFadden. 2009. "Attrition in Online and Campus Degree Programs." *Online Journal of Distance Learning Administrators* 12 (2). https://www.westga.edu/~distance/ojdla/summer122/patterson112.html. Accessed 4 May 2021.

Rice, Rich. 2015. "Faculty Professionalization for OWI." In *Foundational Practices of Online Writing Instruction*, edited by Beth L. Hewett and Kevin Eric DePew, 389–410. Fort Collins, CO: The WAC Clearinghouse.

Russo-Gleicher, Rosalie J. 2014. "Improving Student Retention in Online College Classes: Qualitative Insights from Faculty." *Journal of College Student Retention: Research, Theory & Practice* 16 (2): 239–60.

Schmidt, Stephen W., Christina M. Tschida, and Elizabeth M. Hodge. (2016). "How Faculty Learn to Teach Online: What Administrators Need to Know." *Online Journal of Distance Learning Administration* 19 (1). https://www.westga.edu/~distance/ojdla/spring191/schmidt_tschida_hodge191.html. Accessed 3 May 2021.

Seaman, Julia E., I. Elaine Allen, and Jeff Seaman. 2018. *Grade Increase: Tracking Distance Education in the United States*. Babson Survey Research Group. PDF file. https://onlinelearningsurvey.com/reports/gradeincrease.pdf.

Warnock, Scott. 2015. "Teaching the OWI Course." In *Foundational Practices of Online Writing Instruction*, edited by Beth L. Hewett and Kevin Eric DePew, 151–81. Fort Collins, CO: The WAC Clearinghouse.

Warnock, Scott, and Diana Gasiewski. 2018. *Writing Together: Ten Weeks Teaching and Studenting in an Online Writing Course*. Urbana, IL: National Council of Teachers of English.

5 It Takes a Village to Create Successful Online Composition Courses

Elizabeth Burrows, Samantha McNeilly, and Matthew Kemp

In this chapter, we show how designing and delivering a first-year writing course online embodies (a) the collective efforts of multiple units on campus and (b) rich, multi-layered communication and interaction among various parties: student-student, student-teacher, student-library, student-learning center tutors, and more. We are particularly interested in demonstrating our experience designing and delivering online composition courses that capitalize on the affordances of online platforms (within a Learning Management System [LMS] and outside of it) for teaching and learning. We strongly believe that an effective and successful online course *should seek* the sort of interaction and communication that is characterized by "high authenticity . . . high interactivity, and high collaboration" (D'Agustine 2012, 148). These authentic, interactive, and collaborative needs necessitate that instructors create these online student-centered classes with intentionality, and while we can never guarantee that these things will always occur in any course, let alone an online one, these goals remain consistent. These courses should connect students to the resources available to them, specifically the library and campus learning centers. Because an LMS can become a hindrance to authenticity, interaction, and collaboration, we will discuss our village approach within and outside of the LMS. When designing an online course, instructors need to anticipate student needs while engaging students in public and private writing and in alphabetic and multimodal composing practices in the online class environment regardless of where the class is housed. Utilizing such spaces is not only conducive to successful writing instruction and learning, but it also provides transferable skills students need across the university and in the workplace. These features of online courses are necessary for student success in online courses and have implications for retention, a current concern across the country.

THE VILLAGE PEOPLE

Writing instructors don't work in a vacuum, especially, those who teach online; they rely on instructional designers, librarians, and learning center tutors. Together, all these parties create the foundation of online composition courses. Librarians and learning center tutors become a source of guidance and feedback for students in online classes, thus forming a village that supports student learning.

Over the years, our learning center (LC), library, and composition program have enjoyed a long history of collaboration and support. The LC participates in the composition program's trainings, both informing instructors of the scope and ability of the center's tutors while learning about new pedagogies the composition program is utilizing, such as new individual or sequenced assignments, textbooks, or digital writing platforms. Similarly, members of the composition program frequently attend the LC's biannual all-staff trainings or monthly writing-focused trainings to present pedagogical changes or best practices directly to tutors. For example, recently the director of composition led a break-out session at a LC training in which she answered tutor questions about the program's change to a teaching-for-transfer curriculum. This kind of collaboration aims to align LC tutor training with program goals and work for better support of students.

Like the collaboration between the LC and the composition program, librarians have attended composition program professional development meetings to keep instructors abreast of new library initiatives (e.g., a new database of study materials) to pass along to students. For example, Samantha regularly attends composition program meetings, and she recently gave input on a program tied to the information cycle because, if implemented, it would require heavy interaction between instructors and librarians. Moreover, librarians work closely with the composition instructors throughout the semester to schedule library instruction sessions or to update LibGuides as needed for the online classes.

Another layer of collaboration among the village people is between the library and LC. The library has partnered with the LC to provide workshops on topics such as formatting papers, citation styles, avoiding plagiarism, and study skills. These workshops are promoted to the composition instructors and their students. These multi-directional collaboration efforts build our community connections and ideals of working as partners to help students. In the remainder of our chapter, we will discuss how this village works and networks for the benefit of students in our online composition courses. We will also explain ways these networks can work in the larger scope of English studies, especially in our current educational climate.

The Village in the LMS

Recently, our university has increased the number of online composition courses, and advisors have reached out to students during their appointments to offer these options, especially given the student population at Auburn University at Montgomery. Many of our students work full time, have children, and deal with a number of other life circumstances that make attending traditional face-to-face classes difficult. Regardless of student population, online English courses are becoming more attractive to students and university administrators.

John Barber (2000) defines the online writing classroom as "a site for teaching and learning where multiple individuals can create social presences and realities that are both interactive and collaborative" (243). At the core of this definition is student social presence through interaction and collaboration with other members of the class community, traditionally the instructor and other students; however, in the model we describe, students interact with their peers, the instructor, library staff, and LC tutors. This web of interactive relationships expands students' connection to campus beyond the LMS and mimics the interactions of students in on-campus courses.

The Teacher's Role

Barber's (2000) use of Feenberg's "teacher-moderator" model is key in online writing classrooms within and outside the LMS, as we'll discuss later. Modeling and moderating conversations and interaction in an online class is crucial. Contrary to face-to-face classes where students can retain privacy of much of their writing, the online class leaves the student with little choice because writing happens in an online space and becomes visible to the class community. A teacher modeling the length, rhetoric, language choice, and other features of effective online writing can give students an example to emulate, at least at the beginning, until they've developed the confidence needed to produce writing in that novel environment. Students need to learn how to write within the required length mainly to avoid the "information overload" typical in online classes relying heavily on reading and writing (Barber 2000, 258). For example, in her courses, Elizabeth uses a rubric for discussion posts and replies, along with a sample discussion/reply for students to see so they can gauge their writing against the example at first. As the students become more adept at discussions and less nervous about others reading their writing, they don't need to resort to reading the sample again. Ongoing feedback from Elizabeth also helps the students grow as participants in the discussion forum, and in online spaces in general.

Barber (2000) also advocates for "chunking" information or "using shorter written messages" on selected points instead of writing lengthy messages on all points of discussion (258). Participants in Barber's (2000) study found shorter, more concise written messages more accessible and comfortable to read. In Elizabeth's courses, feedback to students in discussions is short but direct. She gives the students one thing to keep doing because they did it well in addition to one way to improve the next week. For example, some students have an interesting perceptive, and/or a creative response to a reading, but they often fail to point to the place in the text where those points arise, even though it's required in the discussion prompt. This is an easy place to give direct feedback because, as Barber notes, these shorter messages are more impactful than a long paragraph about the entire post. Offering this kind of feedback is not limited to a particular writing space and can certainly happen in public digital spaces. Moreover, playing the moderating role is significant, especially when the course theme or readings are controversial and prone to heated debates. Elizabeth has taught courses with themes that involve subjects like serial killers, private prisons, institutionalized racism, and police brutality. Students respond to and write about these topics in discussion posts, journals, and drafts that require peer review and comments. Being a moderator is imperative, especially when personal opinions can be strong; many people feel comfortable writing things online that they might not say to someone's face. Elizabeth uses peer review questions to guide students toward avoiding writing such opinions. She also gives examples of what to do and what not to do in peer review. She uses American Idol judges to show the various kinds of comments ranging from off topic (Paula Abdul) to mean (Simon Cowell) to uncritical (Steven Tyler). In the end, she hopes these models and student examples of excellent peer review help them hone their critiquing skills.

The Library's Role

Library instruction and online library resources are a critical component of any composition course, but it is especially true with regards to online courses where students will not necessarily have in-person contact with the library/librarians or have easy access to the physical library. Librarians are aware that they're expected to "integrate library resources into the systems students use most" (Jackson 2007, 455). Relevant library resources and other helpful information can be provided in a LibGuide. Customized LibGuides embedded directly into Blackboard, our campus LMS, deliver library resources directly to online students without the need for students to visit multiple websites or click on endless links. The LibGuides also make online courses outside an LMS easier to navigate because all of the research information is housed in one place. Virtual references services are also available to students via LibChat, where students are able to chat online with librarians for research help.

To assist the instructor in creating support structures for students, the librarians at AUM have worked closely with the English composition instructors to create specific LibGuides called research guides, for their online classes. The research guides contain specific databases related to the student's topics, as well as links to other scholarly and popular sources. Video tutorials are also a part of the guide since the students do not receive the same instruction on database searching as the face-to-face students. The virtual reference services are also widely used by students. For example, within the LibGuides, there is a virtual chat widget that asks students if they need help each time they log on.

Alternatively, there is a button that students can click to launch the chat session on their own without being prompted. Shank and Dewald (2003) state that the "closer the link between course assignments and library resources to help with those assignments, the greater likelihood that students will access library information" (41).

LibGuide Views: Jan. 1ˢᵗ-Mar. 30ᵗʰ 2019

Guide Id	Guide Name	Views
637570	AUM Library Research Help	580
905713	ENGL1020: Technology (A. Fowler) Online Class	226
612838	MKTG 4360: Marketing Research	225
51489	ENGL1020: Heroes & Villains (Elizabeth Kent-Burrows) Online Class	222
776925	NURS 3150: Evidence Based Practice in Nursing	185
802475	ENGL1020: Locklear Online Class	162
796763	CMDS 3500 Research Help	133
809268	BIOL 1010: Cells, Molecules, and Life	84
51506	Queen Elizabeth I of England	76
802487	ENGL1020: Death (Juanita Barrett)	76

Figure 1: LibGuides with total views from the first half of the Spring 2019 semester

Moreover, by having multiple points of access to library resources, students have more opportunities to contact librarians to inquire about research, whether via email, chat, phone call, or texting. When students are conducting their research online, they have instant access to library resources within the LibGuide, eliminating the need to go out and search for them on their own. The availability of these tools and services encourages instant communication and interaction between students and the library staff, which instructors can reinforce. This close connection secures student access to research help from partners in the online writing class, making librarians a crucial component to the village. Students benefit from having direct access to library resources, regardless of potential changes to instructional models/modes (as in the sudden pivot for many in spring 2020 with the onset of COVID-19 shutdowns). In fact, providing these online tools provides consistency for all courses. Instructors benefit from these as well; rather than teaching the library resources, the librarians handle this so the instructor can focus on the writing happening in the classroom, pointing students to the LibGuide for instruction and support. The LibGuides are customized to fit the instructor's theme, assignments, and outcomes/goals for their class. As students write research proposals, these topics are shared with the librarians so specific resources can be added to the LibGuide.

In addition, the LibGuides have valuable resources such as the CRAAP test. This evaluative tool was developed by Sarah Blakeslee (2004) in conjunction with the librarians at California State Chico in early 2004: "CRAAP is an acronym that most students don't expect a librarian to be using, let alone using to lead a class. Little do they know that librarians can be crude and/or rude, and do almost anything in order to penetrate their students' deep memories and satisfy their instructional objectives" (6). While there were methods to evaluate sources prior to this, Blakeslee wanted something that would stand out to students; currency, relevance, authority, accuracy, and purpose thus become the CRAAP test. Students in Elizabeth's courses are directed to the LibGuide to learn about the CRAAP test, but it doesn't end there. To reinforce the valuable knowledge in the LibGuide, Elizabeth has students post a link to a web source. Then, in a discussion post, students complete the CRAAP test for another student. This builds connections between students and the materials they are working on at the time. Moreover, by working with instructors on creating the LibGuide, the librarian will have an opportunity to discuss any difficulties and assignment details with the faculty member, improving both assignments and library assistance for students. The faculty member will perhaps see the librarian as a consultant, improving information access and students' information literacy skills both within the course and beyond it (Shank 2003, 42).

When students are working on finding sources, for example, the librarians can reach out to the instructor to give a heads up on trouble areas and vice versa. In fact, a few years ago, Elizabeth and Samantha worked with a student via email to locate sources for a research paper on child sociopathy. This collaborative work between the instructor and the librarian helped solve issues for students, and the student was appreciative. This kind of support shows students how the community works together for student success, and it is just one example that has repeated itself through the years.

Finally, having an embedded, or dedicated librarian, in online classes gives students yet another access point to library resources. This arrangement is a benefit for everyone involved—students have their own personal librarian who is familiar with their assignments and classwork, faculty members have an information literacy expert collaborating on the assignments and classwork, and the librarians have an opportunity to make an impact on student's information literacy skills that will benefit them in all of their academic classes. Librarians have been, and should be, a crucial component of any composition classroom, especially if the class is online.

The Learning Center's Role

Another important component in the online writing class is our campus Learning Center (LC). To better engage students in online material, LCs must foster a sense of community and interaction in their pedagogy in order to aid students and faculty. An easy approach to supporting online students is for the LC to be a repository of information, handouts, or worksheets (a "storehouse" as Lunsford calls it) for specific writing tasks. For example, our LC produces short videos on various writing topics such as formatting the header for the APA stylesheet. However, it is important to note these passive materials do not encourage interaction and connection among tutors, the center, and students. There must also be active communication, especially between students and tutors.

We seek ways to create living discourse with students in which they grapple with the content. A great way to encourage this type of discourse is through interaction with a tutor. However, online writing tutoring does encompass a different set of approaches and needs in comparison to face-to-face tutoring (F2F) that must be considered. Centers may support students synchronously or asynchronously. Asynchronous models can work well when implemented correctly. This cannot be overlooked, as many centers may lack the staff, funds, and technological resources to facilitate synchronous tutoring. Both approaches are valid, and the decision of which to employ in an LC must be made with all variables considered as with any pedagogical choice (Mick and Middlebrook 2015, 145).

On our campus, F2F writing tutoring occurs in thirty-minute, one-on-one appointments, while online writing appointments are asynchronous with a maximum turnaround of forty-eight hours. Students must create an online appointment and email their document(s) and assignment sheet to our LC. The documents are then sent to a tutor specifically selected to work with online writing classes, and the tutor returns the document with bubble comments and/or holistic feedback. Tutors avoid making comments on every single error or item in a student's paper. Rather, they comment on higher order concerns, giving holistic comments primarily and lower-level suggestions as needed. In this way, students are not overwhelmed by a wall of comments and feedback with no direction on how to sort them, creating more accessible and comfortable messages (Barber 2000). Through the partnership of cross-training with the composition program, tutors know the pedagogical goals of class assignments and units and can give more informed, effective feedback to strengthen the lessons and guidance of the instructor. Additionally, the tutor can refer the student back to a resource already provided on a research guide for the course or link to a database within the library. Working with tutors to receive feedback builds our students' sense of community and support by both interacting with other campus entities outside of the LMS and seeing how those units collaborate to create and share resources. These tutor interactions give online students valuable collaborative experience, helping create the kind of collaborative social presences Barber (2000) uses to define the online writing classroom.

Within this context, one strength of online writing tutoring (OWT) is that it mimics the desired educational goals of engaging students to more deeply consider the rhetorical choices of their writing, something many online students may miss in thinking their writing exists in a vacuum on the LMS. Public and online writing modes push students to think of "real" readers in a general audience. OWT mimics this dynamic. In a synchronous session, this is clear to imagine as a student submits a text to an unfamiliar reader with no knowledge of course content or assignment choice. There exists an opportunity for the tutor to lead the student to a point of reflection about the purpose and organization of the text. While Mick and Middlebrook (2015) postulate that asynchronous tutoring would lead to "a sense of participant isolation, or . . . loss of social presence," the separation of tutor from student does allow the tutor to emulate a public reader, or an "interested by abstract reader," thus helping the student in fact participate in the interaction similarly to the synchronous session (131; Remington 2006, 2). The student, knowing the tutor will not have access to course materials, lectures, or content, is confronted with the idea of considering an abstract reader, with no opportunity for her/him to explain textual choices. The act of submitting a text to a disembodied reader, with no immediate knowledge of course content or assignment specifics (or a chance to explain them face to face), forces the student to consider their rhetorical choices, phrasing, and text organization. This submission also mimics the act of posting a written text in a public online space, one where the audience's knowledge levels are unknown.

A tutoring session with a skilled tutor, synchronous or asynchronous, will aid writers to "consider the needs of their audience, as well as the purpose and language of their writing" (Barber 2000, 244). This is due to tutoring sessions creating the opportunity for self-reflection and dialogue between the writer and reader. For example, Elizabeth allows her students an opportunity to revise and resubmit particular assignments. In this case, students can reflect on the feedback from a tutor, self-reflect on those comments in relation to their own rhetorical choices, adapt their text, and then create a new tutoring session for another round of feedback. In the second session, the student has the ability to dialogue with the tutor, informing of certain changes and seeking guidance on any new ideas. Now, the student has the opportunity to dialogue with a librarian for resources and information as well as with their instructor and tutor.

Like cleverly conceptualized online writing instruction, OWT can provide students a sense of community and engagement when they are disconnected from the physical campus. Encouraging this kind of connection between students and the LC also offers consistency to a course regardless of instructional model/mode. For example, when Elizabeth swiftly moved her face-to-face courses online during the beginning of the coronavirus pandemic, she didn't have to introduce a new mode of learning for those students. Elizabeth's integration of the online LC options made the transition easier for everyone involved. The aforementioned collaboration between the three units allows tutors to have a better idea of the composition curriculum and assignments they will encounter. We believe this familiarity gives tutors the chance to build bridges with students that, on the one hand, minimize the use of statements such as "I'm sorry I don't know a lot about this assignment," and on the other, encourage more personalized communication geared toward students' needs. Similarly, the LC's knowledge and partnerships with the library also allow tutors to recommend specific resources to students. This creates a net of support where students do not have to exist in vacuums of the LMS or tutor center or library. Students' sense of campus community grows when campus constituents are connecting and communicating among themselves and with students. In addition, instructors can incorporate and reinforce this piece of the village throughout the course. In Elizabeth's classes, students write revision plans between the rough and final drafts. This plan requires students to synthesize feedback from peers and tutors and serves as the basis for teacher-student conferences.

THE STUDENT'S ROLE

In addition to communicating with their instructor, peers, and possibly public audiences, students get to interact and communicate with other parties on campus: library staff and LC tutors. Besides serving as other channels of authentic communication that allows students to practice the rhetorical skills developed in the open writing spaces, these interactions serve an equally significant purpose: supporting students in their academic endeavor and providing opportunities for success in what can be an overwhelming environment.

Students are active participants in this community. All village components reinforce and encourage student interaction with each other. For example, Elizabeth incorporates LC PowerPoints and videos in her courses, posts announcements about LC events and activities, and sends emails to students to remind them to use the LC as a resource throughout the semester. The LCs scheduling system sends emails to the instructor after each student visit with a tutor's summary of what happened during the session, which further cements the connection between the two as well as creating a communication channel that includes the students themselves.

Similar interactions happen between instructors, librarians, and students. Samantha and Elizabeth often have email chains with students to assist in locating, evaluating, and synthesizing sources. Students are encouraged to seek out the librarians for help during any stage of the research/writing process, but it is important for instructors to make student expectations clear from the beginning. While Elizabeth does not grade students on interactions with the library resources, she does (through lectures and course materials) explicitly tell students that they are expected to use and engage with the LibGuide and other library resources to support their research and writing. Comments and feedback are the most common and efficient way to remind students of these things.

We believe these close-knit interactions between our three units create more diverse and engaging digital spaces that help students better "create social presences and realities . . . both interactive and collaborative" (Barber 2000, 243). Our dialogues with each other through course materials and resources also mimic to students the interplay of different groups and people so commonly found in society. We ask our students to collaborate and work together, and we model these goals with our actions as well. By leveraging our resources and skill-sets, we are better able to help our online students in coursework but also connect with campus departments, giving a face or voice to otherwise often anonymous web links, email addresses, or syllabus sections stating to "use campus resources."

THE LARGER VILLAGE

We believe many readers identify with Jason Snart's (2015) argument that teachers become disheartened when some students refuse to engage fully in the online course even though they had spent a long time thoughtfully designing an engaging learning experience. While he encourages instructors to aspire for ideal engagement and interaction, he acknowledges that such full emotional and intellectual engagement may not be always possible (Snart 2015, 116). Moving the class to a public writing space, especially social media sites/websites, can be a step in the right direction toward the intellectual and emotional engagement and interaction all teachers hope to achieve in their online classes. Students often lose work because of the locked nature of an LMS. These alternate pathways allow for the more authentic interaction described in this chapter without leaving the village behind. Instead, the village also leaves the LMS behind with ease. Campus resources like writing tutors and library resources are not inherently tied to an LMS, so they can be used regardless of where the course and the writing happens.

Nitin Agarwal theorizes that sound conceptualization of the online class lies squarely on the instructor's shoulders because they are responsible for planning, designing, and delivering the materials to students. Once students receive these materials, the second phase of "experience, reflection/observation, and application" requires student active engagement and interaction with these carefully designed materials, peers, the instructor, and possibly public audience (Agarwal 2011, 42). This phase is what Barber describes as an actualization of writing as a social activity that encourages "new forms of writer-audience interaction" (243). When writing moves to a public platform, students begin to consider their public audience more carefully because writing is not addressed solely to the instructor or their classmates any longer; the online writing class becomes "contact zones" where "cultures meet, clash, and grapple with each other" (Pratt 1991, 34). By writing in public spaces, more voices representing more cultures can join the discourse community of the class, nuancing and complicating the perspectives students have already brought to the online open discussion. As Barber (2000) argues, this open-to-the-public writing requires students to "consider the needs of their audience, as well as the purpose and language of their writing" (244). The instructor must then consider the needs of their students and carefully construct connections to the campus village in ways that address this new space.

Furthermore, student writing accrues a longer lifespan that transcends the limited life of the writing class. Their writing continues to live on that public platform, thus having the possibility of being read, and sometimes commented on, by wider audiences that include mere strangers. This extended availability of writing results in what Barber (2000) calls a "multivalent discourse in the online classroom" (250). This complex discourse, we argue, encourages more reflection on the writing produced by the student and by others in that discourse. Because the discourse is alive, students are able to visit it after the course has ended and they have the opportunity to engage with the writing in more nuanced ways that may result in reconsidering some of their earlier expressed ideas or pursuing others further through research. Such rich and long experience is not possible when writing happens in the confinement of an LMS because students lose access to that site after the semester has ended. Barber (2000) uses the Bakhtinian concept of "heteroglossia" to describe that level of interaction between writers and the meaning of written texts residing in the online class public space (250). This multi-layered interaction between instructor, other students, and public audience becomes a vehicle for student's deeper comprehension of the course content (Cooper and Selfe 1990) and a site for reflection on their writing as well as their social presence and practices. While not all instructors have the option of moving writing outside the LMS, some of the examples might be adaptable to LMS activities and embedded elements, depending on the LMS in use. D2L, for example, is a fairly open and adaptable LMS while Blackboard is relatively closed.

Some writing teachers have the choice of staying within the LMS or one of thousands of online public spaces to which they can move their online writing class; for those who choose to leave the LMS, websites like Wix and Weebly and social media sites like Facebook remain among the more prominent and favorite platforms where writing, interaction, collaboration, and learning happens. Several scholars suggest the use of social media platforms for various reasons, and we argue that using social media as sites of public writing creates authentic forums where students practice group-work activities as well as learn about privacy and civic discussions, both skills required in future workplaces. Using social media also builds on student familiarity with these sites and applications while helping combat the isolation many students feel in the online class. Using one or a mixture of these options allows for more possibilities, but it also requires some additional planning for all members of the campus village.

Orchestrating the Village Outside the LMS

In her Chair's Address to the Conference on College Composition and Communication (CCCC), Kathleen Blake Yancey (2004) spoke about what scholars and instructors face as "never before has the proliferation of writings outside the academy so counterpointed the compositions inside" (297–98). This was a warning for us to reevaluate what we teach and how we teach, which was later echoed by Cynthia Selfe (2004), who wrote "if our profession continues to focus solely on the teaching of alphabetic composition—either online or in print—we run the risk of making composition studies increasingly irrelevant to students engaging in contemporary practices of communication" (72). Much has changed in the fourteen years since Yancey and Selfe warned instructors about the need to evolve and adapt to teaching new composition practices in an ever-increasingly digital world, but there is always room for more. Composing in digital modes, through Wix, Weebly, Google Sites, and other sites, supports this growing need to address the complex composition practices of contemporary students. In her classes, Elizabeth has students create a website on Wix (or one of the many free online website generators) so students write in real time for a real audience rather than for an imagined audience supplied by the instructor. While there is no way to account for a real audience outside of the classmates, there have been several instances throughout Elizabeth's time using these platforms where "random" people have followed, commented, and otherwise interacted with her student's work. Strangers also follow Elizabeth's YouTube channel that hosts her lectures and other instructional videos. Because this is a possibility, it is something she discusses with students prior to their publishing the website/work.

In the past, Elizabeth's students also have used these sites to keep research journals along with final research projects. While students can compose alphabetic text on these sites, there is a wider range of possibilities of what can be composed and shared on these public writing spaces. In other classes, for example, students edited and remixed video presentations, music and movie clips to connect their ideas with inspiration behind them (they end up looking like VH1's show *Pop Up Video*).

Figure 2: Screenshot of a Pop-Video Style Project on Lana Del Ray's "Paris"

One student fully immersed her website in grunge culture; each page included images, music, and video related to the various aspects of her argument about the cultural impact of grunge on the world. Another student regularly used pictures to accompany her blog posts for the class.

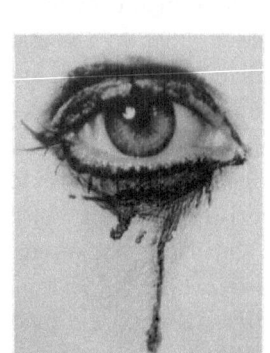

Figure 3: Screenshot from a Student's Blog with Images

These websites allow students to create beyond the alphabetic text as Selfe points out. These kinds of assignments are often more difficult to submit in an LMS due to size and file restrictions, which is why the authors believe public platforms are also important to discuss when developing an online writing course with a village of campus resources to support the students who take them.

When students create projects like websites or write online, they don't have to rely on an LMS for their work to be published. This "real world" application also pushes students to reflect on and make critical choices about their rhetorical situation. George Pullman (2016) suggests that through learning to write online, writers need to develop more digital rhetoric skills that will enable them to think of content as well as the design of that content. He argues that even if the content created to reside in an online platform becomes stale or irrelevant over time, the rhetorical skills and digital literacy acquired along the way remain a "lifelong digital learning" asset for the online writer (Pullman 2016, xvi). Empirically supporting Pullman's (2016) contention, Jose Albors-Garrigos and Jose Ramos Carrasco (2011) studied learning curves and found that learners who engage in education that capitalizes on the affordances of technology and interaction develop lifelong learning skills and are able to continue learning and development of knowledge and skills years after taking that course. Instructors who choose to create assignments like these must communicate with the library and the LC so the support network stays current. When Elizabeth includes assignments like these, she emails them to the LC and the library. In those emails, Elizabeth explains the purpose and audience and asks for feedback and questions so that everyone is on the same page.

Relying on the Village in Public Spaces

In these public digital modes, students come face-to-face with the possibility that someone is going to find and read their work. Instead of an imagined audience for a project, these public writing spaces provide "real" audiences, thus pushing students to think about what they write and create in different ways. Wix, Weebly, and Google Sites offer a way for students to play with and practice the composing and literacy skills of the twenty-first century. It is also an ideal site for learning by doing. To do this, instructors and students interact with the library and the LC in a myriad of ways.

The library can help instructors with more than LibGuides focused on research; they can also create guides for instructors and students that address the digital resources and technology they ask their students to use. Likewise, the writing center can prepare tutors to assist students with these new assignments.

Utilizing open online spaces as platforms for the online writing class comes with its own caveats. The first one has to do with the instructor level of comfort with technology. Some instructors are more technologically adept, but these websites are meant for broad audiences/users who don't have coding skills. For example, Elizabeth doesn't know how to code, but she has several websites on several platforms that she's used in and out of class. While online courses are being lauded for their advantages for students, it's essential that instructors consider the needs of students in these spaces. Part of the village that hasn't been a focus so far is the Center for Disability Services (CDS). They often offer resources for students with documented disabilities, and they are exceptionally significant in terms of a village support network for students. As Beth Hewett (2015) notes, moving the online class to spaces outside the LMS may result in being in spaces that are not ADA compliant, thus alienating these students and affecting their learning experiences. Mick and Middlebrook (2015) suggest surveying students about their possible "invisible disabilities" that may compromise their comfort and/or learning and participation in public spaces (145). In Elizabeth's syllabi, she goes beyond the statement from CDS to include a section about accessibility. Acknowledging that students have varying degrees of experience and comfort with these public spaces and programs is important, especially for those with disabilities. However, CDS often reminds instructors during the composition program's pre-fall training that many students do not self-identify, meaning that there are often students with various disabilities in our classrooms that don't have official documentation. The village we've created at our university assists with all students in an effort to support every student as much as possible.

Because of this, instructors can rely on the campus village for help in this area in addition to their own pedagogical practices. As online instruction becomes more and more in demand, instructors should look at all the options available to them, in terms of instruction, lines of communication, and potential assignment modes. Instructors can rely on the village for help here as well. Carlito (2018) explains that

> librarians are already well-versed in many literacies, including information, visual, and media . . . librarians are experts in the paradigm shift from print to multiple modes; therefore, by teaching faculty and students to locate, evaluate, use ethically and cite various modes, librarians become the primary resource on campus for creating multimodal artifacts. (165)

There is potential for librarians to work with instructors to create and lead activities to assist with course content. Carlito's article can, in fact, serve as an example on how to utilize the village for both instructors and students. Our composition program is doing just that. Our spring 2020 professional development aims to further integrate this support network from the library into an instructor's toolkit. Including the writing center in these professional development opportunities can ensure that all parts of the network work to support all student needs.

Building Your Own Village

Utilizing these technologies and social media sites allows instructors to heed the call of Kathleen Blake Yancey, Cynthia Selfe, and other writing scholars. Building and delivering a successful online writing class is largely a collaborative effort that capitalizes on campus resources, particularly the library and the learning center. This laborious effort enhances student learning and writing experience. Furthermore, making decisions regarding moving the online writing class to open spaces requires much thoughtful planning and conceptualization in order to avoid what Yancey (2009) described as a disconnect between students' writing in and out of the academy. What she noted in that report was that students were becoming writers outside of the classroom in digital spaces like blogs, social media, comments sections and threads, and in chat rooms, but the school writing that students do isn't being connected to that outside writing. She suggested then, and we are reissuing the call here, to elevate these kinds of writing tasks in these digital environments so that we may "help our students compose often, compose well, and through these composings, become the citizen writers of our country, the citizen writers of our world, and the writers of our future" (Yancey 2009). Moving the online writing class to public spaces represents what Barber (2000) calls "an extension into new and challenging dimensions" (254). This move, if planned and conceptualized properly, can bring many benefits to students in these classes.

The combination of campus resources and faculty create a community with support for the students. As the students encounter problems, they have multiple options for help. This can be replicated in other areas of English studies. While this chapter focuses on English composition courses, the entire university can benefit from this kind of campus resource community. In Elizabeth's literature survey courses, for example, LibGuides and writing tutors can still be beneficial, with information dedicated to that specific course. LibGuides with resources specific to the covered time periods help students avoid the intimidating amount of library resources available so they can focus their efforts.

Elizabeth's revised Survey of World Literature II course uses the campus village as a foundation. One of the assignments for the course is a re-mix, where students will have options for taking a course reading and re-mixing it into a different mode. Elizabeth and the LC will communicate so the tutors are prepared to assist students with this assignment. In addition, students will be required to give small group presentations. Elizabeth and the library will coordinate LibGuides and other course materials to facilitate this assignment. At the beginning of the course, Elizabeth will also invite the village into her Blackboard course using video introductions so students can put a face to a name. Designing her literature course with the village as the foundation makes it easier to support the students throughout the semester.

As we navigate into unknown territory (with the pandemic and other pressures and factors affecting education) we should lean into this idea of community. English studies can use a variety of technologies and techniques to build connections. During the second half of the spring semester of 2020, we all put our theory to the test. Elizabeth spent much of her spring break creating tutorials and writing instructions for her colleagues on how to move their classes online. To do this, she explained the importance of the library and the LC. She also discovered new possibilities for English studies online. While Zoom has become a primary resource for professional development and training for Elizabeth since March, 2020 (and the pivot to online-only), she sees the possibilities for utilizing Zoom and Zoom breakout rooms for English studies instruction. The library also had to adapt quickly to provide virtual reference services when the campus closed. Although the physical building was shut down, they were still providing services to students and faculty via their virtual helpdesk. The library had been providing chat services prior to the pandemic, however, once the library went virtual it upgraded its subscription to Libchat to include an integrated Zoom option, so librarians could screenshare with students, and vice versa, if they were having technical issues or if they just wanted a more personalized session with the librarian. Similarly, the LC pivoted to synchronous sessions hosted on the campus LMS. Zoom and LMS-integrated technology can offer more opportunity to connect the campus community with students when they can't be in the same room (for whatever reason). As Elizabeth designs the fall 2020 courses, she is in talks with the library and the LC to schedule more time with each in her course schedule. The "asynchronousity" described earlier in the chapter is just the tip of the resource iceberg. The pandemic has pushed all of us to find new avenues to pursue. The benefit to this is twofold: the more resources and technologies we discover offer more options for the instructors, and as we begin to integrate these into the (virtual) classroom, we can ensure that we build structures that cater to student success.

Doing so also has some important implications for retention, which is on the minds of everyone from the faculty to the administration. Berger (1997) wrote about the relationship between student performance and a sense of community, and Clink (2015) writes "the library can support the institution's retention efforts, then, are to provide spaces, personnel, and collections that help students create a sense of community . . . and to validate students who . . . are on their way to successful completion of a college degree" (22). As we have described, the ways in which the library supports online writing students falls in line with what other scholars are requesting. In addition, Griswold (2003) discusses writing centers' link to retention noting, "writing centers represent a unique blend of academic and student affairs approaches. It is such a blend that much of the retention research identifies as important" (278).

In fact, there are opportunities to increase the connections between and among the various members of the campus village. The library and the LC can replicate many of the teacher's course components. Elizabeth incorporates PowerPoint presentations, audio feedback, and video-conferencing in all of her classes, but these are especially important in online courses. What we'd like to see as we move forward is more of this kind of interaction with the library and the LC. We can capitalize the structural components of the LMS and other public spaces to further cement this village approach to education and instruction. Building these support structures is important on so many levels, and with the national interest in retention, these villages can support student success more completely than without the integration of the separate resources.

REFERENCES

Agarwal, Nitin. 2011. "Collective Learning: An Integrated Use of Social Media in Learning Environment." In *Social Media Tools and Platforms in Learning Environments*, edited by Bebo White, Irwin King and Philip Tsang, 37–52. New York: Springer.

Albors-Garrigos, Jose, and Jose Carlos Ramos Carrasco. 2011. "New Learning Paradigms: Open Course Versus Traditional Strategies. The Current Paradox of Learning and Developing Creative Ideas." In *Social Media Tools and Platforms in Learning Environments*, edited by Bebo White et al., 53–80. New York: Springer.

Bailey, Nathan et al. 2011. "Mylearningspace: Engaging Education." In *Social Media Tools and Platforms in Learning Environments*, edited by Bebo White et al., 419–35. New York: Springer.

Banks, Adam. 2015. "Ain't No Walls behind the Sky, Baby! Funk, Flight, Freedom." *College Composition and Communication* 67 (2): 267–79.

Barber, John F. 2000. "Effective Teaching in the Online Classroom: Thoughts and Recommendations." In *The Online Writing Classroom*, edited by Susanmarie Harrington et al., 243–64. Cresskill, NJ: Hampton Press.

Berger, J. B. 1997. "Students' Sense of Community in Residence Halls, Social Integration, and First-year Persistence." *Journal of College Student Development* 38 (5): 441.

Blakeslee, Sarah. 2004. "The CRAAP Test." *LOEX Quarterly* 31 (3) https://commons.emich.edu/loexquarterly/vol31/iss3/4.

Bosman, Lisa and Tom Zagenczyk. 2011. "Revitalize Your Teaching: Creative Approaches to Applying Social Media in the Classroom." *Social Media Tools and Platforms in Learning Environments*, edited by Bebo White et al., 3–15. New York: Springer.

Carlito, M. Delores. 2018. "Supporting Multimodal Literacy in Library Instruction." *Reference Services Review* 46 (2): 164–77.

Clink, Kellian D. 2015. "The Academic Library's Role in Student Retention." *PNLA Quarterly* 80 (1): 20–24.

Cooper, Marilyn, and Cynthia L. Selfe. 1990. "Computer Conferences and Learning: Authority, Resistance, and Internally Persuasive Discourse." *College English* 52 (8): 847–69.

D'Augustino, Steven. 2012. "Toward a Course Conversion Model for Distance Learning." *Journal of International Education in Business* 5: 145–62.

Griswold, Gary. 2003. "Writing Centers: The Student Retention Connection." *Academic Exchange Quarterly* 7 (4): 277–81.

Hewett, Beth L. 2015. "Grounding Principles of OWI." *Foundational Practices of Online Writing Instruction*, edited by Beth L. Hewett and Kevin Eric DePew, 33–92. Fort Collins and Anderson: The WAC Clearinghouse/Parlor Press.

Jackson, Pamela Alexandra. 2007. "Integrating Information Literacy into Blackboard: Building Campus Partnerships for Successful Student Learning." *The Journal of Academic Librarianship* 33 (4): 454–61.

Lunsford, Andrea. 1995. "Collaboration, Control, and the Idea of a Writing Center." *The St.Martin's Sourcebook for Writing Tutors*, edited by Christina Murphy and Steve Sherwood, 36–42. New York: St. Martin's Press.

Mick, Connie Snyder, and Geoffrey Middlebrook. 2015. "Asynchronous and Synchronous Modalities." In *Foundational Practices of Online Writing Instruction*, edited by Beth L. Hewett and Kevin Eric DePew, 33–92. Fort Collins and Anderson: The WAC Clearinghouse/Parlor Press.

Pratt, Mary Louise. 1991. "Arts of the Contact Zone." *Profession* 33–40.

Pullman, George. 2016. *Writing Online: Rhetoric for the Digital Age*. Indianapolis, IN: Hackett Publishing Company.

Remington, Ted. 2006. "Reading, Writing, and the Role of the Online Tutor." *The Writing Lab Newsletter* 30 (5): 1–5.

Schoper, Sarah E and Aaron R. Hill. 2017. "Using Facebook to Promote Learning: A Case Study." *Journal of Learning Spaces* 6 (1): 34–39.

Selfe, Cynthia. 2004. "Toward New Media Texts: Taking Up the Challenges of Visual Literacy." In *Writing New Media: Theory and Applications for Expanding the Teaching of Composition*, edited by Anne Frances Wysocki, Johndan Johnson-Eilola, Cynthia L. Selfe, and Geoffrey Sirc, 67–110. Logan: Utah State UP.

Shank, John D., and Nancy H. Dewald. 2003. "Establishing our Presence in Courseware: Adding Library Services to the Virtual Classroom." *Information Technology and Libraries* 22 (1): 38–43.

Snart, Jason. 2015. "Hybrid and Fully Online OWI." In *Foundational Practices of Online Writing Instruction*, edited by Beth L. Hewett and Kevin Eric DePew, 33–92. Fort Collins and Anderson: The WAC Clearinghouse/Parlor Press.

Yancey, Kathleen Blake. 2004. "Made Not Only in Words: Composition in a New Key." *College Composition and Communication* 56 (2): 297–328.

Yancey, Kathleen Blake. 2009. "Writing in the 21st Century: A Report from NCTE." Urbana, IL: National Council of Teachers of English.

6 Teaching "Teaching Technologies in English Studies": Training a New Generation of Teachers

Stephanie Hedge

In a small dark room in the back of the library, huddled around an old, outdated desktop, a group of graduate students pokes and prods at the guts of the Blackboard site for their own class, clicking around the assignment features, the gradebook, the announcements and blogs and videos, changing the theme and the layout. Most students express dismay at the limitations of the features, or frustration at the unintuitive layout, while others are overwhelmed at the possible classroom configurations. This same group will later debrief on Slack, sending emoji-filled messages that tentatively, hesitantly, nudge at the boundaries of English studies and technology. They argue for using different features in different classrooms, the wiki pages that might work for a literature class, the groupings that would work for a creative writing seminar. They consider their own positions as students, working and learning in online spaces, and imagine the possibilities of their own online classrooms, guided by their own pedagogies, perspectives, and skills.

These students are enrolled in "Teaching Technologies in English Studies," a graduate-level course taken as part of the Digital Pedagogy track in the English studies MA at the University of Illinois Springfield. This course, taken alongside content-specific pedagogy courses, prepares students for the realities of teaching in 2018 and beyond. Through acknowledging that teaching, writing, and reading are increasingly mediated by emergent technologies, this course aims to prepare graduate students for a shifting job market and changing English studies landscapes, positioning these emergent scholars as potential leaders regarding online teaching[1.]

This chapter explores that course, arguing for pedagogy courses that explicitly focus on teaching that is supported by and mediated through technologies and suggests that this course might become a foundational course across English studies disciplines, taking up the role of introducing students to new perspectives and possibilities of teaching. Reflecting the balance between theory and practice that serves as the backbone for "Teaching with Technologies," this chapter will begin by exploring three guiding beliefs that shape this course: (1) digitally mediated teaching is fundamentally different from teaching face to face, and these teaching practices should be supported by dedicated pedagogies; (2) emergent teachers should be armed with digital literacies grounded in digital pedagogies so that these teachers will be able to adapt to shifting emergent technologies; and (3) English studies as a field is uniquely positioned to grapple with the intersections between word and technology. Following this discussion of the theory, I will share details of what this course looks like in practice, with suggested outcomes/objectives, assignments, and readings.

Guiding Belief #1: Digitally Mediated Teaching Requires Dedicated Pedagogies

The act of mediating instruction through emergent digital technologies fundamentally changes that instruction. Strategies, activities, assign-

---

1. This chapter was written just prior to the global pandemic that has upended education in 2020, an unprecedented circumstance that has forced on-ground classes into online and remote modalities with little warning. This addendum is written in the middle of that ongoing crisis as institutions weigh the necessity of continuing remote instruction for the near future, and instructors are working hard to adjust their classes to facilitate remote and blended learning. I mention these particular circumstances because they highlight the need for a theoretically grounded digital pedagogy for teaching online—graduate students and instructors are better prepared to make challenging pedagogical decisions in the face of unprecedented challenges when they have a teaching philosophy and grasp of theory that is untethered from the specifics of individual technologies and applications. Adding classes like "Teaching Technologies in English Studies" to English graduate curricula is increasingly necessary as the relationship between education and technology continues to shift and change, and as our students and instructors are faced with unprecedented circumstances.

ments, discussions, teacher personas—all of the features that make up face-to-face classrooms are fundamentally changed when they are mediated through technology. Beginning with McLuhan's claim that "all media work us over completely" (1967, 26) to Bolter and Grusin's arguments about remediation (1999), the idea of technologically mediated teaching as fundamentally *changed* is a belief that grounds pedagogies dedicated to online teaching. Pedagogies designed for face-to-face may not be successful in online teaching; instead, teachers need pedagogies designed or adapted for online teaching to be successful. Beth L. Hewitt (2014) offers a glimpse at the challenging moving parts to online writing pedagogies, pointing out a laundry list of "building blocks" that make up the online writing classroom: "course setting, pedagogical purpose, digital modality, medium, and student audience" (196). These blocks represent the spaces where the teaching experience is mediated—our voices, bodies, texts, discussions, and thoughts—by the learning management system, the discussion boards, the blogs or tweets or videos or voice memos or Google Docs we employ to teach. Navigating this digital *ecology* requires a dedicated pedagogy that embraces such complexity. Kristie Fleckenstein (2005) argues for an understanding of the online classroom as a complex system, an "emergent identity, a gestalt of transacting elements that cannot be reduced to a sum of its parts" (150), a classroom that is greater than the individual technologies that comprise its parts. This ecological model speaks to the necessity of a pedagogy that acknowledges the online writing classroom as a space unique from F2F instruction. The understanding that mediation fundamentally changes the teaching process is not a new one; for example, decades ago, Joanne Buckley (1997) writes as a woman with a disability about the freedom she experiences teaching online in a setting where her body is not visible. This reality is the exigence for much of the writing and research about teaching online, as Scott Warnock (2009) points out in the introduction to *Teaching Writing Online*, a text dedicated to helping instructors think about "migrating" their teaching practices to online writing instruction. Building from this belief, then, the "Teaching Technologies" course I designed supports students as they develop their own pedagogies and approaches to the online classroom. The teaching philosophy and ePortfolio assignments described below facilitate the creation of individual online pedagogies supported by theory.

Guiding Belief #2: Digital Literacies Should Be the Foundation of Online Pedagogies

J. Elizabeth Clark (2010) has argued for a twenty-first century pedagogy that is founded on the flexibility afforded by digital literacies. She calls for the profession to be able to "morph" and embrace emergent technologies, pointing out that there will always be new technologies: "We cannot understand or embrace this digital imperative without the notion of flux: the ever-changing landscape of Web 2.0 platforms and applications. In this regard, the 'greatest hits' of the current digital world—ePortfolios, blogs, wikis, Twitter, social networking software, Second Life—are not the final development in composition pedagogy" (27). As an instructor who moved away from incorporating Twitter in all my classes because of increasing harassment faced by women and people of color on the platform, I keenly feel the swift changes in technology pointed out by Clark here. A pedagogy rooted in technologies must be flexible enough to adapt to constant change, and this flexibility is best facilitated through fostering the growth of digital literacies in students. Calling on teachers to "pay attention" to the technologies surrounding education, Cynthia Selfe (1999) defines technological literacy as "a complex set of socially and culturally situated values, practices, and skills involved in operating linguistically within the context of electronic environments, including reading, writing and communicating" (11). Selfe describes a digital literacy that is grounded in social use and context, a literacy that is in keeping with how English studies as a field approaches texts and serves as the grounding for the digital literacies developed in "Teaching Technologies." This course provides space for students to develop heuristics for approaching technologies with a pedagogical bent, building from Stuart Selber's construction of three literacy categories: functional, critical, and rhetorical. Selber (2004) points out that technology "and its constitutive contexts are dynamic, contingent, and negotiable by nature" (29) and offers his three literacies as heuristic. Functional literacies focus on the ability to use technology, understanding "computers as tools" (25). Critical literacy emphasizes the social contexts for technologies, encouraging questions and analysis (81), while rhetorical literacies understand the persuasive and productive power of technologies, building on the skills of functional and critical literacies (166). Given the realities of swift and profound changes in emergent technologies for teaching (remember MOOCs?), this course uses Selber's literacy frameworks to support student-created heuristics for using, analyzing, and teaching with emergent technologies. The analysis and demonstration assignments, discussed in more detail below, are specifically geared toward developing digital literacies.

Guiding Belief #3: English Studies Is Uniquely Situated to Engage with Online Teaching Pedagogies

As Selfe and Hawisher (1999) argue in "The Passions that Mark Us: Teaching, Texts, and Technologies," English studies as a discipline has always been concerned with texts, language, words, and the ways that those artifacts are embedded in culture. This attention to literacies and their contexts give English studies a unique vantage point for interrogating emergent technologies and thinking about how those technologies are tied to communication, teaching, and research. They remind us that technological artifacts are central to English studies not because they are merely communication tools, but because they "embody and shape—and are shaped by—the ideological assumptions of an entire culture" (Selfe and Hawisher 1999, 2). Perhaps no discipline is better suited to thinking through the cultural contexts of emergent technologies, particularly those technologies that are mediated through writing and language. Our skills in thinking through alphabetic texts can (and have!) been expanded to visual and other multimodal texts (Selfe 2004; Kress 1999; Arola and Wysoki 2012), and our field is increasingly expanding into digital humanities (Burdick et al. 2012). Our disciplinary approach to understanding the ways words do work in the world, coupled with our focus on pedagogy, makes English studies well-suited to grapple with the challenges of online teaching and teaching through technologies.

There are also two key practical reasons that this course belongs in English studies. The first is that many graduate programs are already structured to include graduate-level pedagogy courses, given the realities that many graduate students in English studies teach first-year writing or other gen-ed courses. We have already established pedagogical training as central to the work of English studies, and widening that work to include the realities of online teaching is a necessary step in preparing our emergent scholars. As Anthony Atkins (2005) reminds us,

> TA training is crucial for every new teacher, but especially for those inexperienced with digital technologies and new literacies. It is still abundantly clear that many writing programs use TAs

and contract/adjunct staff to teach the first-year composition courses, and it is the program, department, and university's responsibility to see to it that, one, the TAs are trained properly and, two, students in the first-year composition classroom have fully prepared and qualified teachers. Specifically, writing programs, departments, and universities have academic/professional goals, and without proper TA training teachers of first-year writing cannot help facilitate those goals and agendas.

Pedagogy courses frequently introduce students to new aspects of English studies; many former literature students begin their "conversion narratives" (Kopelson 2008) to composition studies in their pedagogy classes, for example, and these classes not only prepare our students for the realities of the job market, but offer a space for expanding the boundaries of what we understand English studies to be. This is tied to the other practical reason for including a course specifically geared to teaching online or teaching with technologies in an English studies graduate program: the need for English studies programs to remain relevant in a digital world. Kristine L. Blair (2016) unpacks the need for digitally literate English studies as she describes the move to an online MA program at Bowling Green State University, arguing that the needs of contemporary students are not only best met by online courses, but also by programs and departments that embrace technologies. She writes, "we must remediate and transition our profession into a new model of higher education that both emphasizes professionalization and sustains the relevance of a language arts degree beyond the academy" (Blair 2016, 38), and goes on to suggest that online teaching is one path to disciplinary relevance. A pedagogy course geared toward creating online teachers is both immediately practical for the teaching landscape our students will encounter, and as a core part of English studies programs creates room for future scholars and educators to draw new boundaries around English studies departments and degrees.

Moving Between Theory and Practice: The Role of the Instructor

The role of instructor for this course is a potentially challenging one—that of practitioner, expert, facilitator, and guide to thinking about teaching with technologies and teaching online. The instructor has to create a course that marries theory with practice and meaningfully demonstrates best practices for online teaching (potentially in a F2F or blended course, which adds to the challenge). This is a unique challenge for many programs, particularly those that do not have a dedicated digital or online pedagogy expert, made potentially more complex through faculty resistance to and reluctance toward online teaching. In her chapter "TextSupport: Incorporating Online Pedagogy into MA English Programs," Abigail Scheg (2016) discusses these challenges, pointing toward small steps that departments could take to incorporate online pedagogies in their terminal English MA programs, including dedicated online sections in pedagogy courses, and reliance on guidebooks and other practical features. Scheg (2016) points out that "small steps toward incorporating online pedagogy make for significant learning opportunities for potential teachers" (134), and these small steps might be the right place for departments to begin before implementing a course like "Teaching Technologies," to build faculty buy-in for and confidence in teaching online pedagogies. Part of that buy-in comes from making space for instructors who may not feel as though they are experts in online teaching to facilitate a course like "Teaching Technologies."

Based on my own experience teaching this course, I have two inter-related suggestions for instructors who might lean into their uncertainty to concerns about a course dedicated to online pedagogies. The first is to be transparent about your own online and digital pedagogies and practices and transparent about your own expertise and growing edges. As I talked about the choices I made in designing this course, students were invited to respond critically and thoughtfully. Similarly, with the Blackboard shell they were invited to experiment with, students were encouraged to play with, challenge, and explore my teaching strategies as the semester went on. My willingness to be open about the challenges of crafting an online class let students feel better about their own struggles and growing edges and allowed us to learn best practices and approaches together.

My second suggestion is to create an online space for experimentation and play regardless of the delivery mode for the course. This provides an environment where instructors might demonstrate some best practices in online teaching while also inviting students throughout the semester to deconstruct, challenge, and re-make parts of the course based on what they are learning. For me, this meant developing a Blackboard shell for a F2F course that mimicked my online courses in format and structure and allowing students to experiment with format. We re-wrote several assignment sheets to account for digital delivery, for example, providing students with a low-stakes yet practical space to adjust to the realities of online delivery modes. Structuring the course delivery modes as transparent, flexible, and experimental gives both the instructor and the students room to learn and grow together.

Theory into Practice: A Look at "Teaching Technologies in English Studies"

The description of "Teaching Technologies in English Studies" on the current syllabus is this:

> This course is situated at the intersection between pedagogy, English studies, and emergent digital technologies, and begins with the assumption that engagement with digital technologies is an inherent, crucial part of developing a contemporary online pedagogy in English studies—both in fostering digital literacies skills in students and engaging in digital literacies as instructors. This course walks the line between theory and praxis, introducing you to critical theories on the production and analysis of text(s) in digital contexts and critical theories on engaging with digitally mediated pedagogies, while also providing opportunities to think about those theories in lived online classroom practices. This course will also look at the ways technologies are situated in the world, as inherently political, social, and historical artifacts that both shape and constrain our lived realities, and invite you to think through challenges of access, identity, and cultural engagement as you design and implement your online pedagogy.
>
> Given the challenges of engaging with emergent digital technologies, which change and update constantly, this course is geared toward providing you with a broad heuristic for engaging with technologies, rather than teaching specifics. In other words, you will be given the tools and skills to seek out, assess, analyze, and implement new and emergent digital technologies in varied online pedagogical contexts. Therefore, the reading, writing, and research work you do within this course will be influenced by your own interests, history, and personal pedagogical approach. You will also have an opportunity to learn collaboratively with your peers, as you lead discussions, contrib-

ute to our blog, engage in teaching demonstrations, and share your analysis, writing, and design practices with the class.

The objectives for this course stem from this description: they are focused on ensuring that students are comfortable articulating theories of teaching online and with technologies, and that students are putting those theories into practice as they consider their own online teaching classrooms. They are currently written on the syllabus as:

> As a teacher-practitioner, this course asks you to engage in a wide variety of pedagogical readings and practices. By the end of the semester, you will:
>
> - Be able to define digital literacies and digital pedagogies as both theories and lived practices in the world, and articulate the ways in which these technologies are tied to social, cultural, and historical ideologies and practices
> - Be able to articulate the need for a technologically informed pedagogy, both for students and for instructors, and be able to demonstrate the lived practices of this pedagogy through designing and implementing assignments and classroom practices for online courses
> - Be able to advocate for Online courses, and demonstrate readiness for teaching in online spaces
> - Be able to critically analyze and assess diverse emergent digital technologies, both for their potential as pedagogical tools and for grading and assessment purposes
> - Draft a thoughtful, critically complex digital teaching and learning philosophy, informed by both theory and practice
> - Complete a fully annotated digital online teaching portfolio, demonstrating your ability to turn theory into practice and preparing you for future teaching, as well as demonstrating your ability to design and publish digital documents

I am sharing the course description and objectives not as a prescriptive suggestion but rather to illustrate the approach that I have taken to create a course centered on the guiding beliefs articulated above. One key feature that I would like to highlight is the student-led choice in technologies, English studies focus, and philosophy. As I will discuss in the assignments section below, the types of digital artifacts that we study, and the particular classes they envision, are all driven by the interests, experiences, and beliefs of the students enrolled in the class. This student-led philosophy is appropriate both for a graduate-level course and for shaping future scholars and instructors.

Assignments

There are four broad categories of assignment for "Teaching Technologies in English Studies": technology analysis, teaching demonstration, teaching philosophy, and ePortfolio. I will discuss each category below, offering concrete examples of the kinds of assignments that might fall under each category. Each category of assignment asks students to define for themselves what effective online and technology-supported teaching looks like and provides space for students to pair theory with practice. These assignments are weighted roughly equally, with the ePortfolio taking a slightly larger share of the overall grade as it acts as a cumulative assignment for the course.

Technology Analysis: The first category of assignment is an analysis, which grounds our semester in theory with an eye toward practice. I have asked students to analyze or discuss different types of technology throughout the years, but the grounding purpose of this assignment is an explicit focus on the affordances, constraints, underlying systemic beliefs, and potential for pedagogical application of a piece of emergent tech. There are a few different approaches that I have taken to the analysis papers, depending on the semester and the needs and interests of the students.

- One approach is a **student-led emergent tech analysis**, where students are asked to find and analyze emergent technologies that are not necessarily explicitly created for teaching and consider how and why they might fit into an online and technologically supported pedagogy. Students share their discoveries through a class blog or in class discussion, and frequently choose to use these technologies in their teaching demos. Students have found places for civic engagement (like the Facebook TownHall feature), editing and sharing work (like Xodo or Dropbox Paper), publication and presentation (like Fold or Soundcloud), and classroom organization (like Lino Corkboard or Classcraft).
- Another approach to the analysis assignment is a directed analysis of **CMS and LMS systems** currently in use at different institutions. Students are directed to analyze Moodle, Blackboard,

and Canvas, and then invited to find an additional LMS to analyze on their own. Students are invited to explore more than just the features of the site and dig into the histories and contexts of the companies behind these classroom systems. I have found that this variation of the analysis assignment is most useful for students who are currently teaching online or are planning to teach online in the immediate future.
- A slightly different approach to the analysis paper is to have students create either an **ecology discussion** or a **dream LMS proposal**. Both of these assignments ask students to think creatively about their classrooms and the kinds of technologies they either use or would like to use.
  - The ecology discussion invites students to think of the online classroom as an ecology, supported by many technologies beyond the LMS they use through the school. I invite students to analyze all of the technologies supporting a single classroom, which may include discussion features like Slack or Blogger, may include places like Twitter or Facebook, and may include teaching and writing technologies like Prezi or YouTube or class-created wiki pages. The goal is for students to interrogate their own classroom ecologies, and to understand how all of this tech works both individually and as a cohesive whole to create an online classroom.
  - The dream LMS proposal asks students to build their own LMS, based on what they know of current LMSs and what they want their own classroom to look like. This can be a concluding assignment in a sequence focused on analyzing an existing LMSs, or a stand-alone assignment that asks students to pivot from analysis to invention. Students are required to articulate their understandings of both effective online teaching and their own pedagogies and approaches, as well as demonstrate an understanding of the affordances and constraints of varied technologies.

These varied approaches demonstrate how flexible the analysis assignment can be to meet the needs of different programs and students.

In all analysis assignment sheets, I include a heuristic for the students to follow, offering a slew of guiding questions across broad categories for analysis. As students complete analysis work over the semester, they are invited to add their own questions or categories, and following the submission of each piece, we take time in class to share as a group what additions or changes students have made to my original heuristic based on their own analysis and discussion. Regardless of which type of technology the students are analyzing or what shape their analysis takes, all assignments end with a pivot toward lived classroom practices. Students are invited to think about these technologies in the context of teaching, and the heuristics provided in the assignment sheets consistently include a "practice" category that invites students to think about how these technologies might intersect with their own pedagogies and goals for the classroom. Here is a sample heuristic from the student-led technology analysis assignment sheet:

> Affordances and Constraints: What does this technology allow or invite you to do? What kinds of writing or work does it explicitly support, and what kinds of work is made possible through this platform (What are the official vs unofficial uses of this technology)? As well, what kinds of things does this technology prevent or make difficult? What kinds of work is not possible through this platform?
>
> Barriers to Participation: What are things that would prevent students or instructors from using this technology? Consider access, financial burdens, ease-of-use, accommodating students with disabilities, and platform/operating system limitations.
>
> Embedded Values: What assumptions does this platform make about the work or about the people who use it? Who wrote or created this platform? How do the design choices make arguments about the world? These values are often tied to the barriers and affordances/constraints—What does this platform think is important or worth doing? How does it make money or otherwise support itself? What other platforms is it affiliated with?
>
> Pedagogical Implications: How are you going to use this technology in an online English studies classroom? How does it fit in with your larger assumptions about what and how students should be learning? How does it contribute to the purposes of a Liberal Arts education? Why this technology

specifically? What specific assignments, activities, or classroom management might this technology support?

The goal of these analyses is to ask students to *pay attention* to the emergent technologies they might use as they teach and to think through the creation of heuristics for engaging critically with technologies. Students should complete this assignment with the confidence to assess new technologies and incorporate them in their teaching, becoming flexible and digitally literate instructors who are prepared for the challenges of teaching in the quickly-changing world of online teaching. This is particularly important for students who may take jobs in varied online teaching environments. I cannot teach students all of the features of every LMS, for example, and therefore this assignment is geared toward helping students assess, discover, and then make use of emergent or unfamiliar learning management systems guided by their own pedagogies and perspectives.

Teaching Demonstration: The second category of assignment for this course focuses explicitly on the practice of teaching and asks students to prepare twenty-minute online teaching demonstrations that take place throughout the semester. These teaching demonstrations are tied to their teaching philosophies and analyses, in that students are required to highlight a specific technology or online teaching strategy for their demo, and to articulate how this demo is grounded in their own teaching philosophy. There are three key components to these demos: a lesson plan, a reflection, and the demo itself, structured as a workshop model where peers participate in the online lesson before class and then come together to respond following the demonstration, which I explain on the assignment sheet as follows:

> One of the keys to strong, engaged teaching is the ability to balance theory and practice: to understand, internalize, and theorize best teaching pedagogies, and subsequently channel those pedagogies into lived online classroom practices. These practices must also adhere to course and program goals, taking into account the requirements of other stakeholders across the university. A related requirement of strong, engaged teaching is the ability to reflect on one's teaching practices, honestly assess the strengths and weaknesses of any given pedagogy and practice, and make careful adjustments to teaching based on these assessments. No teaching strategy or specific lesson is perfect, and

the ability to locate, articulate, and assess individual teaching practices is key to critically engaged teaching. This is particularly key when thinking about technologies—remember, as we've talked about, including technology should be done to support a pedagogy or best teaching practice. This demo is designed to give you a space to play with a technology, and to use technology to support what you want to teach. You will each be given 20 minutes to teach a short online lesson, relevant to English studies (creative writing, composition, literature, or linguistics) and that incorporates technology, to your peers. After the lesson, we will offer immediate feedback (think of this as similar to a writing workshop: you are, in effect, workshopping your teaching activity for peer critique).

For many students, this is their first experience in teaching in an online space. I set up a separate Blackboard shell for the demonstrations, and invite the students to add, change, and explore existing structures on the site as they create their lesson plans and teach their assignments. For this assignment, students turn in **lesson plans** before they do their demonstration. These lesson plans have both a practical and theoretical purpose: (1) for students to prepare their lesson strategically and (2) for students to articulate their philosophy and pedagogical approach as they craft their lesson. Although students structure the lesson plan in their own style, they are required to articulate the goals of the lesson, the strategy for including technologies and online tools, and to relate these goals and strategies to their pedagogies. Following the demonstration, students turn in a **reflection** where they think critically about both their own experiences as the instructor and feedback from their peers. Students are asked to articulate both what worked well in the lesson and what their growing edges might be, developing individual heuristics to test how technology-mediated lessons are received by students and adjust their own practices in response. Important to this reflection is the **workshop-style feedback** given to students after their demonstrations. Following the demonstration, the student is given a chance to ask questions or share their own perspective before sitting silently as their peers offer feedback and brainstorming. I ask three questions of the room: What are things that were particularly successful about this lesson? What are specific growing edges or changes for this lesson? Based on this lesson, how might you incorporate this technology or strategy in new or different ways? This discussion is frequently lively and engaged and allows all of the students to practice thinking critically about their teaching using the language and heuristics of the course. The ultimate goal of this assignment is to provide a relatively low-stakes space for students to experiment with technology-mediated teaching, allowing students to both develop their own styles and approaches, and to provide space and guidelines for students to become reflective and critical teachers.

It is particularly important that these demonstrations are given in *online* spaces, where students can experiment with different tools, the challenges of asynchronous teaching, and the realities of creating contained lessons in digital spaces (very different from a teaching demonstration in F2F teaching). In my classes, students have taught an online lesson between course sessions, and the feedback was given at our next F2F meeting, but Slack or other dedicated chat platforms can be useful for facilitating this feedback in online classes. For my students, this assignment is often the first time that they have been given the power and position of *instructor* in an online space, and opens up the opportunity to both reflect on pedagogies in practice, and discuss the challenges of online teacher personas, creating community, and taking control over technologies and learning spaces.

Teaching Philosophy: The third category of assignment for this course focuses explicitly on theory and invites students to craft their own online teaching philosophy. Teaching philosophies are a common genre in academe, frequently forming the backbone of cover letters, and are included in job applications and tenure files. Creating an online philosophy (particularly grounded in technologies and digital literacies) positions students as practitioners in the field and invites students to enact a theoretically grounded digitally literate instructor identity, putting into words their explorations from the teaching demonstrations. These philosophies ask students to envision an "ideal" online classroom and to position themselves within it, to define their own understanding of teaching online, and to offer specific examples of their own best practices and approaches. In addition to acting as a professionalizing document, this philosophy requires that students articulate the need for a digitally literate approach to online teaching.

To illustrate the kinds of considerations that students bring to their "Teaching with Technology" philosophy, I am sharing three excerpts from student submissions. Articulating the tensions between her own digital literacies and fostering the same in students, Rebecca* writes,

> Emergent technologies afford new types of student compositions; simultaneously they require engaged critical attention. As an instructor, I choose to position myself as a coach for two primary reasons: 1) it makes space for student decision-making and agency, and 2) it recognizes my limitations as an instructor. I cannot know every technology or envision every possible multimodal composition, but I can make space for students to bring that expertise into the classroom. By compassionately walking alongside students as they embrace their identities and agency as composers in new media, I aim to prepare them for critically engaged composing practices with emergent technologies.

Here, Rebecca positions herself as a teacher-coach, exploring the persona that she can best adopt in the unique space of the online classroom and forwarding the possibilities of teaching with and through new and emergent media. Like the ideal instructor for "Teaching Technologies," Rebecca recognizes that she is unable to know or teach to every technology and instead grounds her approach to online teaching in the need for digital literacies driven by student agency. Her sense of the online classroom mirrors the goals and outcomes of this graduate course. Rebecca recognizes that her role in an online space may not look the same as in an on-ground class. This idea is echoed by Theresa, who positions her classroom as a way to interrogate some of the key differences between online and on-ground teaching. As she grapples with the ways that student/teacher bodies are mediated through technologies, Theresea writes,

> To explicitly demonstrate the necessary role of embodiment in democratizing standards of literacy, my classroom examines the body as context for all writings (Dolmage). This work begins with myself, through an open presentment of my lived reality and experiences with emergent technology. In a classroom space that gestures ever-outward through digitization, the body is always behind the writings we encounter in public, and often digital spheres. Foregrounding of the body assures students see their own potential in acquiring technological literacies, and their ability to offer new perspectives on literacy broadly. These perspectives are weighted with rhetorical, critical interrogative skills, and are capable of crafting new worlds by troubling extant discourses via emergent digital technologies. The work of

> my critical classroom is this: to send forth student writers who create, and challenge, and change the face of literacy.

In this philosophy, Theresea articulates a common goal for English studies courses—creating engaged and critical thinkers—but acknowledges that the (dis)embodied nature of an online course gives her a unique way to do so, beginning with her own identity as instructor in the (online) room, and the ways in which her students do and do not embody that same space. Theresa's philosophy demonstrates the potential for this assignment to encourage students to think about the online classroom as at once a unique, demanding pedagogical space while also being an English studies classroom, with the attendant learning outcomes and goals that go with that space. Similarly, Liam discusses a technology focused assignment that grounds his online students in a discussion of the medium by which they learn. As an illustration of his student-centered philosophy, Liam writes,

> I begin the semester by asking students to write a "technology narrative" in which they reflect on the ways in which they have learned with, through, and about technologies in public and private contexts. This narrative encourages students to recognize that technology is not incidental to their lives but rather forms an integral part of sharing, listening, and communicating in society and that rhetorical practice "mobilizes the imagination, the emotions, and the body" (Sheridan, Ridolfo, and Michel 152). Their narratives also help me understand the variety of experiences, expertise, and learning opportunities students bring to the classroom. When students ask for help accomplishing tasks in certain platforms, I can direct them to peers who have some expertise in those areas. Students, as rhetors, are thus positioned as "point[s] of articulation" (Sheridan, Ridolfo, and Michel 72), critically mediating through their subject positions the contributions that human and non- human actors make to their compositions.

Using students' own voices and experiences, Liam centers his classroom on what students know already about how they write with and through technology, and how his online course can complicate, challenge, and expand that relationship. While writing through technology is not exclusive to online courses, Liam is using the mediated nature of online classes as a lens to begin interrogating this relationship, while also creating a student-centered and digitally literate space for learning.

These examples show the complexity of the online teaching philosophy as a tool for inviting students to consider the complexities of the online classroom and how they might intersect with digital literacies, English studies, and writing. Overall, the goal for this assignment is to require students to articulate the theories that support their own personal approach to online and digitally mediated teaching in a professional, outward-facing document.

ePortfolio: The final project for this semester asks the students to build and annotate an online English studies course in an ePortfolio (and, optionally, in a full course shell on an LMS). There are three key pieces to the portfolio that students will develop: the critical introduction and annotations, the course documents, and the design of the portfolio. The **critical introduction and annotations** allow students to articulate their approach to their portfolio and explain the choices that they have made while crafting their course. On the assignment sheet, I ask, "If your teaching philosophy spoke broadly about the theories that govern your approach to pedagogy, your introduction should do much of the same work *in context*—how have you then applied that philosophy in practice?" Crucially, this is a space where students are able to explore their choices in building an *online* class; students are encouraged to reflect on the theories, pedagogies, and readings that shape their choices, and to explore why and how this course functions as an explicitly online class. Working from the theories that underpin their teaching philosophies, and the lived experience of their teaching demonstrations, students are invited to showcase their understanding of what makes an online class effective. The critical introduction and annotations require students to provide the theoretical grounding for their decisions and provide space for articulating how all of the individual pieces work together.

The **course documents** make up the bulk of the portfolio and represent the types of work that make up a course. Importantly, while some of these documents will be in a genre that exists across course delivery modes, students are asked to craft documents that are geared toward an online classroom. There are four types of course documents required for this portfolio, although students can choose the type and number of submissions across the categories. The first requirement is a *syllabus* for an English studies course. This syllabus should be explicitly student-facing and ask the students to think about their objectives, goals, and policies that support online teaching. Next, students include *course structure documents*, which outline places where technologies support the overall running of the class, and might include discussion board or peer review strategies, attendance apps or grading and assessment strategies, and overall course policies. Crucially, these documents cover the pieces that make an online course run, moving beyond the syllabus to implementation. The third requirement is student-facing *assignment sheets* that walk through how the students will be assessed on their work and learning throughout the course. Again, while the assignments themselves may be used in F2F classes, the design and delivery should be geared toward online classes. The final requirement is *in-class activities*, where students envision the realities of in-class online engagement. This one is typically the most challenging for new teachers, as they create week-by-week or unit-specific activities for an online class, and these frequently build from the work of the teaching demonstrations or the technology analyses as students seek theoretically grounded digitally literate strategies for student engagement and learning.

In addition to the content of the portfolio, the students are also asked to think carefully about **design**:

> As a digital document, one of the things you will consider as you create your portfolio is overall design. You should think about what you want this document to do in the world, and who your audience might be. Is this for prospective employers? For students? How will those different audiences shape how you craft this site and its documents? I also encourage you to think about things like tabs, sections, and overall structure—how are you going to put this portfolio together in a way that makes it easy for the reader to move through your documents? How are you going to make plain your annotations and your approach to developing this material? And where are you going to put each document: how are you going to frame this portfolio? The platform and organization are up to you—the only requirement for this portfolio is that the design is clearly *thoughtful*, and that I can easily navigate between sections, documents, and annotations.

This assignment is the cumulative project for the course, and explicitly puts the theories learned throughout the semester into practice. The goals for this assignment are two-fold: the first is the same as the goal for the course—to create digitally literate instructors who are prepared to teach English studies courses online in emergent digital contexts, and the second is to create a professional, public portfolio that students can adapt for use as part of a job search or tenure file.

Conclusion

Thanks to the role of first-year composition in many English Departments, pedagogy classes have become a staple of many English studies graduate programs as our students teach composition courses as part of their graduate experience. This incorporation of pedagogy as an integral part of English studies broadly writ has led scholars from our field to be pedagogy leaders across institutions and campuses. As higher education continues to embrace the possibilities and potential of online education, English studies programs have an opportunity to consider online pedagogies as a cornerstone of pedagogy courses, or—as this chapter advocates for—a standalone pedagogy course dedicated to online pedagogies. And we have an opportunity to continue to be leaders in higher education related to online courses.

The curricular choices that we make in our English studies programs have a ripple effect across institutions—Liam, for example, has gone on to be the writing center director at a large state college, and is transforming their tutoring program to include online pedagogies that he began to develop in this course. Another graduate from our program has created award-winning online general education courses, beginning from their experience of teaching first-year composition courses that were developed in Teaching Technologies, while another student at a small liberal arts college is leading online teaching fellowship workshops for teachers of online courses across campus.

The pedagogical foundation provided by this course showed itself to be useful even for those graduates who had never intended to teach in online spaces—as the global pandemic in 2020 that required all classes to abruptly switch to remote modalities demonstrated, all instructors can benefit from a solid grounding in digital pedagogies. In the Spring of 2020, several former students reached out to share their stories of adapting to remote learning, and all of them said that they had an easier time transitioning to remote learning than their colleagues because they had a theory of practice guiding their decisions. Two former students became leaders on their campuses, guiding other instructors in the shift to remote learning, sharing some of the resources from "Teaching Technologies" and helping others devise teaching philosophies in line with remote learning. Although this pandemic is a wildly unique circumstance, instructors with a solid foundation in the theories and practices of digital learning are well positioned to meet any challenges that come up, and well positioned as leaders in education.

Understanding digital pedagogies as a foundational part of English studies education has the potential to shift theories and practices about online teaching across higher education, while broadening the boundaries of English studies and positioning our graduates for the realities of the job market in a digital age.

Note

*Student names are pseudonyms

References

Arola, Kristin L., and Anne Frances Wysocki, eds. 2012. *Composing(Media) = Composing(Embodiment): Bodies, Technologies, Writing, the Teaching of Writing*. Logan: Utah State University Press.

Atkins, Anthony T. 2006. "Writing/Teachers and Digital Technologies: Technology/Teacher Training." *Kairos* 10 (2). https://kairos.technorhetoric.net/10.2/binder.html?praxis/atkins/introduction.htm.

Blair, Kristine L. 2016. "English Online/On the Line: The Challenges of Sustaining Disciplinary Relevance in the Twenty-First Century." In *Degree of Change: The MA in English Studies*, edited by Margaret M. Strain, Rebecca C. Potter, and National Council of Teachers of English, 22–40. Urbana, Illinois: National Council of Teachers of English.

Bolter, Jay David, and Richard Grusin. 2003. *Remediation: Understanding New Media.* . Cambridge, MA: MIT Press.

Buckley, Joanne. 1997. "The Invisible Audience and the Disembodied Voice: Online Teaching and the Loss of Body Image." *Computers and Composition* 14 (2): 179–87. https://doi.org/10.1016/S8755-4615(97)90019-0.

Burdick, Anne, Johanna Drucker, Peter Lunenfeld, Todd Presner, and Jeffrey Schnapp, eds. 2012. *Digital Humanities*. Cambridge, MA: MIT Press.

Clark, J. Elizabeth. 2010. "The Digital Imperative: Making the Case for a 21st-Century Pedagogy." *Computers and Composition* 27 (1): 27–35. https://doi.org/10.1016/j.compcom.2009.12.004.

Fleckenstein, Kristie S. 2005. "Faceless Students, Virtual Places: Emergence and Communal Accountability in Online Classrooms." *Computers and Composition* 22 (2): 149–76. https://doi.org/10.1016/j.compcom.2005.02.003.

Hawisher, Gail E., and Cynthia L. Selfe. 1999. "The Passions That Mark Us: Teaching, Texts, and Technologies." In *Passions Pedagogies and 21st Century Technologies*, edited by Gail E. Hawisher and Cynthia L. Selfe, 1–12. Logan: Utah State University Press. https://doi.org/10.2307/j.ctt46nrfk.

Hewett, Beth L. 2014. "Online and Hybrid." In *A Guide to Composition Pedagogies*, 2nd ed., edited by Gary Tate, Amy Rupiper Taggart, Kurt Schick, and H. Brooke Hessler, 194–211. New York: Oxford University Press.

Kopelson, Karen. 2008. "Sp(l)Itting Images; Or, Back to the Future of (Rhetoric and?) Composition." *College Composition and Communication* 59 (4): 750–80.

Kress, Gunther. 1999. "'English' at the Crossroads: Rethinking Curricula of Communication in the Context of the Turn to the Visual." In *Passions Pedagogies and 21st Century Technologies*, edited by Gail E. Hawisher and Cynthia L. Selfe, 66–88. Utah State University Press. https://doi.org/10.2307/j.ctt46nrfk.

McLuhan, Marshall, and Quentin Fiore. 2001. *The Medium Is the Massage: An Inventory of Effects*. Berkeley, CA: Gingko Press.

Selber, Stuart A. 2004. *Multiliteracies for a Digital Age*. Studies in Writing & Rhetoric. Carbondale: Southern Illinois University Press.

Selfe, Cynthia L. 1999. *Technology and Literacy in the Twenty-First Century: The Importance of Paying Attention*. Studies in Writing and Rhetoric. Carbondale, IL: Southern Illinois University Press.

—. 2004. "Toward New Media Texts: Taking Up the Challenges of Visual Literacy." In *Writing New Media: Theory and Applications for Expanding the Teaching of Composition*, edited by Anne Frances Wysocki, Johndan Johnson-Eilola, Cynthia L. Selfe, and Geoffrey Sirc, 67–110. Logan: Utah State University Press.

Scheg, Abigail, G. 2016. "TextSupport: Incorporating Online Pedagogy into MA English Programs." In *Degree of Change: The MA in English Studies*, edited by Margaret M. Strain, Rebecca C. Potter, and National Council of Teachers of English, 120–37. Urbana: National Council of Teachers of English.

Warnock, Scott. 2009. *Teaching Writing Online: How and Why*. Urbana: National Council of Teachers of English.

7 Virtual Literature Circles: Re-Embodying Discussion in Online Literature Courses

William P. Banks

As the director of a university-wide writing across the curriculum program at East Carolina University, I engage regularly with many faculty from diverse disciplinary backgrounds. We work together in professional development workshops, individual discussions around pedagogy, and at writing retreats, and in all of these settings, when discussions of online and face-to-face instruction have arisen, I sense the ongoing tensions that they feel about teaching online. While many disciplines outside of English seem to worry a lot about issues like cheating on exams and how to replicate lab-based activities, English faculty often share with their colleagues around campus the concern that fully online classes cannot recreate the robust in-person discussions/question-and-answer dialogue they feel happens in their classrooms. Classroom-based researchers have repeatedly critiqued this illusory notion of what happens in college classrooms, which far too often fall back on lectures, PowerPoint presentations that are read to students, and Q&A's that are less dynamic conversations than they involve mini-assessments where faculty *initiate* questions they already know the answer to, wait for students *respond* to that question with the right answers, and then *evaluate* out loud whether the answers are correct; Cadzen (1988) refers to this as the I-R-E model for "discussion." Of course, this is no discussion; it's an oral testing framework (see Spangler, this volume).

I would contend that what many faculty feel is missing in online spaces is less the dynamic give-and-take of in-person conversation than the affective and embodied engagements that for many of us make teaching a fundamentally human and humane project. While I enjoy teaching fully online courses, I cannot deny that I personally feel less connected to the students in those courses; as part of my own way of being in the world, I often rely on facial expressions, tones of voice, and the type of energy I feel emanating from others to understand the situation I am in. Far less than on students' spontaneously asking for clarification or my asking a question that goes unanswered, I modulate my instruction based on what I'm feeling from the class, the looks in students' eyes, the embodied and affective sense I have of them and the room. What some have framed as "soft skills" (OECD 2015, Klaus 2008) or "emotional intelligence" (Coleman 2005), I think of as an ability to read the room. No doubt most of the skills I may have in this regard come from my time spent in theater and performance, where improvisation activities taught us the importance of staying tapped into the other bodies on stage with us, and multiple public performances taught us how to feel the audience's approval or contempt with our performances. Whether other teachers have had similar experiences to my own is not important; the reality is that nearly all of us have spent our formative years surrounded by other students and our teachers, and then we became teachers, and throughout these experiences, many of us have developed some tacit skills with understanding when instruction is working or not, when students are learning or not—and those soft skills do not translate very easily to fully online teaching contexts.

To that end, I'm tremendously sympathetic toward faculty in my own English department when they resist teaching online. Not unlike the students who study abroad in a foreign country and can quickly become overwhelmed by some of the most basic day-to-day activities like shopping for groceries and managing money, when we move online—particularly when we do it suddenly as faculty around the country found themselves doing in 2020 as COVID-19 moved us nearly all online—our mental and emotional energies are taxed by the loss of those interpersonal frameworks we have come to rely on. I feel that sense of loss myself, and I've spent considerable time trying to think about how to balance the ostensible loss of those more embodied experiences with the many great things that online teaching affords me and the students I teach.

In this chapter, I report on my use of virtual literature circles in two different literature courses—an undergraduate children's literature course and a graduate gay and lesbian literature course—and how these circles function as a middle-ground for using some synchronous digital strategies in a primarily asynchronous online pedagogy. In the 2020 pandemic, many of my colleagues were unable to imagine an asynchronous version of their courses and ended up requiring students to participate in once- or twice-weekly synchronous class lectures. While there are numerous reasons this sort of strategy was riddled with problems and, at times, created insurmountable obstacles for non-campus-based students (Darby & Lang 2019; Levy 2020), some faculty in English studies still felt they needed synchronous lecture/discussion in order to think they were actually teaching. With virtual literature circles, I have been able to offer students and myself purposeful and focused in-person discussion opportunities that remain cognizant of and responsible to many of the ongoing inequities and problems that may exist within fully online teaching and learning contexts.

Discussion Bored?

There is no shortage of criticism in online teaching contexts for the now ubiquitous online discussion board, and in many ways, this criticism arises in no small part because discussion boards were not designed or originally imagined as spaces for teaching and learning. By wholesale importing this type of digital tool into school-based contexts, we have often failed to understand why they were created and what they were developed to do, and thus have also failed to imagine how teaching and learning contexts might re-envision "discussion" in more meaningful ways.

Typically displayed visually as a type of tree structure where responses to previous posts are placed directly below that post and indented five to ten pixels from the left, and responses to responses are then indented another five to ten pixels in order to "thread" the discussion and help readers keep up with which writers are responding to which comment/post, discussion boards have a long and robust history in online communities. In fact, as a digital genre, discussion boards pre-date the online teaching and learning contexts we know by several decades. Ward Christensen and Randy Suess are credited with launching the first computer-based bulletin board system (CBBS) in 1978 (Gilbertson 2018). Not surprisingly, Christensen claimed he conceived of the idea during the 1978 blizzard in Chicago, which kept him house-bound for several days, and he was looking for ways to engage with others online where in-person options were limited. As consumers at the time had access primarily to a dial-up internet, which did not allow for always-on network connections, the idea of asynchronous online discussion picked up quickly. The early 1980s saw the global emergence of Tom Truscott and Jim Ellis's Usenet framework, which introduced the idea of threaded discussions; users participated in discussion forums/newsgroups that were designed around topics or ideas of interest to discussants. These organic, networked discussions continued to evolve as Internet Relay Chat (IRC) channels made both large group and private messages a common option for users. BBSs, forums, and message boards began to merge in the 1990s with the W3 Consortium's creation of WIT, which Lee (2012) argues was the first forum protocol developed for the World Wide Web. Then the late 1990s and early 2000s witnessed a proliferation of open-source online bulletin board platforms like phpBB, myBB, and VBulletin, which look most like what contemporary users think of when they imagine the discussion boards that are available in large learning management systems (LMS) like Blackboard, Canvas, D2L, etc.

What had begun as a tool to let physically distant users engage each other around topics of interest and shared values by the twenty-first century had become the de facto method in online learning spaces for discussion. In 2020, my campus switched from Blackboard to Canvas for our official LMS, and one of the things I was critical of immediately was the fact that "out of the box," Canvas does not provide any digital tool built for student writing and discussion except for discussion boards—no blogs, no wikis. While teachers can enable students to create their own threaded discussion boards, without adding in additional and/or third-party plugins, teachers and students have little access for writing and engaging with each other outside of this discussion board context, and certainly none of these tools are built to engage readers outside the password-protected space of the Canvas classroom.

For my online classes, I tend to teach outside of our campus-approved LMS, making use of open-source, server-based tools like Drupal and WordPress, so students have access to different digital tools and genres for writing, sharing, and responding. But even in this context, I, too, have felt the need to install a discussion board element so that students engage with certain key questions, topics, or issues related to course materials. Partly, this allows me to use student blogs for longer, more focused writing/new-media composing projects where peer-feedback is important, but where ongoing back-and-forth discussion is not necessary, and still use discussion boards for issues that I want students to unpack and explore through give-and-take that is represented in shorter pieces of individual writing and response.

Despite having the option of engaging students with different digital genres within our online course platform, I still find that I'm missing those more affective and embodied elements that I enjoy. In fact, in fall 2020, I chose to teach in Canvas so that students would have all their courses in one system and would not have to juggle different logins and other inconveniences while learning during a pandemic. What I also quickly discovered was that many of the students in the class were craving that same sort of "face-to-face" experience as well. Several years ago, I began to wonder how I might get the best of both pedagogical contexts. For nearly twenty years, I had been supplementing F2F classes with a host of online tools for pre- and post-class discussions, peer review, etc., so in my online courses, I was wondering how to make that same sort of supplemental approach work by bringing in synchronous discussions that would not also create large problems for students who are working, caring for their families, or engaging in other commitments that have made online learning their best option. For me, that started with asking how teaching practices I have valued and found useful could be re-imagined for online spaces: how could I reimagine traditional literature/reading circles for online digital contexts?

Building the Virtual Literature Circle

In my literature courses, which cater primarily to undergraduates who are soon-to-be teachers (Children's Literature) or graduate students who are already teachers (gay and lesbian literature), I have typically used literature/reading circles because they represent a "best practice" that K–12 teachers can carry back to their own classrooms and use. I know from long years of teaching teachers that when teachers have themselves benefited from a strategy, they are more likely to use it with their current or future students. Teachers who learned as students to engage in productive, content-focused peer review of writing, for example, are more likely to implement it effectively in their courses. Likewise, teachers who have been part of literature circles (or their non-academic cousin, book groups) are often more willing to disrupt their own place as the center of knowledge-creation in a classroom and allow students more choice and more input in how and why they read books.

Literature circles (book groups, book clubs, reading groups) represent an intervention into traditional literary pedagogies that were overly focused on an authority (the teacher) proclaiming which books were valuable (or not) and what was valuable or important about those books, and a too-frequent focus, particularly in high school settings, on identifying rhetorical tropes and figures at work in exemplar texts. In this model, the reason we read is to figure out how authors use metaphor or alliteration, or how they construct the setting of the novel, which of course, is not the primary reason most readers read at all. Literature circles, as Harvey Daniels (2001) notes, "combine two very important educational ideas: collaborative learning and independent reading" (3). The focus is primarily on encouraging life-long readers who find pleasure in reading, not as a scavenger hunt, but as a way to enrich their lives by seeing themselves and their world through diverse lenses. In his early formulation of literature circles, Daniels (2002) offers the following "key ingredients":

1. Students *choose* their own reading materials.
2. *Small temporary groups* are formed, based on book choice.
3. Different groups read *different books*.
4. Groups meet on a *regular, predictable schedule* to discuss their reading.
5. Kids use written or drawn *notes* to guide both their reading and discussion.
6. Discussion *topics come from the students*.
7. Group meetings aim to be *open, natural conversations about books*, so personal connections, digressions, and open-ended questions are welcome.
8. The teacher serves as a *facilitator*, not a group member or instructor.
9. Evaluation is by *teacher observation and student self-evaluation*.
10. A spirit of *playfulness and fun* pervades the room.
11. When books are finished, *readers share with their classmates*, and then *new groups form* around new reading circles. (18)

Clearly, the focus here is on student choice and small group interactions around shared interests in a text; likewise, students direct the conversation and are only moderately influenced by facilitative suggestions from the teacher as they move from group to group. In my classes over the years, I have employed a variety of different models for literature circles: in some models, I have limited students' choices based only on the course topic and/or appropriate genres, while in others, I have allowed students to self-organize around books I have pre-selected, typically in shorter summer courses where there is not time to survey student interests and order books. In my F2F classes, these work particularly well, and as the teacher, I can move among the different literature circles to see what reading strategies they are using while also paying attention to how themes from the novels/discussions might further influence other class discussions.

The first time I taught children's literature online, I wondered how I might do something similar with students, and if doing so might also afford an opportunity for synchronous discussion. At the time, Google (n.d.) had just developed Hangouts-on-Air, which allowed up to ten individuals to participate in a synchronous group chat that could be watched by others in real time. These "hangouts" were also recorded, and once finished, the video could be shared through YouTube with various privacy settings. Capitalizing on the informal framing Google had created by naming them "hangouts," I created the following assignment for a summer children's literature course:

> **Reader Hangouts**
>
> Each Wednesday, a group of students will host a Google Hangout-on-Air for 30 minutes in which they discuss the novels and stories we've read over the last week. The goal of these Hangouts is to make connections between/among the various texts and to help others in the class to see how ideas from course "lectures" and presentations, as well as the stories and novels themselves, connect. Each member of the class will sign up to be hosts for one Hangout. These will be recorded and can be watched live or after they have been completed.
>
> *Expectations*: Hosts for Hangouts are expected to make notes about the connections they see among the stories, novels, and course materials in advance of the Hangout and then to use those notes to host the Hangout. Perhaps you could think of these as Talk Shows for Children's Lit. Other students in class are expected to sign up and participate in at least 2 Hangouts that they're not hosting by listening live and posting questions to the hangout on the video.

These Reader Hangouts are not exactly literature circles as traditionally defined, as digital tools offer lots of interactive options that classroom-based circles cannot really make use of. Reimagining these activities as online projects allowed me to think through some of the more ephemeral elements of literature circles—like the fact that conversations for each group are not recorded and no one but group members can know what happened in the discussion—and design methods for learning that would amplify the best of both in-person circles and our digital tools:

- Student Choice: as with traditional circles, students enjoyed some degree of choice in terms of which book group they ended up in. I used a Google Form to let them request the top three books they most wanted to discuss live with other classmates, and based on their selections, I divided the students fairly evenly in five groups across the term.
- Preparation: since these discussions would be broadcast to others in the class, I followed Google's suggestion that the discussants prepare some questions in advance and develop a plan for how their group would move. While lags in conversation and umm's and uhh's are expected in F2F discussions, those same elements can exhaust viewers' patience in online environments. Likewise, while literature circles tend to meet multiple times to discuss books as they read them, our Reader Hangouts were a one-shot opportunity to discuss the book, and thus were more like traditional book clubs in that regard.
- Engagement: Google's Hangouts-on-Air platform allowed for two different types of viewer engagement, and my assignment tried to leverage that to improve engagement around these video discussions. Students who were part of leading other Reader Hangouts were required either to view the hangout live and ask questions for the group to respond to and work into their discussion, or to watch the recorded video within two days of posting it online and offer feedback on the discussion (extend ideas, challenge assumptions, forge new connections across texts, etc).
- Teacher Involvement: undoubtedly, one of the benefits of literature circles is that students develop independence with reading away from a teacher's prying eyes; this also helps stop teachers from forcing everyone to read through one predetermined lens. However, given that these groups met only once and were working with shared course texts, I decided that participating in each group by helping them to frame their discussion topics in ad-

vance and then also serving as a resource during the discussion could be useful. As much as possible, I tried to keep my voice out of the discussion, but from time to time, it was useful to offer them an insight to extend their ideas or a framework for understanding the text and its cultural history they may have been missing.

Because I taught that children's literature course during a short, six-week summer semester, there were a number of time limitations to contend with that shaped my choices. Since the students knew well in advance that the course would be fully online, I knew that trying to schedule anything that everyone would have to participate in would be difficult, but I also knew we did not have a lot of time to choose various dates and times for hangouts. My workaround was to have students choose the one Wednesday night they could participate and sign up for that night, which also meant I had to be flexible and not force even-numbered groups, and not requiring all the other students to watch live allowed for greater flexibility with the timing, too.

A year later, I was offered the chance to teach a graduate-level special topics course on gay and lesbian literatures; this course would be fully online during the regular fifteen-week semester, and it would be offered as part of ECU's online master's degree program in multicultural and transnational literatures. The increased time and freedom of the longer semester allowed students to meet multiple times over the semester, but since we would be reading books as a whole group over the term, I re-imagined the Reader Hangouts for this course to be focused on secondary research and queer theories. Many graduate courses require students to read secondary work either as recommended readings or to build annotated bibliographies throughout the semester that would then inform their seminar-style papers. What if I created reading groups for collaboratively reading and understanding those secondary texts? These reading groups would choose their readings from those materials available through our university library so that all students had access, and I could serve as a guide-on-the-side to help them locate resources based on their interests, and perhaps supplement through PDF book chapters unavailable through our library's online offerings.

Whereas I felt I needed to be present for all of the undergraduate one-shot Reader Hangouts, for the graduate students, I required them to have at least three hangouts over the first three months of the course and to invite me to at least one of them. But I encouraged them to meet as often as they wanted since one thing that our online graduate students sometimes feel they miss out on is the in-person camaraderie and the sense of a cohort working together on the difficult and often stressful learning experience that is graduate school. To further support their cohort experience, for each group I created a wiki-type page in my online course platform; groups posted their Hangout-on-Air videos there so that they and their classmates could watch them, and because it was a wiki-style page, they could add additional materials as needed, for example, building a shared bibliography of resources. As the teacher, I simply checked periodically to see what they were discussing and to offer any additional resources that might be useful. When I have taught LGBTQ-themed courses F2F, one of the things that students have really struggled with has been engaging queer theory in their longer course projects. We spend so much time talking about the literature and culture in class, and various queer theories seem most useful at the moment they are relevant to the ideas we are discussing; in the end, I have struggled to meld these two types of texts to make them seamlessly part of course meetings. In the online course, where students were using traditional discussion boards and blog posts to respond to the novels, plays, and poems, the Reader Hangouts created a scaffolded alternative space for engaging secondary research and queer theory in meaningful ways. Because I was not always present, this space also allowed students to fumble and stumble through the texts and wrestle with meaning in ways that are useful for first-time readers of queer theories. In terms of scaffolding learning, this framework also allowed students space to practice with ideas before asking an often more focused or nuanced question of me as the more experienced reader of queer theories.

Hangups with Hangouts

I've used variations of the Reader Hangouts several times since those early attempts, and in general, these have been wildly successful. Students appreciate the flexibility of how and when they sign-up to participate in synchronous discussions, and while this sort of engagement may seem "natural" for more extroverted students, introverted students have also appreciated the fact that the groups are small and tend to focus on more in-depth discussions rather than what some introverted students have seen as the superficial discussions that occur in many F2F classrooms (Jensen & DiTiberio 1989; Cain 2013; Kris 2018). Most of the undergraduates I teach in online courses are campus-based students, and they already feel they are part of an in-person educational experience. While they appreciate the Reader Hangouts as something different, they are not as enthusiastic about them as the fully online students who live at some distance from campus and who are often seeking ways to feel more connected to their classmates. This need for connection has been most pronounced for the fully online graduate students I teach, and for them, having a space to discuss the often more complex writing they encounter in critical theory and secondary research has been a powerful contribution to the coursework.

Unfortunately, as is often the case with online technologies, Google discontinued Hangouts-on-Air in 2019 and forwarded Google Meets as its new platform for video conferencing. While Google Meets allows users to record meetings, that option is only available at the moment to those with education accounts linked to their school or organization. While none of the alternatives I've found offer the simplicity of live broadcasting (with discussion), recording, and then automatically posting the video to a video-hosting site like YouTube, most video conferencing platforms offer a number of built-in options that come close to providing the same functionality. Since I made a commitment to use the campus LMS (Canvas) during the 2020 pandemic, I looked for video options that would do something similar and settled on using Microsoft Teams's Live Events option. Since we are a Microsoft campus, we can easily place Teams video conferences into our Canvas course, or we can create course-related Teams groups with different "channels" for each Reader Hangout group. In those channels, student groups can collect materials relevant to their group, prepare transcripts and/or talking points on the Notepad, and host their live video events. With the live events, they can select which students are the presenters and producers of the event and which students are only viewers. Viewers still have the option to ask questions during the live event, and the video stream can be automatically recorded for later viewing from Teams or through Microsoft's online streaming platform, Streams.

READER-WRITER HANGOUTS ACROSS ENGLISH STUDIES

Over the last several years since I created my first online Reader Hangouts project, I've also found ways to use them in other F2F and online courses, as have many of my colleagues in English studies. A colleague in writing studies, Stephanie West-Puckett, introduced me to Google Hangouts-on-Air when we were working together as part of the Tar River Writing Project, an ECU-based site of the National Writing Project. We had used this tool as part of a grant-funded project for connecting writing to informal science projects that area K–12 and college students were doing together: "Remix, Remake, Curate" (https://trwpconnect. wordpress.com/). When she began to imagine how she might use the Hangouts function in her first-year writing courses, Stephanie saw it as an ideal space for student writing and composing groups. At times, these groups hosted live Hangouts to teach others in class about a writing-related topic, or to get feedback on their group writing projects. Similarly, for faculty who enjoy group writing conferences in their F2F classes, these sorts of Writer Hangouts would also be simple to create in a fully online environment. Where writing teachers typically model peer review through a fishbowl activity in class, using Writing Hangouts that others can view, ask questions of, and then use as models for their own peer review/writing groups seems like a natural fit.

Like my colleagues in film studies and literary studies, I often want to show and discuss short film clips when I'm teaching children's literature, which can be challenging given many of the limitations of online video conferencing. Currently, there are mobile apps like Acapella (https://www.mixcord.co/pages/acapella) that allow small groups of users to share space on the screen; while designed to help people sing together, the app can also be repurposed for discussion up to ten minutes long. Similarly, Netflix Party, a Chrome browser extension, can be used for groups to watch a film and discuss it in real time, though the discussion is limited to a text-based chat window. A new site, TwoSeven (https://twoseven.xyz/), now offers a free platform that seems similar to Google's Hangouts-on-Air but is focused on a small group of users in a video conference all watching and discussing the same movie or video clip. Just like with the Reader Hangouts, film studies faculty could host video viewing hangouts in which they guide students through scene construction and analysis, modeling terms and concepts that then students could demonstrate mastery of in a later video hangout.

Making synchronous work effective in fully online courses, as we know, cannot simply be replicating the fifty- to ninety-minute whole group lecture/discussion, but if faculty and students want to engage in real time, there are certainly ways we can re-imagine what synchronous discussion/chat looks like. Having done synchronous video chats with both undergraduate and graduate students over the last decade, I have found that what has worked best has been these smaller hangouts that meet some key goals for synchronous online work: (1) because groups are small, there is much greater flexibility for both students and teachers to choose times that work equitably for all involved, which at times may even involve rescheduling so that everyone in the group can participate; (2) smaller groups also make it more efficient to norm group behaviors and to establish expectations for discussion, which invariably leads to higher quality discussions overall; (3) having a recorded archive of the hangouts that group members or others in class can return to and view as often as they want prevents me as the teacher from having to fill in students who miss something or repeat parts of discussions that students missed while taking notes or simply zoning out as we all sometimes inevitably do in large group discussions.

So far, I find that these smaller, more focused discussions are often richer and more nuanced than those I can orchestrate in large classrooms, and as such, they have significant potential to improve learning transfer throughout the course and after. Certainly it takes time for me as the teacher to be involved in multiple synchronous discussions, but as a more extroverted and social teacher, I also feel more connected to and aware of the students in my online classes when I use these hangouts. I remember their names more quickly, and many of the details of the discussion boards, blogs, wikis, and other written projects in class "stick" in my head far better than if they are only textual. Students in online classes, particularly the graduate students, report greater satisfaction and a sense of connection, as well, in student evaluations of instruction at the end of the course. For many of them, seeing a teacher's face and hearing their voice indicates a presence, a being-there-ness, that text alone does not. For faculty who fear losing aural discussion frameworks, modifying the Readers Hangouts to meet their own contexts might be one way to overcome the felt sense that online learning is too difficult or too disembodied.

References

Cain, Susan. 2013. *Quiet: The Power of Introverts in a World that Can't Stop Talking*. New York: Broadway Books.

Cazden, Courtney B. 1988. *Classroom Discourse: The Language of Teaching and Learning*. Portsmouth, NH: Heinemann.

Coleman, Daniel. 2005. *Emotional Intelligence: Why It Can Matter More than IQ*. New York: Bantam.

Daniels, Harvey. 2002. *Literature Circles: Voice and Choice in Book Clubs and Reading Groups*, 2nd edition. Portsmouth, NH: Stenhouse Publishers.

Daniels, Harvey. 2001. "Looking into Literature Circles Viewing Guide." Portsmouth, NH: Stenhouse Publishers.

Darby, Flower, and James M. Lang. 2019. *Small Teaching Online: Applying Learning Science in Online Classes*. San Francisco: Jossey-Bass.

Gilbertson, Scott. 2010. "Feb. 16, 1978: Bulletin Board Goes Electronic." Wired. Accessed 25 September 2020. https://www.wired.com/2010/02/0216cbbs-first-bbs-bulletin-board/.

Google. (nd). "Google+ Hangouts On Air." Accessed 25 September 2020. https://services.google.com/fh/files/blogs/Hangouts_On_Air_Technical_Guide.pdf.

Jensen, George H. and John K. DiTiberio. 1989. *Personality and the Teaching of Composition*. Norwood, NJ: Ablex Publishing.

Klaus, Peggy 2008. *The Hard Truth about Soft Skills: Workplace Lessons Smart People Wish They'd Learned Sooner*. New York: Harper Business.

Kris, Deborah Farmer. 2018. "Six Strategies to Help Introverts Thrive in School and Feel Understood." KQED. Accessed 25 September 2020. https://www.kqed.org/mindshift/51811/six-strategies-to-help-introverts-thrive-at-school-and-feel-understood.

Lee, Joel. 2012. "How We Talk Online: A History of Online Forums, from Cavemen Days to the Present." Make Use Of. Accessed 25 September 2020. https://www.makeuseof.com/tag/how-we-talk-online-a-history-of-online-forums-from-cavemen-days-to-the-present/.

Levy, Dan 2020. "The Synchronous vs. Asynchronous Balancing Act." https://hbsp.harvard.edu/inspiring-minds/the-synchronous-vs-asynchronous-balancing-act.

OECD (Organisation for Economic Cooperation and Development). 2015. *Skills for Social Progress: The Power of Social and Emotional Skills*. OECD Skills Studies. Paris: OECD Publishing. https://doi.org/10.1787/9789264226159-en.

University of Waterloo. 2020. "Synchronous and Asynchronous Online Learning." https://uwaterloo.ca/keep-learning/strategies-remote-teaching/synchronous-vs-asynchronous-online-learning.

8 Redesigning Assignment Sheets for Online Teaching: A Case Study in Universal Design and Multimodality

Ashley J. Holmes

In July 2018, the Association of Departments of English (ADE) released a report about "A Changing Major," highlighting a number of trends in the evolving nature of the English major in colleges and universities across the US. Some of the major findings of the report suggest the growing prevalence of concentrations within English departments and, thus, moves to make changes to curricular requirements for the major. While the report does not fully address the role of hybrid[1] and online course offerings, it does make the perhaps surprising claim that English departments have "not made digital and media studies visible parts of the major or the curriculum" (ADE 2018, 20). Digital skepticism certainly remains within many English departments; however, as the ADE report argues, "There is no doubt that electronic and other new media loom large in the landscape of reading, writing, editing, design, and (increasingly) literary study" (20). While the ADE's study of English departments found a smattering of course offerings in digital literacy and examples of assignments in digital genres, the committee ultimately concluded that "English departments . . . generally lag behind in this curricular area," and they suggest increased attention to media studies, digital literacy, and online platforms as "obvious possibilities for future growth" (2018, 20).

As teacher-scholars in English studies, we have likely experienced changes to the English major in our own departments: the literary studies

---

1. Hybrid courses typically involve some form of "reduced 'face-time' that is replaced by time spent outside the traditional classroom" (Caulfield 2011, 20). While scholarship on hybrid courses emphasizes that this time outside of the classroom could include experiential or community-based projects instead of or in addition to online activities, my use of "hybrid courses" in this chapter refers to courses that mix traditional face-to-face classroom instruction time with significant online instruction outside of the classroom.

concentration in my English department, for instance, recently initiated major curricular changes to course sequencing and titles and significantly expanded special topics course offerings. Whether faculty in English departments initiate these changes themselves or are required to make changes from top-down mandates, we know that to remain relevant, to entice English majors, and to more successfully place majors in jobs or graduate school, we must be able to communicate our humanistic values and ideals within the changing nature of society. In agreement with the ADE's "A Changing Major" report, English departments should seriously consider the role of digital media in the requirements for majors; for many departments, offering courses in alternate formats such as hybrid or fully online would give majors and other students taking courses in English the opportunity to hone their skills in reading and writing for digital contexts, genres, and audiences. In the Spring of 2020, many of us found ourselves unexpectedly and hurriedly moving classes to fully online, hybrid, and blended models because of COVID-19. As we transition out of emergency instruction, we now have the opportunity to plan ahead and anticipate alternate formats, not as improvised stopgaps but as theoretically informed and effectively designed online courses.

Within my specialization of rhetoric and composition, studies of digital writing have grown considerably over the last two decades, and, based on sound pedagogical research, more English teachers are inviting students to compose in multiple modes and to publish in ways that take full advantage of Web affordances (Alexander 2004; Palmeri 2012; Selber 2004; Selfe 2007). However, I have found that even as English teachers ask students to compose in some of the most innovative and technologically advanced ways, we rarely turn the lens on ourselves to consider the ways digital tools might transform one of the most ubiquitous pedagogical genres: the assignment sheet. Most English teachers—myself included—begin writing assignment sheets with the software program we know best, Microsoft Word. Many of our assignment sheets for English courses rely on traditional alphabetic text formed into complete sentences and paragraphs in what The New London Group (1996) would identify as the linguistic mode of communication. In reflecting on my teaching materials, I noticed a disconnect between what I ask of students in their writing—multimodal and interactive digital compositions such as infographics, blogs, or digital stories—and what I model as their instructor and writer of course assignment sheets; this disconnect was even more pronounced when I transitioned to teaching a fully online version of one of my courses.

In this chapter, I draw on my experiences with teaching online as a case study to analyze the evolution of an assignment sheet from a course I taught as face-to-face, hybrid, and fully online. I analyze the various versions of the assignment "sheet," narrating the revisions I made to convert my fairly traditional, Microsoft Word, text-heavy assignment sheet to formats more conducive to online instruction, and I reflect on how approaching redevelopment of teaching materials from a Universal Design for Learning (UDL) perspective was productive. For example, I highlight how reconceptualizing my assignment sheets for the Web challenged me to incorporate more visual modes and interactive genres, to be more concise and engaging in my explanations, and to consider issues of accessibility and the diverse needs of learners. I conclude the chapter by highlighting best practices in designing assignment sheets for online courses—many of which are also applicable for face-to-face or hybrid courses—in English studies and the role of professional development workshops in promoting these best practices, especially as world events in 2020 have rapidly increased the number of courses shifting to online modes.

This study contributes to the dearth of research on teaching-related genres, especially as they intersect with digital and online technologies. Calling for more research into the role of technology in teaching genres, Jennifer Grouling (2018) comparatively studied the genre of teacher comments when shifted from paper commenting to digital comments via iPad. Grouling's study—which found that some features like "marginal comments" were significantly different—suggests that we still have much to learn about the ways we design, enact, and perform genres of the classroom. While some genre studies scholars (Giltrow 2002) have argued that "meta-genres" within institutional contexts can serve "to discipline genre performances within activity systems" (Reiff and Bawarshi 2016, 4), my experience suggests that translating the genre of the assignment sheet into digital and online contexts invited less predictability and conformity with genre performance. As Mary Jo Reiff and Anis Bawarshi (2016) indicate in their introduction to *Genre and the Performance of Publics*, the dynamism and instability of the revised assignment sheets for my online course may have been bolstered in part by their digital publication. Before delving into analysis of the assignment sheets themselves, I first provide some background information on my institution, the course, and some of the underlying theories informing the analysis.

INSTITUTIONAL CONTEXT AND COURSE

Georgia State University (GSU) is an urban research institution with its main campus located in downtown Atlanta. GSU has one of the most ethnically diverse student bodies in the country and is a leader in graduating students from underprivileged backgrounds. In 2015, the Board of Regents in Georgia voted to merge GSU with Georgia Perimeter College, combining the mission of a research institution with a commitment to serve the needs of community college students across six other campuses. Now, with over fifty-one thousand students across the metro-Atlanta area, GSU has moved quickly to offer courses in a variety of formats to meet the needs of its diverse and geographically-dispersed student body through hybrid and fully online options to complement its face-to-face offerings. Prior to consolidation, Georgia Perimeter College had (and continues to have) a robust set of online and hybrid course offerings and programs, and the GSU campus downtown has been working to expand online options post-consolidation. Even prior to consolidation, however, administrators at GSU were encouraging departments to develop their hybrid and online courses and programs for reasons ranging from enticing new students and better serving commuters to alleviating scheduling issues by maximizing the limited resources of classroom space on an urban campus. Then, in early 2020, GSU's Provost announced increased support for the development of fully online programs and "master course" curricula and appointed an inaugural associate provost for online strategies. This injection of administrative support for pedagogically-sound and well-designed online instruction was well underway when the university shifted to online instruction because of COVID-19.

Within the English department on the main campus—my home department—the move toward hybrid and online courses came at a slower pace until we were all forced into online teaching during the pandemic. In 2013, our department first began experimenting with hybrid courses that met face-to-face for seventy-five minutes each week with additional online content for what would have been the second class each week. From 2013 to 2018, the English department consistently offered a few sections of English courses in the hybrid format each semester, though the corps of instructors teaching hybrid remained relatively small. The majority of the hybrid course offerings were in lower-division studies (courses in English at the 1000 and 2000 levels), with only a few 3000-level courses in the major within the concentrations of rhetoric and composition, and literary studies. In the 2018 summer term, English offered its first fully online courses, and I was one of the instructors to first teach an online class in our department. In fact, the original offering of one section of English 3120: Digital Writing & Publishing (ENG 3120) filled so quickly the dean's office requested we add two more sections; each filled quickly to the cap of twenty-five students. Clearly, GSU students were interested in registering for fully online English courses.

My own experiences with teaching ENG 3120 began in 2012 through a traditional face-to-face course format, and, since that time, I have taught ENG 3120 four times face-to-face, three times hybrid, and three times fully online. This upper-division English course typically enrolls a mix of majors in English, drawing from our concentrations in literary studies, rhetoric and composition, creative writing, and pre-education English, as well as in majors such as journalism, film and media, and business. Students learn about best practices for digital writing style, visual layouts, accessibility, attribution and copyright, and multimodal composing through digital writing and production assignments such as blogs, infographics, websites, and maps. Because the course content is deeply enmeshed with best practices for digital writing and online publishing, I became increasingly concerned with how my own assignment sheets for the course were not instantiating the practices I was teaching and expecting of students. While this case study came out of what I saw as a significant disconnect between pedagogical theory and practice, my experience with incorporating Universal Design in my assignment description has led me to begin transitioning some assignment sheets in other English courses I teach—ones without an emphasis on digital writing—to be more accessible, multimodal, and interactive. Indeed, I hope to make the case that redeveloping our assignment sheets is a valuable, inclusive practice whether we are teaching digital writing or literature, whether online or face-to-face.

Theories of Universal Design for Learning and Multimodality

As an educational framework first developed in the 1990s, Universal Design for Learning (UDL) began as a way to accommodate the diverse needs of learners. As David Gordon, Anne Meyer, and David Rose (2014) state, "the goal of UDL is to make sure everybody"—not just traditional learners, nor only those learners on the margins—indeed, everybody "has the opportunity to develop into an expert learner" (89). As a guide to aid in the development and selection of teaching and learning tools, early UDL theorists created three guiding principles:

1. "multiple means of engagement (the 'why' of learning),"
2. "representation (the 'what' of learning)," and
3. "action and expression (the 'how' of learning)." (Gordon, Meyer, & Rose 2014, 89)

As UDL and disability studies researchers emphasize, Universal Design teaching practices are essential for some students but can benefit all student learners (Dolmage 2014; Gordon, Meyer, & Rose 2014; Walters 2010; Yergeau et al. 2013).

In English 3120: Digital Writing & Publishing, I have been teaching the importance of accessibility in digital design for many years. As a previous editor with *Kairos: A Journal of Rhetoric, Technology, and Pedagogy*, I helped prepare webtexts for digital publication by checking for accessibility, such as the presence of transcripts for audio clips or text-heavy images, and I ask students in my courses to follow many of these same procedures in their use of alt tags, transcripts, and other accessible digital layout and design features. As Douglas Eyman et al. (2016) argue in "Access/ibility," adhering to standards of accessibility provides benefits ranging from "legal compliance" and "findability" to enhanced "usability and navigation"; Eyman et al. support the Universal Design principle that "designers who take into account the needs of people with disabilities actually improve usability for all people." While I had a statement about accommodations and learning differences on my syllabus, I had not done much to proactively design assignment sheets with accessibility and Universal Design in mind. Like many other instructors, I was approaching accessibility in my assignment sheets from a retrofit model by "add[ing] a component or accessory to something that has already been manufactured or built"; as Jay Dolmage has eloquently argued, retrofitting does not "necessarily fix a faulty product, but it acts as a sort of correction" (2008, 20). Universal Design provides the framework by which we can reconceptualize, from the ground up, our development of teaching materials such as assignment sheets, syllabi, and rubrics.

Alongside accessibility, multimodality is an important course concept in English 3120 that I also began to realize I was teaching but not modeling through the pedagogical materials I had developed. As outlined by the New London Group (1996), we communicate and make meaning in texts through five modes: Linguistic (alphabetic words, phrases, and sentences), Visual (images, page layouts), Aural (music, sound effects), Gestural (body language, sensuality), and Spatial (environmental and architectural spaces). In fact, many of the texts we encounter in our everyday lives are what the New London Group would call multimodal, combining two or more of these modes; this is especially true with digital texts that may include embedded video or audio clips, inviting users to interact with digital space by clicking through self-selected content. At the time of their writing in the late 1990s, the New London Group argued that "Increasingly important are modes of meaning other than linguistic," and that claim is echoed even more so over two decades later in the ADE report "A Changing Major." English majors are expected to be able to compose and publish in formats beyond academic essays that use primarily linguistic modes to communicate meaning, and courses like English 3120: Digital Writing & Publishing are intended to help prepare them to write in multiple modes and publish using best practices of accessibility. Students in English 3120 are given a brief introduction to the concept of *multimodality*, and their digital writing assignments are intended to give them practice with composing in multiple modes while also adhering to what they have learned about accessibility and attribution.[2]

As I began rethinking my assignment sheets for teaching online, multimodality seemed like a logical next step in the redevelopment of my teaching materials. In the following section, I describe the series of revisions I made to the description for a blogging assignment I teach in English 3120. What I initially envisioned as a transition from a linguistic-heavy Microsoft Word document to a more multimodal format resulted in an entire reconceptualization of the assignment description using Universal Design as a guiding principle.

---

2. Like many digital writing scholars, I use the term *attribution* to explain how students should give credit for borrowed or remixed digital content. As opposed to *citation*, which implies an academic style such as APA, MLA, or Chicago, attribution leaves open-ended the format but emphasizes the importance of attributing and giving credit when using other media or sources in digital publishing.

The Evolution of an Assignment Sheet

Blogging has been a major unit in all of the sections I have taught of English 3120 over the last seven years; students create individual blogs using WordPress and post a series of entries on a topic of their choosing, often with a focus on a local niche or issue. Appendix A shows the blogging assignment sheet from a face-to-face version of the course. As readers can see from a quick visual skim of Appendix A, the assignment sheet is extremely text heavy, with only a few layout features—bold-faced section headings—to help break up the wall of paragraphs of text describing the assignment. My attempt to add a bit of visual design to this Word document happened in the header at the top of the assignment sheet, which progresses from a bright orange block to a series of lighter and smaller orange, yellow, and pink blocks. From the perspective of a typical English course assignment sheet, I thought I was doing pretty well adding a splash of color. However, considering my assignment sheet design in relation to the course content, I was not at all modeling the kinds of digital writing practices I was expecting of students—the very "best practices for digital writing" I mention in the blogging assignment sheet.

As students in the course learn through course readings and discussions, users read differently when reading content online. For starters, we read more slowly—counterintuitive to what feels like a fast-paced experience—but we also read significantly less of the text (Carroll 2017). As Farhhad Manjoo explains in "Why You Won't Finish This Article," published online in *Slate*, 38 percent of Web readers who land on an article will be gone nearly immediately, engaging with no content on the page, and those who stay on a page with an article very rarely make it to the end (2013). We also know from user-experience and eye-tracking research that Web readers tend to skim content, rather than reading content word-for-word (Nielson 2006). To help keep readers on a webpage, one of the concepts I teach students in digital writing is "chunking," which "makes content easier to comprehend and remember," especially when Web readers are skimming quickly and not always able to comprehend content deeply (Moran 2018). I also teach students to incorporate additional visual and design layout features to help break up content, such as bullet lists, embedded media (e.g., images, video, audio), and hyperlinks (Carroll 2017). However, my original assignment sheet about blogging did not include any of these Web design or embedded media features. Thus began the first revision of my blogging assignment sheet.

When I began teaching a hybrid version of English 3120, it was becoming more important for me to model good digital writing practices as students were engaging with more of the course content through our Course Management System (CMS), iCollege, a version of Desire2Learn. Instead of passing out a print version of my text-heavy Word-based assignment sheet, students were encountering the assignment sheet through online reading, likely skimming the content quickly as research suggests most of us do with Web reading. Appendix B shows a revision of the assignment sheet for the blogging project when I began teaching the course as hybrid. Instead of writing and designing the assignment sheet in Microsoft Word, I composed, edited, and published the assignment sheet within an HTML webpage in iCollege. In this revision, I worked to model some of the digital writing practices I assign students, avoiding large blocks of text and instead breaking content out into bullet lists under the bold-faced headings. I also added a large text box at the bottom with a list of some of the features that students should incorporate to compose an effective blog entry. I hoped to catch their attention with the formatting of the text box content because it is essential to their success with the blogging assignment. To be clear, my goals were not to let students off the hook of having to closely read assignment sheets for my class simply because the format shifted from F2F to online; rather, my intention was that these layout and design features would more clearly communicate the assignment to students—that seeing a bullet list of the course goals to which the assignment connects, for instance, would help them more quickly and easily see, read, and understand the rationale for this assignment rather than burying a list of those course goals within a paragraph in a block of text. For your own reading experience, compare the opening paragraph of Appendix A with the opening section of Appendix B.

With this revision of the assignment sheet, the blogs students submitted demonstrated that they better understood the assignment instructions and they noticed the significance of specific features that make a good blog entry. The original text-heavy version of the assignment sheet (Appendix A) resulted in students spending more time on developing a niche for their blog, without as much attention to best practices in Web writing; indeed, the section that takes up the most visual space and has the longest paragraph in the assignment sheet is the "Choosing a Blog Niche and Localizing the Issue" section, suggesting to students that this component of the assignment was especially important. However, the revised version (Appendix B) helped demonstrate through the visual layout—particularly the use of the large text box with a bullet list at the bottom of the screen shot—that students should focus their energies not only on content and developing a niche, but also on Web design and layout features in their blog posts. This revision more effectively, specifically, and concisely communicated to students my expectations for the blog assignment. While this revision began to better model some of the writing for the Web features I was asking of students, it still lacked considerably in its use of visual, aural, and gestural modes, and it did not model the kind of interactivity and multimodality I was also asking of students in their digital writing assignments. As I prepared to teach a fully online version of the course, I saw this as an opportunity to better model multimodality, which in turn led me to also re-conceptualize the genre of the assignment "sheet" and move toward principles of Universal Design.

Moving Toward Multimodality in Online Teaching

Knowing that multimodality was so central to the course concepts in English 3120, my first thought as I prepared my teaching materials for a fully online version of the course was to make them more multimodal; in particular, I wanted to move beyond the linguistic mode to better incorporate visual, aural, gestural, and spatial modes. Not only would these multimodal pedagogical materials be more engaging, but I also surmised that they would be more accessible for users needing accommodation. As Shannon Walters (2010) notes, "from an impairment-specific perspective, multimodality seems inherently accommodating to the material needs of users, audiences, and students of dis/abilities. A student or user experiencing difficulty in one mode can express or receive information in another mode" (437). However, as Walters and her technical writing students found in their experimentation with various approaches, multimodal revisions can work well for impairment-specific accommodation, but "situated in the larger conversation of disability studies, [multimodal approaches] may continue to be inaccessible to the audiences for which they would seem most useful, such as disabled users with varying levels of impairment, nondisabled users with varying levels of abilities or learning styles, and anybody with a cognitive or invisible disability" (440).

Reinforcing the limitations of multimodality to address accessibility is Stephanie Kershbaum's contribution to the co-authored article "Multimodality in Motion." Kershbaum critiques multimodal environments for being inhospitable because many multimodal texts are "not commensurable across modes"; "inaccessible multimodal spaces are too often remedied by a problematic turn to the retrofit"; and "texts and environments are rarely flexible enough to be manipulated by users" (Yergeau et al. 2013). Kershbaum argues that what she calls "multimodal inhospitality" occurs "when the design and production of multimodal texts and environments persistently ignore access except as a retrofit," and she makes the case for considering issues of access at the early stages of designing and developing multimodal texts (Yergeau et al. 2013). In particular, Kershbaum recommends designing multimodal texts that "incorporate redundancy across multiple channels" to make digital texts more flexible and to "enable customization and manipulation of these texts by readers" (Yergeau et al. 2013).

As I revisited my blogging assignment sheet for the online version of the course, I first decided to reframe the assignment sheet as a short video of me describing the assignment instead of a static, linguistic text formatted on a Word document or embedded into an HTML document on iCollege. I created the approximately three-minute video using QuickTime and the built-in camera on my laptop; the video shows my head and shoulders and captures footage of me speaking into the camera, describing the blogging assignment. The video gave me the chance to better mirror the ways I describe assignments during class time: offering quick asides about how to approach defining the blog's niche and emphasizing the visual layout and design features that factor prominently into the blog's evaluation. My initial plan was for the video to replace both the earlier Word document description of the assignment (Appendix A) and the revised version placed on iCollege (Appendix B), modeling multimodality, interactivity, and embedded media in effective digital writing. For students in the course to be able to access the video clip, I first published the video as unlisted on YouTube—which offers an auto-captioning feature and/or allows users to post transcripts—and then embedded the YouTube video within our CMS iCollege.

Publishing the video to YouTube provided a platform that supports possibilities for captioning and/or a transcript to be fully accessible to students who may need accommodation and to better serve the needs of all students and the diverse ways they learn.[3] Users interested in YouTube's auto-caption feature may see it as a time-saver; however, the software has

---

3. YouTube helped me address some of the limitations of working within my university's CMS; however, many genre-related decisions for development of

been critiqued for its inaccuracies (Yeargeau et al. 2013). Moreover, double-checking for errors and making corrections to auto-captioning may be more labor intensive than simply creating the transcripts for oneself.[4] Janine Butler (2018) argues for yet another approach to captioning videos; as a self-identified deaf instructor, Butler demonstrates how "hearing composers can reimagine the design of their captioned videos, and appreciate students' embodied responses to new rhetorical situations," challenging teachers and students to move beyond seeing captions as "the two lines of text at the bottom of the screen" to instead incorporate captioning in the design of the video itself as "dynamic visual text" or "embodied captions." While I have not yet been able to experiment with these recommendations, Butler's suggestion to incorporate embodied design seems especially fruitful when creating instructor videos for online courses.

While the video accomplished many of my initial goals to move toward multimodality in my assignment "sheet" design, I soon realized the limitations of choosing only one mode of delivering information. While I described the assignment in the video, the level of detail I could achieve through the linguistic mode was not matched in the aural, visual, and gestural modes of the video; students needed both components: a linguistic description of the assignment that they could revisit and read through alongside a descriptive video of me providing context for the assignment. I needed to re-conceptualize the assignment description, to fully move away from the Microsoft-Word-assignment-sheet style that I had been using for years.

BEYOND THE SHEET: CHECKLISTS, CHUNKING, AND REDUNDANCY IN ASSIGNMENT DESCRIPTIONS FOR ONLINE TEACHING

The final set of revisions I made to the blog assignment sheet actually became more of a reconceptualization by exploring new possibilities in assignment design; as I experimented with affordances of digital and on-

---

my pedagogical materials continued to be impacted by "the politics of the [CMS] interface" (Selfe and Selfe 1994).

4. With new technologies evolving so quickly, my approach to recording these videos has shifted yet again. During the time between teaching my first fully online version of this class in 2018 and my most recent version in summer 2020, my university embedded Kaltura, a video management platform, within our CMS. Kaltura has eliminated the need for me to post videos on YouTube and has greatly enhanced the ease of creating captions for my instructor videos.

line tools, I began to see this teaching genre as less of a sheet and more of a multi-layered assignment description, with different modes and points of access and redundancy of information across modes of delivery. Three approaches guided the final design: checklists, chunking, and redundancy. These approaches align with some of the suggestions Shannon Haley-Mize (2018) makes for how instructors can incorporate Universal Design in their development of online teaching materials: "clear, interactive course headings and icons; grouping content into small, logical modules; incorporating checklists for monitoring progress; and providing self-check quizzes and activities with immediate feedback" (124).

Checklists functioned on multiple levels within the CMS course design for my online teaching, and I had checklists for students to track their completion of each course module and for assignments and tasks within each module. Appendix C is a screen shot from the CMS that shows a student's view of the blogging assignment description's checklist. This combined set of components, as listed below and in a checklist in Appendix C, represents the final, revised blogging assignment description for my online course:

- the Blog Project Assignment Sheet (already revised for the hybrid version of the course, pictured in Appendix B),
- the Instructor Video Introduction,
- the "What Makes a Good Blog Entry?" lesson, and
- the Blog Project Grading Rubric (pictured in Appendix D).

Creating this set of digital documents involved breaking some pieces of the original Word document into different online files, as well as adding some new details to enhance students' understanding of the assignment. It is the checklist style, though, that helps unify the set of documents and encourages students to explore the assignment description in multiple modes and formats. While some students may prefer a linear model and/or a linguistic mode by beginning with the first item listed—the redesigned linguistic description of the assignment, as shown in Appendix B—other students may choose to click around and start by viewing the Instructor Video Introduction or looking at student examples in "What Makes a Good Blog Entry?" The status bar built-in to the CMS (see the top of the image in Appendix C) invites users to eventually move through and read/view/listen/interact with the full set of assignment materials, tracking the percentage of topics completed and showing "X of 4 topics complete." Part of what made the checklist possible in the first place, though, was "chunking" the assignment description into smaller components.

Chunking was a guiding principle in the first revision of the assignment (from Appendix A to Appendix B), but it also became a valuable tool in the final set of documents for the assignment description. For example, one of the sections on the original blog assignment sheet was "Writing a Good Blog Entry" (See Appendix A), and this was where I described how students' blog entries would be evaluated. When I redeveloped the assignment description for online teaching—creating the instructor video paired with the assignment description—I decided to pull out a couple of the components of the assignment sheet into separate "chunks" of content. I created an entire new page of content for "Writing a Good Blog Entry," which—in the revised version—shows an excerpt from a sample student blog in a previous semester, describing and pointing directly to evidence in the sample of what the student had done particularly well in the blog entry. In this way, I was able to demonstrate in more detail how to be successful with this assignment—something that did not quite fit into the original version of the Word assignment sheet but worked quite well in this re-visioning of the assignment description into multimodal chunks of interactive pages.

These moves toward increased multimodal and interactive designs of the assignment description also meant that I needed to be mindful of Kershbaum's valid concerns about multimodal inhospitality. Redundancy across channels—in other words, repeating content but in slightly different ways, modes, or methods so that users have more agency in how they access content—became a way to address potential inaccessibility and to embrace Universal Design for the benefit of all learners. As one example, the Instructor Video Introduction on YouTube reinforces and extends information on the "Blog Project Assignment Sheet," and users can access that content by watching the video and/or by reading the transcript on YouTube. To take another example, the Blog Project Grading Rubric appears as a hyperlinked HTML page from the "Blog Project Assignment Sheet," is visible as a separate HTML page on the Blog Assignment checklist (see Appendix D), and is also accessible as an embedded, interactive rubric built within the CMS; thus, users can access this content in different places and modes.

In sum, the new set of documents describing the blogging assignment aligned more with a Universal Design approach that proactively incorporates accessibility, rather than retrofitting. As Walters and her students found in their usage of multimodal and Universal Design to address (in)accessibility, Universal Design "resists the simple substitution of one mode for another to accommodate a disability—visual modes for the hearing impaired or aural modes for the visually impaired—and desegregates users by designing for as wide an audience as possible" (2010, 441). Because "normalizing assumptions . . . often drive multimodality" (Walters 2010, 450), multimodality is not the only factor instructors should consider when preparing pedagogical materials like assignment sheets for online courses. Universal Design for Learning's "proactive approach . . . involves designing courses and other student services in a manner that deliberately analyzes and removes barriers . . . [making them] more likely to be accessible to all" (Haley-Mize 2018, 120).

In the summer of 2020, I had the opportunity to test some of these recommendations on a larger scale as I was invited to help lead a series of webinars in our university's "Mastering Online Teaching" (MOT) program. In response to the swift move to online teaching, faculty members were strongly urged—and in some cases required—to participate in the MOT program, resulting in approximately two thousand faculty proceeding through at different times during the summer. In the webinars, I collaborated with instructional designers to encourage faculty to "deconstruct" their syllabi and assignment sheets in many of the same ways I advocate for here—by using checklists to keep students on track, by breaking them into manageable chunks, and by having redundancy across the CMS platform so that students could access content in different ways. My recommendations for reconceptualizing assignment "sheets" in online teaching also meaningfully overlapped with another MOT webinar topic: transparency in learning and teaching (TILT). TILT-ing assignments means more explicitly identifying for students the "purpose," "task," and "criteria," and this often results from chunking the content on assignment descriptions into these areas and using checklists for students to make sure they are meeting the stated criteria for success (see https://tilthighered.com/ for examples and additional resources). Faculty who attended these webinars for the MOT program found the strategies of deconstructing a syllabus and TILT-ing assignments to be extremely helpful in redesigning their course materials for online delivery, and the practices of checklists, chunking, and redundancy were important to that redevelopment work.

WHY UNIVERSALLY RE-DESIGN ASSIGNMENT SHEETS?

While I cannot deny that reworking teaching materials takes time and effort, re-conceptualizing how we design assignment sheets and other teaching genres is essential for enhancing our teaching and aiding in student learning. This is true no matter what specialization within English studies we are teaching and whether we are teaching F2F, hybrid, or fully online. From inclusivity and accessibility perspectives, using Universal Design in the (re)development of our online teaching materials means that all students reap the benefits of engaging with course content through a variety of formats. This might mean redesigning a two-page Word document description of a literary analysis assignment into a teacher's TED Talk, podcast, and/or interactive video, or it may simply mean revising a text-heavy assignment description to use chunking or other visual layout and design features to better communicate the assignment to a diverse set of learners. Additionally, UDL results in proactive approaches to making pedagogical documents inclusive for all learners, so that in the event a student enrolls with an identified disability (or in the very likely event that students enroll with undocumented disabilities and learning differences), instructors need not retrofit those materials or revise for an impairment-specific scenario. The same federal protections for students with disabilities apply within F2F, hybrid, and online courses; therefore, making the investment now to begin redesigning our assignment sheets, syllabi, handouts, and exams with UDL in mind means that we will enhance the teaching and learning experiences for all learners in F2F courses we are currently teaching, as well as help us prepare to transition into possible hybrid and online course formats.

One lesson I learned from this assignment redesign experience is that it is okay to start small. I have not yet been able to redevelop all my assignment sheets to adhere to the principles of Universal Design, with the considerations of multimodality, interactivity, and inclusivity outlined here. I started with one teaching component—the blogging assignment—as a way to experiment with the affordances and limitations of various technologies and the CMS. Starting small allowed me to pilot these changes and make adjustments before putting in the labor of revising an entire set of teaching materials. In her arguments about the importance of UDL, Haley-Mize (2018) maintains that the syllabus and assignment sheets are perfect starting points for (re)design work because they shape "the students' initial impressions of the type of learning environment the instructor will establish" for online or face-to-face teaching (121). My goal is to continue working on redeveloping the syllabus and another major assignment "sheet" in preparation for the next fully online iteration for the course, with the ultimate goal of having all pedagogical documents redesigned over the next two to three iterations of the ENG 3120 course. In the meantime, I have also begun redesigning documents for the F2F courses I am currently teaching that do not necessarily share the writing for the Web content of ENG 3120, but that nonetheless benefit from UDL and attention to multimodality, interactivity, and inclusivity.

Looking back on my first experiences teaching fully online, I found that taking the time to rework my blogging assignment sheet resulted in better student engagement and fewer complications for me as an online teacher. Because students could access the blogging assignment description in multiple formats and because the content was broken into smaller chunks, students had a stronger grasp of the blogging assignment, especially compared to other assignment sheets in the course that I was not yet able to revise. For example, students in the online course created digital stories as a final project, and I had to field many more questions on the discussion board and via email about what to do and how to do it, as well as how students' work would be evaluated. With the blogging assignment, students had fewer questions and better met the assignment expectations, and I believe this can be attributed in part to the redesigned assignment description, the chunked content on the assignment description (Appendix B) and within the online course module (Appendix C), and the student examples that demonstrated how to succeed with the assignment. As Claire Battershill and Shawna Ross (2017) recommend in their guide to digital humanities in the classroom, "be aware of any information that is not included in readymade tutorials but that your students will need to know," such as technical instructions, tutorials, or even submission instructions (124). Not including detailed and clear descriptions can result in confusion for students. In other words, taking the time to universally redesign your assignment sheets in advance may save you the time and labor of responding to individual student questions because the assignment's description will be clearer and more accessible to all.

Finally, a major benefit of redesigning assignment sheets using Universal Design and increasingly multimodal designs is to enhance the coverage of digital humanities in our English departments. We will be doing a great service to our English majors by modeling the kinds of digital writing they will be expected to compose beyond graduation and providing them hybrid and online course spaces to practice these skills. Perhaps most importantly, incorporating these principles for redesigning our assignment sheets positions English departments as proactive leaders in inclusivity and accessibility. Regardless of whether we are already teaching hybrid or online, our face-to-face classes in early American literature, contemporary poetry, or Enlightenment rhetoric would all benefit from redesigned assignment descriptions. Taking a closer look back at our genres of teaching—re-examining the documents we use to communicate on paper and online with our students—means confronting that we may not always be as effective as we think at explaining to students how to succeed in our classes. Indeed, the best practices for assignment sheet (re)design outlined below are worth considering for all of our English studies classes offered in all formats.

Best Practices in Assignment Sheet (Re)Design for Online Teaching (With Benefits for Face-To-Face Teaching, Too)

1) *Make it scan-able, skim-able, and more concise.* Knowing the research about how users read online should prompt online instructors to cut back on long, linguistic-heavy descriptions of assignment expectations. Online readers are more likely to skim linguistic content, so keeping all the essential components but trying to shorten them for online formats will encourage students to keep reading. However, "chunking" and incorporating multimodal and interactive designs—numbers 2 and 3 below—will also help you create texts that give students multiple ways to engage with and read/watch/listen to your assignment description. Regardless of whether we are preparing to teach online, revisiting our assignment sheets for classes we have been teaching F2F for years—descriptions that may have grown longer and longer with time—to check for concision and to revise for scan-ability would improve the way we articulate assignment descriptions and goals for students.

2) *Chunk components of the assignment into parts.* One way to help make your assignment description shorter and more scan-able involves breaking it into parts. What may have originally been a two-page Word document with sections describing different components of the assignment may be re-conceptualized as a series of short texts spread across different

modes and platforms. Again, regardless of whether you are teaching online, hybrid, or face-to-face, chunking may be a good first step in redeveloping traditional, text-heavy, Word document assignment descriptions.

3) *Consider how incorporating multimedia, multimodality, and/or interactivity may enhance your ability to communicate the assignment effectively to students.* Creating materials that are click-able with embedded media and that engage with multiple modes of communication will create a more engaging learning experience for students. This might involve hyperlinks to online resources or scholarly articles; short videos that explain course concepts; or podcast-style audio segments, among other multimodal options.

4) *Keep Universal Design and inclusivity as guiding principles in redesigning assignment sheets.* While multimodality may be a way to engage diverse learners, we cannot assume that making our assignments multimodal will make them accessible and inclusive for all. Remembering that multimodality can be inhospitable to some learners, we must approach the revision of assignment sheets from the ground up—Universal Design invites us to prepare documents that are interactive and accessible, multimodal and inclusive for all learners.

These strategies for redesigning assignment sheets for online teaching are based on my experiences with teaching hybrid and online courses over the last few years. During the start of the COVID-19 pandemic in the US, many of us had to transition quickly into online teaching with little or no time to prepare our materials for this new mode. Without the pressures of triage-style teaching, instructors can be proactive in more mindfully preparing their online assignments using these recommended best practices as they—by necessity or choice—may increasingly find themselves teaching in hybrid, blended,[5] or fully online modes.

The suggestions outlined here contribute to an emerging set of practices within English studies that deserves more attention and more empirical research so that we can better understand the impact of teaching English studies online. Moreover, by embracing the changing nature of the English major through our redesigned pedagogies, we can help stu-

---

5. "Blended" instruction has emerged as a term used by many institutions to indicate socially-distanced models of learning which are necessary during world health crises. At GSU, our administrators defined blended learning as a kind of hybrid but where in-person class meetings are held at 50 percent or less capacity of students to allow for social distancing.

dents better understand the relationship between humanistic study and the ever-evolving technologies of literacy in our society.

References

ADE (Association of Departments of English). 2018. "A Changing Major: The Report of the 2016–17 ADE Ad Hoc Committee on the English Major." ADE. https://www.ade.mla.org/content/download/98513/2276619/A-Changing-Major.pdf.

Alexander, Jonathan. 2014. *On Multimodality: New Media in Composition Studies*. Carbondale: Southern Illinois Press.

Battershill, Claire, and Shawna Ross. *Using Digital Humanities in the Classroom: A Practical Introduction for Teachers, Lecturers, and Students*. New York: Bloomsbury Publishing PLC, 2017. ProQuest Ebook Central, http://ebookcentral.proquest.com/lib/gsu/detail.action?docID=4931522.

Butler, Janine. 2018. "Embodied Captions in Multimodal Pedagogies." *Composition Forum* 39. https://compositionforum.com/issue/39/captions.php.

Carroll, Brian. 2017. *Writing and Editing for Digital Media*. 3rd ed. New York: Routledge.

Caulfield, Jay. 2011. *How to Design and Teach a Hybrid Course: Achieving Student-Centered Learning Through Blended Classroom, Online, and Experiential Activities*. Sterling: Stylus Publishing.

Dolmage, Jay Timothy. 2014. *Disability Rhetoric*. Syracuse: Syracuse University Press.

Dolmage, Jay. 2008. "Mapping Composition: Inviting Disability in the Front Door. In *Disability and the Teaching of Writing*, edited by Cynthia Lewiecki-Wilson & Brenda Jo Brueggemann, 14–27. Boston: Bedford-St. Martin's Press.

Eyman, Douglas, et al. 2016. "Access/ibility: Access and Usability in Digital Publishing." *Kairos: A Journal of Rhetoric, Technology, and Pedagogy* 20 (2). http://kairos.technorhetoric.net/20.2/topoi/eyman-et-al/index.html

Gordon, David, Anne Meyer, and David Rose. 2014. *Universal Design for Learning: Theory and Practice*. Wakefield: CAST Professional Publishing.

Grouling, Jennifer. 2018. "The Genre of Teacher Comments from Hard-Copy to iPad." *Journal of Response to Writing*, 4 (1). http://journalrw.org/index.php/jrw/article/view/103/66.

Haley-Mize, Shannon. 2018. "Addressing Learner Variability on Campus through Universal Design for Learning." *Learning from Each Other: Refining the Practice of Teaching in Higher Education*, edited by Michele Lee Kozimor-King, and Jeffrey Chin, 116–29. University of California Press, 2018. ProQuest Ebook Central. http://ebookcentral.proquest.com/lib/gsu/detail.action?docID=5452027.

Manjoo, Farhad. 2013. "You Won't Finish This Article: Why People Online Don't Read to the End." *Slate*. Accessed 13 Dec. 2018. https://slate.com/technology/2013/06/how-people-read-online-why-you-wont-finish-this-article.html.

Moran, Kate. 2018. "Why Chunking Content is Important." Neilson Norman Group. Accessed 12 Dec. 2018. https://www.nngroup.com/videos/chunking/.

Neilson, Jakob. 2006. "F-Shaped Pattern for Reading Web Content." Neilson Norman Group. Accessed 12 Dec. 2018. https://www.nngroup.com/articles/f-shaped-pattern-reading-web-content-discovered/.

The New London Group. 1996. "A Pedagogy of Multiliteracies: Designing Social Futures." *Harvard Educational Review* 66 (1): 60–92.

Palmeri, Jason. 2012. *Remixing Composition: A History of Multimodal Writing Pedagogy*. Carbondale: Southern Illinois University Press.

Selber, Stuart. 2004. *Multiliteracies for a Digital Age*. Carbondale: Southern Illinois University Press.

Selfe, Cynthia, ed. 2007. *Multimodal Composition: Resources for Teachers*. Cresskill, NJ: Hampton Press.

Selfe, Cynthia, and Richard Selfe. 1994. "The Politics of the Interface: Power and Its Exercise in Electronic Contact Zones." *College Composition and Communication* 45 (4): 480–504. doi:10.2307/358761.

Walters, Shannon. 2010. "Toward an Accessible Pedagogy: Dis/ability, Multimodality, and Universal Design in the Technical Communication Classroom." *Technical Communication Quarterly* 19 (4): 427–54. https://doi.org/10.1080/10572252.2010.502090.

Yergeau, Melanie et al. 2013. "Multimodality in Motion: Disability and Kairotic Spaces." *Kairos: A Journal of Rhetoric, Technology, and Pedagogy* 18 (1). Accessed 14 December 2018. http://kairos.technorhetoric.net/18.1/coverweb/yergeau-et-al/pages/access.html.

Appendix A

Text-Heavy Version of the Assignment Sheet for Face-to-Face Course

[Microsoft Word document]
ENG3120 Local Public Issue Blog (25%)
Blogs are a popular and user-friendly way for citizens to quickly publish to the Web. For our course, you will create a blog using your sites.gsu.edu account (which is a version of WordPress for educational purposes) in order to practice good research and digital writing skills, become a better reader and reviewer of your peers' digital writing, and to engage

your role as an academic citizen through social media. While easy to create, not all blogs are created equal, and we will spend some of our class time discussing what makes an interesting topic for a blog, how to keep your eyes open for and brainstorm blog post ideas, and how to design and write in an effective style for the Web.

Choosing a Blog Niche and Localizing Your Issue
The most interesting blogs offer something new for readers, even if they are on topics that are seemingly familiar. Thus, a major task for this assignment will be identifying your unique niche or take on your chosen issue. I would like for you to choose an issue or cause that has some connection to the local area *and* that is meaningful to you personally, that you don't currently know much about but are interested in, or that you currently have a bit of expertise in. Your cause or issue might be anything from homelessness to cystic fibrosis, from education to immigration. Whatever you choose, though, you must be able to connect the issue locally in some capacity. Sometimes localizing your issue means simply making the issue personal to you; you might also take a broader national or global issue and localize it by researching its impact or instantiation in the local area or with local community members. Once you've selected your niche, each of your blog posts should relate to that topic in some way.

Formatting Your Blog Post Titles
For each blog entry, please include the blog number in the title. For example: "Blog 1: Homelessness in Downtown Atlanta" or "Blog 5: An Interview with State Senator X."

Writing a Good Blog Entry
Each of your blog entries will be evaluated considering best practices for digital writing that you will read more about as the semester progresses. Your work will be evaluated in the following categories: length, audience and purpose, ethos and credibility, and effective digital writing style.

Drafts
Starting June 25, you will post a digital copy of a draft blog entry to Google Drive (what used to be called Google docs) before class each Wednesday. During class, you will take some time to read and respond to drafts of your peers using Google Drive's commenting feature, and you will then use that feedback to revise that entry in advance of the final draft due date (the following Monday). Blog drafts and peer review

of drafts will be evaluated as pass/fail, and you will earn 5 points each (pass) for bringing a draft and/or responding to peer drafts or 0 points each (fail) for failure to bring a draft, missing peer review, and/or not providing a thorough and thoughtful review.

Grading Cycle & Feedback

You will receive staggered feedback and grades on your blogs. You will receive a grade and feedback on 1–2 entries. Your feedback will be posted through D2L; you can check your grade through the gradebook and then you should be able to click for a more detailed assessment with comments from me. I will post an announcement on D2L when I've completed the assessments for each grading cycle.

Appendix B

A Revision of the Assignment Sheet

> **Blog Project Assignment Sheet**
>
> Blogs are a popular and user-friendly way for writers to quickly publish to the Web. For our course, you will create a blog using WordPress to meet the following course goals:
> - demonstrate your understanding of effective design and style for the Web,
> - become a better reader and reviewer of your peers' digital writing,
> - and develop professional skills that would be applicable for social media, content development, copy writing, and other digital writing and online publishing jobs.
>
> **Choosing a Blog Niche and Localizing Your Issue**
>
> The most interesting blogs offer something new for readers, even if they are on topics that are seemingly familiar. Thus, an important task for this assignment will be identifying your unique niche or take on your chosen issue. Once you've selected your niche, each of your blog posts should relate to that topic in some way.
> - I would like for you to choose an issue for your blog's niche that has some connection to the local area and that is meaningful to you personally, that you don't know much about but are interested in, or that you have a bit of expertise in.
> - Whatever topic you choose, you must be able to connect the issue locally in some capacity. Sometimes localizing your issue means simply making the issue personal to you — as long as you're explicit in your own local positioning; you might also take a broader national or global issue and localize it by researching its impact or instantiation in the local area; or you could simply localize your issue by targeting a local readership. Other blogs may specialize in local topics related to the history of a place or contemporary local issues.
>
> **Writing a Good Blog Entry**
>
> Each of your blog posts should be 250 - 500 words and employ effective digital writing style. Below is a list of components you may use to enhance readability and scan-ability in your blog posts, though don't try all of these at once and feel free to include other ideas not here. Use the grading rubric at the end of this page to guide the development of your posts, too.
>
> | | |
> |---|---|
> | - Subheadings | - Use of color |
> | - Highlighted keywords | - Bulleted lists |
> | - Typeface variations | - Short paragraphs that use "chunking" |
> | - Use of tags or categories | |
> | - A sentence or paragraph that is set off visually to stand out from the rest of the entry | |
> | - Strategically placed and appropriately chosen hyperlink(s) to external websites | |
> | - Strategically placed and appropriately chosen image(s) or video clip(s) | |
>
> **Evaluation**
>
> See the Blog Assignment Grading Rubric for details about how your blog posts will be evaluated.

Figure 1. Screen shot from within the online CMS

Appendix C

Checklist of Items for Blogging Assignment Description

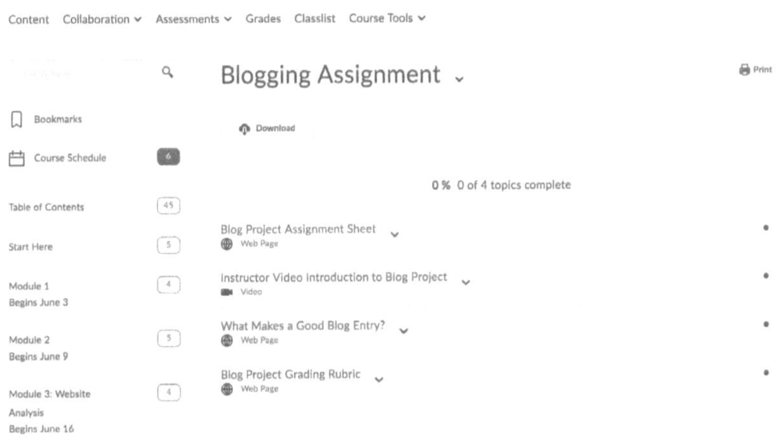

Figure 2. Screen shot from within the online CMS

Appendix D

Blog Project Grading Rubric

	20 points	15 points	10 points	5 points
Length of entry	Blog posts are clear and concise, typically 250 to 500 words each.	One or more blog entries are somewhat verbose (too long for the genre).	One or more blog entries are somewhat underdeveloped (too short).	Several blog entries are significantly underdeveloped (too short).
Purpose and Audience	Blog entries have a clear purpose and focus related to the niche and that would be of interest to a local audience.	Blog entries have a clear purpose but may seem unrelated to blog niche OR not engaging for a local audience.	Blog entries have a clear purpose but may seem unrelated to blog niche AND not engaging for a local audience.	Blog entries have an unclear purpose or focus, seem unrelated to the blog niche, and/or do not seem engaging to a local audience.
Blogger's ethos and credibility	Blog entries are error-free and present the writer as trustworthy, transparent, credible, and accountable. The entries clearly link to relevant online content used to help write the entries. The posts give credit to other authors and artists when using portions of their writing, images, and/or other media.	Blog entries contain some typos/errors but still present the writer as trustworthy and credible. However, because the writer may not link to relevant content and/or may not clearly identify sources for borrowed or referenced material, the transparency and credibility may be questioned.	One or more blog entries do not link to relevant content, may include broken or blind links, and/or do not clearly identify sources when material has obviously been borrowed.	Blog entries contain significant errors or typos and cause readers to question the transparency, credibility, and/or accountability of the writer.
Effective digital writing style	The entries successfully demonstrate effective digital writing style by incorporating several purposefully selected components (not too many, but not too few) from the list above to enhance readability and scan-ability and to demonstrate effective digital writing style.	The digital writing style is average. The entries may incorporate either too many or too few of the components from the list above to enhance readability and scan-ability.	The digital writing style is muddled, possibly detracting from the content. The entries may incorporate either too many or too few of the components from the list above to enhance readability and scan-ability.	The entries do not demonstrate effective digital writing style.
Effective layout, use of media, and hyper-linking	The layout and design for the entries are clear, effective, and usable. The entries adeptly use visuals and/or audio to engage readers. Hyperlinks are styled appropriately and are rhetorically meaningful to the content.	The layout and design are average could be enhanced. The use of visuals and/or audio is present and meaningful. Hyperlinks are styled appropriately.	The layout and design could be clearer or more user-friendly, and the style of hyperlinks could be enhanced.	The layout and design for the entries need significant improvement. The use of visuals and/or audio needs improvement. Hyperlinks may not be rhetorically meaningful and/or may not be styled appropriately (long URLs, typing "Click here," hyperlinking an entire sentence, etc.).

Figure 3. Blog Project Grading Rubric

9 Experimental Research and Reflective Teaching Practice in Online Writing Instruction

Joanne Addison

In 1997, I taught my first fully online writing course—a section of core composition. While most of my colleagues were skeptical, piloting online learning in one of these courses was an easy sell. After all, what did my department have to lose by turning one section of core composition over to this folly? As my students and I fumbled our way through a crude precursor to today's learning management systems, we ended the semester both frustrated by the limitations and intrigued by the possibilities of online learning. Slowly, more and more of my department's courses went online, learning management systems matured, and by 2005 I had been awarded a grant to develop a fully online version of our English Writing, Rhetoric, and Technology major. Across the country today, more than one out of every four students is enrolled in an online course each semester, making online courses "a common part of the course delivery modality for many students" (Seaman et al. 2018, 12).

Despite this relatively long history with fully online courses and the growth of online learning overall, significant skepticism remains in my department, mirroring that of the larger academic community concerning the effectiveness of online education. Couple this skepticism with seemingly intractable complaints about the quality of student writing and it becomes difficult to convince others that digital spaces can offer engaging and effective educational experiences for students and faculty in English studies. But it would be a mistake to simply attribute this to a Luddite-like resistance to educational technology overall. Rather, I would argue that we have yet to make the case for what counts as effective online writing instruction and the ways this might inform English studies in general. Unabashedly, this article is guided by George Hillocks Jr.'s admonition that "Some practices and approaches are clearly better than others and we had better not ignore the differences" (2009, 23). The differences, I think, have yet to be clearly articulated for digital environments.

Many people would argue that there is no significant difference between the outcomes in online and face-to-face courses overall and, therefore, we should continue to expand our online offerings (see, for example, *No Significant Difference*). But comparing generalized outcomes is not the same as identifying, classifying, and comparing various types of instruction in digital environments to determine which modes of instruction are most effective. Indeed, we have been content to project modes of instruction identified using experimental research in face-to-face classrooms onto digital classrooms. But digital environments entail opportunities and constraints not present in face-to-face classrooms that are likely to alter or even erase face-to-face instructional modes at the same time that they engender new modes. Thus, we need ways to identify the modes that are actually in use and measure their effectiveness. Examining the state of online instruction in writing studies can inform future directions for English studies as a whole.

EMPIRICAL KNOWLEDGE ABOUT TEACHING WRITING ONLINE

In 1986 George Hillocks, Jr. published *Research on Written Composition*. The meta-analysis included in this book was based on experimental and quasi-experimental research and was the first large-scale synthesis of its kind in writing studies. It remains a landmark touchstone for arguments about what works in teaching writing and is used to differentiate modes of teaching in English studies overall. For example, in response to one of the latest articles in the *Chronicle of Higher Education* lamenting the state of student writing abilities (Teller 2016), Douglas Hesse (2017) references *Research on Written Composition* in arguing that we do, in fact, know what works in teaching writing. Hillocks's meta-analysis was based on seventy-three experimental studies and allowed him to identify and evaluate four modes of instruction[1]:

---

1. Hillocks (1986) differentiates between Mode of Instruction and Focus of Instruction. Mode of Instruction primarily focuses on the activities of the classroom and the teacher's orientation toward her students as well as the students' orientation toward each other. Focus of Instruction primarily concerns the con-

1. Presentational: Focused on lecture and teacher-led discussions about the qualities of good writing and reviewing examples of good writing with feedback almost exclusively in the form of evaluative comments from the teacher for a final grade, students positioned as passive recipients of knowledge and skills. *Least effective mode, half as effective as all other modes.*
2. Natural Process: Focused on student-led interests, freewriting, feedback from peer review groups and teacher, with an emphasis on multiple drafts and revision. Little to no focus on the study of models, rules for good writing, or highly structured activities, teachers seen as facilitators, not evaluators. *About 50% more effective than Presentational Mode, equally effective as Individualized Mode.*
3. Environmental: Focused on objectives that are clear and specific, balances peer group activity with whole group activity using structured problem-based learning, revision is emphasized, rules of good writing are taught through structured activities, teacher is both facilitator and evaluator, balances teacher, student, and activities. *"On pre-to-post measures, the environmental mode is over four times more effective than the traditional presentational mode and three times more effective than the natural process mode"* (1986, 247).
4. Individualized: Focused on individual instruction of students in a tutorial or even whole class format, student activities include significant variation but the defining feature is a lack of student interaction with other students and an emphasis on individualized interaction between teachers and students or, more commonly, tutors. *Included primarily because of inclusion of writing centers and tutors—the first three modes are those most commonly referenced.*

Hillocks's book was considered so important, and for some so controversial, that in 1988 a significant part of *Research in the Teaching of English* (Vol. 22, No.1) was turned over to a discussion of its methods and conclusions by leading scholars such as Sandra Stotsky, John Hayes, and Alan C. Purves. Unfortunately, we'd be hard pressed to name a study such as Hillocks's today that can be used as a touchstone for arguments over what works in teaching writing online. We lose more than just one

---

tent of the classroom instruction or disciplinary approach—for example two primary approaches today are genre studies and rhetorical studies (Hesse 2017).

methodological approach to knowing in this situation. In fact, we lose an important window into our history, philosophical underpinnings, and the ongoing development of our field. As Hillocks outlines for us in summarizing his meta-analysis:

> To some extent, these three modes of instruction represent an historical progression. The presentational mode is undoubtedly the oldest and certainly the most widespread . . . . The natural process mode has intellectual antecedents in Rousseau's *Emile* and in some interpretations of Dewey's work. . . . its more recent roots can be traced to the Dartmouth Conference . . . and to the work of Emig. . . . what I have called the natural process movement, dating from the 1960's, was and is a reaction against the dominant presentational mode with its often arbitrary assignments. . . . Environmental instruction has intellectual antecedents in the work of Herbart and Dewey. In composition, however, it appears to be relatively recent. . . . Environmental instruction, then, incorporates elements of both the presentational and the natural process modes, but moves beyond both to suggest more powerful approaches to teaching composition (1986, 247–48).

Continuing Hillocks's meta-analytical work by incorporating our movement into digital spaces can help us track our progress and articulate the ways that teaching practices in digital spaces should continue to be grounded in rich philosophical and empirical histories rather than being perceived as simply reactions to current market forces. Further, knowing what characterizes the most effective modes of instruction is crucial to ensuring positive student outcomes and driving policy decisions. But is a meta-analysis designed to identify and measure modes of instruction possible for online writing instruction at this moment in time? As will be shown in the research review to follow, it seems the answer is "no."

Review of the Research 2001–2010

In 2013 the Conference on College Composition and Communication Committee for Best Practices in Online Writing Instruction released "A Position Statement of Principles and Example Effective Practices for Online Writing Instruction." This documents details fifteen principles for effective online writing instruction. Principle 15 calls on administrators, teachers, and tutors to commit to ongoing research into their programs and classes (31). As an example of an effective practice the authors suggest, "Quantitative studies that investigate student performance in terms of learning outcomes or benchmarks, grades, and course retention should be designed and deployed" (31). More specifically, I would call for experimental studies. Why focus on experimental research? Because experimental research that utilizes a control group in testing the effects of a pedagogical treatment between comparable groups remains one of the best ways to validate which practices are better than others. It allows us to establish causal relationships even when absolute standards don't exist in order to make informed decisions about what works in teaching writing. Despite its widespread acceptance across fields in the social sciences and education, experimental research is one of the least used methodologies in English studies.

The decline in experimental research has been evidenced through recent accounts offered by Haswell (2005), Webb (2006), Anson (2008) and Bowie and McGovern (2013). This situation is even more pronounced when we focus specifically on fully online writing instruction. In 2001 Susan Kay Miller assessed the state of distance learning research in *Computers and Composition*—the journal in which we would expect to see some of the earliest research in online writing instruction in our field. From 1994, the year in which the first article on distance education appeared, through 1999, twelve articles were published. Only one of the articles employed quantitative research, none focused on fully online writing classes, and none were experimental in approach. In 2013 Bowie and McGovern assessed the types of research published in *Computers and Composition, Computers and Composition Online, Kairos*, and *College Composition and Communication* from 2003 to 2008. Of the 365 articles reviewed, almost 289 were related to computers and writing and 35 met their definition of empirical research (258). Of those, only two were experimental.

The lack of empirical research in general and experimental research in particular has led many of us to rely on a meta-analysis conducted by the US Department of Education (2010) in arguing for the efficacy of online writing courses despite the fact that only three of the studies included focused on writing, and more importantly, were conducted in very specialized writing classes. One was a technical writing class in agriculture, one a writing class for students with disabilities, and one a writing class in English as a foreign language. Thus, no studies were included that might be considered the types of "standard" writing courses in which most online/hybrid students enroll. This Department of Education study sought to determine if student outcomes in fully online courses differed from those in face-to-face or hybrid courses and identified just over one thousand empirical studies of online learning from 1996 through 2008. Of these studies, the authors found that 176 could be classified as experimental or quasi-experimental. Of these, only fifty included a comparison of outcomes between fully online courses and either face-to-face courses or hybrid courses as well as a significant effect size. The meta-analysis of these fifty studies "found that, on average, students in online learning conditions performed modestly better than those receiving face-to-face instruction" (ix). However, a number of researchers disagreed with the analysis and upon updating the results with additional studies concluded:

1. That there is no concrete evidence to conclude that fully online instruction, in a standard full-term-length, for-credit college level course, is either superior to or inferior to in-person instruction.
2. That the current status of research in online learning is very weak: the field has produced very few rigorously conducted experimental studies, while even fewer of them were both carefully designed and tested in relevant contexts. (as quoted in Phan 2012, 1–2)

One significant factor that we don't know about these results is whether or not the face-to-face instruction being used for comparison engaged a mode of instruction that was highly effective. For example, if the face-to-face class used a presentational mode and the online class could also be classified as presentational, then even though the outcomes were the same neither is likely to have had the best outcomes possible given what we know about the presentational mode of teaching. This is just one example of why we need to be able to identify and assess the modes of online writing instruction—after all, if we are basing our efforts primarily on comparative studies where few or none of the classes involved are employing the most effective modes of instruction, then our comparisons are of little use and may even be harmful.

Like the Department of Education report on which so many of us rely, Warnock's 2013 research bibliography is also short on experimental studies of online writing classes that measure effectiveness beyond surveys of student satisfaction or self-reports. While this bibliography includes a sample of nineteen studies from 1997 to 2013 focusing on comparisons of student outcomes in fully online, hybrid, and face-to-face courses, it is not focused exclusively on writing courses (e.g., studies of courses in statistics, social studies, education, the corporation K12, Inc. etc. are included). Of the relatively few studies included that were conducted in a composition or writing class of any kind, only three could be classified as experimental or quasi-experimental.

REVIEW OF THE RESEARCH 2010–2018

This review picks up just after where Bowie and McGovern and the Department of Education left off by considering articles published from 2010–2018. To be included in this review, the research must have been conducted using fully online writing courses (excluding MOOCs) and must have focused on some effect of student learning. The research must have been experimental in nature (i.e., comparing two groups of online writing students who are generally similar with one designated as the control group and the other as the experimental group, controlling for variables to the extent possible in natural educational settings) and must have met MacNealy's criteria for rigorous empirical research as outlined by Bowie and McGovern:

1. Was planned in advance: the researcher planned the research before conducting, as opposed, for example, to having taught a class using a new technology and retroactively deciding to write about the experience.
2. Demonstrated systematic collection of data: the researcher collected data systematically—there was a sampling method in place for at least some of the data collected in the study.
3. Produced a body of evidence that others could study: the research resulted in videos, survey results, interview transcripts, a collection of documents, observations notes, or other data that others could study if they wished. (249)

I began with a consideration of Section 5 of the "Bedford Bibliography of Research in Writing Instruction: Publications Regarding Research and Investigation in Online Writing Instruction." This bibliography catalogues publications focused on online writing instruction from 1990 to 2015. It is inclusive of work conducted in writing centers as well as classes taught in a face-to-face format using some type of educational technology. There are a significant number of empirical articles listed, but of the

135 studies included at the time of this writing, not a single one met the minimal criteria set above. While this does not diminish the importance of the research that is included, it does suggest a narrowing of the types of research we value, a discussion we will return to later.

Since Bowie and McGovern's review, there has been an increase in journals focused on online learning. So, my second step was a broad database search using the very general terms "online writing " to begin to identify the range of journals publishing work in this area in order to cast a wide net when identifying possible studies for this review. The journals included are

- *Computers and Composition*
- *Computers and Composition Online*
- *Journal of Computer-Assisted Learning*
- *Kairos*
- *Journal of Computers in Education*
- *Research in the Teaching of English*
- *English Education*
- *Distance Education*
- *Composition Studies*
- *WPA Writing Program Administration*
- *Assessing Writing*
- *Journal of Technical Writing and Communication*
- *College Composition and Communication*

Through reading the abstracts of all articles published in these journals, only one was identified that employed an experimental design and met the criteria established earlier. "Comparison of Online and Face-to-Face Peer Review of Writing" (2017) concludes that while most of the rules for effective peer review are the same in online and face-to-face learning environments, there are some differences to which we need to pay attention.

This continued shift away from empirical research in general has many implications. For example, Takayoshi finds herself arguing in 2018 that as a field we have abandoned data-based research of how people write at a moment when "contemporary writers' composing processes explicitly weave together culture, the individual, and literacy in ways that are inadequately explained by the composing process research that does exist" (552). Similarly, I would argue that our abandonment of data-based research, and even more so experimental research, prevents us from identifying and measuring modes of online writing instruction in ways that can significantly shape the pedagogical, political, social and economic future of online writing instruction. Instead, institutional decisions to move classes online are likely to be made primarily based on economic factors, not what's best for students, teachers, and the future of English studies, thus marginalizing our departments and limiting our practice. Equally important, as mentioned earlier, is that data-based research serves as an important window into our past, present, and future as it allows us to understand concrete teaching practices within the context of their philosophical and historical underpinnings.

There is likely another significant contributor to this situation, one that is much more difficult to uncover and even more difficult for many of us to contemplate. That is, current labor conditions in higher education, especially in fields where large numbers of part-time faculty teach the introductory courses, has a silent but certain effect on our research practices. While I haven't been able to find valid statistics on the number of part-time vs. tenure track faculty teaching fully online courses, it is likely that the vast majority of online courses are taught by part-time faculty that have neither the resources nor the time to conduct empirical research. This relationship between research and labor conditions in the US is a matter that deserves significant attention, and although that is beyond the scope of this article, it is most certainly related to the lack of experimental research in online education.

Do Modes of Instruction Still Matter?

I'd like to return to George Hillocks Jr.'s admonition that "Some practices and approaches are clearly better than others and we had better not ignore the differences" (2009). The Conference on College Composition and Communication Committee for Best Practices in Online Writing Instruction outlines their beliefs on which practices and approaches are better than others in "OWI Principle 4: Appropriate onsite composition theories, pedagogies, and strategies should be migrated and adapted to the online instructional environment" (2013, 13). Here they argue that foundational approaches to teaching writing can and should be used in online writing classrooms, and their example practices focus on a learner-centered, problem-based, highly interactive mode of instruction very closely aligned with the environmental mode outlined by Hillocks in 1986.

The Department of Education meta-analysis also discusses modes of instruction (called "learner experiences"). Their analysis revealed three modes of instruction with two of them paralleling Hillocks's presentational and environmental modes:

1. Expository instruction: This mode is marked primarily by the transmission of knowledge through digital devices in a lock-step fashion with little interaction between students and other students as well as between students and teachers. Evaluation is generally summative in nature. Often referred to as "canned" courses.
2. Active learning: In this mode the learner gains knowledge through inquiry-based interaction with digital artifacts such as online drills, simulations, or games. In both Expository and Active learning the technology delivers the content.
3. Interactive learning: This mode of instruction differs significantly from expository and active in that learners gain knowledge "through inquiry-based collaborative interaction with other learners; teachers become co-learners and act as facilitators." (3)

While the expository mode parallels Hillocks's presentational mode, the interactive mode parallels Hillocks's environmental mode, because of the degree to which teachers and learners engage in problem-based, interactive learning. It seems that the active mode may differ significantly enough from those offered by Hillocks, and to which composition studies still largely adheres as an organizing principle, that it should be considered a new mode worthy of further study.

But let's look at this a bit more closely. As already mentioned, CCCC has taken the position that online writing instruction should closely mirror the environmental mode of instruction. However, unlike Hillocks, we don't have the research needed to make a strong claim for this mode of instruction in online learning environments; instead, we are relying on research conducted in very different contexts. The Department of Education study does include a mode of instruction meta-analysis based on seven studies:

> Four studies (Cavus et al. 2007; Dinov, Sanchez and Christou 2008; Gao and Lehman 2003; Zhang 2005) provide preliminary evidence supporting the hypothesis that conditions in which learners have more control of their learning (either active or interactive learning experiences in our conceptual framework) produce larger learning gains than do instructor-directed

conditions (expository learning experiences). Three other studies failed to find such an effect (Cook et al. 2007; Evans 2007; Smith 2006)." (41)

With inconclusive results such as these, a potentially new mode of instruction unique to online learning that may be both under utilized and under researched in composition studies (active), and with no significant research base of our own upon which to draw, it seems problematic at best to be positioning one mode of instruction strongly over others at this point in time. As mentioned earlier, the result of our inattention to this situation has real material consequences for students, teachers, and institutions. After all, if the research to date shows no significant difference between expository classes and interactive classes in student learning, then why not choose the much more cost-effective expository mode of instruction?

All is not lost as there is some evidence upon which we can begin to build a case for the environmental/interactive mode of instruction. However, this case would largely be built on the use of online technologies in onsite classes that are designed to facilitate student-to-student and students-to-teacher interaction (e.g., an online peer review system used specifically to facilitate interaction between students as they help each other revise essays). In other words, we would still be left to infer much of our conclusions and resulting practices.

Research Designs and Reflective Teaching

Digital educational spaces offer a number of research challenges and opportunities, but perhaps the most significant advantage online courses offer is in the way they lend themselves to data collection and analysis processes as well as to reflective teaching practices. Experimental research, whether conducted by a teacher in her own classrooms as part of a reflective practice or by a team of researchers with the goal of publication, can significantly improve teaching practices in English studies and allow us to make a strong case for the types of digital spaces we want to build for and with our students and to counter increased efforts to allow online education to be driven primarily by market forces.

Hillocks's book provides compelling evidence that some teaching practices and modes of instruction are better than others in writing classrooms. While there is some evidence from the Department of Education study outlined earlier that the same may be true online, the seven courses used to identify modes of instruction offered mixed results and were not centered on English studies. While we can and should use these studies as a starting point for future research, there is much work to be done.

In designing experimental or quasi-experimental research there are four minimum criteria that must be met. First, the outcomes of one group of students must be compared to the outcomes of another group of students with only one of these groups receiving some sort of treatment (that is, they engage in some type of learning activity or mode of instruction in which the first group doesn't engage). Second, a reliable assessment process must be established such as the use of a pretest and posttest with clear scoring criteria to measure change. Both the pretest and posttest should be scored by at least two people, with significant differences between scores negotiated or decided by a third reader. Third, while in a true experiment students would be assigned randomly to each class, in most cases we will be conducting quasi-experiments as many of us have little control over how students register for classes. So, it is important that we account for differences to the extent possible and, again, employ a pretest and posttest to gauge students' level of ability before the experiment begins.

Finally, we must account for teacher bias to the extent possible. Teacher bias refers to differences among teachers in terms of philosophy, experience, and ability. While you can never eliminate teacher bias, one way to minimize it is to work with larger groups of teachers—for example, three teachers in three different classes instruct students using an existing method while three teachers in three different classes instruct students using a new method (the treatment), with comparisons of outcomes being made across all six classes. There are at least two interesting aspects to teacher bias that digital environments alter. First, as Hillocks points out, it can be difficult to know if the treatment was carried out in the way described by the researcher. In fact, less than 5 percent of the studies in his meta-analysis presented evidence that the treatment was instructed as described (99). Because almost all the activities and learning that take place in a digital classroom are recorded, it becomes easier to authenticate whether or not a treatment was administered as described. Further, it also becomes possible for a single teacher to more reliably conduct an experiment between two of her own classes as an outside teacher or researcher can review and assess the extent to which one class is designed as a control group and another as the experiment group, thus opening up possibilities for valid experimental research to become part of a teacher's ongoing professional development in meaningful ways and putting experimental research within reach of far greater numbers of teachers who may not have the resources or time for larger projects.

For example, a faculty member teaching two sections of the same class at the same school might assign students to write an argument by definition or literature review. Students can be given the basic format for the assigned writing and asked to write a brief essay following this format. This pretest should be scored by at least two people using valid criteria. Given the widespread use of rubrics and standards not as readily available when Hillocks published his book, establishing these criteria is likely to be relatively straightforward.

In an experiment comparing a presentational/expository mode (Class A) of instruction with an environmental/interactive mode (Class B) of instruction, clear distinctions between learning activities can be made and assessed by two or more classroom researchers. Class A might be given model essays to review, required to complete a lock-step planning process often using graphic organizers, engage in minimal interaction with other students and the teacher, and receive primarily summative evaluation both during planning and on the final draft. Class B might also be given models but would then be asked to work in groups to identify how and why the model constitutes an effective argument by definition or literature review; engage in group discussions that include the teacher as facilitator to further refine criteria for an effective argument or literature review; invite students to list the top five criteria for an argument by definition or literature review with the teacher synthesizing the results; write a mini-essay as a group that is given formative feedback by both other groups and the teacher; and submit at least two drafts of a final essay, the first one of which receives formative feedback via audio or text and/or the use of a rubric. The posttest, which should be the same as the pretest, would be assessed by two readers again and the difference in gain between the two classes measured. This particular process might not lead to widely generalizable results appropriate for publication, but it does lay the groundwork for larger studies and can form the backbone of a rigorous and engaging professional development opportunity for faculty that can lead to school-wide change.

In a large setting—say an entire school district or program within a university—teachers could be sent a descriptive questionnaire that allows researchers to begin to determine what modes of instruction might be most prevalent. From there, researchers could begin to group the teachers' classes according to known modes as well as emerging modes and then closely review each course to further refine the classification and determine research participants. The next steps in the process could be similar to those outlined earlier, with those teaching the same classes using a common assignment but different activities or modes of instruction.

Future Directions

It's clear that our turn largely away from data-driven research, and experimental research in particular, leaves us in a precarious situation when it comes to making a case for effective teaching practices in English studies online. The active mode of instruction not only deserves more attention from English studies but should be informed by the scholarship of Les Perelman and others working in the area of automated essay scoring less we find ourselves coming to the table too late when this mode of instruction is adopted as a viable middle-ground between the expository and the interactive. It might be argued that a similar event has already occurred with the use of tests such as Accuplacer to allow students to opt out of essential writing courses in the name of improving students' time to degree by use of a "good enough" test.

The current state of data-based research also leaves us relying more on practitioner lore than the type of reflective practice that can lead to improved teaching. As Hillocks reminds us, "Efficient reflective practice is dependent on being able to construct clear objectives and their criteria, to identify reasons for failures, and to invent better approaches to reach the objectives" (29). The robust nature of many current learning management systems offers opportunities for us to conduct writing research at a pace and on a scale that previously was quite difficult. Equally importantly, those of us teaching in fully online environments are in a unique position to make experimental research part of a reflective teaching practice that can benefit our immediate students as well as the field of English studies at large.

References

Bowie, Jennifer L., and Heather A. McGovern. 2013. "De-coding Our Scholarship: The State of Research in Computers and Writing from 2003–2008." *Computers and Composition* 30 (3): 242–62.

CCCC Committee for Best Practices in Online Writing Instruction. 2013. "A Position Statement of Principles and Example Effective Practices for Online Writing Instruction (OWI)." https://prod-ncte-cdn.azureedge.net/nctefiles/groups/cccc/owiprinciples.pdf.

Harris, Heidi. 2017. "The Bedford Bibliography of Research in Online Writing Instruction." Macmillan Learning. http://community.macmillan.com/docs/DOC-5039-the-bedford-bibliography-of-research-in-online-writing-instruction.

Hesse, Doug. 2017. "We Know What Works in Teaching Composition." *The Chronicle of Higher Education*, January 3, 2017. https://www.chronicle.com/article/we-know-what-works-in-teaching-composition/.

Hillocks Jr, George. 1986. *Research on Written Composition: New Directions for Teaching*. Urbana: National Council of Teachers of English.

Hillocks, George. 2009. «A Response to Peter Smagorinsky: Some Practices and Approaches are Clearly Better than Others and We had Better not Ignore the Differences.» *The English Journal* 98 (6): 23–29.

MacNealy, Mary Sue. 1999. *Strategies for Empirical Research in Writing*. Boston: Allyn and Bacon.

Means, Barbara, et al. 2009. "Evaluation of Evidence-Based Practices in Online Learning: A Meta-Analysis and Review of Online Learning Studies." Association for Learning Technology. http://repository.alt.ac.uk/629/.

Miller, Susan Kay. 2001. "A Review of Research on Distance Education in Computers and Composition." *Computers and Composition* 18 (4): 423–30.

Phan, Bao Quoc. 2012. "Online Learning Literature Review: Effectiveness and Outcomes." Office of the Registrar, Reed College. https://www.reed.edu/registrar/pdfs/online-learning-literature-review.pdf.

Russell, Thomas L. 2004–2019. "No Significant Difference—Presented by WCET." *No Significant Difference—Presented by WCET*. DETA. http://www.nosignificantdifference.org/.

Seaman, Julia E., et al. 2018. "Babson Survey Group: Grade Increase: Tracking Distance Education in the United States." *OLC*, onlinelearningconsortium.org/read/grade-increase-tracking-distance-education-united-states/.

Takayoshi, Pamela. 2018. "Writing in Social Worlds: An Argument for Re-searching Composing Processes." *College Composition and Communication* 69 (4): 550–80.

Teller, Joseph. 2016. "Are We Teaching Composition All Wrong?" *The Chronicle of Higher Education*, October 3, 2016. https://www.chronicle.com/article/are-we-teaching-composition-all-wrong/.

Warnock, Scott. 2013. "Studies Comparing Outcomes Among Onsite, Hybrid, and Fully-Online Writing Courses." *WPA-CompPile Research Bibliographies*, no. 21. PDF file.. http://comppile.org/wpa/bibliographies/Bib21/Warnock.pdf.

10 More Than Replication: Online Pedagogy Informing Face-to-Face Writing Instruction

Michael Neal, Amy Cicchino, and Katelyn Stark

Although online education has the potential to extend access to diverse and growing student populations, some educators—including many in English and the humanities at large—remain skeptical of online learning. Even when they assume online education can work for technical, informational, or skills-based courses, many seem less convinced that online education can work for the interactive, collaborative, discussion-based humanities classes they teach. These assumptions are loaded with humanistic values, deep-seated beliefs, and perhaps even some experiential knowledge or hearsay about online teaching, which is rife with examples of mechanized classroom pedagogy; canned, video-based lectures; self-paced learning modules; large class sizes with little support for students or instructors; objective, multiple-choice tests to assess factual information; and the lack of a classroom community for students and instructors. The 2020 COVID-19 pandemic, which caused institutions across the world to rush to remote instruction, has, in many ways, reinforced this skepticism. Without warning or preparation, educators hastily made the mid-semester transition to delivering learning online to students who had registered for face-to-face instruction. Many educators finished the semester exhausted and frustrated, still wondering how they could achieve learning in the video-based or learning management system (LMS) classrooms. These poorly constructed and supported examples of emergency remote instruction conjure images of educational technitization and the reduction of active learning to standardized correctness, lengthy and mandatory video meetings, inflexible formulaic approaches, and rote memorization.

While online learning like this certainly has existed and will continue to exist, other models of online education proliferate, even in the humanities. Kristyn E. Harman, a history scholar, prioritizes the design of her classes with the "imperative that students be active knowledge-generators who assume responsibility for constructing and managing their own learning experience" (2018, 3). Harman's work goes beyond lecture recordings, assigned readings, and mandated discussion boards, and illustrates that online courses can be interactive, collaborative, discussion-rich, and engaging (2018, 4). Scholars in online writing instruction (OWI) have developed principles that advocate for models that promote engagement and interaction (see, for example, the College Composition and Communication / National Council of Teachers of English "Position Statement of Principles and Example Effective Practices for Online Writing Instruction (OWI)" found at https://cccc.ncte.org/cccc/resources/positions/owiprinciples).

However, the purpose of this chapter is not to argue for a certain kind of online teaching since that has been done well by many others (Blythe 2001; Hewett 2006; Kiefer 2006; Dockter & Borgman 2016; Cummings et al. 2017); rather, we would like to unpack the assumption that the ideal standards for online humanities classes and pedagogies are located in face-to-face (F2F) classes and that the measure of success in online instruction is contingent upon the degree to which they replicate F2F practices and pedagogies. We want to challenge the fallacy that F2F pedagogy is worth replicating simply because it's known and, therefore, must be ideal.

In our experiences developing a graduate course on the topic of hybrid and online writing instruction (OWI), participating in that course together, and having other online educational experiences, we were pleasantly surprised to find that OWI—when properly supported and designed—provides an exigence to reflect on, critique, and even revise our F2F pedagogies as much as it has dissuaded us from merely replicating them in a new medium. In fact, we found several instances in which our OWI pedagogy has informed our F2F pedagogy. In this chapter, we explore three specific F2F pedagogical practices that we have reimagined in light of our OWI experiences: classroom homespaces, class discussions, and writing workshops. However, before we jump into an exploration of those practices, we will first establish the institutional contexts and exigencies that prompted our journey into OWI.

Institutional Context

We enter into this conversation as members of an English department at a large, research-oriented, southeastern state institution that has exerted little pressure to pursue online education. With a stable undergraduate population of over thirty thousand students, we are considered a selective but not elite school, and we draw students from states where tuitions are significantly higher and temperatures are significantly lower. Despite large student enrollments, we have not had a corresponding push for online classes in English until 2018 when college composition course caps were lowered in efforts to improve our national ranking. With little warning, the English department suddenly needed significantly more sections of composition to accommodate these smaller classes. While we were able to find enough instructors, we didn't believe we had the physical space needed for these classes, which prompted the solution: online teaching.

We had offered a select-few number of online composition courses in the past several years, but we had not developed a thoughtful and scalable approach to delivering writing instruction online. These courses were typically developed in isolation with the instructors doing their best to adapt the curriculum online with little departmental support or visibility. Within a matter of weeks, however, we transitioned from blissful ignorance to near panic over the need to deliver dozens of new, online courses by the following semester. No time to pilot courses. No time for pedagogical preparation for the instructors of these classes. No new funding in the department to accommodate these changes. No fundamental change in our beliefs and assumptions about online education. While we have an Office of Distance Learning that provides generalized university support for online teaching, it focuses more on legal (e.g., Americans with Disabilities Act, security, copyright), technical (e.g., course management systems, recording lectures), and institutional issues (e.g., registration, submitting grades). We wanted educational best practices that could work effectively for small writing courses. We also feared a crisis implementation would likely lead to an impoverished model of online teaching that would simply reinforce the predilection for face-to-face instruction. Fortunately, the university eventually located classrooms to accommodate the additional courses face-to-face (F2F). Crisis averted—until, of course, the COVID-19 pandemic in 2020.

While relieved that we had evaded the problem of having to launch many sections of online writing without the requisite time or financial resources needed in 2018, the three of us remained determined to prepare instructors to teach writing online for several reasons: (1) We wanted to critically explore OWI now that we had the time to develop a theoretically and pedagogically informed approach to online instruction; (2) We wanted our graduate students, who will likely move into positions at institutions that have embraced online learning, to be both effective online teachers and competitive on the job market; and (3) We were curious about the ways in which OWI can inform our composition program in terms of curriculum, accessibility, interactivity, and digitality. Therefore, despite the lack of institutional exigence, the three of us designed a hybrid graduate-level course that focused on online writing instruction: Michael taught this course and Amy and Katelyn enrolled in it as advanced graduate students. The hybrid course was designed to begin and end with F2F classes but held a totally online window in the middle. In this course, GTAs read theory about online and hybrid pedagogies, developed an online and/or hybrid syllabus for an existing course, designed an online composition course calendar to use within our program, participated in online peer review and conferencing, and developed an ePortfolio specifically focused on their identities as online and hybrid teachers (this included a theory of online pedagogy). We hoped the hybrid course would provide us with opportunities to experience and critically reflect on the affordances and constraints of both online and hybrid spaces.

Affordances of Digital Technologies

Forays like ours into OWI often begin with attempts to replicate F2F courses, which are assumed to be worth copying. We initially looked for technologies that would closely mirror F2F practices: If we typically begin F2F classes with announcements, we looked for digital space where we can broadcast announcements; if we spend time giving notes on or explaining difficult concepts in the readings, we looked for how we might deliver recorded lectures using slides or narration; if we conference or workshop in our writing classes, we looked for platforms that allow students to share and comment on their writing. While some of these platforms are interactive (e.g., Google Docs, Zoom, or discussion boards), others are one-way communication (e.g., video lectures, slides, assignment sheets, announcements, rubrics). We found no shortage of available technologies that facilitated our attempt to replicate the F2F classroom. However, while our inclination was to mirror the F2F practices, our experiences reading for, participating in, and reflecting on the graduate course prompted us to rethink this approach.

When our own course transitioned from the F2F classes to online instruction and we began to engage in online technologies, our engagement waned, and the quality of the class suffered. We found the interaction on discussion boards disappointing; the posts were less engaging than our F2F classroom conversation, and students often responded in required ways but no more. The remediated discussion didn't mimic dialogue, even among hyper-literate graduate students who knew each other and interacted well during the F2F class sessions. As students viewed videos that attempted to replicate instructional knowledge delivery, they became bored viewers. Even when students became makers of such presentations, they struggled to produce compelling presentations that did more than summarize the materials. We noticed that even though it was relatively easy to import technologies that mimicked F2F practices into the online learning environment, the interaction didn't measure up. Thus, our online classes, when delivered in this way, became a poor substitute for F2F learning.

To put it bluntly, we were stunned. After all, we had spent several weeks interacting together in a F2F setting and had prepared ourselves for the online portion of the class. The vast majority of students in the class self-identify as proponents of engaged, online education. We were all relatively technologically savvy and all certainly eager to learn more. Plus, as faculty and graduate student participants, we had more than the requisite skills as readers and writers, ideal candidates for such engaged, online learning. Yet we struggled. Was it just us? Or were these strategies losing something in their translation into the online medium? In asking how we might change our own approaches to OWI, we looked to principles 3 and 4 from the 2013 "Position Statement of Principles and Example Effective Practices for Online Writing Instruction (OWI)" to focus our goals as teachers:

- Principle 3: Appropriate composition teaching/learning strategies should be developed for the unique features of the online instructional environment.

- Principle 4: Appropriate onsite composition theories, pedagogies, and strategies should be migrated and adapted to the online instructional environment.

These two principles in conversation prompted us to ask what meaningful engagement with others and with the course content might look like in a F2F classroom and what they might look like online. We had acknowledged that affordances and constraints of physical and digital pedagogical spaces are significantly different, so why had we assumed that the best online class would merely mirror the F2F classroom? Once we began re-imagining online teaching and interactive spaces as having unique affordances and constraints, it allowed us to do two things: (1) imagine a broader array of possibilities for the online writing classes than simply replicating pedagogies from our F2F courses, which led us to (2) see how our new, online writing practices inform our F2F pedagogy rather than the other way around. So, as we explore in each section below, first our online pedagogy changed so that it was no longer beholden to mirroring our F2F writing classes, and then conversely—at least in these instances outlined below—through our critical reflections of OWI scholarship and experiences, we began to see our F2F pedagogy evolve as a result.

Homespaces

In F2F classrooms, students and teachers interact in a physical space for a set amount of time each week. This class time becomes a "homespace" that serves as a hub where teachers explain and clarify assignments, discuss readings, remind students of approaching due dates, establish and gauge class morale, discuss and explain challenging concepts, engage in invention for writing projects, focus students on the upcoming work for the class, and read and respond to each other's writing. In an online class, this homespace may be lost to some degree, which may be one reason online courses are characterized by a "thrive or dive" student culture (Sapp and Simon 2005, 473) where certain students can adjust to these new interactions while others cannot. Sapp and Simon link lower rates in student retention and success in online learning environments to "settings in which teachers cannot rely on face-to-face interaction to motivate students and build rapport" combined with a lack of "interpersonal accountability" in students (2005, 476–77). Put differently, homespaces—whether in F2F or online classrooms—structure student learning, create routines and accountability, support interpersonal communication, and moderate access to important classroom practices and policies (see Cummings et al. 2017).

Online writing teachers employ a variety of strategies for re-creating a classroom's shared homespace. Scott Warnock and Diana Gasiewski (2018), for example, mention a combination of weekly course announcements and detailed weekly plans to forge regular communication patterns with students, point to upcoming due dates, and offer tips and encouragement. This two-pronged system of communication curates what they characterize as the "vast corpus of texts" that immerses students in online courses (168). Other online writing instructors create class websites and blogs that will direct students to the information, activities, and interactions they will need to complete the course. Learning management systems (LMSs) can serve as another option for homespaces in online classes. In our graduate course, Michael took a two-pronged approach: first, he used the module function in Canvas to organize weekly files; second, he sent weekly announcements—sometimes in written form, other times in video—to direct, instruct, encourage, and remind students of expectations. Even though students could navigate the LMS in many ways to locate what they needed, the everything-everywhere approach has weaknesses: (1) many students want a routinized space or structure for consistency, such as Michael emailing a video announcement that included an overview and instructions at the beginning of each week; and (2) for students with diverse processing and neurological needs, hunting and searching amidst the "vast corpus of texts" felt ineffective and overwhelming. Michael's modules and announcements organized and delivered the digital activities of the class thereby creating the homespace of the shared F2F classroom.

After experiencing the importance of the homespace in online course settings, we understand its significance in F2F classrooms in new ways. Not only did the creation of electronic homespaces in our online class motivate us to create similarly structured hubs in our F2F courses, but it also challenged us to question if the ephemeral announcements and conversations we have in the F2F classroom are the best methods for delivering important information. What if students aren't present or aren't concentrating well during this F2F delivery? When and how can students access this information outside of the class? What might students record, remember, and/or forget between when the explanation was given and when they need to use the information? To create a more intentional and effective homespace for our F2F courses, we now consider several advantages to using video announcements, announcement boards, weekly modules, and other instructional materials that will remain accessible beyond the boundaries of the few minutes we have in class together each week. While students can still receive assignment descriptions in their syllabi and on assignment sheets, we now better understand the value in reinforcing them with content they can access repeatedly and outside of class when they need it most. These videos could be used to introduce an entire assignment or be broken-down into shorter segments, which students can encounter at different moments in the assignment process.

For example, an assignment for the graduate course prompted Michael to reconsider how he introduces and discusses assignments in his F2F courses. Regularly, his practice would be to introduce the assignment and explain the steps to complete it at the very beginning of the process. In fact, his syllabi and course calendar mark the days in which an assignment is assigned because it is important for students to know that day will include this introduction and explanation. On that day in the F2F homespace of the shared physical classroom, he introduced an assignment on developing, editing, and captioning videos, and students asked technical questions about the process of completing this assignment. What he realized later is that most students weren't ready to hear or apply some of the technical instruction he supplied during that introduction because they weren't at that stage in the project. Instead, they would especially need the instruction on closed captioning late in the project. From the OWI experience, we now see the value of breaking down the instructions and recording them to place in a digital homespace that students can access when *they* need it. Further, Michael regains the time he would spend initially explaining and revisiting the instructions to perhaps help students where they are in the process. These videos also provide consistency and thoroughness to the F2F instruction since we know from experience and observation that instructors are prone to forget something or present it in different ways to different classes.

Even as we like the idea of more structured and accessible homespace materials for a F2F classroom, we are aware of the labor issues in developing videos or other supplementary materials. However, instructors can start with a few, strategic videos and build a library over time. As we discovered in our class, certain videos can easily be shared with other instructors or for other classes. A video on integrating sources into an essay could be in multiple classes or over multiple semesters, reducing the workload over time and fostering a community among online and F2F teachers. Of course, all this documentation puts students and instructors at risk for information overload. When we think about all the announcements and instructions we tend to provide in a F2F class, access to all that information can become overwhelming. In addition, these media files require storage space, which is not always accessible or inexpensive. Instructors need to be aware of the infrastructure available at their institutions to address these practical concerns as well as what will happen to the materials in terms of ownership and copyright if they are stored on and accessed through institutional LMSs (Rielly and Williams 2006, p. 70). Even so, these issues can be mitigated by starting small, prioritizing, and building intuitive infrastructures, something we may be able to do now that we are not being rushed into online instruction.

Discussion

In addition to developing clear homespaces, we discovered other online pedagogical strategies that have challenged our assumptions and practices in the F2F classroom. Perhaps one of the most ubiquitous pedagogical activities in English classes is discussion, which can include everything from discussing the content of a reading to discussing ideas for papers or projects. Replacing the more traditional lecture model, class discussion is widely used in English classes, filling large portions of limited F2F class time. While online instructors have several technological options to foster or replicate this practice, discussion boards—digital spaces that allow students to respond to a prompt, create prompts, or respond to one another's text asynchronously through a threaded discussion—are perhaps the most familiar. Every LMS we know has this type of tool to facilitate discussion, and many other options, such as blogs, exist as LMS-alternatives.

When compared to F2F class discussion, it's reasonable to think online discussion boards can be more equitable and advantageous: writers have the opportunity to communicate simultaneously and at their own pace without interruption, unlike the classroom where voices vie for limited airtime, advantaging aggressive discourse styles such as those who speak first, interrupt, or talk over others. In the F2F class, others remain relatively silent when one person (often the teacher and a few dominant students) inhabit most of the communication space. Depending on how it is set up, discussion boards can subvert the initiation, response, evaluation (IRE) model where the teacher is the center through which all discussion is moderated and redirected (Cazden 2001). From a logistical standpoint, classroom discussion happens in a finite time and usually produces no written record outside of students' notes, whereas online discussion allows all students to participate, gives students more time to formulate responses and consider others' ideas, provides a transcript of the conversation that can be archived for future access, and helps students navigate the challenges of voicing their ideas in a physical space.

Since discussion is so valued in English and discussion boards are low-bridge technologies that have been in place for decades, it's only natural, then, that English instructors would turn to them to facilitate discussion in online teaching. When working ideally, discussion boards boast great potential for both F2F and online classes. However, our reading and experience cause us to question how well these digital platforms actually support dialogue and knowledge making. While we understand the potential values of the boards, they often deteriorate into performativity and forced responses. The instructor may not be engaged in IRE, but they can still dictate the content of discussion, the structure, and even "force" dialogue through requirements. Many of the posts on discussion boards are also performative—students engaging inflated language, hyper-critical perspectives, stream of conscious ramblings for the sake of impressing the teacher or silencing other voices. These aren't necessarily effective rhetorical moves that invite dialogue and exchange.

We understand discussion as a means to an end, not an end in and of itself. Our observation, though, is that class discussion and discussion boards seem too much like an end rather than a means. Just talking about what students think about a text or requiring them to post messages a certain number of times a week suggests that speaking or posting a message often substitutes for a pedagogical purpose rather than seeing it as helping students meet larger course or project goals. Once our class started to critique and question discussion board pedagogy, we came to re-evaluate the pedagogical purposes of class discussion more generally. While in some cases, discussions harken back to Socrates and an ancient pedagogy of inquiry-based knowledge making, they can also function as a "thinly veiled lecture" in which "teachers, not students, determine the viability of answers" (Paulsen and Copeland 2018, 27). They can also get bogged down in the performative aspects we describe earlier. More so, F2F discussions often operate under the assumption that once something is said orally, students can process that information in tandem with the class lesson or discussion. This assumption not only privileges one type of learning, it has us questioning our F2F scaffolding processes. Rethinking discussions has us rethinking deeper aspects of our pedagogies and what assumptions we make about student learning. Even when discussions are better, they still limit participation and don't provide a transcript of the response. Especially in the writing classroom, we have concluded that discussions are overused and overvalued in both online and F2F classes.

While we don't suggest that writing classes should abandon all uses of discussion and discussion boards, our use of discussion boards in the online class prompted us to turn a critical lens to discussion in both class types. For our online classes, instead of individuals posting to discussion boards, students participate in a series of reflective and discursive steps to help them work through course content, assigned readings, and more difficult theory. These steps could take different forms at different times. For instance, students could be required to call or Skype a peer to discuss a reading before they answer questions individually or together, or students could work together in Google Docs to discuss questions or course content. Instead of answering teacher-initiated prompts in class or on the discussion boards, we began to think of them as corresponding with the current work of the class. For example, Katelyn hosts student clusters, where the class is broken down in small groups to discuss answers, investigate texts, and then visually report their findings. The clusters provide safe, small group spaces for students to exchange ideas that they can share with the class and/or apply to their current work. In these spaces, each student has access to these collective materials (either by taking notes, taking pictures of the boards, or saving the shared Google Doc). Even though Katelyn initially developed the idea for these in our online class, we also see this cluster model being advantageous to students in F2F classes, especially when compared to traditional turn-taking discussion.

When students interact with one another in ways that forward their work in the class, not surprisingly they interact more naturally, and they remain engaged because of its usefulness. We hope these student clusters can become a pedagogical tool to replace much of our class discussion where students are encouraged to interact with one another to produce knowledge, skills, and texts that help them achieve their goals in both F2F and online classes. We're excited to imagine all the more engaging interaction that can happen in our classes as we rely less on large class discussion and encourage more meaningful interactions.

WORKSHOPPING

Many F2F writing classrooms engage in structured or semi-structured collaborative groups whose primary purpose is to provide and receive feedback on a piece of writing at some stage in the process. These workshops in F2F classes can be heard and seen through the embodied movements of and interactions between students: they are speaking and listening actively to one another and typing or marking comments on a paper. Because every class member is in the same physical room, the F2F teacher can walk from group to group, ask and answer questions, and observe the kind of feedback being exchanged. As the circulating teacher observes recurring issues, the class has the ability to come together to review concepts together before breaking back into smaller workshop groups. Delivering workshops in this way is inherently tied to F2F classrooms. But what does this activity look like in an online space? As in each of the other instances, we began by searching for technological tools that could replicate F2F classroom peer workshops. Just like the last two examples—homespaces and discussions—we read scholarship and then experienced workshops both in F2F and in online settings. In reflecting on these ideas and experiences, we began to re-think our traditional classroom workshop models as well as the ways we attempted to replicate them online.

An effective online workshop, in our minds, has two needs: (1) a way for the class to collectively come together to receive direction and review recurring questions and problems, and (2) a peer-to-peer interaction that allows for sharing and responding to students' writing. In "Kairotic Design: Building Flexible Networks for Online Composition," Cummings et al. describe a pedagogical strategy of delivering "ad hoc" online videos to their courses wherein they discuss recurring issues they are viewing across drafts, respond to students' questions, and take up unanticipated or "unfolding" content. These videos are informal as they are designed and delivered week-to-week by the teacher as issues arise, thus the kairotic element of their title. When we first encountered this reading in the context of our graduate class, we considered how this *ad hoc* video strategy might provide one aspect of the workshop for students: the collective addressing of common issues and questions. The videos not only met this need, but they also utilized the technological affordances to improve upon the existing F2F pedagogical strategy as students can review as needed the concept being addressed.

We, next, needed to replicate the interactive feedback common to workshopping. While workshopping serves as an important part of the writing process in that students receive formative feedback needed for their drafts to progress, it similarly has a social function in F2F classes. As students sit down with one another in the F2F classroom, they can encounter and read faces as well as hear and interpret voices within a shared and related context. Cummings et al. point to the value of the synchronous components in an online course to "build social rapport and support social interaction," "enhanc[e] motivation to respond to others," and "create social 'glue' that can make asynchronous exchange more productive" ("Starting Assumptions and Assets"). We, similarly, wanted workshops to remain a space where students could interact, thereby contributing to an overall classroom community. If this couldn't occur synchronously, we wanted the asynchronous interactions to still be personable and engaging. When we tried to conduct an online workshop that embodied these values—community-building and interpersonal engagement—certain problems arose.

For our class, students were assigned workshops during the time in which the class was online. In addition, Michael and several students were traveling during this time, two other students were high school teachers still in session, and another student was also a full-time teacher at a nearby community college. Put differently, outside of the shared class time we had in our F2F sessions, we had many time and energy constraints. Even though our F2F class held a traditional "class time," during the online time we could not assume students would have continuous availability. Thus, we needed a workshop model that was either flexible or asynchronous to accommodate our varied schedules. So, we did not plan for synchronous peer feedback sessions.

Before the online classes began, students were paired randomly and given the option to determine their own preferences, platforms, and needs for workshopping. The VARK learning styles had surfaced in class conversations after reading Kristine Blair's chapter, "Teaching Multimodal Assignments in OWI Contexts." Consequently, students had been thinking about their own preferences for processing and presenting information, and this topic was extended into our approach to planning workshops. While Michael provided expectations and checkpoints for the workshop—students had to exchange drafts and give detailed feedback, discuss that feedback, and send him a joint reflection following the workshop—students were allowed to develop exactly how they would workshop in a way that considered their individual preferences for learning and their availability. Students could work synchronously by trading paper drafts or using a free technology like Google Hangouts or Facetime to live chat with another while sharing digital drafts; alternatively, they could work asynchronously by exchanging drafts and giving in-line feedback using the comment feature on Word or Google Docs, or exchanging drafts and creating informal videos to deliver discussion-based feedback.

Many of the workshopping groups employed a mixture of these strategies. Amy and Katelyn, who were paired to workshop, for instance, planned to view each other's drafts in advance of a digital meeting using Google Hangouts. To facilitate this process, they set two times across their schedules: one deadline to exchange texts giving ample time to read and review before a synchronous meeting and a second shared time when they could digitally meet to discuss that feedback. Although planning a class-wide synchronous event might have demanded all members of the class carve out the same forty-five minutes, organizing a synchronous component across a two-person group was much easier. After workshopping two documents—a text-based teaching philosophy and a drafted teaching ePortfolio—they completed the following reflection sent to Michael providing rationale for the decisions of how they chose to conduct the workshop:

> Katelyn and I used Google Hangouts because we wanted to use the screensharing option. In advance of our digital workshop, we read each other's documents and provided feedback on a Google doc. This gave our digital workshop clear structure and helped with putting the advice into action afterwards. While [the peer reader] offered feedback, the writer took additional notes at the bottom of the Google document. Our feedback spanned design, content, and functionality (links and organization). I think we both walked away with clear direction as to how to strengthen the ePortfolio—philosophy included.

While some of the same markers of the traditional workshop emerged through the reflection, such as the feedback process (for instance, where one student speaks while the other takes notes), other affordances were unique to delivering the workshop in this digital medium and Google Hangouts, specifically. During one point in the workshop, Amy mentioned that Katelyn could embed her Creative Commons license icon using the embedded HTML markup language provided, but Katelyn had never done this on the Wix website platform before. Using the Screenshare feature on Google Hangouts, Amy was able to share her own screen and walk Katelyn through the process. Screensharing is a feature found on many digital video conferencing platforms such as Zoom and Skype, but Google Hangouts allows this affordance without demanding the student download software or purchase a membership.

This same affordance would have been possible in a F2F workshop only if students were working in technology-enhanced classrooms or had access to their own personal devices in class. In working within the context of the online course, however, they were able to use their personal technologies—although Amy or Katelyn could have gone to a public library if they did not have access to their personal computers—and they had the additional advantage of a quiet workshopping atmosphere. This was a specific benefit for Amy who struggles to hear and focus in a F2F classroom workshopping setting due to the simultaneous conversations. However, this workshopping method benefitted more than this particular group. During a discussion of their personal learning preferences, another group realized that they both struggled to recall exactly what was said in workshops when the time came to revise their texts. To respond to this shared struggle, they developed a similar process of asynchronously exchanging texts then synchronously meeting over Zoom and recording their peer workshop so that the feedback could be revisited days later. So, while we began our excursion into digital workshopping asking how we might replicate the F2F workshop environment, we came to realize that the F2F workshop was not always conducive to our individual learning needs and appreciated that the digital workshopping environment gave us a greater agency in tailoring the peer feedback protocol to those needs.

In "Complexity, Class Dynamics, and Distance Learning," Kate Kiefer (2006) discusses the role of the teacher in shaping which actions are seen as possible in the online writing classroom. While she is clear in stating the classroom dynamic evolves and grows uniquely within each individual course, she goes on to write, "teachers do have much influence in shaping the dynamic that emerges because they can impose structures that limit choices students might make" (130). Without realizing it, we had been limiting what was seen as possible in our F2F courses by only allowing students one way to workshop, an approach to workshopping that often reflected our own experiences as students in writing classrooms. Moving online allowed us to ask what was important about the workshopping process, what was unique about the digital learning space, and how we might begin to use the affordances inherently located in those digital spaces to enhance the learning being done.

Amy, for example, now allows students in her F2F advanced composition course to decide how they will complete the workshopping activity asynchronously over the weekend. Before the workshop, she helps students assess their learning styles and work through coordination aspects, asking students to practice accessing files and testing the technology they would be using, set deadlines for when they would respond and meet, and create writer profiles that detailed their own thoughts on this particular draft and how they wanted their peers to respond. They record these deadlines, writer profiles, and draft files on the LMS discussion board. Students then workshop in groups of three following their self-determined plans. Following the workshop, Amy uses a reflection activity to gauge the student reception of the process and identify recurring issues and questions to which she can respond in the following class. This sequence of activities captures the synchronous, whole group discussion aspect of the workshop environment but still allows group members to work on their own timelines in flexible settings that complement their preferences and needs. If teaching online, however, Amy would use a Google Doc to compile a list of student questions and issues then make an ad hoc video in response to them.

While we've detailed positive workshopping experiences, this was not the case across the entire graduate class or even across the advanced composition course Amy taught the following semester. In both cases, some students fell out of contact during workshopping: when they encountered issues, they did not reach out to instructors and, in some extreme cases, they did not respond to the instructor's attempt to communicate with them. Moving the workshop outside of the context of the F2F class relies on student accountability and trust. While instructors can put certain structures in place to help students see the workshop as a series of smaller tasks and deadlines, when a student goes off the grid, another student's learning is affected by a lack of peer response. To respond to this, we suggest organizing students into groups of three or four so that writers have multiple sources of feedback. We also want to stress the importance of structuring peer feedback sessions in such a way that both direct the workshops to the most important details and provide an immediate record to all parties (including the instructor) for accountability and content sharing. While both instructors in the scenarios above did take measures to articulate specific tasks and deadlines, having students post their feedback to shared classroom spaces (like discussion boards or shareable Google Docs) allows teachers to immediately see who has (and has not) met the expectations for the workshop and reach out. In creating environments that support transparent workshopping and open pathways for communication, showing up as an engaged peer responder is key.

Conclusion

No pedagogy is perfect. No classroom setting is perfect. While we cannot offer a panacea to transmedia pedagogy in this chapter, we argue that all pedagogies demand critical reflection and constant revision and should be informed by the course's unique environmental, technological, and mediated affordances. As well, we hope we have called attention to the hierarchy that exists between F2F and online pedagogies in which the F2F is upheld as the ideal standard for teaching and learning. Though the impulse is great to attempt to replicate F2F classroom spaces and pedagogies with which we are most comfortable and familiar, we have discovered that direct migration of one to the other produces significant limitations. However, we're grateful for our inability to replace the F2F classroom in our online teaching because our failure to do so resulted in turning a critical lens on not only our online but also our F2F classroom pedagogies. Our failures and frustrations evolved into generative ways to reconsider long-held assumptions about teaching and learning in our classes. Therefore, instead of lamenting about what is "lost" in the move from F2F to online instruction or obsessing about what practices we should "preserve" from F2F environments, we have offered three examples in which our accessible and digital-focused online pedagogies have informed our F2F practices to yield potentially more effective and equitable practices. Furthermore, as we realize that our experiences are unique to our particular context, we hope these examples will counter the belief that online classes are only effective if and when they successfully replicate the F2F classroom.

What isn't unique is the continued movement—voluntary or involuntary—toward more online education. In some ways, COVID-19 has made us all online instructors, which makes the need to support all instructors in developing thoughtful online pedagogies more pressing than ever before. Our programmatic goals were not merely to move our writing courses online, but to provide thoughtful preparation before teaching online, support structures while teaching online, and spaces to reflect on and revise teaching strategies after online courses. While each of us found the online and hybrid course useful, we were pleasantly surprised that this reflective teaching filtered into our F2F teaching as well as our online courses. In 2020, the abrupt norm became online instruction, but often without the advantage of strategic planning and scaled implementation. As universities navigate how to approach remote, hybrid, or F2F learning in the future, we believe that online teaching is a valuable site of learning and professional development that requires reflective practice and purposeful planning. We have as much to learn from online teaching as we have learned teaching F2F.

References

Blythe, Stuart. 2001. "Designing Online Courses: User-Centered Practices." *Computers and Composition: An International Journal for Teachers of Writing* 18 (4): 329–46.

Cazden, Courtney B. 2001. *Classroom Discourse: The Language of Teaching and Learning*. Portsmouth, NH: Heinemann.

Cummings, Lance, Renea Frey, Ryan Ireland, Caitlin Martin, Heidi McKee, Jason Palmeri, and James Porter. 2017. "Kairotic Design: Building Flexible Networks for Online Composition." In *Making Space: Writing Instruction, Infrastructure, and Multiliteracies*, edited by James P. Purdy and Dànielle N. DeVoss. Ann Arbor: University of Michigan Press. https://doi.org/10.3998/mpub.7820727.

Dockter, Jason, and Jessie Borgman. 2016. "Minimizing the Distance in Online Writing Courses through Student Engagement." *Teaching English in the Two-Year College* 44 (2): 213–22.

Harman, Kristyn E. 2018. "The Transformative Power of Digital Humanities in Teaching Family History Online." *Journal of University Teaching & Learning Practice* 15 (3): 1–16.

Hewett, Beth L. 2006. "Synchronous Online Conference-Based Instruction: A Study of Whiteboard Interactions and Student Writing." *Computers and Composition* 23 (1): 4–31.

Kiefer, Kate. 2006. "Complexity, Class Dynamics, and Distance Learning." *Computers and Composition: An International Journal for Teachers of Writing* 23 (1): 125–38.

Paulsen, Jenny Cameron, and Matt Copeland. 2018. "Socratic Learning Conversations: Ancient Practice Meets New Technology." In *Toward a More Visual Literacy: Shifting the Paradigm with Digital Tools and Young Adult Literature*, edited by Jennifer S. Dail, Shelbie Witte, and Steven T. Bickmore, 27–38. Maryland: Rowman and Littlefield.

Reilly, Colleen, and Joseph John Williams. 2006. "The Price of Free Software: Labor, Ethics, and Context in Distance Education." *Computers and Composition* 23 (1): 68–90.

Sapp, David Alan, and James Simon. 2005. "Comparing Grades in Online and Face-to-Face Writing Courses: Interpersonal Accountability and Institutional Commitment." *Computers and Composition* 22 (4): 471–89.

11 A Tale of Two Courses: Class Discussion Issues in English Studies Online

Susan Spangler

When I started teaching online about ten years ago, some of my colleagues in English commented that they would never want to teach online because they would miss the discussions that consumed the majority of their time with students. They felt students would miss a learning opportunity they could only get through the dynamic, back-and-forth exchange of face-to face, synchronous interaction in their classrooms, and therefore they were hesitant to take their courses online. As I've read through my colleagues' syllabi over the years as part of our course evaluation process, I've seen the value they put on class discussion, featuring it prominently in their syllabi and assigning weighty participation points as part of the course grade.

I think some instructors thrive on class discussion because they feel it energizes them or their students, or they feel it proves that students are engaged with the material and with their classmates. Others may relish discussions because they get feedback from students or can gauge their understanding of the material easily in person. Some may prefer class discussion as a way of conducting class because that is the method they experienced and enjoyed as students. Yet, in our disciplines, we share most of our important work through writing (or think we do), through publishing articles, book chapters, and books. We assume that dynamism can come in writing and reading and writing back—so why do we struggle to imagine that students in our classrooms might also be part of that dynamism in written formats?

Perhaps instructors assume, as Riggs and Linder (2016) assert, that they are better able to engage students in active learning in face-to-face environments. English studies instructors certainly have reason to favor effective face-to-face discussion over online discussion. Traditional class discussion, in many English studies instructors' minds, embodies democratic ideals and builds community. Beers and Probst (1998) explain that through classroom talk, students can learn the skills necessary for a productive, adult social life. We learn through classroom talk to experiment with and test our own beliefs. We have to summon the courage to voice our own thoughts in front of others, a sometimes terrifying thought for insecure young adults. We have to support our opinions with well-reasoned evidence. We also learn to explore and consider adopting others' perspectives and points of view when we are exposed to new ideas. We of course learn to test those against our own, and perhaps we learn to appreciate the differences and commonalities between our own opinions and those of others, but at the very least, we should learn to treat our differences with others respectfully through discussion.

When done well, class discussion can prepare learners to sustain that kind of free exchange of ideas into adulthood, and that's why, I think, most teachers of English studies value discussion as a learning tool in the classroom. They see it as a way for learners to develop critical thinking skills and confidence in opinions and to get used to explaining them to others. Class talk is a way to develop the courage to offer ideas in the first place and then defend them. Many instructors want students to engage in the kind of idea exploration with texts that will help them later contribute to the democratic values and principles we in education espouse. As Beers and Probst (1998) point out, "If students are to flourish in and contribute to a democracy that values freedom and hopes to preserve the dignity of individuals, then they must be taught to read, think, write, and discuss intelligently" (19). Face-to-face class discussions can provide learners one way to explore, to think, to question what they and others have to offer.

McCann et al. (2006) discuss the power of "talking in class," describing what they call "authentic" discussion. This kind of discussion is one in which the teacher does not already have the answer, a discussion that is dialogic instead of monologic. Authentic discussion invites speculation and invites all to participate in inquiry by advancing theories and testing claims. It begins by asking the kind of questions that don't have a ready answer, that often involve a dilemma or debatable point. The best kinds of face-to-face discussion can inspire learners to engage with texts, issues, and the world around them; that engagement produces knowledge.

Effective class discussions produce thoughtful, respectful opinions and responses, challenge ideas, build from one idea to another organically, and encourage collaboration to keep the conversation going.

THE MYTH OF DYNAMIC DISCUSSION IN FACE-TO-FACE CLASSROOMS

The problem is that orchestrating an effective class discussion in face-to-face classrooms isn't easy. So many obstacles prevent class talk from contributing to ideal learning situations, but these obstacles aren't usually addressed or even acknowledged by face-to-face instructors, the same ones who are reluctant to teach online. I'd like to convince these instructors that the idea of a democratic, community-building discussion is more often a myth than a reality in classrooms and that online discussions can be more effective if we approach them with a more pedagogically open mind.

While teachers and students both like the idea of free-flowing and dynamic conversations, teachers also feel pressured to meet objectives they set for the discussion, which may lead them to rely on a more structured class discussion model. Courtney Cazden (1988) studied classroom discourse and found the most common type of discussion across all grade levels was something she termed the IRE sequence. This style involves more "recitation" than discussion, though in most teachers' minds, IRE is the default method for a successful discussion. Teachers *initiate* the classroom talk by asking questions, lecturing, or giving assignments. Students *respond* to the initial question, often repeating information that was previously given to them. Then, instead of the discussion becoming an actual free exchange of ideas, the teacher *evaluates* the answer the student has given. Exchanges occur mostly between the teacher and students, not student to student. When students disagree or extend each other's comments, they tend to look to the teacher for validation, which keeps the authority on the teacher alone. It's little wonder that students don't know how to engage in an open discussion when they've become inured to this kind of communication pattern, one in which the teacher talks so much.

The IRE sequence persists in schools because it exists as an idealized schema in teachers' minds for the way class discussions should work. It's how the teachers themselves may have been educated, and it's a way for them to maintain control of the "conversation" in the classroom. Perhaps the IRE sequence evolved from the agonistic rhetoric popular in classrooms before women were given access to higher education, ones in which young men recited in classrooms in order to "win" an argument as evaluated by the professor (Connors 1997). Black-and-white television programs like *Leave It to Beaver* show us a middle ground between IRE and agonistic rhetoric when we see young Theodore Cleaver in this classroom, standing when called upon to recite some information the teacher has demanded. Wherever this IRE sequence came from, it has entrenched itself as the de facto discussion model in Western schools, and it is probably the kind of discussion most instructors are thinking of when they say they value engaged discussion, in spite of its obvious faults.

Because of its tenacity, however, IRE is easy to recognize as a formal kind of classroom talk. Students can easily learn the IRE sequence, and through participation in it, they can become "competent communicators" in the school setting. They are socialized into thinking the IRE sequence is the ideal method for classroom discussion, just as the teachers are. Part of developing competence in this form of classroom communication is learning the norms of the situation. There may be consequences for actions such as talking out of turn, interrupting, or talking off-topic, and the IRE pattern may be disrupted if students advance the discussion in a way the teacher deems appropriate. Once students learn the appropriate behavior for the IRE sequence, it's easier to focus on the academic content, which is probably why teachers continue to value this discussion method: They think students are learning more, but they are actually confusing style (performing the IRE pattern) with substance.

What we seem to be missing when we privilege the IRE recitation framework is that students are having a "discussion" only with the teacher, which is just about as inauthentic a discussion as one can have. During this recitation-type of discussion, students make eye contact primarily with the teacher, especially if they are in rows. They speak only loud enough to be heard by the teacher. Even if they refer to what another student has said, they rarely talk directly to that student. This kind of discussion is hardly what most English studies instructors have in mind when they say they value authentic discussion: peers who address each other, make eye contact, and share ideas with each other. But perhaps the myth of open classroom discussion persists because IRE is safe and known: The teacher stays comfortable with where the discussion is headed. It is not really open to inquiry, investigation, and creativity because the teacher controls it. It functions as a discussion with training wheels, but ones in which the wheels are never removed.

Even if teachers avoid the IRE model of discussions in face-to-face classrooms, they still face obstacles in leading effective discussions. The answerless questions that begin dialogic debates aren't always enough to get a discussion going. Sometimes those kinds of questions elicit a snarky or facetious comment from a class member, and the rest of the class dissolves into giggles. Discussion over. Questions that work well in one class fall flat in another. The combination of students and their personalities and backgrounds make dissent or consensus impossible. They all end up agreeing with each other, or disagreeing quickly, and yet many instructors still cling to the idea that online discussions could never be as engaging or productive a learning experience as face-to-face discussions.

Whether in online or face-to-face courses, discussing sensitive issues like socio-economic class, race, gender identity, and religion can make so-called "safe spaces" of English classrooms feel more like oppressive environments, especially for students in the minority on those issues. Even the best-intentioned teachers can offend or incense students, and it's even more likely that students will offend each other, because they are just at the developmental stage of learning to participate in class discussions respectfully, and they're bound to make missteps. Teachers of English want to engage in class discussions of provocative texts, and yet they often cannot lead them effectively so that students feel valued and affirmed in the discussion.

Then there are the times when class discussions do not follow the IRE framework. Ineffective leadership allows strong personalities to dominate the discussion. There's one person in the back who wants to take over. One person may change the topic slightly, and another student builds on that until the discussion ends up in irrelevant places. Yes, the discussion is free-flowing, organically building on ideas, but it's off-topic to the text and issues initially being discussed. How is this kind of discussion, democratic as it may be, valued and valuable in the classroom?

Productive classroom discussions are also affected by race, gender, personality types, and other identity issues, though again, not many instructors acknowledge these as obstacles in leading class discussions. Research has shown repeatedly that males are privileged in discussions, whether at work or in school. Boys are shown to raise their hands in discussion quickly, whether they know an answer or not, whether they've thought about what they want to say or not, and whether the teacher has finished asking the question or not. Because they are quicker to volunteer, they get called on more frequently than their female counterparts. These habits of talking more frequently in school continue into the working world, as we'd like them to do in ideal situations, but more often with the biases of society attached.

Sociolinguist Deborah Tannen (2017) posits that men take up more verbal space than women, not only because they are called on more or are quicker to volunteer answers, but also because women give them the space to do so. Women sometimes don't speak up because they make a conscious choice to remain silent. Some women feel that they'll be seen as "aggressive" if they talk "too much." In a Yale University study, Victoria Brescoll (2012) found that male executives who spoke more than peers earned 10 percent higher competence ratings, but when female executives spoke more than peers, they earned 14 percent *lower* competence ratings. Fair or not, it's a reality that women encounter and will likely take into consideration, even in the class discussions they are participating in. Perhaps some female students consciously hold back in discussion because they fear being punished with poor grades for talking "too much," just as the female execs are "punished" with lower competence ratings.

Discussions also privilege extroverts, who process information by speaking, or those who will raise a hand before they fully know what they want to say. Some people aren't engaged in the discussion at all, or they may be taking notes instead of talking, as some introverts are wont to do. In face-to-face courses, students can hide during discussion for any number of reasons. The reasons for their lack of participation aren't clear, but how many times have nonparticipants sat through classes without contributing and there been no reflection of their silence in their grades? Certainly I'm not advocating that quieter students or students who like to process in their heads before speaking should receive lower grades, and most teachers I know would also not make that claim, but we need to be more critical about this obvious disconnect between our values and our actions. Instructors who believe in the power of classroom discussion don't necessarily reflect on evaluating the discussion accurately or fairly, or articulate the course goals or objectives involving class talk to students. How does an instructor grade traditional discussion or participation? Many instructors have percentages of the final grade designated for class discussion, but how is this grade calculated? Instructor's discretion? A holistic impression? Points per class? Points per contribution?

Like many teachers, I've tried different methods in my courses to engage students in meaningful conversations and to reward those who do. After hearing a conference presentation by Adrian Frana (1995) from Rich East High School near Chicago, I tried his system for continuous evaluation and crediting of class participation. I was teaching a speech course at the time, and I wanted students to practice contributing to class discussions as well as let them know that each contribution was valued. During discussion, I kept the seating chart of students handy, and I assigned quality points to each participant according to my perceived value of each contribution. The grading scale suggested by Mr. Frana went from 6 (for clearly original thinking, considerable depth of though, citing textual or other evidence, responding directly to others, or relating the discussion to a meaning experience or historical event or other literature) to 1 (for asking a question, agreeing or disagreeing with no elaboration, or talking out of turn). My scale went from 5 to -2 (for inappropriate questions or comments).

The plan was to assign points to participants as the discussion was happening. Then at the end of the grading period, I'd add up the points and assign a letter grade for participation based on the points. In theory it sounded great, or at least different from what I had been doing before, which was pretty much nothing with grading discussion. What I found in actually practicing this method was that I was too busy assigning points to really pay attention to what the students were saying. This method simply rewarded the same students who dominated the class discussion. Even a few students who occasionally contributed extremely thoughtful ideas to the discussion couldn't compete with the students who made more, but more average, contributions. Eventually, I abandoned this grading method as ineffective and inefficient.

How Online Discussions Can Overcome Face-to-face Discussion Obstacles

Clearly, my face-to-face class discussions and grading schemes have gone through multiple iterations in an effort to "perfect" them, that is, to make the discussions democratic, thought-provoking, and useful as a learning tool, and to make the assessment of students fair and reflective of their contributions to the classroom talk. Through the years, I've tried Socratic seminars and small group circles and giving each student three (and only three) tokens that they *had* to use during class discussion to get credit. Yet with each of these different iterations of discussions, I've still felt unsatisfied with the results. None of the changes in the ways I've designed discussions, or the questions I've posed, or the assessments I've tried, or the number of tokens I've passed out, or the way I've arranged the seats has made me feel as though students had reached that democratic ideal of a dynamic, free exchange of thought in a face-to-face class. And if the teachers I talk to in my own department and elsewhere at conferences are any indication, I am convinced that most instructors aren't really getting the most out of their F2F class discussions in spite of their avowed dedication to this traditional method.

As I considered what teaching English studies online could offer in terms of class discussion, I thought about the opportunity that English studies teachers have in those online spaces to model discussion and design different types of discussion among all students, not just the most extroverted or gregarious or impulsive. There's no hiding in an online course discussion because simply "being present" doesn't exist. Students have to post/contribute to get credit for the class discussion. All voices must be expressed instead of just the confident ones. The IRE method is not the default method for responding, especially when students are directed to respond to each other. The students become their own mediators instead of the teacher moderating the discussion.

When I started designing my courses to go online, I knew I wanted students to do more with discussion than they could do in a face-to-face course. I wanted discussions to become another text that students could revisit and reflect on, just as they could other course material, and just as I did. If class discussions are truly valuable, as many English studies instructors argue, then they would be treated as such, and with online class discussions, this goal is possible.

Just as with face-to-face courses, the way that I design discussion for online courses depends on the purpose for the interaction or response and learning outcomes I'm trying to help students achieve. My graphic literature course has a variety of discussion goals, which I'll explain here in an attempt to show the reasons for the variety of discussion forums.

Discussions in Graphic Literature

In my graphic literature course, I want students to do several things:

- to demonstrate an appreciation and understanding of graphic literature
- to develop the ability to respond to verbal and visual arts in meaningful ways
- to read attentively, closely, and critically
- to write thoughtfully, coherently, and persuasively
- to develop and challenge their own thinking through scholarly research
- to express honest, original thoughts about the reading,
- to show that they have actually read the material,
- to interact with others and respond to their thoughts

No one kind of discussion forum can do all those things, or do them all well, so I've categorized my discussion forums into two main kinds: first impressions and second thoughts.

First Impressions. For each graphic text that they read, students in my graphic literature course post in the "First Impressions" forum. Here, I want students to give me their honest first impressions of the literature they have read. I want to know about their reading process because reading graphic literature takes a few different reading skills than reading word-only texts. I also want them to show that they have, indeed, read the text. My directions for this reading response look like this:

> After you finish the text and look at your reading notes, take about 15–20 minutes and write about what you've read (notice it's a time limit and not a word limit). I want this to be an informal type of response. I'm most concerned that you just get your thoughts down first and foremost, and then that you get them posted so that we all have an opportunity to take a look at them.
>
> Here are some suggestions for what to write about, although feel free to take off on other thoughts, too.
>
> a) What are your initial thoughts on this text? How did you respond to it as a reader? What did you enjoy? What puzzled you? What did you want more/less of? What questions do you have about the text?
> b) Connect the assigned text to other articles, books, and authors you have read. How does this text inform others' writing, or spring from it?

> c) [The above questions are the same for each text, but question C varies according to the specific text they are reading. This third question usually has something to do with their reaction to a unique feature of the graphic text and the specific graphic technique we are studying along with that text.]

> This activity helps you meet several course goals, as shown on the course rubric. Your post should show me that you have read and thought about the text as an interested reader of graphic literature.

The "First Impressions" discussion forum is similar to the face-to-face class discussion in which students are expressing their opinions about the topic, doing some exploratory thinking. They are working toward these course goals:

- to develop the ability to respond to verbal and visual arts in meaningful ways
- to demonstrate an appreciation and understanding of graphic literature
- to write thoughtfully, coherently, and persuasively
- to express honest, original thoughts about the reading
- to show that they have actually read the material

This is the forum in which students demonstrate they have read and thought about the material, just as in face-to-face classrooms where peers hear each other's comments and pay attention (or not) to what they have to say.

Second Thoughts. For each text that students in my graphic literature course read, they also post in the "Second Thoughts" forum. It is here that I know that interaction among students is actually occurring, because here students are to read all the other posts to get an overall impression of others' thoughts, and then juxtapose them with their own. Here are the instructions for the second-thoughts forum:

> After everyone has posted (or the majority of people) go back to the discussion board and read what everyone has written on the text. While reading through the First Impressions posts, respond to at least two of your classmates' posts by 1) making a

connection, 2) asking a follow up question, or 3) providing an alternative viewpoint.

Then in the Second Thoughts forum, write a post that puts you in the class conversation about the text. Synthesize your classmates' overall impressions about the text if there is a consensus, or summarize the main threads of competing ideas if there isn't. Discuss others' responses to the texts, give your thoughts on their questions, and respond to their overall initial responses. Mention people by name and give credit in your synthesis to especially insightful or meaningful posts as you see them.

This Second Thoughts post should show that you can respond to verbal and visual arts in a meaningful way (a course goal), as shown on the course rubric. The best posts will synthesize main ideas from everyone's posts and thoughtfully discuss a specific post from the first impressions.

It is in this "Second Thoughts" forum where students treat the "First Impressions" discussion forum like another text, reviewing what other students have said about the texts and demonstrating that they have actually paid attention to their ideas. They also see how other students react to their post. As students read others' posts and respond in this forum, they are ultimately exposed to more ideas, check their synthesis of the first impressions against others,' and get ideas for the "final answer" response.

The "Second Thoughts" discussion allows students to demonstrate these course goals:

- to demonstrate an appreciation and understanding of graphic literature
- to develop the ability to respond to verbal and visual arts in meaningful ways
- to read attentively, closely, and critically
- to write thoughtfully, coherently, and persuasively
- to express honest, original thoughts about the reading
- to show that they have actually read the material
- to interact with others and respond to their thoughts

This kind of reflection on a previous discussion doesn't happen often in face-to-face classrooms, and it certainly can't happen with the specificity of reading and synthesizing everyone's posts, as it does in an online classroom.

Final Answer. After we have finished reading and discussing the major graphic texts for the course, We have one more major discussion forum, the "Final Answer," in which students synthesize the texts we have read throughout the semester, taking into consideration all the discussion they've read about each text. Here is an excerpt of that assignment:

> After you have read **all** the texts, write **one** final reading response that puts all the texts in conversation with each other, and reflects on your conversation with others. You might address similar themes or techniques in the works. You might notice similar reactions to different texts by you or classmates. You might have strong feelings about which texts are worth keeping in the course and which ones you would drop. Or you might have suggestions for other texts to complement the ones we've read.
>
> Start gathering ideas for this discussion by revisiting what you and others have said about the individual texts in the First Impressions and Second Thoughts posts for each major work. Where can you make connections between and among the works based on what you or others have previously written?
>
> Whatever you write, it should show that you have thought about the texts *collectively, as a whole* instead of just individual works as well as how the class as a whole responded to them.

The "Final Answer" helps students meet these course goals:

- to demonstrate an appreciation and understanding of graphic literature
- to develop the ability to respond to verbal and visual arts in meaningful ways
- to read attentively, closely, and critically
- to write thoughtfully, coherently, and persuasively
- to express honest, original thoughts about the reading
- to show that they have actually read the material
- to interact with others and respond to their thoughts

This Final Answer discussion allows students to interact with each other in much the same way as the second thoughts posts. They read through others' responses and find similarities or trends, and then they synthesize that information in crafting their final answer. And again, they treat the discussion forums like other texts to revisit and reflect on.

In the literature course, these discussion forums are a way to hear students' ideas and a place for them to figure out their own thoughts on a particular work. Through posts, students hear what others have to say and weigh those ideas against their own. They have a chance to learn and grow in an understanding of the text by considering ideas that had not occurred to them. More importantly, students have a chance to articulate how the discussion changed them as readers of literature. In a typical face-to-face discussion, students don't have the opportunity for that reflection. They simply "participate" in a class discussion, whether that means simply sitting and listening or actually volunteering their thoughts on the subject of discussion. This extra step in the discussion helps make the online discussion not only different from a face-to-face discussion, but it also has the potential to make the discussion more meaningful than simply experiencing a discussion and moving on. Because the discussions are written, there is a record of who participated and who wrote what. It lasts, and the reflection on the initial discussion helps make it last even longer in students minds. This kind of discussion also reflects disciplinary values in English studies, where we as scholars build our own knowledge by reading other scholars' articles and then synthesizing those into something that reflects where we stand now. This model teaches students a methodology that is often absent in F2F "discussion" because it doesn't lend itself to that level of processing and reflection.

Students understand this difference, too. Online discussions require a greater investment of thought and engagement. One student wrote, "It was interesting to learn what other people thought about the novels that we read and to see how their ideas and perspectives differed from or were similar to mine. The format of required postings meant that everybody's opinions were expressed, unlike a traditional classroom, where some people could sit for an entire semester and not say one word. . . . I also think that the relative anonymity of an online class enabled me, at least, to be more open in expressing my opinions than I probably would have been in a classroom setting." This student recognizes the democratic potential of online discussions and the purpose of treating the discussion as a text.

Discussions in Rhetoric for Writers

Discussions work a bit differently in my online Rhetoric for Writers course. There, I have students keep blogs, which are created on Blogger since we are a Google campus. Unlike the literature course in which student posts are available only to other students in the course, the blogs are public to honor the tradition of ancient rhetoric, practiced in public forums. Every week, students either write or respond to blogs. In order to keep the discussion that results from the blogs manageable for students, I put them in teams of eight to ten and then break those into groups of bloggers and responders. That way, students are reading the same four to five blogs every other week when they respond. Because of the small number, they can develop a knowledge of other students' bodies of work, topics they like to write about, and rhetorical elements they have written on in the past.

Here is an excerpt of the blog assignment:

> Every other week, you will find a news story and rhetorically analyze the current event using one or more of the concepts we have discussed in class. Utilize at least one rhetorical concept you have learned during this course in your analysis (kairos, stasis, commonplaces, etc.). Be sure to explain the concept(s) in your blog and refer to the textbook (or other reference material) accordingly. Apply the chosen concept(s) to the news story. Give the rhetorical situation of the text by saying where it's from and when it was published.
>
> Develop your post with adequate support for your analysis by citing and quoting from the text(s) you've read. Conclusions might center on how effective the piece was in reaching a particular audience, speculation on why this particular approach was taken, whether the approach was common or innovative, and so forth.
>
> You will then post your analysis and your own persuasive argument about that story (about 200 words) on your blog. The post should be written for an audience that is critical and objective, open to being persuaded, and it should be written in Standard American Written English unless there's a point you want to make that requires you to use another form. Really excellent blog entries extend beyond the entries themselves; they include

links to other people, resources and images that help your readers process the ideas.

On the weeks you are not posting, you will read and respond to one or more of your classmates' posts. The goal for responding is still 200 words, whether you post 50 words on 4 blogs, or a couple of 100-word responses, or 1 long response. I expect the responses to be thoughtful and respectful, and to add meaning to the discussion the other person has begun. A note: I will read all of the posts and keep track of the discussions. However, I won't be commenting on your posts unless you ask me a direct question or I feel I need to step in. I'm doing that for 2 reasons. The first is that somehow, as soon as the professor weighs in, everyone else stops. The second is that I will likely say something that one of you would have said, and I've taken away the space for you to say it.

The blog will help you demonstrate these course goals:

- analyze foundational rhetorical concepts and techniques in written discourse (read attentively, closely, and critically, SLO #1)
- become familiar with major theories in composition-rhetoric
- apply rhetorical theories and strategies in producing written texts (write thoughtfully, coherently, and persuasively, SLO #2)
- practice written, oral, and visual delivery skills individually and in collaboration with others.

My method for dividing students into teams and groups developed over the years when challenges occurred. Without the teams and groups, students would have about ten blogs to read and respond to. Some blogs would get a lot of attention from the others (usually the ones who posted on time), and others would not get any responses. Students simply did not read everyone's blog before choosing whom to respond to. The smaller number of blogs to read makes the workload reasonable, and students get to know each other's work more in depth, which makes for better discussions over the term.

In forming the groups, I'm also conscious of the research in computer-mediated communication and its implications for academic online discussion groups. From Herring's (2000) and others' work, two things are clear: People display features of gendered communication styles in their posts, and conventionally feminine communication styles are at a disadvantage. It's important to note for creating online discussions that when a discussion group is moderated to maintain order and focus, women participate more actively. If posting is limited to a particular number or length, or posts are monitored for insensitive language, women tend to flourish in online discussions. Just as in face-to-face classrooms, the facilitator must be aware of who gets the most attention and "talk time" in the class and work to make the discussion equitable for all involved. This is the reason for my note on the assignment page, to let students know that their blogs are specifically for this course, and the discussion on them should reflect classroom standards of civility and academic thought.

Another interesting finding by Herring (1996) is that in mixed-gender discussion groups, minority gender's communication style tends to shift toward the majority gender's style. That is, women tend to communicate more aggressively in male-dominated groups, and men less so in women-dominated groups. Though at this point I don't actively divide students into groups according to perceived gender, I try to make sure most groups are relatively balanced from what I can tell of students' gender identities as reflected on the course roster (as rudimentary as that may be). It might be worth purposely rearranging groups by gender for future research purposes.

INTENTIONALITY IN ONLINE CLASS DISCUSSIONS

As I continue teaching online English studies in literature, writing, language, and pedagogy, and revising my course components, I understand that I need to be intentional about the kinds of discussions I create in order to maximize the learning experiences for the students and effect the sort of critical and engaged thinking we say we want from students in English studies classrooms. Instead of operating under the aegis that good discussion just naturally occurs, as so many instructors do, I know that I have the ability in an online course to disrupt that natural assumption because I can planfully construct discussions in a number of ways. To do that, I need to think about the purpose of the discussion forums—To see if students read the material? To have students come to a consensus about what something means? To freely exchange ideas?—and the goals that students can achieve through the various ways of responding to each other. I know I need to match the purpose of the class discussion with appropriate ways of posting and responding, and because I am critical of traditional F2F discussion models, I work to find ways for online technologies to make the mythical democratic discussion a reality.

Intentionality is what I have also stressed to instructors who are suddenly called upon to teach remotely, as they were in the spring of 2020. As an experienced online instructor, I was recruited for my university's Digital Instruction Support team to help all faculty migrate to emergency remote teaching during the COVID-19 pandemic when our campus was closed. The DIS team offered workshops for instructors on a variety of teaching subjects. During the discussion forum workshops, I urged instructors to think about the purpose of their discussions as well as practicalities like the class size and length of discussions. Classroom instructors who are used to discussing an issue for 50 minutes with only about half of the students actively engaging in the discussion didn't understand that every student would have to respond to a discussion topic in order to "get credit" for that activity. I also showed how to set the forums to display the way they wanted. Did the instructor want the students to be able to see what others had posted before they posted their own, or did they want them to have to post first so as not to be influenced by other students' posts Did they want students to respond to others, or would they be the only one commenting? Did they want a blog-like display, or each one individually? These are all choices that instructors must decide before they set up a discussion forum. And how are they to be graded? Rated? Points awarded?

I'm looking for ways to create opportunities for sustained discussions and responses with more exchanges between students to get an ongoing correspondence. Right now, students are required to respond to others in the course on different discussion forums, but there isn't a sustained exchange. I'm looking for ways to encourage more natural exchanges even if it's not required of students. Inspired by research on gender performance in computer-mediated communication, I'm also thinking of experimenting with group membership, allowing self-selection, forming homogeneous and/or heterogeneous groupings to study the effects on discussions, or designing unmoderated spaces where students can post freely.

And as someone interested in and troubled by assessment, I am looking for flexible and fair evaluation methods for assessing discussions in online settings. My overriding question is "how does one grade it fairly?"

and I've been slowly changing my assessment to holistic rubrics that describe top discussions, competent discussions, and undeveloped discussions. I've recently created a holistic rubric for discussions in the Graphic Literature course, and it worked well for me, but I'd like to get student feedback to see how they felt about its implementation.

Teaching online also affects my thinking on F2F class discussions because I'm more cognizant of people who aren't participating, and I'm doing more paired/group work to encourage students to be fully engaged with the material and each other instead of perpetuating the IRE model of discussion in my courses. I also give time for students to write before they talk so introverts can process information in ways they prefer. It's a constant experiment with class discussion now to maximize learning opportunities instead of just taking F2F discussion for granted.

The COVID-19 pandemic has been a revelation for both students and instructors on the benefits of online discussion forums. A graduate student and instructor in an MFA program for popular fiction, Anna Burke, told me in a phone conversation on July 20, 2020 that she noticed two benefits of online discussion forums. First, as an instructor, she noticed that the international students in her first-year writing course benefited from online discussions, which she characterized as more "egalitarian." While the international students' classroom interaction during whole-class discussions was sporadic and minimal, they impressed her dramatically in online discussions. Burke hypothesized that during class, they may have been too busy processing English to make meaningful contributions to the discussion in real time, but in the online format, they were more engaged in the discussion, with time to process others' comments, formulate their own opinions, and even fact-check posts before responding.

From the student side of the discussion coin, Burke found that when her courses went suddenly remote, she felt that she "was in class for the first time in the semester" because she found ways around "that guy in the back of the class." One male student in Burke's MFA course dominated F2F discussions, verbally attacking other students as well as the instructor, making them reluctant to add to the class conversation. When courses moved online, the discussions put a stop to Isaac's domination, as the other students in the course conveniently ignored or minimized his posts and went on to have meaningful discussions without his participation. Burke reports that the quality of the discussions increased because of the online format. Hopefully instructors will recognize similar results from teaching remote courses and will continue to incorporate online discussion forums as a supplement to F2F discussions even when they return to the classroom.

Thoughtful teachers in English studies have designed productive, meaningful class discussions that are successful in helping students reach the democratic ideals on which they are based. Going online can call attention to assumptions we have about F2F courses that are merely assumptions, not rooted in careful study or reflection on our teaching effectiveness in the classroom. Moving online requires instructors to re-imagine "discussion" and also therefore calls out F2F discussion's many limitations. Implementing online discussions requires instructors to examine how we can construct different discussions for different purposes instead of merely doing what we've always done in F2F classrooms. We must continually examine our online discussions to see what makes them work (or not) and how we as effective teachers might improve them. When we do, we may unleash the potential for online discussions to eclipse those of face-to-face.

References

Beers, Kylene, and Robert Probst. 1998. "Classroom Talk about Literature or the Social Dimensions of a Solitary Act." *Voices from the Middle* 5 (2): 16–19.

Brescoll, Victoria. 2012. "Who Takes the Floor and Why: Gender, Power, and Volubility in Organizations." *Administrative Science Quarterly*, 56 (4): 622–641.

Cazden, Courtney B.1988. *Classroom Discourse: The Language of Teaching and Learning.* Portsmouth, NH: Heinemann.

Connors, Robert. 1997. *Composition-Rhetoric: Backgrounds, Theory, and Pedagogy.* Pittsburgh: University of Pittsburgh Press.

Frana, Adrian W. 1995. "Speech in the English Classroom: Zeroing in on the Contribution." Presented at Heads of Illinois Secondary English Departments, Normal, Illinois, April 28.

Herring, Susan C. 1996. "Two Variants of an Electronic Message Schema." In *Computer-Mediated Communication: Linguistic, Social and Cross-Cultural Perspectives*, edited by Susan Herring, 81–106. Amsterdam: John Benjamins.

Herring, Susan C. 2000. "Gender Differences in CMC: Findings and Implications." *Computer Professionals for Social Responsibility Newsletter* 18 (1). https://www.researchgate.net/profile/Susan_Herring3/publication/246291970_Gender_Differences_in_CMC_Findings_and_Implications/links/55453b2c0cf24107d397b0e5/Gender-Differences-in-CMC-Findings-and-Implications.pdf.

McCann, Thomas M., Larry R. Johannessen, Elizabeth Kahn, and Joseph M. Flanagan. 2006. *Talking in Class: Using Discussion to Enhance Teaching and Learning*. Urbana, IL: National Council of Teachers of English.

Riggs, Shannon A. and Kathryn E. Linder. 2016. "Actively Engaging Students in Asynchronous Online Classes." IDEA Paper# 64. *IDEA Center*.

Tannen, Deborah. 2017. "The Truth About How Much Women Talk—and Whether Men Listen." *Time*, June 28. https://time.com/4837536/do-women-really-talk-more

12 It's on the Syllabus: Notes from a Black Professor Teaching English Studies Online

Cecilia D. Shelton

The idea that the course syllabus is an important, and even a controlling document for a college course is not a new proposition. A syllabus is the best reflection of what will happen (or has happened) in the teaching and learning experience. It is the document that professors ask to borrow from colleagues for inspiration and modeling when they are preparing to teach a new course. It is the document that students exchange amongst themselves and request via email during registration periods to determine if they want to take a course. As the broad and diverse field of English studies grapples with various iterations and interpretations of online pedagogy, attention to the syllabus is not only a natural, but also a practical consideration. What do instructors and students need from a syllabus? More pointedly for the focus of this collection, how do those needs change when our pedagogy is digital and our courses happen online? Ultimately, how might we orient our syllabi toward more inclusive, anti-racist, justice-oriented practices in English studies courses?

To answer this question, I think the syllabus deserves not necessarily more attention, but *fresh* attention. That is, how can instructors and students see the syllabus anew? And how might a fresh perspective offer an entry point for thinking about English studies online? In this short meditation on the syllabus, I want to offer a fresh perspective by examining the syllabus through the lens of technical and professional communication (TPC). Technical and professional communication scholars think about how communication facilitates action. We are concerned with how communication solves problems in work-place, organizational, and institutional spaces. We think deeply about how genres operate in these systems and how their variation and evolution reflect contextual and rhetorical nuance that often goes unnoticed. I argue that TPC offers language and methods to think about and to compose syllabi in ways that are usable and useful, particularly in a turn toward greater, more intentional engagement with the internet and other digital technologies.

Placing the syllabus within its institutional context helps to orient and focus instructors as syllabus writers. TPC positions instructors to consider the rhetorical situation that the syllabus responds to, attend more critically to the genre conventions that comprise that response, and to engage with intentionality in how the genre participates in the functioning of the institution that contextualizes it. Britt (2006) identifies the role of technical communication as one way that institutions do their "cultural work," which pushes any examination of a genre's function within an institutional context toward a simultaneous consideration of its impact. In other words, we should be thinking not just about what the syllabus does in our classes and programs, but also how it reproduces and/or resists the institution's ideas about teaching and learning.

In this discussion, I use Britt's (2006) claim that "technical communication is the means by which institutions define themselves and conduct their cultural work" (148) as a frame for thinking about the narratives that are constructed around and through the syllabus and how they point toward institutional cultures that can be reproduced or disrupted in our English studies programs and courses. I see the shift toward online coursework and digital pedagogies in English studies as an opening for generative disruption across our field, and I discuss how three basic TPC concepts can help instructors operationalize these productive tensions in their course syllabi.

The metaphors that define and animate the syllabus are important reflections of the narratives that define the culture of higher education. Exploring them provides a window into the syllabus as an important nexus of reproduction (and potential disruption). The syllabus-as-artifact is a common trope that reflects how we understand the document's purpose and function in a course. The metaphor compares the syllabus to the social science concept of an artifact: something made by people that reflects the culture of those who created and used it. That idea tracks with how syllabi function in the academic sphere; they point us toward the culture of teaching and learning at a particular moment in time and in particular disciplinary, institutional, social, political, and economic contexts. Syllabi have evolved over time alongside the culture of higher education, and many of the major shifts are apparent in syllabi. When the internet becomes critical for access to materials and information, we see hyperlinks appear on syllabi; as colleges and universities are increasingly corporatized, we see a growing list of administrative and legalistic common policies; when school shootings become commonplace, we see active shooter protocols appear on syllabi; when a once-in-a-century pandemic takes hold, we see facemask and social distancing requirements appear on syllabi. Syllabi are packed with cultural information that informs how teaching and learning are taking place in context. Even though I think some academics would hesitate to admit this, I would argue that syllabi often do say important things about the identities of their creators and users—instructors and students. Although syllabi might be romanticized as neutral receptacles of the course content, a syllabus says a lot about who created it, what they value, and how they understand their various audiences. The syllabus-as-artifact metaphor suggests that a syllabus should not only announce the fact that the course is occurring online, but it should also document and facilitate the interactions among the people, topics, and contexts—including and especially the digital context(s)—that mediate teaching and learning.

Another prominent syllabus metaphor in academic discourse compares the syllabus to a contract. This metaphor seems rooted in commerce and exchange, where education becomes transactional and a contract is necessary to document what will be exchanged and how. In this instance, the syllabus is identified as a binding agreement between instructor and student for how the course will proceed. It outlines the rights and responsibilities of each party and is the document that is deferred to in the case of a dispute. The syllabus-as-contract metaphor prompts us to think about how the teaching and learning process is operationalized. What exactly are the terms of engagement for how teaching and learning will happen, how will work be completed and submitted, and how will learning be assessed? Instructor and student practices with the syllabus are telling indicators of how pervasive and influential this metaphor is, too. Instructors' choices to have students sign syllabi to indicate understanding and include disclaimers that have legalistic resonances (i.e., "the syllabus is subject to change" or "by remaining enrolled in this course you implicitly agree to these terms") adhere to this business-like approach. Students' use of the syllabus to strategize their labor and exploit perceived loopholes and extra credit to achieve their desired grade outcomes (sometimes independent of the announced learning outcomes) reflects a similar transactional tone. Even a critical stance toward the metaphor's uptake of a business-like stance toward teaching and learning must also acknowledge that the notion of a contract is a familiar way to think concretely about labor and how we do what we do in a classroom.

The digital landscape of the twenty-first century is evolving with breakneck speed, complicating the narratives and cultures implicit in the metaphors described above. Scholars and teachers have spent the first twenty years of this century adding nuance to our discussions of the digital divide, making strides toward the integration of technology across disciplines and levels of education, and tackling so many topics in between. The possibilities for inquiry focused on digital pedagogy are wide-ranging and interdisciplinary. As we enter the third decade of the twenty-first century, an emergent focal point is thinking about how digital, online spaces are pushing and pulling on the rhetorical and social dynamics of our various discourse communities at any given time and how we responsibly represent these tensions in our English studies courses. In the forward to *Critical Digital Pedagogy: A Collection*, Ruja Benjamin (2020) echoes this emphasis on the need for attention to the social work that digital pedagogy demands in the midst of a digital environment that amplifies, rather than escapes, oppressive systems. She argues that instructors should "be champions of the social contract and . . . model and cultivate caring forms of sociality that are everywhere under siege" (x). In other words, how can we train students to not only consume and produce digital content critically, but to also pay close attention to the ways that digital tools and platforms are entering and interrupting our disciplinary work, which is to theorize, create, and critique in response to the universal human themes embedded in language and literature that we explore to make meaning of the human experience? A challenge like the one I've described here means that digital spaces and online delivery is not the backdrop, but is instead at centerstage in the pedagogical conversation about English studies classes online.

Britt's (2006) framing of technical communication in institutional spaces as "cultural work" enables a reading of the syllabus metaphors I've discussed as not only culturally situated but also indicative of the syllabus as integral to the definition of the institution vis-á-vis the course. The syllabus-as-artifact and syllabus-as-contract surface the institutional cultural narratives that animate this technical and professional document in our collective imaginations and reveal themselves in material form. The online learning environment complicates these existing dynamics by mediating and participating in those cultural narratives. So, if we understand the syllabus as a record of what we know, how we know, what we value, who we are, and how we labor, then how should that inform our intentional approach to its composition, particularly when we teach fully online English studies courses?

The notes below are ruminations that focus less on the completed syllabus as an essential course document and turn to the question of how composing the syllabus operationalizes the goals of the course. By organizing my notes in three sections—content management, user experience, and document design—I hope to provide the language and conceptual frames for a fresh perspective on the syllabus as an example of technical and professional communication. Such a view certainly raises pedagogical questions, but also requires us to question how we communicate in our profession as educators and how we convey our expertise in the form of a course plan.

Content Management

Technical and professional communication is concerned with how the content within deliverables and documents is managed so that it is repeatedly useful and usable. Instructors often invest significant time, research, and labor into composing a syllabus, precisely because the content will be useful again when the course is repeated (among the other scenarios described earlier in this discussion). A TPC orientation to composing the syllabus is an effective way to think about both intellectual content and course management in order to approach the composition of the syllabus strategically based on how and in what forms the content will be used.

Many content management considerations are quite practical. What written content can be drawn from or routed to other sources or documents? For example, oftentimes, content such as policy, resource information, and course descriptions are taken up by instructors from sample syllabi, departmental or college templates, or course catalogs and repurposed for the syllabus. Similarly, the blurbs that instructors draft to describe major assignments, document assessment standards, or office hours also get transferred to assignment sheets, course management platforms, and signage on office doors. Thinking about the multiple places where content might show up in a course, especially one that is being delivered online, means considering how to compose content most efficiently so that it can move across contexts and platforms in a course to maximize its usability. Managing content also means attending to the organization of the content that is being presented in the syllabus. The order in which information is presented can weigh heavily on whether or not and how it gets used.

These practical factors ensure that the syllabus operates as a reliable source of information for its multiple audiences—students, colleagues, administrators, and even sometimes broader publics. But Britt's (2006) claim prompts us to think about what kind of cultural work happens in the management of syllabus content and how that cultural work defines the institution. Here rather than focus on inclusions, I want to invite readers to think about exclusion. That is, what content *don't* we include on our syllabi, but that we maybe should include. If we approach the syllabus through the artifact metaphor, for example, if the syllabus documents who creates and uses it, then how instructors' identities (as the creators) and students' identities (as the users) show up on the syllabus become essential considerations.

There have been some important developments that can be understood as a kind of critical take on content management on syllabi. For example, the move toward including one's pronouns or making land acknowledgements on syllabi are important steps toward considering the identities of instructors, students, and other stakeholders—such as traditional stewards of the land on which universities stand or instructors and students live—as a kind of content to be managed. In addition to these things, I would argue that we should resist the urge to allow the way that an online delivery of a course might seem to obscure identities and embodiments to distract us from the ways that the syllabus always already gives clues about its creators and users. Syllabi should respond to institutional contexts that serve particular student groups (e.g., HBCUs, community colleges), and they should foreground the positionality of the instructor as a relevant factor in how a course takes shape. While technical and professional communication traditionally value objectivity, the social justice turn in the field takes up positionality as "a way of conceiving subjectivity that simultaneously accounts for the constraint and the conditions of context while also allowing for an individual's action and agency" (Walton, Moore, and Jones 2019). Positionality is one way that the syllabus can attend to the constraints of the generic conventions of a syllabus while allowing for an instructor's agency to interrogate the ways that identity impacts the social and cultural contract of the learning experience.

User Experience

The syllabus serves a wide array of audiences, but the primacy of the student audience is imperative to the function of the document. In the truest sense, the students are the original users of the syllabus. While a syllabus can help various stakeholders make critical institutional decisions, students are most explicitly implicated into the action that the document facilitates: learning. The syllabus is often students' first point of interaction with a course. Not only does it orient them to the content of the course, but it also articulates—sometimes unwittingly—how students will be oriented to the instructor, to one another, and to the institution.

One traditional approach to understanding students' user experience of the syllabus is to assess their ability to glean key information from it. Common practices such as the syllabus quiz, where students answer questions about the syllabus after reading it, may provide some insight into how well the syllabus functions as a source of course information; however, quizzes aren't the best assessment of a student's perceptions and emotions about the experience of interacting with the syllabus. Because of the power dynamic between the creators and users of the document, it can be hard to directly observe a student's truthful user experience while there's still time to adjust; often course evaluations reveal a confusing or misleading policy too late.

A shift away from a traditional classroom to deliver a course online adds more dynamics to a student's experience of the syllabus. There are many possible changes in such a shift: a heavier reliance on digital tools and platforms; synchronous and/or asynchronous modes of instruction; the variability of access, quality, and availability of technology (with no assumed minimum standards based on campus computer lab availability); and a range of motivating personal and/or professional circumstances which motivate the choice to learn online, among others. One proactive approach to thinking about the students' user experience is to focus on the ways that the syllabus language constructs the interactions and dynamics that students should anticipate in the course.

Everything from the pronouns that instructors use to articulate the syllabus' point of view to the wording of important policies can shape a student's perceptions and emotions as they use the syllabus. In traditional face-to-face instruction, it is not uncommon to hear teachers refer to students and classroom spaces with the personal possessive pronoun *my*. In many cases, this decision is like a mundane linguistic choice, but it also alludes to the instructors' authority to physically monitor and control the classroom space and to discipline the bodies within it. When a class is being taught online, spaces and bodies are distributed differently and access is virtual, completely changing the face-to-face dynamic. Online courses provide opportunities to more precisely name an instructor's role as a facilitator and to describe their role in terms of its function (teaching) rather than authority and possession.

The often boiler plate language that comprises course management policies do a similar kind of cultural work for the institutional construction of authority and expertise. Policies that foreground ADA legalese rather than accessibility orient students to the institutional requirements for particular kinds of documentation and substantiation that can problematically privilege those with class status and healthcare access while simultaneously limiting access for those without these resources. Policies that discuss academic integrity in terms of the methods and procedures for evaluating a student's guilt can construct students as not being trustworthy and subject their labor to surveillance and seize control of student intellectual property. From a more constructive perspective, a policy governing class discussion of challenging topics can be explicit in its stance on what "respect" means and the kinds of "disrespect" (racist, sexist, homophobic and trans antagonist, classist, ableist, etc.) that won't be tolerated. Connecting these expectations to the themes and topics of the course helps students to identify the expectations for how they are expected to manage and communicate about their perceptions and emotions.

Just these few examples illustrate the ways that instructors can use the syllabus to interrogate their own relationships to the cultural work that reproduces educational institutions and imposes their norms onto students. Instructors can choose to be explicit about the places where they are disrupting those norms to mitigate harm. These examples also prompt students to be aware of how they are (dis/re)oriented to the culture of the institution in particular ways.

Document Design

The presentation of documents is also an important variable for how technical and professional communicators make choices that move users to action. While design might not seem a priority for the intellectual work that syllabi document, some attention to basic design principles can ensure that the emphasis, distinctions, relationships, and tones that instructors aim to convey to students and other audiences happen successfully. One important aspect of designing syllabi for online courses that instructors must hold themselves accountable to is making syllabi accessible for users across the ability spectrum. This work might require some skill and attention to elements of the document that are not student-facing, but that have enormous impacts on how well we are serving students, and all of the various audiences for our syllabi.

Document design principles can offer syllabus users visual rhetorical cues that provide meaningful guidance as to the use of the document. The most basic introduction to design principles are summarized in the CRAP acronym: contrast, repetition, alignment, and proximity. Each of these elements helps designers determine how to lay out information on a page in such a way that users can quickly sort, navigate, organize and interpret information. Consulting a user-friendly resource such as the *Non-Designer's Design Book* can help instructors apply these principles to even the most basic, black and white, word document syllabi (Williams 2015).

The affordances of online instruction open up a range of possibilities for design. Opportunities to incorporate color, typography, and graphics into syllabi that will be read digitally may seem overwhelming, but alongside the visual rhetorical potential, options for formatting and file type, among other formatting choices, these digital affordances also hold the potential to achieve accessible design. Captioned images, tables with headers, image descriptions, descriptive buttons, screen-reader friendly fonts, and lots of other accessible design features are available in the digital platforms and tools that we rely on for online education. When we compose syllabi that take advantage of these design tools and functions, we include the widest and fullest range of possible students, which is a valuable characteristic for the syllabus' function as an artifact that documents all of its creators and users rather than erases or excludes some of them.

Conclusion

This short reflection takes up the syllabus as a focal point for designing and executing an inclusive, anti-racist, justice-oriented English studies course by asking instructors to apply a technical and professional communication lens to the syllabus genre to operationalize these goals. In discussions about teaching and learning online, lots of attention goes to how information is digitally mediated. My argument here is that the syllabus is also mediating the course. What kind of screens are instructors building for students to enter the learning space that they're facilitating? How does it constrain and inform their bodies, their thinking, and the work that they produce?

The syllabus is a technical/professional document that should be oriented toward inclusion, equity, and justice. As a Black woman instructor in a digital/online teaching context, foregrounding my own critical orientation to the syllabus' function in the institutional narratives and their cultural work is a critical part of my pedagogical commitment. In English studies, a field in which the seemingly subjective nature of literature, writing, and language topics already lead many students to think that everything is just "opinion" in these courses, when those courses go online, it can be even more difficult to address real problems in students' thinking, reasoning, comments, and writing. While instructors' instincts can be to lean away from subjectivities—their own and their students'—in favor of some kind of feigned objectivity, instructors might consider the opposite: what if, instead, we lean into these subjectivities and make them apparent to students, *especially* when we're learning online and tempted to think we can mask them or get around them because we're not "seeing" each others' races/ethnicities among other (marginalized) identities. As a professional document, the syllabus can both make that argument *and* operationalize it in our courses, as well.

References

Benjamin, Ruha. 2020. Forward to *Critical Digital Pedagogy: A Collection*, edited by Jesse Stommel, Chris Friend, and Sean Michael Morris, ix-xi. Washington, DC: Hybrid Pedagogy.

Britt, Elizabeth C. 2006. "The Rhetorical Work of Institutions." In *Critical Power Tools: Technical Communication and Cultural Studies*, edited by J. Blake Scott, Bernadette Longo, and Katherine V. Wills, 133–50. Albany: State University of New York Press.

Walton, Rebecca, Kristen Moore, and Natasha Jones. 2019. *Technical Communication After the Social Justice Turn: Building Coalitions for Action.* New York: Routledge.

Williams, Robin. 2015. *The Non-Designer's Design Book: Design and Typographic Principles for the Visual Novice.* New York: Pearson Education.

13 Expanding Instructional Contexts: Why Student Backgrounds Matter to Online Teaching and Learning

Catrina Mitchum, Marcela Hebbard, and Janine Morris

Previous research has shown that online courses consistently have a lower rate of student persistence despite having equivalent learning outcomes as face-to-face (F2F) courses (Stack 2015; U.S. Dept. of Ed. 2010; Dietz-Uhler, Fisher, and Han 2007; Morris and Finnegan 2009). Although there are many reasons why students start and stop online courses, there are two that we address here. First, faculty in online contexts are often not given additional time, space, or support to develop online-specific pedagogies (Warnock 2009). Faculty in English studies, for instance, are often tasked with developing innovative curricula to engage students while combating particular institutional and personal constraints (Kayalis and Natsina 2010; Lancashire 2009; Manzolillo 2016). Second, programs and instructors teaching online, at times, do not consider how student background characteristics and external factors impact student perceptions, commitment, and persistence (Bean and Metzner 1985; Metzner and Bean 1987; Cabrera et al. 1992). What we offer in this chapter comes from our research on implementing effective practices in online writing instruction—research that builds on past distant learning studies and more recent online writing instruction research—long before the global situation. What we offer in this chapter is especially relevant given our current moment, when instructors are tasked with shifting teaching modalities quickly and often with little training and support.

Getting to know students on an individual level can be difficult in large English studies classes (both F2F and online). Nonetheless, the benefit of attempting to do so can greatly enhance student success in those courses. In online contexts, while instructors are often committed to building community (Lenard 2005; Tschudi, Hiple, and Chun 2009), community-building endeavors fail to include getting to know students individually as one might in face-to-face classes. In this chapter, we advocate and articulate the importance of learning about student backgrounds and expectations in online English studies classes to enhance student success and minimize instructor frustration throughout a term. Specifically, we suggest implementing a "Getting to Know You" survey at the beginning of the semester to help instructors learn more about students' linguistic and educational backgrounds, expectations for course engagement and performance, and anticipated support systems[1] (see Appendix A for survey questions). The survey questions we crafted were intended to investigate online first-year writing (FYW) courses; we recommend that the questions in Appendix A be adapted to fit the background information that will be more relevant for the online courses being taught.

For us, learning about our students' linguistic and educational backgrounds, expectations, and support systems has changed our own pedagogies and raised awareness about how we use technologies to engage with our students. Drawing from our experiences and data from 154 "Getting to Know You" surveys collected during Fall 2017, we offer nine practical suggestions to address student expectations across three dimensions: (1) Linguistic backgrounds, (2) Educational backgrounds, and (3) Institutional support.

Many of the suggestions in this chapter provide nuanced insights into areas of student experience that can be overshadowed by the work instructors put into constructing online classes. For instructors new to

---

1. We support these suggestions with previous scholarship as well as with preliminary results from a larger mixed-methods multi-institutional study that began in the fall of 2017 that investigates student backgrounds and expectations in online First-Year Composition courses at the University of Texas Rio Grande Valley (UTRGV) and the University of Arizona (UA). Both institutions are designated Hispanic-Serving Institution (HSI). Data outlined here comes from fifty-question surveys given to students during the first weeks of classes (UTRGV n=83; UA n=72). Descriptive statistics were used to analyze the quantitative data, and the qualitative data was analyzed using InVivo and Descriptive coding (Saldaña 2016), and then normed.

online environments, particularly contingent faculty or those teaching large sections, it's easy to get lost in day-to-day course logistics and planning, especially without opportunities to get to know students as individuals. Getting to know students by building a community of inquiry (Garrison, Anderson, and Archer 1999) is an important part of teaching and learning in online courses. This chapter seeks to support current English studies online practitioners by proving ideas for their teaching as well as to reassure instructors who might be reticent about making that move to online instruction by providing them with ideas for building stronger online communities. We encourage faculty to pay attention to student backgrounds and expectations in the initial stages of the course, which can ultimately result in better learning experiences and greater retention for them and their students.

Suggestions for Addressing Students' Expectations Based on Linguistic Background

Within English studies, language policies that recognize and set standards for linguistic diversity at the K–12 level have been developed and adopted for some time (NCTE 2000). However, in higher education the responsibility of working with multilingual students has fallen to certain fields such as applied linguistics and English education; however, we argue that language issues are a concern for all English studies faculty for at least two reasons. One is that we use language as a tool for learning and knowledge-production in our respective areas, including creative writing, critical theory, or literary studies (McComiskey 2006). The other is that, in online contexts, language becomes even more central because communication takes place largely through writing (Harrington, et al. 2000; Warnock 2009). Therefore, while it is important to understand students' linguistic backgrounds in face-to-face classrooms, for a variety of reasons, it is particularly important that instructors learn students' linguistic backgrounds in online contexts and consider the impact language has on their pedagogies (Craig 2014; Wojahn et al. 2017). The following suggestions can help faculty and administrators in English studies to anticipate student expectations without placing constraints on students because of their backgrounds.

1. Investigate students' linguistic backgrounds and cultural heritages to gauge the landscape of students in the course.

To learn about student language backgrounds, instructors could ask the following two questions in their "Getting to Know You" survey: (1) List the languages and/or dialects you can read, speak, and or write well; (2) What language(s) do you consider your first language and why? Between the two institutions in our study, 72% (n=56) of students from the University of Texas Rio Grande Valley (UTRGV) listed "English and Spanish" as the languages they can read, speak, and write well," 2.5% (n=2) responded "English and a language other than Spanish," and 20 (25.5%) wrote "English." From the University of Arizona (UA), 67% (n=48) listed "English," 11% (n=8) wrote "English and Spanish," and 22% (n=16) responded "English and a language other than Spanish." The languages "other than Spanish" included Turkish, Arabic, Chinese, Japanese, Tagalog, French, Vietnamese, Russian, Italian, and American Sign Language (see Figures 1 & 2).

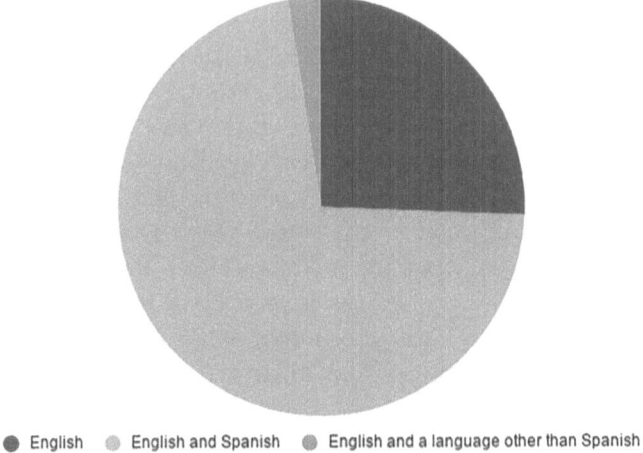

Figure 1: Student Selected Languages (UTRGV)

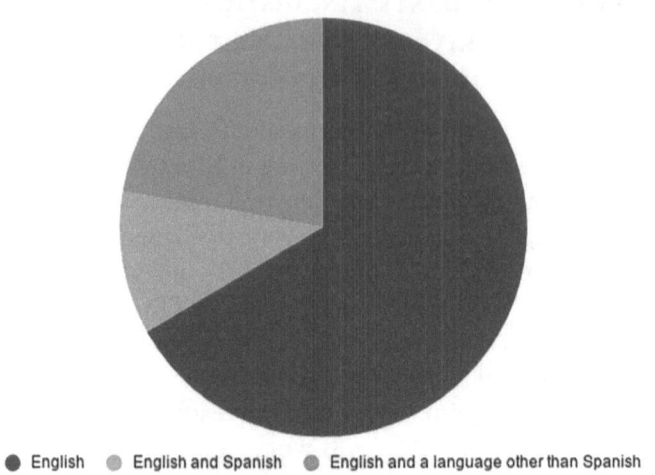

● English ● English and Spanish ● English and a language other than Spanish

Figure 2: Student Selected Languages (UA)

As this data shows, UTRGV and UA are quite different culturally and linguistically. This finding suggests that even at institutions with a large percentage of Hispanic enrollment, like UTRGV (89%), assuming a linguistically homogenous student population may be misleading (Matsuda 2006). As Figures 1 and 2 demonstrate, many Hispanic students self-identified as English monolingual. These results suggest that making assumptions about our student populations based on big data can be problematic. An online English instructor might use these results to ensure that their interactions with their online students, which are largely written, are culturally and linguistically sensitive. This is important for all English courses, but is particularly important for online English courses because instructor interaction is linked directly to online student success (Lammers and Gillaspy 2013). Exploring students' linguistic backgrounds can also help online English instructors identify the unique cultural and linguistic landscape of their particular courses.

2. Integrate elements of culturally sustaining pedagogies framework in online classes that consider student diverse sociocultural and linguistic backgrounds.

Instructors can use the information about students' linguistic backgrounds to develop culturally sustaining pedagogies that see, value, and support students' rich bilingualism/multilingualism as an asset for learning (Rosa and Flores 2017). In sociolinguistics and bilingual education, language is viewed as a shaper of personal and cultural identity (Dicker 2003; Holmes 2013; Norton 2016). *Identity* is considered a lived experience that is fluid and constructed based on the context (Hughes 2007) and linguistic and discursive representation (Ivanic 1998; Hyland 2002). From this perspective, when students—monolingual and multilingual alike—enter online environments, they already bring with them heritage-based cultural and linguistic practices that will continue to be expressed, revealed, or created through language (Gee 2011). However, despite language playing a major role in students' learning and construction of knowledge, in many online classrooms, students' cultural practices, home languages, and/or language varieties are ignored, devalued or deemed "improper," "uneducated," or "intellectually deficient" (Bucholtz, Casillas, and Lee 2017; Lippi-Green 2012). This is not so in a F2F classroom, where oral language is the primary means of communication; students are not deducted points for oral language barriers.

A recent pedagogical theory and practice that can help online educators to recognize and support students' agency, especially multilingual ones, is called culturally sustaining pedagogy (CSP) (Paris and Alim 2017). CSP first appeared in 2014, building from previous conceptualizations of asset pedagogies (Ladson-Billings 1995; Moll and Gonzalez 1994; Valdés 1996). Asset pedagogies are defined as instructional approaches that reposition the linguistic, literate, and cultural practices of working-class communities of color as resources and assets. CSP expands these notions and aims "to reimagine schools as sites where diverse, heterogeneous practices are not only valued but *sustained*" (Paris and Alim 2017, 3).

While CSP takes different forms across different contexts, at its core, it sees students' languages and cultures as something to be sustained in educational contexts because they are "sources of sustenance for identity" (Bucholtz, Casillas, and Lee 2017, 55). In online contexts, instructors can help sustain and develop students' identities by designing classroom activities that connect course content with students' languages and cultures. Some examples include asking students to explore texts across languages and cultures by completing a comparative rhetorical analysis, using a cross-cultural framework to analyze texts in translation, allowing students space to select readings in their preferred first language, assigning authors in translation and asking students to use Google translate to analyze both texts and translation technologies. Each classroom activity should include a reflective piece. By incorporating reflection pieces, instructors are stimulating active participation and learning because students are given the opportunity to connect their personal experiences through discourse to comprehend and clarify the subject of discussion at hand (Ke, Chávez, and Causarano 2011).

By incorporating socio-cultural elements (i.e., language, culture, age, gender, ethnicity, background, professional experience) when designing online course activities, instructors help students see their languages and cultures as resources for learning and shapers of their identities.

3. Offer Frequent Opportunities for Students to Write Without the Concern of Standard "Correctness" and Encourage Students to See the Value and Differences Between Approaches to "Correctness."

In F2F contexts, we can identify linguistic backgrounds faster than in online contexts. For example, instructors can rely on cues such as eye contact, gestures, oral participation, synchronous peer-to-peer interaction; we can see student understanding. However, in online courses, because we rely heavily on written text (Lee and Jenks 2016), we are at risk of making assumptions about students' intelligence and academic ability based on their written linguistic performance. To lessen this possibility, we need to intentionally bring out and interrogate our linguistic ideologies so they don't cloud our view of student writing. Language ideologies are shared belief systems about specific language, language varieties, or language practices that are explicitly articulated or implicitly embodied in everyday actions, language policies, and institutional practices (Irvine 1989; Bloomaert 1999; Leeman 2012). Jerry Won Lee and Christopher Jenks (2016) claim that the preconceived ideologies of "standardness" and "correctness" of a particular variety of English are not inherent to the language itself. Instead, they are sustained through the work of institutional agents such as postsecondary education. Scholars in composition studies have argued that many classrooms operate from a monolingual ideology (Horner et al. 2011) in which students who are nonnative speakers of English and students who speak nonstandard English varieties are expected to write in dominant Standard English (Nero 2006). The danger of this ideology is to deem students' language varieties as "deficient" or "inferior" and to assume Edited Standard English is the norm when in fact it is another language variety (Coleman 1997). Hence, it is crucial that instructors develop rhetorical awareness about their own linguistic ideologies and recognize whether they make assumptions about students' intelligence or academic fitness based on their written linguistic performance (Asao 2015; Asao 2019).

A place where language ideologies become visible in online courses is in discussion boards. Because class discussions, posts, and responses are considered the driving force of a course—the entryway to new learning (Jones and Jones 2014)—students are required to actively participate in them. As a genre, discussion boards are considered informal places for writing (Manzolillo 2016; Warnock 2009). However, if online instructors see discussion boards as sites for formal writing, then beliefs of standardness, correctness, and legitimacy of the standard form can hinder students' learning (Lee and Jenks 2016). One suggestion is for instructors not to place heavy penalties when discussion responses/posts fall short of a well-conceived or well-written post because it can de-motivate students (Jones and Jones 2014). Instead, faculty can use scaffolding strategies (Cho & Cho 2016) and ask follow-up questions to provoke a more in-depth response or clarification without over-burdening students to the point of frustration. Likewise, developing online discussions or "literature circles" can be a mechanism to enhance community-building and engaged reading (Bowers-Campbell 2011). Students don't often get to orally hash out ideas, and when questions are convoluted in writing, it can make student understanding both more difficult and more time consuming because of the asynchronous aspect of the course. Instructors might consider allowing video or audio responses so that students who feel more comfortable communicating orally might do so.

In sum, implementing a "Getting to Know You" survey can provide online instructors a better understanding of students' sociocultural and linguistic backgrounds. As a result, faculty and administrators can consider ways of teaching online that are not only linguistically and culturally sustaining, but that also promote equality and inclusion by considering students' perspectives of their linguistic identities. However, linguistic identity is just one piece of the complex interplay of student characteristics that can impact student success. Understanding students' past educational experiences with writing and online courses is another piece that can help instructors and administrators to improve the student experience.

Suggestions for Addressing Students' Expectations Based on Educational Background

Understanding students' educational backgrounds with both writing and online spaces are important because, despite multimedia incorporation (Estrada 2011; Webb 2012), most online courses rely very heavily on text-based submissions from students. Prior scholarship has shown that students' past writing experiences and beliefs about writing (positive or negative) can affect their confidence and perceived writing ability, influence their beliefs and attitudes toward writing, and impact their expectations about courses and performance in those courses (Boyd 2008; Daly 1978; Faigley et al. 1981; Liao 2017; Petric 2002; Rose 1980; Sanders-Reio et al. 2014). Therefore, learning about students' prior experiences with writing, their self-perceptions as writers, and their previous online experiences can allow English studies faculty and administrators to improve students' experience as well as to address misconceptions about online English course expectations and performance. The following are suggestions for how to learn and address these experiences and misconceptions.

4. Begin understanding students' previous writing experiences to offer space to address writing insecurities.

Understanding Writing Insecurities. Using the "Getting to Know You" survey, instructors can ask students about their strengths and weaknesses in writing, how they feel about themselves as writers, and how those self-perceptions came to be. Understanding student self-perceptions as writers is important in online English studies courses because, regardless of the variety of written genres in English studies, students feeling less than confident about their abilities to write a memo or a critical analysis essay can impact their success. The goal of the questions in this survey is to get a contextualized snapshot of the students in each online course. For example, in our "Getting to Know You" survey, when we asked students to select a statement that encapsulated their ability as a writer, we found out that 75% (n=115) of students selected "I am an okay writer who knows something about writing." This may suggest that most students feel like there is more to learn or that they feel they can/should improve. After selecting a statement, students were asked what contributed to their thoughts about themselves as writers. The majority of students selected positive previous writing experiences overall: "As and Bs in English in high school" (73.1%, n=114), "Positive feedback from teachers" (62.8%, n=98), and/or a "Good understanding of the English language" (51.3%, n=81) were most frequently selected as contributing factors to their perceptions of themselves as writers. For us, the follow up was important because our results suggest that, when considered with students' rating of their writing ability, experiences that are positive, like good grades, positive feedback, and a good understanding of English, are being selected by students who only feel *okay* about their writing and understand they have a lot more to learn.

Another way to explore students' self-perceptions as writers and the experiences that shaped them can be to have students create a mindmap that reflects their experiences and the connection between those experiences and how they feel as writers. They can start with how they view themselves as writers in the middle (using their own language), and use the outer circles to write their past writing experiences and make connections between them. Visualizing their experiences can allow space for students to consider why they have this specific understanding of themselves as writers.

Addressing Writing Insecurities. Online English courses create a unique space where students are writing and submitting work consistently and so creating a breadcrumb trail of their writing and learning growth throughout a course. When we asked our participants to discuss their previous experiences with online courses, some identified what they learned. Of those 99 responses, 35.4% (n=35) expressed learning things beyond course content. Of all the types of learning happening, students remembered what they learned about themselves with 18.2% (n=18) of students learning personal responsibility or independent skills. Thus, crafting distributed activities asking students to reflect on their learning can help satisfy the need for internal validation of writing ability and motivation to continue (Demitriou and Schmitz-Sciborski 2011; Pajares 2003) in ways that can address writing insecurities.

While the reflection opportunities can occur in discussion boards, it is important to have students go back and reread their previous reflections and posts as well as what their classmates shared at specific times during the semester. By "interleaving" (Lang 2016) reflections, instructors can ask students to reflect on the goals they set out in each piece (the outline, the introduction, etc.) and how they met those goals. Archiving and reflecting on work throughout the course can encourage students to see their learning as a process and assist with preparing a final portfolio by using audio, video, or written reflection. As a result, students may improve their self-perceptions as writers. Expecting their effort to be rewarded is an important factor in continuing motivation (Friedman and Mendell 2010).

5. Investigate Student Online Backgrounds in Order to Address Student Misconceptions.

Lacking experience, having negative experiences, or having experiences with a different institution or LMS in online courses can impact student expectations for subsequent online courses, which can, in turn, impact success (Nash 2005). In addition, students might have misconceptions about what to expect in an online course, and those students also tend to be less successful (Herbert 2006; Nash 2005). Thus, understanding expectations is important because whether or not those expectations are met can influence students' success (Plietz et al. 2015). Michael Herbert's 2006 study investigated connections between student expectations and student satisfaction in online courses. He found out that "With a decrease in meeting course expectations comes a corresponding decrease in engagement and motivation necessary to complete an online course" (sec. *Discussion*). If students have misconceptions about what online learning entails, this may impact their performance, overall.

In the "Getting to Know You" survey, instructors can ask the following questions to explore student online backgrounds: Have you ever taken online courses before for college credit? Briefly tell me about your experience (e.g., Which course did you take? Did you like it? Was it difficult/easy? What did you learn from that experience?). In our study, 34.4% (n=51) of the 151 respondents said "no" they hadn't taken an online course before and 65.6% (n=99) said "yes." Students were then asked to describe their experience (see Table 1).

Experience Level	Number of Online Courses	Percentage of Students
Somewhat Experienced	1–2	60.4% (n=58)
Experienced	3–4	24% (n=23)
Very Experienced	5+	15.6% (n=15)

Table 1. Responses that addressed experience level to "Describe Your Experience" follow up question.

Not all respondents identified specific courses taken, but 17.7% (n=17) of the respondents who indicated the approximate number of courses taken identified a previous English studies course such as a composition, literature, creative writing, or linguistics course. This suggests that, in our study, most students that have taken online courses before have only taken one or two and much of that experience falls outside of the discipline. Because student experiences in online courses vary discipline to discipline (Finnegan, Morris, and Lee 2009), knowing which classes they've taken can help instructors address misconceptions about the course they're currently enrolled in by posting video announcements that clearly explain the course and its goals or asking students to write a memo of understanding explaining what they think the course will entail. It might be useful to add a follow up question to the survey that asks students their perceptions of the type of English studies course being taught so that instructors are able to address misconceptions early in the class. While disciplinarity impacts online experiences, simply having different navigation or a different LMS can impact the experience. Understanding previous experience can help instructors to make explicit connections between those experiences and the one students will have in the current course.

6. PROVIDE ACTIVITIES BOTH EARLY AND CONSISTENTLY IN THE COURSE THAT ALLOW STUDENTS TO FOCUS ON MANAGING TIME.

Scholarship has shown that online student retention is lower than face-to-face courses (Parry 2010; Jenkins 2012). A factor that contributes to this is students lacking effective time management skills (van der Meer, Jensen, and Torenbeek 2010). In our survey, when we asked students about their learning experiences in previous online courses, 51.5% (n=51) of students mention time as something they learned. Specifically, 70.6% (n=36) of those students mentioned learning about time management, 17.6% (n=9) of students mentioned learning to work daily, and 15.7% (n=8) of students mentioned learning that online courses took the same amount or more time than face-to-face courses. It is not surprising that time management is an important lesson learned in previous online courses as students often struggle with time management (Wandler and Imbriale 2017; Macan et al. 1990) and some suggest this is due to not understanding "how" to manage time (van der Meer, Jensen, and Tandorenbeek 2010). Providing spaces where students can focus on specific time management tasks may help students more successfully complete our courses.

Specific time management tools and activities could provide students space to reflect on and enhance time management skills. For example, starting the course by having students complete a weekly calendar where they fill in all of their responsibilities and discuss the time it takes to complete the coursework and live their lives can help drive home the point that balance is important in time management, especially in online courses. Asking students to set goals about the specific course, establishing how they will reach those goals and how those goals connect to their specific academic progress, and returning to those goals consistently throughout the course is another way to build in positive time management tasks. Finally, multiple due dates a week might prompt students to complete scaffolding with enough time to understand certain concepts before moving on. How many due dates should depend on the length of the course (accelerated courses of eight weeks or less, may need more due dates in order to prevent cognitive overload).

While understanding student experiences with writing (a student earning As and Bs) and in online courses (Yes—I've taken a class) are not enough data points to fully understand how students perceive themselves as writers and whether or not they're ready for (more) online learning, they do provide a helpful snapshot of the student. Thus, exploring students' past educational experiences with writing and online courses can help faculty and programs anticipate student expectations that might not fit with what the online experience will actually be (Hewett and Warnock 2015). Writing and online expectations are, like linguistic backgrounds, just one piece of complex student experiences. Investigating more nuanced areas of online education, such as students' expectations about peer-to-peer and student-instructor interactions, as well as other forms of institutional and external support can provide an understanding of additional areas where students may need/expect more.

Suggestions Based on Institutional Support

At both course and programmatic levels, it is important to draw on different types of support to help students succeed. Studies of student persistence have established that the relationships students build with academic sources (like their instructors or the institution) are key to their retention and success (Grillo and Leist 2013; Herbert 2006; Morris and

Finnegan 2009; Nichols 2010; Roberts and Styron 2006). Other studies that have investigated online student retention have found that student perceptions of faculty involvement and interaction are the leading factors in a student's decision to stay or drop out of a course (Herbert 2006; Morris and Finnegan 2009). While these relationships are important in F2F contexts, they are especially important online because of their impact on student retention and success in the course. Thus, learning about what students know about institutional support networks and the interactions they expect from instructors can assist English studies faculty with crafting an approachable persona, make their communication practices explicit, and integrate university resources into their classes as part of the curriculum.

To explore student knowledge of institutional support, English studies faculty can incorporate questions in the "Getting to Know You" survey such as, "Besides your instructor and classmates, who else do you expect to interact with this semester that will contribute to your learning?" and "Did you receive advice before entering this class? If so, from who?" These questions could reveal where students' knowledge of available support systems might be lacking. As a result, faculty could plan interventions to reduce potential student feelings of isolation or devise ideas to explain to students how these courses might differ from face-to-face sections. We offer the following suggestions to help students understand expectations for course-based interactions and gain a sense of community with their classmates and the institution.

7. Establish clear expectations for students to navigate, participate, and interact with the instructor, the LMS, and each other.

Although it is not possible to fully measure student readiness (Meloncon and Harris 2015), there are many ways instructors can help students familiarize themselves with the course and outline how their participation will be assessed (Lancashire 2009). While frequency of interactions might vary due to faculty preferences and course length (e.g., eight weeks vs. semester), instructors should add a clause in the syllabus telling students how often and what type of interactions from instructors or other support services (like IT, library, or writing center) they can expect in the course. In addition, faculty should model appropriate communication, attention to detail and proofreading, and response expectations when engaging with students in correspondences and on discussion boards

(Meloncon and Harris 2015; Warnock 2009). Unclear expectations and communications full of errors can set up the expectation to students that those behaviors are appropriate in the course.

Along with making expectations clear, helping students navigate the learning management system (LMS) can prevent potential problems and alleviate challenges students have as they move through the course (Meloncon and Harris 2015; Salisbury 2018). At the beginning of the semester, instructors could create a screencast video of the course, showing students how to access different components and discussing where they might find specific items (such as files or assignments). If a variety of tools in the LMS will be used, instructors should consider introducing the tools as they are needed to avoid overwhelming students. Knowing how materials are arranged can assist student navigation through the course and alleviate questions they might have. In addition, a "Getting Started" folder or module that includes the course navigation video, a description of expectations, and access to technology assistance and institutional support that students must complete before accessing other class materials can better prepare them for navigating the course going forward (Meloncon and Harris 2015).

8. Create opportunities for frequent instructor-student interactions.

It's important to give students frequent opportunities to engage with their instructor to combat some of the isolation online students often experience (Arbaugh 2010). In our study, we asked students how frequently they expected to interact with their instructor. The greatest number of students (47.4%, n=73) selected that they expected to interact with their instructor weekly, while fewer students expected to communicate 1–3 times a week or several times a month (25.3%, n=39 and 24%, n=37 respectively). Finally, only 3.2% (n=5) of students expected to interact with their instructor daily. This suggests that students expect to interact with their instructor at relatively the same frequency as they would if they were attending a F2F class. For new online instructors, it's important to create a balance between engagement opportunities and labor and remember that students are not expecting daily interactions with you.

Furthermore, student-instructor interaction doesn't mean commenting on every single post by every single student every single week. There are other ways instructors can interact with students in the course in manageable, yet meaningful ways. For instance, instructors could hold early and mid-semester virtual synchronous conferences with students (one-on-one or in small groups) to check in on the course. Apart from the occasional conference, the primary way instructors and students interact in the online course is through their interactions in the LMS. To vary the kinds of feedback students receive, instructors might create short audio or video responses to student work and request an email response from the student acknowledging they have processed and reflected on the feedback. Sending an overview message to the entire class, focusing on specific themes or ideas brought up in the weekly posts, is another way to show instructor engagement and presence without dominating a discussion thread.

9. Provide students with access to institutional resources and reasons to engage with those resources.

Like the importance of student interaction with their professor, many studies have emphasized the value of online students engaging with institutional support early in a semester to facilitate their success and retention in a course (Grillo and Leist 2013; Morris and Finnegan 2009; Bailey and Brown 2016; Ludwig-Hardman and Dunlap 2003; Newberry and DeLuca 2014; Stewart et al. 2013; Britto and Rush, 2013). Institutional support services include tutoring (Grillo and Leist 2013); IT and library support (Burns, Cunningham, and Foran-Mulcahy 2014; Dolan et al. 2009); guidance counselling, advising, and coaching (Bailey and Brown 2016; Ludwig-Hardman and Dunlap 2003); as well as institutional, departmental, and class-based orientations and training for navigating and working within the online learning environment (Stewart et al. 2013). Student-institution interactions are important, as according to Grillo and Leist (2013) "the quantity of time students spent engaged in academic support contributed proportionately to the likelihood of graduation. As the total number of hours spent using academic support services increased, the likelihood of student graduating increased" (388).

Depending on the class and institutional context, there are many ways English studies instructors can build in opportunities to engage with institutional support. Discussions could focus on student experience with institutional resources, giving them opportunities to share challenges and best practices and start acting as resources for each other. For research assignments, having students complete library modules or inviting a librarian to offer a synchronous session as part of the process can be a helpful way to familiarize students with those resources. Encouraging students to make writing center appointments can also reinforce the collaborative nature of writing. The more opportunities students have to connect with institutional resources in ways that help them answer questions or use those resources purposefully, the more likely they will return to those services in the future. It's important for online instructors to show students how/where to access these resources and for administrators to work with stakeholders to make support accessible to online students.

While building in opportunities to engage with some of the institutional resources (such as advising) might go beyond the scope of an individual course, programmatically, English departments should have conversations with advisors about their online courses to help prepare students early on. In our study, when we asked students if they received advice before entering their online first-year writing class, only 28% indicated they had received advice (n=45). Of the 45 students who had received advice, 49% indicated they received advice from an academic advisor (n=22), 20% received advice from family or friends (n=9), and 38% received advice from another or unspecified source (n=17). These numbers suggest that students in this sample were receiving the majority of the advice about online first-year writing from their academic advisors. However, in their open-ended responses, students who mentioned their academic advisor indicated that the advice mainly pertained to a degree without commenting on course format or delivery. Learning from participants that students may not have received accurate advice or be fully prepared for their online courses has impacted our own pedagogies. For example, one of the authors sends a welcome email to students a week before classes begins where she explains to them differences between fully online and F2F sections and provides them links to helpful sites that offer tips on how to study online. Students need to send an email reply acknowledging they have read her email. Getting to know students and where they're getting information about online English studies classes can result in subtle shifts in practice that can greatly enhance student experiences in the class.

Conclusion

As online instruction becomes more central, understanding the context of each individual online class is vital in helping instructors make adjustments to fit the students in their current course because the class particulars matter. We reiterate again that using a "Getting to Know You" survey won't necessarily make more work for instructors. On the contrary, the results can guide their courses in ways that are more purposeful. However, it is important to emphasize that the results of a survey should not be used to pigeonhole students based on responses. A survey serves just to find out who our students are, what their current contexts are, and how those contexts change. As faculty are asked to adjust to synchronous online or simultaneous face-to-face instruction at different institutions, investing time in getting to know important elements of students' backgrounds can help instructors to meet student needs in a time of uncertainty.

For faculty and administrators in English studies wishing to develop online courses and enhance their online pedagogies, being aware of student experiences and expectations can be beneficial in a number of ways at the course and programmatic levels. First, understanding students' sociocultural and linguistic backgrounds in an online environment allows faculty and administrators to consider ways of teaching online that are not only linguistically and culturally sustaining, but also take into account students' perspectives of their linguistic identities. In addition, learning students' perceptions of themselves as writers and the experiences that shape those perceptions can shed light on student insecurities when entering online English studies courses. With this information, instructors can address these insecurities and meet students where they are, creating a student-centered online classroom. Furthermore, knowing student expectations about support networks, the interactions they expect from instructors, and the institution can encourage instructors to craft an approachable persona, make their communication practices explicit, and integrate these resources into their classes as part of the curriculum. After all, our goal of putting appropriate frameworks in place at the outset of a semester, rather than waiting until students are struggling, can encourage greater student success later on (Grillo and Leist 2013; Morris and Finnegan 2009). We can build these frameworks based on the modality context we have, but it will also be important to continue to check-in as those modalities change in order to ensure student success and retention.

References

Arbaugh, J. B. 2010. "Sage, Guide, Both, or Even More? An Examination of Instructor Activity in Online MBA Courses." *Computers & Education* 55 (3): 1234–44. https://doi.org/10.1016/j.compedu.2010.05.020.

Inoue, Asao B. 2015. *Antiracist Writing Assessment Ecologies: Teaching and Assessing Writing for a Socially Just Future*. Perspectives on Writing. Fort Collins, CO: The WAC Clearinghouse; Anderson, SC: Parlor Press. https://wac.colostate.edu/books/perspectives/inoue/.

Inoue, Asao B. (2019). *Labor-based grading contracts: Building equity and inclusion in the compassionate writing classroom*. Perspective on Writing. Fort Collins, CO: WAC Clearinghouse; Louisville, CO: University Press of Colorado. https://wac.colostate.edu/books/perspectives/labor/.

Bailey, Tabitha, and Abbie Brown. 2016. "Online Student Services: Current Practices and Recommendations for Implementation." *Journal of Educational Technology Systems* 44 (4): 450–62. https://doi.org/10.1177/0047239515616956.

Bean, John P., and Barbara S. Metzner. 1985. "A Conceptual Model of Nontraditional Undergraduate Student Attrition." *Review of Educational Research* 55 (4): 485–540. https://doi.org/10.3102/00346543055004485.

Bloomaert, Jan, ed. 1999. *Language Ideological Debates: Introduction and Postscript*. Berlin and New York: Mouton de Gruyter.

Bowers-Campbell, Joy. 2011. "Take it Out of Class: Exploring Virtual Literature Circles." *Journal of Adolescent & Adult Literacy* 54 (8): 557–67. https://doi.org/10.1598/JAAL.54.8.1.

Boyd, Patricia Webb. 2008. "Analyzing Students' Perceptions of their Learning in Online and Hybrid First-Year Composition Courses." *Computers and Composition* 25: 224–43. https://doi.org/10.1016/j.compcom.2008.01.002.

Britto, Marwin, and Susan Rush. 2013. "Developing and Implementing Comprehensive Student Support Services for Online Students." *Journal of Asynchronous Learning Networks* 17 (1): 29–42. https://eric.ed.gov/?id=EJ1011371.

Bucholtz, M., D. I. Casillas, and J. S. Lee. 2017. "Language and Culture as Sustenance." In *Culturally Sustaining Pedagogies: Teaching and Learning for Justice in a Changing World*, edited by D. Paris and H. S. Alim, 43–60. New York: Teachers College Press.

Burns, Sharon, Joseph Cunningham, and Katie Foran-Mulcahy. 2014. "Asynchronous Online Instruction: Creative Collaboration for Virtual Student Support." *CEA Critic* 76 (1): 114–31. https://muse.jhu.edu/article/540967.

Cabrera, Alberto F., Maria B. Castaneda, Amaury Nora, and Dennis Hengstler. 1992. "The Convergence between Two Theories of College Persistence." *The Journal of Higher Education* 63 (2): 143–64. https://www.jstor.org/stable/1982157.

Cho, M. H., and Y. Cho. 2016. "Online Instructors' Use of Scaffolding Strategies to Promote Interactions: A Scale Development Study." *The International Review of Research in Open and Distributed Learning* 17 (6): 108–20. https://doi.org/10.19173/irrodl.v17i6.2816.

Coleman, Charles F. 1997. "Our Students Write with Accents. Oral Paradigms for ESD Students." *College Composition and Communication* 48 (4): 486–500. https://www.jstor.org/stable/358454.

Craig, Jennifer Lynn. 2014. "Teaching Writing in a Globally Networked Learning Environment (GNLE): Diverse Students at a Distance." In *WAC and Second-Language Writers: Research Towards Linguistically and Culturally Inclusive Programs and Practices*, edited by Terry Myers Zawaki, and Michelle Cox, 369–86. Perspectives on Writing. Fort Collins, CO: The WAC Clearinghouse and Parlor Press. https://wac.colostate.edu/books/perspectives/l2/.

Daly, John A. 1978. "Writing Apprehension and Writing Competency." *The Journal of Educational Research* 72: 10–14. https://www.jstor.org/stable/27537168.

Dicker, Susan J. 2003. *Languages in America: A Pluralist View*. 2nd ed. Buffalo: Multilingual Matters.

Demetriou, C., and A. Schmitz-Sciborski. 2011. "Integration, Motivation, Strengths and Optimism: Retention Theories Past, Present and Future." In *Proceedings of the 7th National Symposium on Student Retention*, edited by R. Hayes, 300–12. Norman: The University of Oklahoma.

Dolan, Sean, et al. 2009. "Supporting Online Learners: Blending High-Tech with High-Touch." *Online Learning Exchange*, (Nov–Dec): 90–94. https://eric.ed.gov/?id=EJ864776.

Dietz-Uhler, Beth, Amy Fisher, and Andrea Han. 2007. "Designing Online Courses to Promote Student Retention." *Journal of Educational Technology Systems* 36 (1): 105–12. https://doi.org/10.2190/ET.36.1.g.

Estrada, Gabriel. 2011. "Native Avatars, Online Hubs, and Urban Indian Literature." *Studies in American Indian Literatures* 23 (2): 48–70. https://doi.org/10.5250/studamerindilite.23.2.0048.

Faigley, Lester, et al. 1981. "The Role of Writing Apprehension in Writing Performance and Competence." *Journal of Educational Research* 75 (1): 16–21. https://www.jstor.org/stable/27539858.

Finnegan, Catherine, Libby V. Morris, and Kangjoo Lee. 2009. "Differences by Course Discipline on Student Behavior, Persistence, and Achievement in Online Courses of Undergraduate General Education." *Journal of College Student Retention: Research, Theory and Practice* 10 (1): 39–54. https://doi.org/10.2190/CS.10.1.d.

Friedman, Barry A., and Rhonda G. Mandel. 2011. "Motivation Predictors of College Student Academic Performance and Retention." *Journal of College Student Retention: Research, Theory and Practice* 13 (1): 1–15. https://doi.org/10.2190/CS.13.1.a.

Garrison, D. Randy, Terry Anderson, and Walter Archer. 1999. "Critical Inquiry in a Text-Based Environment: Computer Conferencing in Higher Education." *The Internet and Higher Education* 2 (2–3): 87–105. https://doi.org/10.1016/S1096-7516(00)00016-6.

Gee, James Paul. 2011. "Discourse Analysis: What Makes It Critical?" In *An Introduction to Critical Discourse Analysis in Education*, 2nd ed., edited by Rebecca Rogers, 23–45. New York: Routledge.

Grillo, Michael C., and Cathy W. Leist. 2013. "Academic Support as a Predictor of Retention to Graduation: New Insights on the Role of Tutoring, Learning Assistance, and Supplemental Instruction." *Journal of College Student Retention: Research, Theory and Practice* 15 (3): 387–408. https://doi.org/10.2190/CS.15.3.e.

Harrington, Susanmarie, Rebecca Rickly, and Michael Day, eds. 2000. *The Online Writing Classroom*. Cresskill: Hampton.

Herbert, Michael. 2006. "Staying the Course: A Study in Online Student Satisfaction and Retention." *Online Journal of Distance Learning Administration* 9 (4). http://www.westga.edu/~distance/ojdla/winter94/herbert94.htm.

Hewett, Beth, and Scott Warnock, eds. 2015. *Foundational Practices of Online Writing Instruction*. Fort Collins, CO: The WAC Clearinghouse; Anderson, SC: Parlor Press. https://wac.colostate.edu/books/perspectives/owi/.

Holmes, Janet. 2013. *An Introduction to Sociolinguistics, 4th Edition (Learning About Language)*. New York: Routledge.

Horner, Bruce, Lu, Min-Zhan, Royster, Jacqueline Jones, and Trimbur, John. 2011. "Language Difference in Writing: Toward a Translingual Approach." *College English* 73 (3): 303–321. https://ir.library.louisville.edu/faculty/67/.

Hughes, Gwyneth. 2007. "Diversity, Identity, and Belonging in E-Learning Communities: Some Theories and Paradoxes." *Teaching in Higher Education* 12 (5–6): 707–18. https://doi.org/10.1080/13562510701596315.

Hyland, Ken. 2002. "Authority and Invisibility: Authorial Identity in Academic Writing." *Journal of Pragmatics* 34: 1091–112. https://doi.org/10.1016/S0378-2166(02)00035-8.

Ivanic, Roz. 1998. *Writing and Identity: The Discoursal Construction of Identity in Academic Writing*. Amsterdam: Benjamins.

Irvine, Judith. 1989. "When Talk Isn't Cheap: Language and Political Economy." *American Ethnologist* 16 (2):248–67. https://www.jstor.org/stable/645001.

Jenkins, Rob. 2012. "Online Classes and College Completion." *The Chronicle of Higher Education*, March 13, 2012, sec. Run Your Campus. http://chronicle.com/article/Online-ClassesCollege/131133/.

Jones, Elwin L., and Ronald C. Jones. 2014. "The Online Discussion Board: Opening the Gateway to New Learning." *Faculty Focus–Higher Ed Teaching Strategies from MAGNA Publications*. https://www.facultyfocus.com/articles/online-education/online-discussion-forum-opening-gateway-new-learning/.

Kayalis, Takis, and Anastasia Natsina, eds. 2010. *Teaching Literature at a Distance*. New York: Continuum.
Ke, Fengfeng, Chávez, Alicia, Causarano Pei-Ni L., and Causarano, Antonio. 2011. "Identity Presence and Knowledge Building: Joint Emergence in Online Learning Environment?" *Computer-Supportive Collaborative Learning* 6 (3): 349–70.
Komarraju, Meera, Sergey Musulkin, and Gargi Bhattacharya. 2010. "Role of Student–Faculty Interactions in Developing College Students' Academic Self-Concept, Motivation, and Achievement." *Journal of College Student Development* 51 (3): 332–42. https://doi.org/10.1353/csd.0.0137.
Ladson-Billings, Gloria. 1995. "Toward a Theory of Culturally Relevant Pedagogy." *American Educational Research Journal* 32 (3): 465–91. https://doi.org/10.3102/00028312032003465.
Lammers, William and Arthur J. Gillaspy. 2013. "Brief Measure of Student-Instructor Rapport Predicts Student Success in Online Courses." *International Journal for the Scholarship of Teaching and Learning* 7 (2): 1–13. https://doi.org/10.20429/ijsotl.2013.070216.
Lancashire, Ian, ed. "Introduction: Perspectives on Online Pedagogy." *Teaching Literature and Language Online*, 1–20. New York: Modern Language Association of America.
Lang, James M. 2016. *Small Teaching: Everyday Lessons from the Science of Learning*. Hoboken: John Wiley & Sons.
Lee, Jerry Won, and Christopher Jenks. 2016. "Doing Translingual Disposition." *College Composition and Communication* 68 (2): 317–44.
Leeman, Jennifer 2012. "Investigating Language Ideologies in Spanish as a Heritage Language." In *Spanish as a Heritage Language in the United States*, edited by Sara M. Beaudrie and Marta Fairclough, 43–60. Washington: Georgetown University Press.
Lenard, Mary. 2005. "Dealing with Online Selves: Ethos Issues in Computer-Assisted Teaching and Learning." *Pedagogy* 5 (1): 77–95. https://muse.jhu.edu/article/177776.
Liao, Fang-Yu. 2017. "The Relationship between L2 Students' Writing Experiences and Their Perceived Poetry Writing Ability." *Studies in Second Language Learning and Teaching* 7 (4): 619. https://doi.org/10.14746/ssllt.2017.7.4.4.
Lippi-Green, Rosina. 2012. *English with an Accent: Language, Ideology and Discrimination in the United States*. 2nd ed. Abingdon: Routledge.
Litterio, Lisa M. 2018. "Uncovering Student Perceptions of a First-Year Online Writing Course." *Computers and Composition* 47:1–13. https://doi.org/10.1016/j.compcom.2017.12.006.
Ludwig-Hardman, Stacey, and Joanna C. Dunlap. 2003."Learner Support Services for Online Students: Scaffolding for Success." *International Review of*

Research in Open and Distance Learning 4 (1): 1–15. https://doi.org/10.19173/irrodl.v4i1.131.

Macan, T. H., Shahani, C., R.L. Dipboye, and A.P. Phillips. 1990. "College Students' Time Management: Correlations with Academic Performance and Stress." *Journal of Educational Psychology* 82 (4): 760–68. http://dx.doi.org/10.1037/0022-0663.82.4.760.

McComiskey, Bruce, ed. 2006. *English Studies: An Introduction to the Discipline(s)*. The National Council of Teachers of English.

Manzolillo, Monica. 2016. "Teaching Literature through Online Discussion: Theory and Practice." *CLCWeb: Comparative Literature and Culture* 18 (2): https://docs.lib.purdue.edu/clcweb/vol18/iss2/.

Matsuda, Paul Kei. 2006. "The Myth of Linguistic Homogeneity in U.S. College Composition." *College English* 68 (6): 637–51. https://www.jstor.org/stable/25472180.

Meloncon, Lisa, and Heidi Harris. 2015. "Preparing Students for OWI." In *Foundational Practices of Online Writing Instruction*, edited by B. L. Hewett and K. DePew, 411–38. Fort Collins, CO: The WAC Clearinghouse; Anderson, SC: Parlor Press. https://wac.colostate.edu/books/perspectives/owi/.

Metzner, Barbara S., and John P. Bean. 1987. "The Estimation of a Conceptual Model of Nontraditional Undergraduate Student Attrition." *Research in Higher Education* 27 (1): 15–38. https://doi.org/10.1007/BF00992303.

Moll, L., and N. Gonzalez. 1994. "Lessons from Research with Language Minority Children." *Journal of Reading Behavior* 26 (4): 23–41. https://doi.org/10.1080/10862969409547862.

Morris, Libby V., and Catherine L. Finnegan. 2009. "Best Practices in Predicting and Encouraging Student Persistence and Achievement Online." *Journal of College Student Retention: Research, Theory and Practice* 10 (1): 55–64. https://doi.org/10.2190/CS.10.1.e.

Nash, Robert D. 2005. "Course Completion Rates among Distance Learners: Identifying Possible Methods to Improve Retention." *Online Journal of Distance Learning Administration* 8 (4). https://www.westga.edu/~distance/ojdla/winter84/nash84.pdf.

NCTE. 2000. "CCCC Language Policy Committee Report "Language Knowledge and Awareness Survey." http://cccc.ncte.org/cccc/committees/languagepolicy.

Nero, Shonder. 2006. "Language, Identity, and Education of Caribbean English Speakers." *World Englishes* 25 (3–4): 501–11. https://doi.org/10.1111/j.1467-971X.2006.00470.x.

Newberry, Ruth, and Catherine DeLuca. 2014. "Building a Foundation for Success Through Student Services for Online Learners." *Journal of Asynchronous Learning Networks* 17 (4): 1–15. https://www.learntechlib.org/p/183761/article_183761.pdf.

Nichols, Mark. 2010. "Student Perceptions of Support Services and the Influence of Targeted Interventions on Retention in Distance Education." *Distance Education* 31 (1): 93–113. https://doi.org/10.1080/01587911003725048.

Norton, Bonny. 2016. "Identity and Language Learning: Back to the Future." *TESOL Quarterly* 50 (2): 475–78. https://doi.org/10.1002/tesq.293.

Pajares, Frank. 2003. "Self-Efficacy Beliefs, Motivation, and Achievement in Writing: A Review of the Literature." *Reading and Writing Quarterly* 19(2): 139–58. https://doi.org/10.1080/10573560308222.

Paris, Django, and Samy H Alim, eds. 2017. *Culturally Sustaining Pedagogies: Teaching and Learning for Justice in a Changing World*. New York: Teacher College Press.

Parry, Marc. 2010. "Wired Campus." *Preventing Online Dropouts: Does Anything Work?* (blog). September 22, 2010. http://chronicle.com/blogs/wiredcampus/preventing-online-dropouts-does-anything-work/27108.

Petric, Bojana. 2002. "Students' Attitudes Towards Writing and the Development of Academic Writing Skills." *The Writing Center Journal* 22 (2): 9–27. https://www.jstor.org/stable/43442147.

Pleitz, Jacob D., Alexandra E. MacDougall, Robert A. Terry, M. Ronald Buckley, and Nicole J. Campbell. 2015. "Great Expectations: Examining the Discrepancy Between Expectations and Experiences on College Student Retention." *Journal of College Student Retention: Research, Theory & Practice* 17 (1): 88–104. https://doi.org/10.1177/1521025115571252.

Roberts, Jalynn, and Ronald Styron. 2006. "Student Satisfaction and Persistence: Factors Vital to Student Retention." *Research in Higher Education Journal* 6 (March): 1–18. PDF file. http://www.aabri.com/manuscripts/09321.pdf.

Rosa, Jonathan & Flores, Nelson. 2017. "Do You Hear What I Hear? Raciolinguistic Ideologies and Culturally Sustaining Pedagogies." In *Culturally Sustaining Pedagogies: Teaching and Learning for Justice in a Changing World*, edited by D. Pari and H.S. Alim, 175–90. New York, NY: Teachers College Press.

Rose, Mike. 1980. "Rigid Rules, Inflexible Plans, and the Stifling Language: A Cognitivist Analysis of Writer's Block." *College Composition and Communication* 31 (4): 389–401. https://www.jstor.org/stable/356589.

Saldaña, Johnny. 2016. *The Coding Manual for Qualitative Researchers*. 3rd ed. Los Angeles: SAGE.

Salisbury, Lauren E. 2018. "Just a Tool: Instructors' Attitudes and Use of Course Management Systems for Online Writing Instruction." *Computers and Composition* 48: 1–17. https://doi.org/10.1016/j.compcom.2018.03.004.

Sanders-Reio, Joanne, Patricia A. Alexander, Thomas G. Reio, and Isadore Newman. 2014. "Do Students' Beliefs about Writing Relate to Their Writing Self-Efficacy, Apprehension, and Performance?" *Learning and Instruction* 33 (October): 1–11. https://doi.org/10.1016/j.learninstruc.2014.02.001.

Stack, Steven. 2015. "Learning Outcomes in an Online vs Traditional Course." *Georgia Educational Researcher* 9 (1). https://doi.org/10.20429/ijsotl.2015.090105.

Stewart, Barbara, et al. 2013. "Online Student Support Services: A Case Based on Quality Frameworks." *Journal of Online Learning and Teaching* 9 (2): 290–303. http://jolt.merlot.org/vol9no2/stewart_barbara_0613.pdf.

Tschudi, Stephen, David Hiple, and Dorothy Chun. 2009. "Fostering Cohesion and Community in Asynchronous Online Courses." In *Teaching Literature and Language Online*, edited by Ian Lancaster, 121–46. New York: Modern Language Association of America.

US Department of Education, Office of Planning, Evaluation, and Policy Development. 2010. *Evaluation of Evidence-Based Practices in Online Learning: A Meta-Analysis and Review of Online Learning Studies.* Washington, D.C.

Valdés, Guadalupe. 1996. *Con Respeto: Bridging the Distances Between Culturally Diverse Families and Schools.* New York: Teachers College Press.

van der Meer, Jacques, Ellen Jansen, and Marjolein Torenbeek. 2010. "'It's Almost a Mindset That Teachers Need to Change': First-year Students' Need to Be Inducted into Time Management." *Studies in Higher Education* 35 (7): 777–91. https://doi.org/10.1080/03075070903383211.

Wandler, Jacob, and William John Imbriale. 2017. "Promoting College Student Self-Regulation in Online Learning Environments." *Online Learning* 21 (2). https://doi.org/10.24059/olj.v21i2.881.

Warnock, Scott. 2009. *Teaching Writing Online: How & Why.* Urbana, IL: National Council of Teachers of English.

Webb, Allen, ed. 2012. *Teaching Literature in Virtual Worlds.* New York: Routledge.

Wojahn, Patti, Beth Burnk-Chavez, Kate Mangelsdorf, Mais Al-Khateeb, Karen Trujillo-Tellez, Laurie Churchill, and Cathilia Flores. "When the First Language You Use Is Not English: Challenges of Language Minority College Composition Students." *Linguistically Diverse Immigrant and Resident Writers: Transitions from High School to College*, edited by Christina Ortmeier-Hooper & Todd Ruecker, 173–88. New York: Routledge.

Appendix A: Getting to Know You Survey

1. List the languages and/or dialects you can read, speak, and/or write well:

2. What language(s) do you consider your first language(s)? and why?

3. How would you consider yourself as a writer? (Check the option that best describes your answer)

a. I am a strong writer who knows a lot about writing (1)
   b. I am an okay writer who knows something about writing (2)
   c. I am not a good writer, I do not know much about writing (3)

4. Describe the type of interaction and depth of interaction you expect to have with your professor this semester. For example, when, how, and why do you expect to interact with your instructor.

5. Describe the type of interaction and depth of interaction you expect to have with your classmates this semester. For example, when, how, and why do you expect to interact with your peers.

6. Did someone advise you before entering this class? (e.g., friend, family member, academic advisor) If so, what advice did you receive?

7. Besides your instructor and classmates, who else do you expect to interact with (such as librarians, IT staff, Writing Tutors, individuals you have a relationship with outside of school, etc.) this semester that will contribute to your learning?

14 Teaching Ethically Online: Using Universal Design for Learning and Predesigned Courses to Increase Accessibility

Dev K. Bose and Rochelle Rodrigo

As long as first-year composition remains a required course at most institutions, writing programs will continue to design, develop, and deliver online writing courses to meet the growing demand of online undergraduate degree programs. Common issues surrounding FYC and writing programs also transfer to online offerings, including considerations about curricular development and alignment, professional development, student retention, and assessment. Newer issues have emerged in relation to teaching online, especially those related to the labor (e.g., Baldwin, Ching, and Friesen 2018; Rodrigo and Ramirez 2017) and expertise (e.g., Moore and Kearsley 1996; Xu and Morris 2007) of designing and developing online courses, as well as the ethics of making online courses accessible (e.g., Novak and Thibodeau 2016). These two newer issues—making online courses accessible and accounting for the labor involved in designing online courses—are deeply entwined. In *Academic Ableism*, Jay Dolmage (2017) acknowledges that designing and developing courses that follow the guidelines for Universal Design for Learning (UDL) take time (120); in fact, he suggests that instructors see it more as a continuing process of becoming an increasingly accessible course, one which takes the needs of diverse learners into account (137).

One of the ways writing and other academic programs have managed exponential growth of online offerings is by implementing predesigned courses (writing: Rice 2015; Rodrigo and Ramírez 2017; others: Johnson-Curiskies 2006; Onodipe, Aydadi, and Marquez 2016). Predesigned courses (PDCs), long the standard in for-profit institutions, are becoming more common in non-profit, private, and state institutions (Magda, Poulin, and Clinefelter 2015). Whereas some scholars talk about PDCs as a way to help design for curricular alignment (e.g., Magda, Poulin, and Clinefelter 2015) and support design and instruction (e.g., Onodipe, Aydadi, and Marquez 2016; Rodrigo and Ramírez 2017), PDCs can also distribute the labor of designing and developing robust online courses while accounting for accessibility—through the UDL framework—as a core value for course design and instruction.

In this chapter, we emphasize the ethical dimension of teaching *good* online courses. By *good* we emphasize designing and delivering courses that are accessible and usable to the largest number of stakeholders (students, instructors, and even administrators) while keeping in mind fair and equitable labor distributions we find in the academy; this issue is especially true in English studies departments, where large numbers of contingent faculty teach. Of course, by *good* we also mean pedagogically sound courses that are grounded in contemporary theory and scholarship about teaching in the various areas of English studies. In the first section of this chapter, we offer Universal Design for Learning (UDL) as one solution for ethical issues related to accessing online courses. We discuss examples of how English instructors might incorporate the nine UDL categories; the three principles of engagement, representation, and action/expression are broken down into three guidelines: access, build, and internalize (CAST, 2018). In the second section, we discuss how PDCs can help with the ethics of labor involved in designing, developing, and teaching online classes, especially those with robust UDL alternatives. We also acknowledge some of the concerns associated with using PDCs and how our institution is trying to address them, with the intention of offering possibilities for other institutions desiring to know more about how to offer online offerings while ensuring sound pedagogy and accessibility.

Designing for Accessibility: Universal Design for Learning

Womack (2017) argues that accommodation "is the most basic act and art of teaching. It is not the exception we sometimes make in spite of learning, but rather the adaption we continually make to promote learning" (494). This important statement reflects the long-held belief by disability scholars that educational stakeholders (including instructors and administrators across the institution) are responsible for making their courses universally accessible for their learners. More importantly, it is necessary to see accommodation as the rule for all learners, not just for the students who have filed for disability accommodations. As Womack asserts, "there is no normal, primary way of learning, only normalized methods made primary through frequent use . . . Every act of teaching is an accommodation because it creates certain conditions for students to learn and display learning" (496).

At the forefront of effective teacher training should be an emphasis on disability awareness. As Dolmage (2008) indicates, "in the case of the basic writer or the learning disabled (LD) writer, the disability is the writer's, and the university thus marks the writer as foreign and irrational" (19). When writers, especially those deemed as "basic," are seen as problematic in and of themselves, they are being relayed the message that they are unable to succeed. Similarly discussing connections between disability and basic writing, Vidali (2008) argues, "expecting basic writers to 'overcome' or 'normalize' themselves excuses institutional responsibility and negates the identity of basic writers" (47). An essential part of the ableist discourse surrounding basic or LD writers is the "overcoming" narrative, recasting the burden of their othered identities in a way that displaces the fault of the institution that perpetuates these burdens.

An example of an institution's shortcomings could be in support systems that may not be useful to every learner and to everybody. One of these places is the writing center, a fundamental area due to its proxy with writing programs as a valuable resource for aiding student writers. Babcock (2008) uses the example of tutoring deaf college students in the writing center, arguing that "common tutoring practices are based on aural/oral processing" of hearing students (28), advocating for increased research in linguistic expansion (e.g., employing ASL interpreters) and technological options (e.g., live captioning systems, CART, and C-PRINT).

For many students, the first-year composition class becomes an introduction to college skills, with learning to write in academic style being one of those core skills. FYC brings in a complex cohort of students, given the diversity of age ranges, work and life experiences, linguistic backgrounds, and disability status. Fully online and hybrid modes bring new issues to the table: these courses often welcome people who have historically been considered "nontraditional," a label which itself is problematic considering that trends of undergraduate and graduate college enrollments now lean further away from students entering directly from high school (to undergrad) or bachelors (to masters and doctorates) toward longer breaks from academia for a variety of reasons. Postsecondary English instructors need to keep all these students' needs in mind, which translates to instructors being taught the importance of inclusivity and access.

As educational practitioners know today, UDL stems from the Center for Applied Special Technology (CAST). CAST founding directors David H. Rose and Anne Meyer (2006) underscore the importance of UDL in terms of good teaching through accommodation:

> Good teachers make adjustments all the time to accommodate diverse learner needs . . . Universally designed, multimedia learning environments extend a teacher's ability to reach individual learners, something that printed textbooks alone cannot do. New technologies are not themselves instructional. However when combined with instructional methods in the UDL model, they offer extraordinary ways to customize teaching and learning. (x)

UDL provides a path forward for teachers, administrators, and instructional designers to create accessible learning environments for all learners, regardless of disability status. UDL guidelines state that course materials need to be provided through multiple means of engagement, representation, and action and expression.

Universal Design has a history in architecture. An often-used example is the curb cut, which allows for people with mobility impairments to use a sidewalk. The curb cut is useful for someone requiring assistive technology with wheels (such as a wheelchair) but can also be useful for those who may not choose to identify as disabled. Curb cuts are great for strollers, too. Take as another example one of the most popular uses of assistive technology: closed captioning. A study at Oregon State University (2,124 students across 15 public and private universities nationwide) found that 98.6% of students said captions were helpful, with 75% of them noting that they used captions as a learning aid in face-to-face and online classrooms (Doherty 2016). For video transcripts, students referenced the tool as a learning aid 85% of the time (Doherty 2016).

Assistive technology, broadly defined, was created for people with disabilities; yet when assistive technology becomes ubiquitous and widely accepted, it essentially becomes normalized for a broader population of users regardless of disabilities: this is the primary justification for Universal Design for Learning. In short, UDL asks instructors to provide multiple alternatives for students to access and learn course content and then allow for different methods to demonstrate content learning.

The UDL framework has nine categories broken down into three principles: *engagement, representation,* and *action and expression*. Each principle is then broken down into three guidelines: *access, build,* and *internalize*. The Center for Applied Special Technology (CAST 2018) defines the three principles:

> **Engagement** channels learning through affective networks. It emphasizes the "why" of learning by providing options for recruiting interest, sustaining effort and persistence, as well as for self-regulation. By focusing on multiple means of engagement, learners become purposeful and motivated.
>
> **Representation** channels learning through recognition networks. It emphasizes the "what" of learning by providing options for perception, language, mathematics expressions, and symbols, as well as for comprehension. By focusing on multiple means of representation, the goal is for learners to become resourceful and knowledgeable.
>
> **Action and expression** channels learning through strategic networks. Doing so emphasizes the "how" of learning by providing options for physical action, expression and communication, and executive functions. By focusing on multiple means of action and expression, learners ideally become strategic and goal-directed.

By committing to UDL principles, online English instructors dedicate themselves to continually revising their courses so that students have multiple opportunities to learn and be assessed. No course is ever perfectly designed or completed with UDL alternatives; they are only always improving over time. While describing the nine categories of UDL, we will provide examples online English instructors might adopt and/or adapt in their online courses.

Engagement

Keeping students interested and engaged in course work is essential for course design in general. Yet for online courses, retention issues especially need to be addressed. A study conducted by Perry et al. (2008) indicated that out of a group of 113 students who had withdrawn from an online graduate nursing program, seventeen who had been accepted did not begin any class work prior to withdrawing. Other studies describe withdrawals from programs even after several semesters (Perry et al. 2008), high mid-semester withdrawal rates (Jaggars 2011), and lower-level students being at a higher risk of dropping out than their higher-level counterparts (Levy 2007). Nevertheless, online education does carry much potential for higher retention, which in turn requires a high degree of labor while underscoring the importance of accessibility. Students need to feel that they belong to a community of learners through elevated dialogue and interactive experiences. According to Lehman and Conceição (2014), some issues behind higher attrition rates in online courses may include lack of intrinsic and extrinsic motivation, need for greater faculty contact, fear or lack of practice with new technology, lack of clarity in direction, and feelings of isolation that result in procrastination and loss of focus.

UDL **Engagement** guidelines ask that instructors provide students options for "recruiting interest, sustaining effort and persistence, and self-regulation" (CAST 2018). To *accessibly* engage students interests, UDL prompts instructors to optimize individual choice and autonomy, make learning relevant, and minimize threats and distractions (CAST 2018). In an online literature course, for example, instructors might allow students to select their own readings, demonstrate how different critical reading strategies are applicable in professional and personal settings, and work with technologies that they already know or that have an easy/intuitive learning curve. Instructors in such a course might also ask that students demonstrate their use of a specific reading and annotation strategy. If the students have been allowed to select their own text and/or access the required text in different modalities (e.g., print, E-reader, web-based), the instructor can help students identify methods for annotating the text and sharing those annotations with the instructor. In this case, students working with a print text might take pictures of their annotations and upload them to the online course site.[1] Students reading

---

1. While we acknowledge that screenshots are unable to be read by screen readers without alternative text image embedded, it may be advisable to ask stu-

in the Kindle application can share their highlights and notes (Amazon, n.d.) and students reading a text on the web might use applications like Hypothes.is or PowerNotes to annotate the web text; both applications have a sharing function. Giving students options to select their texts and the technologies to engage those texts in various ways not only empowers them "to take charge of their own learning" (Amazon, n.d.) but helps defuse anxieties caused by using unfamiliar technologies so that they can focus on learning—a germane skill for online classes, since anxiety due to learning in a potentially isolating environment can happen.

Once students are interested in and engaged with the course, UDL prompts instructors to *build* toward students' sustained effort and persistence. Specifically, UDL suggests giving students options for "heightening salience of goals and objectives, varying demands and resources to optimize challenges, fostering collaboration and community, and increasing mastery-oriented feedback" (CAST 2018). Asking students to peer-review complete drafts of projects is a common activity in English studies courses, yet in online contexts, this practice requires flexibility on the part of the instructor and accountability on the part of the student. Following this set of UDL guidelines, faculty designing and implementing a peer review assignment will want to help students focus on the major learning objectives of the assignment. Faculty might ask students to revise the course and/or assignment prompts and grading criteria before writing and submitting their drafts. Students might also be asked to use a version of the grading criteria as a guiding framework for the peer review activity. When faculty ask students to reflect upon the reviews they have given and the feedback they have received, faculty can ask students to frame their plans for revision in relation to how those plans will help students meet the course/assignment learning objectives. While these practices certainly remain universal to English classrooms, in an online course it is more a matter of scaffolding technology use. For example, students may be tasked with peer reviewing essays through ELI Review, which instructors can program by requiring feedback on multiple essays prior to completion of a self-reflection module. To help vary demands and optimize challenges, faculty can design peer review

---

dents to describe in words alongside the uploaded image, which itself becomes a lesson in writing analysis through image alternative text or captioning. A larger concern bearing further thought is the ethical issue of students' being held to accessibility standards with the content they create in online courses. Instructors, program administrators, and course designers would benefit from building assignments to recognize screen reading access.

activities so that students can pick from a variety of types of feedback and focus of critique they might give, such as identifying strengths, asking questions, using sentence starters, applying the rubric, etc. (see also Haswell, 2006 for instructional response roles). Ideally faculty provide examples of productive and constructive feedback before, during, and after peer review activities.

To support students *internalizing* engagement through self-regulation, UDL prompts instructors to provide student options for "promoting expectations that optimize motivation, facilitating personal coping skills and strategies, and developing self-assessment and reflection" (CAST 2018). One of the best ways to help students internalize engagement is by making it explicit in reflective and meta-reflective activities. A film studies professor might ask students to articulate their goals during the beginning of the course and then prompt them to regularly return and reflect upon both their goals and the course learning objectives, which increases students' awareness of their growth and learning. Asking students to connect what they are learning to other current activities (e.g., asking film students, "Now that you understand how shot composition and sound is used in film, how does this knowledge change how you watch audio-visual media?") prompts meta-awareness of their learning. Prompting students to regularly reflect upon their working and learning processes for the course will similarly help them identify what supports and what distracts from their success as a student. In an online course, students may be required to regularly complete labor logs in Google Sheets after completing major writing tasks; instructors can create student folders in Google Drive and share these labor logs with their online students prior to the start of the course. When students share what they are struggling with and how they are working to overcome their obstacles, students will know they are not alone because they can share ideas and resources with one another. This is particularly important when considering that online students often have little to no face-to-face interaction with the instructor and classmates. Although we may remind students that librarians and writing tutors are available and useful, nothing validates those resources like the instructor's and/or another student's positive endorsement. And, in the name of giving students choice and fostering access, students should be able to develop and represent their reflections in a variety of modes and media.

Representation

UDL **Representation** guidelines ask that instructors provide *accessible* student options for "perception, language and symbols, and comprehension" (CAST 2018). Instructors can provide options for perception by "offering ways of customizing the display of information," as well as offering alternatives for auditory and visual information (CAST 2018). Providing accessible content is a cornerstone of UDL and can be achieved in many ways, including captioned videos, recorded lesson screencasts, embedding alternative image text for screen readers, and adding the ability to decrease and increase font size in learning management system screens (in whole windows as well as in windows embedded into the platform). Online faculty can help facilitate accessible representation in multiple ways. First, they can be sure to provide optional instructional materials to students that demonstrate how to access captions in and control playback speed of videos, locate and read alternative text for images and tables, change font size, and take advantage of any text-to-speech applications available by the institution and/or applications being used. Second, faculty can be sure to internalize basic accessibility formatting and options as they design course instructional materials and assignment prompts. For example, all instructional material and assignment prompts should use heading functions instead of bolding text, as well as provide alternative text for images and tables (these are now the required accessibility formatting options in the 2018 sixth edition of the Quality Matters rubric). However, faculty should also start to get in the habit of providing audio and video alternatives to materials. After all, in online courses, it may not be immediately obvious which students have access needs, and online students need to be reminded that disability resources apply not just to face-to-face courses, but online as well. For example, faculty could use something like VoiceThread to produce a video introduction and overlay to an assignment prompt while also allowing online students the opportunity to ask questions about the assignment using the same technology. Disability resource centers may provide support in the form of access consultants who can work with instructors to ensure that their courses can be accessed in a variety of ways, as well as advise instructors on ways of improving pedagogical techniques for a diverse set of audiences.

Instructors can *build in* options for language and symbols by "clarifying vocabulary and symbols, clarifying syntax and structure, supporting decoding of text, mathematical notation and symbols, promoting understanding across languages, and illustrating through multiple media" (CAST 2018). Writing instructors who have instructed students in multimodal composing practices have already started building in representational options for students. In an argument-based writing course, students might be asked to reframe an essay explaining solutions to an ongoing problem by reproducing those solutions into a remediated form, such as a slide deck, a tutorial, or a website. Students could be asked to think carefully about their design choices based on the audience of the end-product, then walk through each step of the redesign process as a means of reflecting on the genre of their choice. Online spaces necessitate making instructions very clear, perhaps more so than face-to-face classrooms where students can engage teachers in an immediate give-and-take for clarification. As such, it is a good rule of thumb to break down major projects into modules and perhaps sub-modules, activities, or steps, and then instruct students to closely follow them as one might follow the steps to an IKEA instruction manual. UDL and Quality Matters frameworks both emphasize backward design, and we have found that when faculty envision the final project and walk it backward, step by step, students are more able to follow along without an endless string of emails back and forth seeking clarifications.

Thinking about UDL in terms of genre and modality also helps students *internalize* representations of knowledge, by helping students comprehend what they are supposedly learning in class. Instructors can provide options for comprehension by "activating or supplying background knowledge; highlighting patterns, critical features, big ideas, and relationships; guiding information processing and visualization; and maximizing transfer and generation" (CAST 2018). What better way to help technical and professional communication students to internalize the need for accessible representations of knowledge than to prompt them to produce accessible texts. Instead of just asking professional writing students to develop a website, we can provide instructions on accessibility and accessibility testing websites and require students to test and revise their own websites accordingly. Similarly, we can prompt technical writing students to visualize data with tables and charts, and then take the assignment further by having students provide alternative text for the table and visual. Teaching accessible communication practices is germane to technical and professional communication instruction and can further students' skills for document and multimedia design. Designing and teaching courses that ask students to account for accessibility in their own text development processes and products will help instructors to continue revising online courses to do the same. The *representation* area of UDL should not be difficult to master for instructors of English, since on some level, the study of and instruction on representation is what we do.

ACTION AND EXPRESSION

Learners navigate learning environments in different ways, so the way that interaction occurs must be carefully considered. No one means of **action or expression** will be optimal for all learners: some users may be more impacted by physical mobility issues, while others may be able to communicate better through modes of expression other than speaking. UDL action and expression guidelines ask that instructors provide student options for *accessing* content through "physical action, expression and communication, and executive function" (CAST 2018). To facilitate students' internalizing action and expression through access, instructors can provide options for physical action by "varying the methods for response and navigation" (CAST 2018). The UDL guideline of physical action involves interacting with accessible materials and tools. For example, in a literature class, students might be asked to draw a storyboard and present their findings to the class in a formal presentation. Rather than writing a traditional research paper, students could be asked to meticulously draw from existing field research and orally present these findings through videos/narrated presentations, using captions or including a script to ensure accessibility. Such an accommodation works for a variety of learner needs, and for some instructors, may even provide an alternative means to assess whether students have learned what they said they had learned throughout the course. In terms of optimizing access to tools and assistive technologies, material components such as alternate keyboard commands for mouse/trackpad action need to be considered, as well as ensuring that there is voice-to-text and expanded keyboard functionality. Again, in our program, we ask that instructors of online English classes know these options and provide instructions for all students to use these options so that everyone has the opportunity to explore which input mechanisms work best for them. Not all online tools are built for universal accessibility; however, while learning management systems (LMSs) have to meet minimum 504 standards, instructors or program administrators should routinely seek advice from disability resource centers prior to implementation so that they are aware of any changes to accommodation "best practices" or of any new technologies.

Instructors can provide alternative modalities for expression and communication by *building* content as well as assignments that have students "using multiple media for communication, using multiple tools for construction and composition, and building fluencies with graduated levels of support for practice and performance" (CAST 2018). Usage of multiple tools for construction allows for learners to match their abilities to the demands of the task. Consider introducing students to a variety of web-based applications that they might use in lower-stakes thinking and learning assignments. Try having students think and reflect using images or having them summarize and synthesize with word cloud generators (assessing word frequency) or mind-mapping applications. Students might visualize narratives using timeline or mapping applications or analyze texts using highlighters and mobile cameras (to take pictures of their work and upload it to the class) or annotating applications like Adobe Acrobat, Hyptothes.is, or PowerNotes. As important, instructors can model these alternatives in their lower-stakes activities like class announcements and comments upon student homework. The emphasis on *building* improved action and expression is the faculty member's commitment to continually experimenting with and adding options to their online course as it matures over time. At the same time, faculty should themselves be pedagogically trained to educate students about UDL principles, so that when we ask them to use different modalities, they too are working to make their materials accessible.

Instructors can also provide *internalization* options for executive functions of action and expression by "guiding appropriate goal-setting, supporting planning and strategy development, facilitating managing information and resources, and enhancing capacity for monitoring progress" (CAST 2018). Again, especially in relation to assigning multimodal projects in writing courses, writing faculty have been prompting students to internalize their metacognitive awareness through reflective writing for decades (e.g., multimodal composing: Ball and Charlton 2015; Council of Writing Program Administrators 2014; metacognitive awareness: Tinberg 2015, Yancey 1998). Prompting students to reflect upon their learning, both what and how they are learning, helps students internalize options and methods that better facilitate their own learning and communicating.

UDL is about making key learning structures a part of the system, rather than something that individual students with various abilities have to advocate for on their own. So when we think of course design as utilizing multiple means of engagement, representation, and action, we envision English pedagogies within this perspective, not only to accommodate a diverse array of bodies but to focus on access as a core value in pedagogical training. The path forward indicates that both individual classes (especially general education courses) and full degree programs are going online, and, after spring 2020 and COVID-19's impact on education, academic programs will be more likely to offer entire programs online since they have already developed individual online courses to continue educating during the pandemic. Accessibility of content is therefore key. Much of the scholarship surrounding online course design and accessibility is dedicated to the development of technology in ways that are meaningful for helping people with disabilities succeed. However, as demonstrated by the examples listed above, providing accessible alternatives takes time, creativity, and hard work. It is important to acknowledge the labor that goes into developing online courses in general, and even more so to developing *effective* courses that are continuously revised based on evolving technologies and learning research. We also use this moment to recognize some of our complacencies in face-to-face contexts and pedagogies: while enacting a UDL-informed curriculum may involve labor that faculty are accustomed to, it is essential to implement if we hope to make our courses more open and inclusive. We argue that the online environment sets an example of accessibility from which all English studies courses can be based.

Combatting Labor Issues: Predesigned Courses

Many English instructors are faced with teaching multiple classes, often with split preparation, and, increasingly, across different modes. For example, in many programs, it would not be uncommon for a teaching-focused instructor's workload per term to include two online asynchronous sections of composition, one hybrid section of technical writing meeting synchronously one day a week, and one section of literature or media production synchronously meeting two days a week. And many adjunct English instructors are teaching multiple sections across different campuses to earn a living wage. Designing and developing *effective* online classes certainly adds to that labor, which is often uncompensated work for adjunct and non-tenure-track faculty.

We recognize that implementing UDL can seem like even more labor for faculty who are often already teaching heavy loads and who may not be earning the salaries that research faculty are. However, one way that we have worked to combat that issue at the University of Arizona is through predesigned courses (PDCs). Rather than being spaces for mechanized or automatic instruction, we constructed our PDCs in ways that emphasize collaboration across instructors. This section summarizes research on the labor behind teaching and developing online, then suggests how PDCs can function as a method of professional development (training) for teachers who may have limited online teaching experience, or are just unable to develop online courses from the ground up due to time constraints.[2]

The research cited here suggests that labor issues persist across most English studies departments, which can make it seem even more difficult to engage with UDL practices if they require additional training or work. Bates, LaBrecque, and Fortner (2016) observed the time and energy associated with assessment across several online sections. While multiple semesters of prior preparation are required in order to become efficient, the authors found that actually assessing student submissions took much longer. Peruski and Mishra (2004) also acknowledged the labor and anxieties involved in teaching online but noted that this work may also "foreground some critical pedagogical dilemmas that good teachers need to think about" (48). We offer the suggestion that labor issues may be addressed through offering PDCs for instructors. Furthermore, we suggest that building UDL into PDCs allows for "good teaching" in terms of accessibility, which benefits both students and instructors.

---

2. For more on time: A survey (Freeman 2015) studying perceptions of time with online courses found that in general, more faculty begin course development earlier and fewer faculty wait as long to start online course development than their face-to-face courses. Freeman (2015) found that 53% of the respondents (n=165) developed over 90% of the course content themselves (Freeman 2015, para. 16) and that over 75% of the respondents develop at least half of the course content themselves (para. 17). One question asked respondents to indicate their level of agreement with the statement "it is more time consuming to develop an online course than a face-to-face course." Most respondents, 81%, agree with this statement (not including Neutral), with 43% choosing Strongly Agree (para. 20).

Research has also suggested that labor behind developing online courses should be rewarded with career advancement. Bussmann et al. (2017) argue that developing a quality online course is a significant commitment in time and effort and frequently requires learning new skills and pedagogical methods, yet this labor is unfortunately not counted toward promotion and tenure, despite the "academic effort in redesigning an existing online course to meet quality recognition standards [being] similar to the work of preparing a journal article, in terms of time, academic effort, intellectual effort, and the peer-review process" (7). The authors describe a survey across multiple disciplines at nineteen western universities in which "only 16% of the departments that completed the survey specifically include the development of a quality online course in their promotion and tenure documentation" (1). Acknowledging the labor behind online course development, Bussmann et al. (2017) suggest release time as a form of support (12), calling on administrators and promotion and tenure committee members to "understand the time, effort, and rigor required in developing quality online courses"; they also note that, increasingly, "ensuring quality in online courses is an accreditation issue. Thus, administrators and faculty need to understand the investment in online quality by the faculty, department, college, and institution" (12).

For the reasons described above, we are labor rights advocates for teachers (especially adjunct/contingent faculty and graduate students) and accessibility advocates for faculty, students, and staff. These are neither conflicting nor exclusive paradigms but rather work together to create a culture of inclusion within learning environments. The University of Arizona Writing Program is committed to accessibility through UDL and has been developing a set of suggested practices, including the recommended use of captioned videos, moving the accommodations statement up in the syllabus so that it becomes more pronounced (Wood and Madden 2013), and implementing a gender pronoun policy into foundations writing syllabi. It is important to place emphasis on accessibility when developing online curricula and equally important to address the issue of labor implicit in designing accessible courses. We argue that PDCs are one way of achieving this goal. Because of constraints from high teacher turnover (e.g., graduate students' graduating, adjunct faculty moving in and out of positions), PDCs provide scaffolding to new teachers so that UDL is built into course pedagogies from the ground up.

Popular phrases used to describe these types of courses have been "master" (e.g., Rice 2015), "template" (e.g., Brown and Ramasamy 2017), "canned" (e.g., Puzziferro and Shelton 2009), and predesigned (e.g., Keeton 2004). Independent of the name, some scholars in rhetoric and composition have negatively dismissed the use of digital templates (Arola 2010) and, specifically, PDCs (e.g., Cargile Cook 2005; O'Sullivan 1999). Rodrigo and Ramírez (2017) have recognized that much scholarship about the design and production of online courses emphasizes both a well-developed skill set (specifically instructional design) and a team model to distribute various types of expertise (content, instructional design, media and technology, etc.). In this chapter, we are referring to PDCs as online course shells that share a fully developed curriculum (both major assignment prompts and rubrics, as well as scaffolded learning activities) with multiple instructors. In our instance, instructors have full editing access to the course; however, we find that new online instructors usually only minimally adapt the PDC materials while more experienced online instructors enact significant changes to make the course curriculum their own.

We argue for a purposeful shift toward thinking about how PDCs can support online English programs with curriculum design, alignment, accessibility, professional development, and increased student engagement and retention. Common concerns about PDCs can be addressed by emphasizing the continuum between stability and flexibility that PDCs, and the programs that use them, negotiate between designers, instructors, and students. Knowledge of disability studies and UDL interrogates these approaches by inviting online course design stakeholders to openly and inclusively view their practices within their departments as well as the institution and field at large, especially for the sake of highlighting labor inequities. In the following section, we demonstrate how PDCs have helped us enact a UDL-centered pedagogy for our writing program at Arizona, and how other English departments might make use of a similar framework.

Benefits of Pre-Designed Courses

Why are PDCs helpful for use in online English studies programs? To begin answering this question, it is important to address the discipline of rhetoric and composition, as well as the materially inequitable conditions of labor surrounding the field. Hesse (2018) notes the growing number of adjunct and contingent faculty, especially in writing studies, arguing that "a unit's disciplinary lineage mean[s] less than other factors such as salaries and teaching loads" (289). Especially in the current political climate, departments are resigned to producing returns on investment to the neoliberal university in the name of policy and profit, often to the detriment of intrinsic intellectual value, thereby reducing the role of rhetoric and composition to pedagogical value. At many institutions, this shift leads to the ongoing devaluation of instruction. Since adjunct and contingent lines are not, and may never be in a position to become converted into tenure-eligible positions, the next step may just be promoting the kinds of research that brings in more income in the form of students. Yet it is of paramount importance that instructors are provided with an ethically responsible environment where they can help students succeed while living in hospitable conditions.

It is worth noting the time investment into long-term course development planning. Results from a pilot study of a philanthropic course (Shaker, Nathan, and Dale 2014) included separate results from hybrid vs. online. Overall implications suggest that online instructors benefit from pre-course orientations, highly detailed syllabuses-as-course-roadmap, early and often student/faculty interaction, scaffolding of complicated tasks for student success, and passing on the knowledge that online learning will develop new skills (17–18). These results reinforce what is already known about online study, which is that it takes work, can be challenging, and requires communication not only between faculty and students but also across faculty lines as well. Key to this study, however, is the emphasis on collaboration with course developers, who sat down with the instructors in a similar vein to the research conducted by Shaver (2017). Instructional designers can help faculty with revising their courses and pedagogies, especially in terms of carrying forward best practices, anticipating and acting upon the knowledge of student (and instructor) difficulties, and overall assessment of improvement efforts. A continuum between stability and flexibility becomes negotiated between designers, instructors, students, and administrators as a result of long-term collaborative efforts during online course development.

PDCs may allow for greater collaboration between administrators and instructional designers. At the University of Arizona, offices such as the Office of Instruction and Assessment (at many institutions referred to as Centers for Teaching and Learning) and the Office of Digital Learning work with individual instructors to ensure that these courses align with programmatic goals and objectives. However, in the case of the Writing Program, they work with writing program administrators to ensure that predesigned course content is curricularly sound and pedagogically accessible. The PDCs undergo continuous rounds of revision prompted by both quick, surface-level editing suggestions as well as well-planned curricular revisions, all prompted by and planned with instructors using the PDCs. The continuingly improved PDCs are efficiently shared amongst several instructors teaching the same course. The continuous implementation of Universal Design for Learning in these efforts is a crucial first step toward designing accessible learning environments while maintaining a culture of inclusion for both faculty and students.

    The case can be made that predesigned courses become part of that environment of equitable conditions, whereby instructors, administrators, instructional designers, and program/department heads work together as part of a coalition. From this subset of stakeholders, instructional designers play one of the most important roles at the base level of PDC construction. At the University of Arizona, writing program administrators collaborate with instructional designers to ensure that PDCs are being built from the ground up to align with a university-wide online education initiative (Arizona Online) while at the same time meeting quality standards (using the Quality Matters rubric).

    Good instruction takes time and resources; this is particularly true for online course design. Shaver (2017) discusses the need for ongoing revisions as being central to the online course development process, proposing that faculty co-design common courses while taking on the time-consuming work of learning about online pedagogical practices. The authors found that "instructors unaccustomed to online delivery modes often [found] the creation of an online course long, difficult, and frustrating" (439); therefore, it was essential to give instructors adequate time to share their experiences in an effort to defuse resistance. To facilitate co-designed courses, instructional designers were brought in to "ponder instructor approaches . . . review learning outcomes . . . consider assessment and learning activities . . . share syllabus template and contemplate textbook selection" (440). In other words, IDs help them do what they're already good at doing as instructors, but in a way which would facilitate intersections of good teaching through a design perspective.

    Teacher training is important for helping instructors understand how online teaching and learning, as well as PDCs work. Predesigned courses can be helpful for taking out a lot of the work behind basic course development so that instructors can focus more on teaching the content online, especially the first time, as opposed to creation at the most fundamental levels. But the process of asking teachers to just use a PDC in their courses without adequate training is complex. Every learning management system (LMS) works differently, and for instructors to learn how to implement a PDC into their own teaching takes labor. Online administrators can make using PDCs easier for instructors by producing support mechanisms, such as detailed screencast videos and step-by-step written instructions on how to work with the LMS and PDC.

In our program, PDCs are fully built course shells that become copied over into an instructor's workspace. They are generally not one-size-fits-all, but instead include customizable elements. For example, a module that is built around a major writing project would need to incorporate assignment sheets and peer review mechanisms. Administrators share example assignment sheets as view-only Google Doc files. These files, already built using accessible fonts, provide places for instructors to customize specific elements, such as course total percentages, areas to incorporate sub-topic choices, and rubric options. These files are then shared with students as comment-only files, so that students could ask questions and discuss topics directly within the instructor's adapted document.

By consciously having to adopt curriculum designed by others and then having to adapt it to their own curricular values prior to teaching, instructors working with PDCs must consciously ask questions about why and how they teach the way they do. Many new online instructors have told us that they have also incorporated ideas they learned from the PDCs into their face-to-face pedagogies, demonstrating a sort of backward transfer where the sort of pedagogical rethinking and revision work that online spaces require then feeds back into the face-to-face classroom.

Refutations

While some instructors may feel PDCs impinge on academic/instructional freedom, if done correctly and in collaboration with faculty, we believe that program directors can minimize this concern. Of course, this issue concerns not only PDCs: many multi-section survey courses that are part of general education curricula are designed around specific parameters concerning topics and logistics needed to meet department and college requirements. For instance, an undergraduate Shakespeare survey curriculum may be required to cover specific tragedies, comedies, and histories and require students to write three research papers. In other words, institutionally mandated curriculum is not new to either face-to-face or online courses; the building of a curriculum is always a first step in limiting what can and cannot be taught.

More often than not, arguments in favor of institutionally mandated curricula cite the need for aligning student learning outcomes in the name of institutional assessment and accreditation. Predesigned courses have the advantage of having articulation requirements built directly into the course shell so that instructors can focus more on teaching concepts and engaging students. *Effective* PDCs, emphasizing UDL guidelines, are built with flexibility in mind for both faculty and students. Faculty and students should be able to adapt PDCs to better improve teaching and learning for all involved. Administrative teams supporting PDCs should be able to help by providing suggestions and options for adaptation.

Finally, people might consider predesigned courses a solution for regularly offered courses like required writing courses or popular general education classes. In fact, any course that is offered repeatedly, even if only over time, represents a type of a predesigned course. Most individual faculty who design and teach online courses that are likely to be taught only by them, work with instructional designers to build the first version. Those same faculty usually revise the predesigned course (the course shell designed by previous versions of themselves) before each new course offering. By reframing *their* course shell as a predesigned course, individual faculty revise in a more inclusive and systematic way, including suggestions from previous students, instructional designers, even reflections from earlier versions of themselves.

Despite the many possibilities for innovation and academic freedom, we do have some instructors at the University of Arizona who resist teaching the PDCs. However, in most cases, once they have taught the online course for the first time, they realize that the PDC off-loaded numerous hours of course design and allowed them to more quickly and efficiently focus on the projects and activities they want students to engage in as part of the course. To also help mitigate faculty concerns, we have started designing clearly articulated policies about what changes new-to-online and experienced online faculty can and cannot make to the PDCs. Providing course design feedback loops and demonstrating when and how they are implemented in PDC revisions also alleviates some instructor's concerns and empowers their own curricular design abilities.

Conclusion

The 2020 pandemic demonstrated that students and faculty alike suffer when online instruction is unplanned. What we've learned at the University of Arizona over the last six years is that online teaching and learning are complex, requiring critically executed course designs that emphasize Universal Design for Learning. How unprepared many faculty were was emphasized in Spring 2020 when many of our colleagues who had either not previously taught online and/or had not designed their own online courses realized how much time and energy it takes to build an online course, let alone an accessible one. Numerous people mentioned how having taught a Pre-Designed Course (PDC) helped them with their transition to emergency remote instruction.

We believe that PDCs offer one method for building accessible course designs that less experienced online instructors can adapt as they grow more comfortable with online learning. We suggest that more English departments consider developing PDCs as scaffolds for faculty, particularly adjunct/part-time faculty and graduate teaching assistants, who are often underpaid and under-resourced. Doing so supports instructors and students with a better teaching and learning experience. Whereas most teachers have a long history of unofficially sharing curriculum, hopefully the neoteric realization that online course design requires intense labor will allow a discipline that has traditionally promoted and celebrated autonomous instruction to acknowledge the productive worth of shared curricula, particularly PDCs.

References

Amazon. n.d. "Share Notes & Highlights." Accessed September 4, 2019. https://www.amazon.in/gp/help/customer/display.html?nodeId=201242030.

Arola, Kristin L. 2010. "The Design of Web 2.0: The Rise of the Template, The Fall of Design." *Computers and Composition* 27 (1) 4–14. http://doi.org/10.1016/j.compcom.2009.11.004.

Babcock, Rebecca Day. 2008. "Tutoring Deaf College Students in the Writing Center." In *Disability and the Teaching of Writing: A Critical Sourcebook*, edited by Cynthia Lewiecki-Wilson, Brenda Jo Brueggemann, and Jay Dolmage, 28–39. Boston: Bedford/St. Martin's.

Baldwin, Sally J., Yu-Hui Ching, and Norm Friesen. 2018. "Online Course Design and Development Among College and University Instructors: An Analysis Using Grounded Theory." *Online Learning* 22, no. 2, 157–71. http://doi.org/10.24059/olj.v22i2.1212.

Ball, Cheryl E., and Colin Charlton. "All Writing is Multimodal." In *Naming What We Know: Threshold Concepts of Writing Studies*, edited by Linda Adler-Kassner and Elizabeth Wardle, 42–43. Logan: Utah State University Press.

Bates, Rodger, Bryan LaBrecque, and Emily Fortner. 2016. "Teaching Multiple Online Sections/Courses: Tactics and Techniques." *Online Journal of Distance Learning Administration* 19 (3): 1–8. https://www.westga.edu/~distance/ojdla/fall193/bates_labrecque_fortner193.html.

Brown, Victoria, and Rangasamy Ramasamy. 2017. "Changing Faculty Perspective of Distance Learning Through Support." *Distance Learning* 14 (3): 29–35.

Bussmann, Susan, Sandra R. Johnson, Richard Oliver, Kerry Forsythe, Miley Grandjean, Michelle Lebsock, and Tyler Luster. 2017. "On the Recognition of Quality Online Course Design in Promotion and Tenure: A Survey of Higher Ed Institutions in the Western United States." *Online Journal of Distance Learning Administration* 20 (1): 1–14. https://www.westga.edu/~distance/ojdla/spring201/bussmann_johnson%20_oliver_forsythe_grandjean_lebsock_luster201.html.

Cargile Cook, Kelli. 2005. "An Argument for Pedagogy-driven Online Education." In *Online Education Global Questions, Local Answers*, edited by Kelli Cargile Cook and Keith Grant-Davie, 49–66. Amityville, NY: Baywood Pub.

CAST (Center for Applied Special Technology). 2018. *Universal Design for Learning Guidelines (version 2.2)*. http://udlguidelines.cast.org.

Council of Writing Program Administrators. 2014. "Outcomes Statement for First-Year Composition (3.0), Approved July 17, 2014." Council of Writing Program Administrators. http://wpacouncil.org/aws/CWPA/pt/sp/statements.

Doherty, Heather. 2016. "Student Says Closed Captions, Transcripts Aid Learning, Oregon State Study Finds." *Oregon State University: Ecampus News*, October 31, 2016. https://ecampus.oregonstate.edu/news/2016/closed-captions/.

Dolmage, Jay. 2008. "Mapping Composition: Inviting Disability in the Front Door." In *Disability and the Teaching of Writing: A Critical Sourcebook*, edited by Cynthia Lewiecki-Wilson, Brenda Jo Brueggemann, and Jay Dolmage, 14–27. Boston: Bedford/St. Martin's.

Dolmage, Jay. 2017. *Academic Ableism: Disability and Higher Education*. Ann Arbor: University of Michigan Press.

Freeman, Lee A. 2015. "Instructor Time Requirements to Develop and Teach Online Courses." *Online Journal of Distance Learning Administration* 18 (1). https://www.westga.edu/~distance/ojdla/spring181/freeman181.html.

Haswell, Richard H. 2006, Nov. 9. "The Complexities of Responding to Student Writing; Or, Looking for Shortcuts via the Road of Excess." *Across the Disciplines*. https://wac.colostate.edu/docs/atd/articles/haswell2006.pdf.

Hesse, Douglas. 2018. "Redefining Disciplinarity in the Context of Higher Education." In *Composition, Rhetoric, and Disciplinarity*, edited by Rita

Malenczyk, Susan Miller-Cochrane, Elizabeth Wardle, and Kathleen Blake Yancey, 287–302. Logan, UT: Utah State UP.
Jaggars, Shanna. 2011. "Online Learning: Does It Help Low-Income and Underprepared Students?" *Community College Research Center Brief* 52, 1–4. https://files.eric.ed.gov/fulltext/ED517933.pdf.
Johnson-Curiskis, Nanette. 2006. "Online Course Planning." *Journal of Online Learning and Teaching* 2, (1): 42–48. http://jolt.merlot.org/05014b.htm.
Keeton, Morris T. T. 2004. "Best Online Instructional Practices: Report of Phase I of an Ongoing Study." *Journal of Asynchronous Learning Network* 8, (2): 75–100. http://dx.doi.org/10.24059/olj.v8i2.1829.
Lehman, Rosemary M., and Simone C. O. Conceição. 2014. *Motivating and Retaining Online Students Research-based Strategies That Work*. San Francisco, CA: Jossey-Bass.
Levy, Yair. 2007. "Comparing Dropouts and Persistence in E-Learning Courses." *Computers and Education* 48 (2) 185–204. https://doi.org/10.1016/j.compedu.2004.12.004.
Magda, Andrew J., Russell Poulin, David L. Clinefelter. 2015. *Recruiting, Orienting, & Supporting Online Adjunct Faculty: A Survey of Practices*. Louisville, KY: The Learning House. https://www.learninghouse.com/knowledge-center/research-reports/adjunct2015-report/#.
Moore, Michael G., and Greg Kearsley. 1996. *Distance Education: A Systems View*. Belmont, CA: Wadsworth.
Novak, Katie, and Tom Thibodeau. 2016. *UDL in the Cloud! How to Design and Deliver Online Education Using Universal Design for Learning*. Wakefield, MA: CAST.
Onodipe, Grace, M. Femi Ayadi, and Rolando Marquez. 2016. "The Efficient Design of an Online Course: Principles of Economics." *Journal of Economics and Economic Education Research* 17, (1): 39–51. https://www.abacademies.org/articles/jeeervol17no12016.pdf.
O'Sullivan, Mary F. 1999. "Worlds within Which We Teach: Issues for Designing World Wide Web Course Material." *Technical Communication Quarterly* 8, (1): 61–72. http://doi.org/10.1080/10572259909364649.
Perry, Beth, Jeanette Boman, W. Dean Care, Margaret Edwards, and Caroline Park. 2008. "Why Do Students Withdraw from Online Graduate Nursing and Health Studies Education?" *Journal of Educators Online* 5, (1). https://files.eric.ed.gov/fulltext/EJ904043.pdf.
Peruski, Lisa, and Punya Mishra. 2004. "Webs of Activity in Online Course Design and Teaching." *ALT-J* 12 (1): 37–49. https://doi.org/10.1080/0968776042000211520.
Puzziferro, Maria, and Kaye Shelton. 2009. "Challenging Our Assumptions About Online Learning: A Vision for the Next Generation of Online Higher Education." *Distance Learning* 6, (4) 9–20. http://ezproxy.library.arizona.edu/login?url=https://search-proquest-com.ezproxy2.library.arizona.edu/docview/230731994?accountid=8360.

Quality Matters. 2018. *Specific Review Standards from the QM Higher Education Rubric, Sixth Edition.* https://www.qualitymatters.org/sites/default/files/PDFs/StandardsfromtheQMHigherEducationRubric.pdf.

Rice, Rich. 2015. "Faculty professionalization for OWI." In *Foundational Practices of Online Writing Instruction*, edited by Beth L Hewett and Kevin Eric Depew, 389–410. Anderson: Parlor Press; Fort Collins, CO: WAC Clearinghouse. https://wac.colostate.edu/books/perspectives/owi/

Rodrigo, Rochelle, and Cristina D. Ramirez. 2017. "Balancing Institutional Demands with Effective Practice: A Lesson in Curricular and Professional Development." *Technical Communication Quarterly* 26 (3): 314–28. http://doi.org/10.1080/10572252.2017.1339529.

Rose, David H., and Anne Meyer. 2006. *A Practical Reader in Universal Design for Learning.* Cambridge, MA: Harvard Education Press.

Shaker, Genevieve G., Sarah K. Nathan, and Elizabeth J. Dale. 2014. "Sequential Online Course Redesign: When 'It Just Takes Time' Works No Longer." *To Improve the Academy: A Journal of Educational Development* 33 (2): 220–38. https://doi.org/10.1002/tia2.20013.

Shaver, Denise. 2017. "The Added Value of Conducting Learning Design Meeting to the Online Course Development Process." *TechTrends: Linking Research and Practice to Improve Learning* 61 (5): 438–43. http://dx.doi.org.ezproxy1.library.arizona.edu/10.1007/s11528-017-0205-1

Tinberg, Howard. "Metacognition is Not Cognition." In *Naming What We Know: Threshold Concepts of Writing Studies*, edited by Linda Adler-Kassner and Elizabeth Wardle, 75–77. Logan: Utah State University Press.

University of Arizona. 2018. "Writing Program Goals and Student Learning Outcomes (SLOs): First-Year Writing Courses." University of Arizona. https://goo.gl/z8t98M

Vidali, Amy. 2008. "Discourse of Disability and Basic Writing." In *Disability and the Teaching of Writing: A Critical Sourcebook*, edited by Cynthia Lewiecki-Wilson, Brenda Jo Brueggemann, and Jay Dolmage, 40–55. Boston: Bedford/St. Martin's.

Womack, Anne-Marie. 2017. "Teaching Is Accommodation: Universally Designing Composition Classrooms and Syllabi." *College Composition and Communication* 68 (3): 494–525. http://www.ncte.org/library/NCTEFiles/Resources/Journals/CCC/0683-feb2017/CCCC0683Teaching.pdf.

Wood, Tara, and Shannon Madden. 2013. "Suggested Practices for Syllabus Accessibility Statements." PraxisWiki. *Kairos: Rhetoric, Technology, and Pedagogy* 18 (1). http://kairos.technorhetoric.net/praxis/tiki-index.php?page=Suggested_Practices_for_Syllabus_Accessibility_Statements.

Xu, Haixiz, and Libby V. Morris. 2007. "Collaborative Course Development for Online Courses." *Innovative Higher Education* 32 (1): 35–47. https://doi.org/10.1007/s10755–006–9033–5.

Yancey, Kathleen. 1998. *Reflection in the Writing Classroom.* Logan: Utah State Press.

15 Performing Identities in Cyberspace: Imagining the Online Multicultural Learning Community

Richard C. Taylor

The capstone project committee, comprised of members of the Multicultural and Transnational Literatures concentration in our English department, is gathered to assess a student's work and to pose relevant questions. The student teaches in a community college near St. Louis. She has designed a multiethnic literature unit for one of the core courses in English that she regularly teaches. She's written a critical introduction contextualizing the unit; her focus is on introducing African American and African diaspora literatures to her students. Her work includes a theoretical framework, a highly detailed syllabus, and lesson plans.

The committee is gathered separately in a classroom, connected to the student via speakerphone. Faculty members ask her about the choices she's made in her curriculum and make suggestions about new material and strategies for presenting it. Then the subject turns to a shattering event in her own community: the shooting of Michael Brown, Jr. by a police officer in Ferguson, Missouri on August 9, 2014 and the explosive aftermath. We talk about the Black Lives Matter movement. It is a grim—but gripping—background for our pedagogical work.

There has always been some suspicion about the distant education programs in my department. Much of the work is invisible, unrecognized, unrewarded. But it presents an opportunity to be relevant—which is no small matter for some of us in the liberal arts—and to embody and embrace a worldwide scholarly community. Part of the work involves maximizing the reach of the program while minimizing the distance among the participants and instructors. Our faculty, by and large, teaches teachers, and so we have an opportunity to introduce new concepts and theories, new approaches, and a broadly diverse set of texts and authors. We have witnessed only a tiny fraction of what we refer to as our outreach, but we have worked with professionals all over the globe, even though our most immediate impact is with those in our home state—partly a product of the painfully exorbitant cost of out-of-state tuition. Those professionals, in turn, fitted with dozens of new texts and approaches, as well as the energy that comes with a sense of renewed mission, teach others in turn.

For participating faculty members, the price of admission to distance education is an imaginative leap. Instructors have to create or represent themselves digitally—and in my case largely through the exchange of words—and believe in the reality of this human connection. We have to be real for our students, and they have to be real to us. Effective distance education instructors are a positive and unique presence. Weak ones remain invisible: bureaucratic managers who do little more than upload prerecorded content and assign grades. If I am right that distance education will be an enduring part of students' university experiences, and not simply an efficient system of content delivery, then instructors have an obligation to imagine and create a practice motivated by the kinds of impulses that led most of us into a teaching career in the first place: a pedagogy opposed to the infamous "banking system" and authoritarianism, one that is built on a fundamental belief in collaborative learning, the excitement of discovery, and the creative power of our online communities.

The committee puts our MA candidate on hold to discuss her fate. She'd acquitted herself admirably, and we return to our phone conference with the good news. The next step is hers as she advocates for curricular diversity and the value of multiethnic literatures in her teaching career and continues to be an engaged member of the community where she lives and works. The capstone "professional project," after some revisions requested by committee members, usually becomes a successful calling card for our program and for the instructor as she works for change in her own institution or applies what she's learned to a new professional situation.

"The Roar of The Greasepaint"

For those instructors trained in conventional classroom environments and who are either unfamiliar with distance education or actively resistant, online learning is powerfully stigmatized by some rather unfortunate historical forebears (see, for example, http://www.godistancelearning.com/history-of-distance-learning.html). A fair amount of snake oil has been sold in the name of remote education, from the spate of correspondence courses developed in the immediate aftermath of World War II to promise returning soldiers careers in refrigerator repair and the like, to the grotesque hokum of Trump University. I myself bought into one such scheme offered by a muscle-bound superhero named Charles Atlas, who promised I would henceforth never again have sand thrown in my face. The illegitimacy associated with this sort of scheme has attached itself in the public consciousness to admirable efforts such as online general education development programs, as well as the proliferating massive for-profit universities, some of which are perceived as degree mills. On the other hand, most instructors of literature, however sentimentally attached to the smell of old books and the rustle and squeak of desks and chairs, can't ignore the value and reach of TED Talks and online archives and powerful new literacies and textualities easily accessible to our students and colleagues. The internet has irretrievably digitized education, and those who try to ignore it (if that's even possible for instructors of English) fail their students and their disciplines. Yet I'm vividly aware of the continuing resistance to moving one's teaching practice partly or entirely online.

My own entrance into distance education teaching was a matter of being shoved onstage, rather than carefully planning an audition and a systematic rehearsal process. It was the product of departmental strife of the sort that most English departments experienced in the 1990s and beyond, and I carried with me into this new arena a nagging suspicion that I had somehow sold out, betrayed my own educational roots, and abandoned what had been the most joyous aspect of my professional life: the personal interaction with students and the daily drama of the classroom. At the risk of sounding immodest, I had developed a bit of a following as a face-to-face classroom teacher, and the pain of sacrificing reputation paralleled my own sense of loss as my skills as an archival scholar—what seemed to some an uncanny ability to find obscure bits of information and seek answers in the dusty folds of parchment—became less and less relevant, increasingly obsolete. (I also had near secretarial speed and accuracy on my old Underwood typewriter, if any prospective employers are interested!)

This personal history serves as a caution about the risk of retroactive rationalizing. Because of a move to distance education I felt compelled to make, I'm bound to justify it to myself. In considering this transition, I find myself almost daily providing answers to the question, "what's so great about teaching literature online?" But a less frequent corollary, "what's so great about teaching literature face-to-face," also needs to be called into question. What are they holding onto so passionately—my colleagues who teach Shakespeare and Faulkner and Whitman and the like?

"Students learn more in the face-to-face environment." Arguments based on assessment of student learning are rendered moot, at least at this point, by wildly inconsistent data. Part of the problem, especially in the field of literature, is that online instruction is still in its early stages of development and improvement. The arguments for the superiority of face-to-face instruction typically focus on issues of community and engagement and rely on selective reports of student opinion, rather than on student learning data (see, for example Arleen R. Bejerano's comparative essay "Face-to-face or online instruction: Face-to-face is better") which repeats all the clichés without actual evidence, and which comes to a conclusion without context. Most of the comparative studies seem to be based on selective case studies rather than student learning data, which varies widely depending on the course, institution, instructors, students, and so forth. As Barbara Slater Stern notes, "It appears that when the literature comparing online and traditional courses is reviewed, the researcher can make a case for either one or both being more or equally effective, depending on the variables used."

I'll return to my own transitional experience and the initial concerns about what my students and I might be sacrificing. Critics make the case that distance education is a matter of convenience, but of course there are aspects of the conventional classroom that are practically convenient as well. A change in a due date, correction of a misunderstanding, the reward of an approving smile or head nod—these are conventional conveniences not as quickly replicable online. Surely, convenience doesn't account for the allure of traditional instruction, though.

The romance of teaching literature face-to-face may have something to do with performance: the public reenactment of poems and bits of prose instantaneously shared by all. How will I possibly replicate online the experience of my reading Housman's "Loveliest of Trees" to the students and having them struggle with the riddle of the speaker's age? How can I deny them my talent for "doing the police in different voices" when I'm acting out a bit of Dickens or Eliot? One of the requirements of teaching, of course, is the love of one's own voice, but distance education instructors make podcasts for such purposes, and they lack only the inevitable student applause that comes at the end of their performances! These interactions can be just as powerful in the imagined classroom of the internet and need not be "impersonal" or "remote." Intimacy is a creature of the imagination as much as it is a physical, proximal response. Staffed by those of us who are wordsmiths (and which of us aren't?), distance education classrooms can be sites of intense intimacy and a kind of protection not afforded by face-to-face encounters. They can be both safe zones and contact zones, depending on the judgment and curricular needs of the learning community.

Another aspect of face-to-face instruction that, I think, is less easy to dispense with is that of "taking the measure" of a classroom—of instantaneous student feedback. In the distance education classroom, such feedback is usually asynchronous, piecemeal. When students are confused or bored in the traditional classroom, engaged instructors know it quickly. Actors are bound by their scripts and blocking and the need to coordinate with their fellow performers, and yet they respond instantaneously to audience reaction, which is why no two live performances are ever the same and actors can survive long runs without the sense that they have become automatons.

The sad truth is that distance education instructors, like F2F instructors, can let themselves become automatons, dispensers of canned lectures, PowerPoints, lessons stripped of all spontaneity and inventiveness. This phenomenon reminds us again of the problem with anecdotal studies of student learning: I suspect few students really enjoy learning from robots; they don't develop the kind of admiration that leads to the life-changing inspirations that teachers can provide. They don't make the necessary transference between appreciation for a teacher and subject to dedication to a discipline that has been an essential part of the process of education. Again, the best distance education instructors not only affect spontaneity, but resist repeating themselves, force themselves to invent every lesson, every class, and every semester. For many instructors, this mentoring is the *sine qua non* of their professional identities, and I am certain that it can happen with equal power and effectiveness in both kinds of institutional configurations.

As part of my own transition, I worried about whether I would still be able to reach the proverbial student in the back of the classroom, the one who represented the most enticing challenge, the resistant student hardest to reach. I imagined this student lacking the self-discipline to engage regularly and actively in the online environment, in the absence of the physical presence of the instructor (and I suppose the threat of being "called on" and embarrassed) in the conventional classroom. To be honest, though, I'm not sure how many of these students I was able to reach, and classroom discussions were normally dominated by a handful of students who were fearless public speakers and heedless of the risks of humiliation that I'm sure have quieted many otherwise attentive and committed students.

In the well-run distance education classroom, there is no silent student in the back. Everyone must and does participate. Every answer can be researched, reconsidered, and revised in the absence of the pressure to perform instantaneously, with the instructor and classmates looking on. In their posts and in their formal papers, students have a degree of control in the articulation of their identities, a partial anonymity subject to revision and often gradual revelation. Students—and instructors alike—can often create a sort of scholarly avatar, a representation of self that is composed of thought and word rather than image. Some of the "students in the back of the room" find this condition exhilarating, liberating—and it exacts accountability from every member of the learning community.

The theatricality of the physical classroom—the adrenaline it invokes, the tactile excitement and immediacy of the experience, the aggregation of bodies in space—can be joyous. It is also a theatre of control: conventionally linear, exposed, mastered by the presence of instructors, no matter how "student-centered" their pedagogies. The instructor is almost always physically separated from the learning community. The distance education environment, designed mostly by those trying to replicate in cyberspace the well-rehearsed formats that instructors expect, is also a panopticon, a mechanism for control and order. One could argue the practical necessity for the authority figure and the maintenance of control: due dates, grades and other rewards/punishments, and all the apparatus of institutional structure. I would argue, though, that distance education—still in its infancy—affords the opportunity for the radical reinvention of learning communities, a process already underway, but one that has also been stunted by a kind of habitual laziness and conformity by institutions still largely governed by the practices and ethos of the late nineteenth century. My own desire is for a distance education founded in liberatory practices, joy, community, and a shared commitment to social justice. The objection that distance education is "cold, impersonal, distanced, remote" represents an imaginative failure, one that is being overcome by our best practitioners and the communities they help create.

Staging a Revolution

In my own department, the embrace or rejection of distance education marks a sharp delineation that runs roughly parallel to divisions between those professors of literature whose work conforms to the traditionally recognized canon and to those whose professional identity was formed around postcolonial theory and multiethnic literatures. The latter group complained of marginalization and even open hostility and finally discovered in distance education an opportunity for a degree of independence and autonomy. With new programs in distance education formulated around new conceptions of literature and theory, instructors discovered a student audience thrilled to hear voices that had been excluded and marginalized and ready to embrace the access to higher education life circumstances had denied them.

Institutional resistance to the transition (full or partial) to new pedagogical media and newly emerging literatures is understandable. Just as the institution is wedded to historical practices, even abusive ones such as grading, by virtue of its own investments and the momentum of habit, it has made an enormous investment in the status quo in terms of the conservation and deployment of faculty resources. Each tenure track faculty hire represents, potentially, a thirty-year commitment of an area of specialization and a disciplinary perspective. Our literature faculty is still largely a product of the dominant literary historical templates of the mid-twentieth century: periodization and the celebration of British and American nationalism. The tenure process solidifies these commitments, so any kind of dramatic reconceptualization of the disciplinary shape of the department is potentially devastating. As I review our undergraduates' capstone writing portfolios, they look mostly indistinguishable from those produced in the 1950s, except that they are computer-generated. There is the essay on *Hamlet*, the essay on the Great Vowel Shift, and the explication of a Yeats poem. Those of us teaching African diaspora literature or Latinx children's literature look on in dismay.

I am convinced that the resistance to distance education at my own institution was the result of a happy misunderstanding. Administrators got wind of the massively attended online courses offered early in the advent of distance education and smelled dollars and student credit hours. distance education, they imagined, would be a way to overcome declining enrollments and ensure budgetary freedom. So, a remarkable amount of resources was dedicated to distance education start-up activities, inaugurated in my department by professors of technical and professional communication (those of us in multiethnic literature owe them an enormous debt). Those first experiments in distance education revealed that there were tremendous pedagogical advantages to having these programs: improved graduation rates for students who had left the university and were unable to move back to campus, expansion of our student population outside of our region, the prestige that came with being a "wired campus," and so on. But to their horror they also discovered that successful distance education instruction depended on controlling class size, and so in many cases the distance education classes had lower enrollment caps than did F2F classes. But by that point, the commitment had been made, reputations were at stake, a great deal of money and resources had been expended, and there was no turning back.

Coinciding with this development—another accident of sorts—was the increasing ideological tension in our department around the "canon debate" and related issues (the emergence of new literary theories and challenges to the "New Criticism" of the post-World War II era, for example). distance education seemed to provide a separate camp for the malcontents and disturbers of the peace. While the adherents to traditional literature had the votes to suppress curricular developments in "marginal" fields, they were sufficiently convinced that multiethnic literatures and distance education represented passing fads (as they advised our students) and no real threats to their centrality in the department. So our concentration in multicultural and transnational literatures was born. This fusion of distance education and the profession of multiethnic literatures brought in students from around the United States as well as international students, diversified our student population and (in a painfully gradual process) our faculty, brought in needed resources to our graduate program, fostered curricular innovation, and reconnected us in new ways to the regional public schools and other institutions of higher education.

DISTANCE EDUCATION AND DISCIPLINE: "A CHANGE IS GONNA COME"

The concentration in multicultural and transnational literatures that we have built now includes specialists in Native American and world indigenous writing, Latinx and Caribbean studies, Asian and Asian American culture, Middle Eastern literature, African and African diaspora literary history, postcolonial theory—and we have recently added folklore and film studies as a part of our coalition. Creating a coherent program—"disciplining" ourselves and our students in the context of a disorderly profession—is a creative act in itself. Implicit in the idea of academic disciplines is an inevitable tension between order and chaos. By definition, disciplines seek recognizable and stable boundaries and the institutional rewards that come with a fixed and coherent mission, a settled credentialing process, and a knowledge base around which a consensus has formed. For all their protestations to the contrary, academic institutions devalue the interdisciplinary urge that pushes against settled borders and seeks out temporary alliances and the creative synergy they produce. The simple, apparently unambiguous solidity of math or chemistry or English suggests order and an illusory permanence. We, on the other hand, embody a kind of transnationalism—a collection of intellectual migrants transgressing borders as we struggle against old nationalistic assumptions about the profession of literature.

The physics of disciplinarity betrays its own desire for order, as the gravitational force of a changing world and the production and dissemination of knowledge for which disciplines exist inevitably disrupt and rewrite the rules. Even though institutions push back against this kind of change and try to reward those members who stay safely inside the lines, it is a hopeless effort. The ivory tower, imagined perhaps as a world apart, in actuality fails—and must fail—as a sanctuary. The bullet that murdered Michael Brown, Jr. in Ferguson, Missouri, ricochets through our hallowed halls, and we ignore it at our peril.

My aim in this essay isn't to provide yet another narrative of institutional history; I happily defer to such influential works as Gerald Graff's *Professing Literature: An Institutional History* (1989) for this kind of broader overview. And as I was in the early stages of my own transition from a professional identity defined by historical period to one loosely constructed around conceptions of ethnicity and identity, I contributed to Bruce McComiskey's *English Studies: An Introduction to the Discipline* (2006) by giving my own version of the Matthew Arnold to Terry Eagleton lineage of modern literary study (199–222). But a brief reminder of the dramatic paradigm shifts that have transformed English studies in the past might help respond to those who find both distance education and the broad movement away from traditional literary study a disciplinary betrayal, an affront to a supposedly fixed and orderly discipline. This latter phenomenon I will refer to as the "transnational turn" in literary studies, a term popularized by Paul Jay (2010), who borrowed it from scholars in American studies who were responding in large measure to the canon-disrupting changes wrought by Paul Lauter and the *Heath Anthology* (1989). These two movements—away from the industrial classroom and a nationalistic theory of literary study—provide a foundation for my own belief that the fusion of multiethnic literatures as a subject and distance education as a primary means of disseminating that subject represent the immediate future of the discipline, which is in the process of replacing an approach reflective of an unsustainable nationalism and the racist, sexist, and homophobic ideologies that underlay many of our earlier assumptions about the study of literature and its transmission to students.

Our students are sometimes shocked to learn that the earliest study of literature in English-speaking classrooms used classical texts exclusively. Learning Latin and Greek represented erudition—or more fundamentally represented the difference between an educated and uneducated person. Ben Jonson's oft-quoted assertion, in his First Folio eulogy, to Shakespeare's having "small Latin and less Greek" is illustrative. The gradual inclusion of the "vernacular" literature in the nineteenth- and twentieth-century classroom was taken by traditionalists as a derogation of an essential ideal, one that ironically helped define early modern Britain as "neoclassical" and the rightful inheritor of the ancient gift of the Muses. An emerging nationalism helped to justify this shift toward acknowledging and celebrating literary achievements in English, and so by the end of the eighteenth century, British periodicals had identified a still-emerging canon of vernacular poetry, drama, and even the still morally suspect novel. By the twenty-first century, the literatures of ancient Greece and Rome had been dispatched to the moldy basements of the academy, where they linger as a fading relic.

When Robert Frost wrote the poem "The Gift Outright" in 1923, American literature was starting to establish itself as a doctoral concentration in American academies, and Fred Lewis Pattee had staked a reputation as "the first professor of American Literature" at Penn State University (Martine). Frost articulates a case for an American literature emerging from the long shadows cast by its English father in "The Gift Outright" (1923). The presumptuousness and naïve nationalism of the poem are shocking in retrospect:

> The land was ours before we were the land's.
> She was our land more than a hundred years
> Before we were her people. She was ours
> In Massachusetts, in Virginia,
> But we were England's, still colonials . . .
> To the land vaguely realizing westward,
> But still unstoried, artless, unenhanced,
> Such as she was, such as she would become.

Of course, students now ask whom exactly the poet means by "ours"—who are excluded from the "we"? And in what sense did "we" belong exclusively to England? What truth lies buried in his chilling phrase about our "vaguely realizing westward"?

The fundamental justification for the coincidence of British and American literatures in the Western academy is precisely this nationalistic fantasy. The rationale for teaching literature in public institutions was primarily its contribution to promoting citizenship and national pride, as well as producing sensibilities that could demonstrate their refinement by quoting Tennyson and Longfellow. The United States became the inheritor of a literary lineage of genius, birthed in the classical age, reformulated for an England that perceived itself as the "new Rome" in its "Great Age of Empire," and finally reified in the America of manifest destiny. It is a vision that is exclusively white, colonizing, monocultural, almost entirely male, and heterosexual—Leslie Fielder's "Come Back to the Raft Ag'in, Huck Honey!" (1948) notwithstanding.

My own students generally discover the roots of our contemporary study of multiethnic literatures in the social activism of the post-World War II era. The American Civil Rights Movement was certainly one of those piercing bullets that rattled around the halls of the academy in the 1960s and beyond. In Britain, the creation of cultural studies also inaugurated a profound paradigm shift that moved the discipline away from "the text itself" and toward an understanding of texts as they revealed issues of class and identity, for example. Both of these "origins" provided a foundation for the transnational turn, which I would argue represents the dominant and most compelling principle refocusing our attention away from a celebratory nationalism toward concerns such as human migration and intersectional identities. I am not suggesting that this latest paradigm shift will erase the cottage industries that have developed around, say, Shakespearean studies or nineteenth-century American poetry. I do predict that the emergence of transnational approaches to literature and new pedagogical methods will permanently marginalize the older nationalistic constructs. Specialists in Spenser and Faulkner will have offices down the hall from the classics department. The great canon debate, aptly captured in Lillian Robinson's *In the Canon's Mouth* (1997) and written about ad nauseam ever since, will turn out to be the first major tremor in a seismic shift.

I find it highly improbable that English professors will ever again ask students to produce critical papers on Underwood typewriters. Shifts in pedagogical practices, which of course coincide with and sometimes instigate these broader changes in approach and disciplinary understanding, have been equally transformative. Change is seldom total, but it is nonetheless devastating. None of us, however much we romanticize older methods of research and discovery of information—no matter how much pride we took in our cleverness in unearthing the wondrous and arcane—will ever forego the internet and its terrible beauty or the blessed simplicity of cut-and-paste word processing. Luddites take note: in the words of Sam Cooke, "a change is gonna come."

In my own coursework in English, students did almost no memorization. As a student, I had occasion to talk to older people who, when they discovered I was an English major, proudly recited a bit of Frost or rattled off a chunk of Chaucer's "Prologue" to *The Canterbury Tales*. Pedagogies constructed around recitation and memorization are now nearly extinct, however much they had been embraced and valued by earlier generations of professors and students. These approaches were shoveled under by the ascendance of "critical thinking" as an annoyingly amorphous and yet convincingly modern objective. The most recent shift, it seems to me, is an equally hard-to-define ethic of engagement, in which students of English embrace the present, the messy and immediate world in which they live and move about. Many of my own doctoral instructors boasted about not living in the world of the later twentieth century—so consumed were they in their own historical niches and content to let the noise and confusion of post-modernity swirl by unattended. It strikes me that this posture was both dishonest and unhelpful. Personally, as much as I tried imaginatively to live in a world of proscenium arches and men hyper-concerned with cuckolding, and courtiers vying for the affection of a sex-addled king, I couldn't ignore the Challenger disaster and South African apartheid and the suffocation of would-be migrants in airless crates in the hulls of freighters. It strikes me that this shift toward active engagement with a world beyond whatever borders are constructed to keep us insulated is also likely to be permanent. For better or worse, all of us have to contend with globalization, and to ignore it—for those of us charged with preparing people to thrive in the world—is profoundly irresponsible. For our critics who, for the past twenty years, have dismissed us as faddish or trendy, I would respond that environmental awareness—most dramatically a phenomenon such as global warming—has been similarly discredited, but the changes human beings have wrought are the proverbial bell that can't be unrung.

In my first messy steps into distance education as a vehicle for teaching multiethnic literatures, I wondered whether I wasn't rationalizing the connection between subject and system, tenor and vehicle. I am convinced, however, that distance education can convey the same transnational impulse that drives contemporary literary study: toward inclusiveness, cultural diversity, multiplicity of learning styles, anti-authoritarianism, and the fluidity of identity. It is, again, not my intention to try to create a new narrative of pedagogical history, although if I were to do so, I might begin with the specter of Richard Busby (who as an Anglican priest and teacher throttled the backsides of many of the luminaries of seventeenth-century British poetry) and his notorious "headmaster's rod," along with Ichabod Crane's warning about the consequences of sparing it. It might move through the Utilitarian nightmare of Dickens's Thomas Gradgrind in *Hard Times* to Michel Foucault's panopticon in *Discipline and Punish* (1975). Most such narratives see the contemporary classroom as an offshoot of industrialization and a Fordist vision of efficiency for the benefit of the masses. The intellectual framework for my own teaching begins with Paulo Freire's *Pedagogy of the Oppressed* (1970) and might conclude with the distance education chatroom, with its disembodied participants reimagining the learning community.

Much of the contemporary literature we teach embodies this synthesis of technology and human creative connection. In Elif Shafak's *The*

Bastard of Istanbul (2007), the chatroom is both a vehicle for international communication and a conflict zone exploring the Armenian Holocaust and the lingering cultural effects on life and love a century later. Rajaa Alsanea's *Girls of Riyadh* (2007) demonstrates the subversive power of new technologies to disrupt the brutal patriarchy of Saudi rule. The literature we read and interpret enacts the kind of learning and connection the students and their instructors are themselves forging.

While I'm an advocate for and practitioner of distance education, I am mindful of the skepticism Audrey Watters expressed in "The Invented History of 'The Factory Model of Education'": "We tend to not see automation today as mechanization as much as algorithmization—the promise and potential in artificial intelligence and virtualization, as if this magically makes these new systems of standardization and control lighter and liberatory." So too, we've invented a history of "the factory model of education" in order to justify an "upgrade"—to new software and hardware that will do much of the same thing schools have done for generations now, just (supposedly) more efficiently, with control moved out of the hands of labor (teachers) and into the hands of a new class of engineers, out of the realm of the government and into the realm of the market (Watters).

At the start, let me disavow the prospect of distance education as a kind of automatic, corrective panacea. It is no more inherently "liberatory" than the assumptions of those who operate the system. I would argue, however, that it is potentially more democratic and offers, for both instructors and students, a vast field of creative options and learning models unavailable to those managing and enduring the industrial model of instruction. Conversely, it can also represent a dead zone, a return to the bad old days of rote rehearsal and memorization, with a textbook substituting for a human presence and canned, pre-recorded lessons timed to appear once a week with little or no interaction or feedback except for graded papers or tests periodically providing a sort of tepid, fleshless validation or condemnation of the participant. distance education has the potential to tear down the economic barriers erected by universities conceived of as exclusive enclaves: Jude Fawley can finally enter Christminster, Hardy's (1894) Oxford stand-in in *Jude the Obscure*. It can embrace students isolated geographically, culturally, and financially. Or it can become like the long-ridiculed correspondence or mail-order courses of the 1950s and their false promise to all the desperate and frustrated Biff Lomans of the world who flunked math and lost their scholarships.

Cary Grant and the Panopticon

For me, making a quick transition from face-to-face (F2F) to distance education required a rethinking of instructional ethos, both in an abstract and personal sense. As a writing program administrator, I learned that the first concern of most new teaching assistants was establishing their own authority and credibility: "What if I don't know the answer?" "How will students respond to my youth and inexperience?" "What will I do if they act up?" Of course, the irony is that once good teachers have established a level of comfort with their own authority, they spend the rest of their careers trying to cede or delegate it successfully.

For me, much of my own sense of teacherly ethos emanated from my theatrical background—from bodily and vocal control. I knew how to project and modulate sound, how and when to whisper so that every student in a large classroom gets the full, startling effect. I knew how to move in the liminal space between lectern and rows of desks, to dance when required, to stand on my head (in a moment of memorable madness). As I've said, the physical performance of teaching, for me, was nearly always joyful and a source of confidence and authority. Frankly, I felt depressed at the prospect of losing the physicality of my professional work.

The system of electronic boxes that comprise the typical distance education classroom erases identity (at least initially) for both instructor and instructed. This, too, struck me as a kind of irony for those of us whose subject is representations of identity in multiethnic literary works. Each of us is assigned a name—inflexibly so—by the university's registrar, and the name might be somewhat suggestive of gender or national or cultural origin. But in the absence of bodies, we are, again at least initially, ghostly presences gradually made flesh discussion post by discussion post, comment by comment, paragraph by paragraph—and the ways we identify or (re)create ourselves. Given this freedom—as a short, overweight, middle-aged, white male—I decided to become Cary Grant, and posted the actor's picture as a representation of myself. The students didn't seem to mind this preposterous bit of fraudulence and chose their own self-representations that may or may not have borne any resemblance to physical reality.

As the system permitted a degree of playfulness and experimentation around our identities, it also (at least temporarily) obscured whatever our bodies suggested to others about our ethnic identities and sexualities. Some students enjoyed that novel form of anonymity; others "came out" quickly and specifically in their online engagements. I found the distance education environment a safe space, where students could be both intellectually challenging and also courteous and collaborative. I did my best to treat each student with respect and gentle guidance, and in response I discovered that there really was no need for a written lecture on the importance of respectful engagement. In terms of authority, my experience and facility with writing provided it. It's one way in which this system is not particularly democratic: those with confidence in their writing skills have an enormous advantage as members of the community.

As I've argued, removing the punitive aspect of education—whether in the industrial classroom or cyberspace—has proven an almost insuperable task, in part because, to coopt Foucault, the nexus of discipline and punishment seems so easy and natural, almost irresistible. Fear is a tempting shortcut to authority and obedience. My hope, for those like me making this kind of pedagogical transition, has been that the opportunity prompts a reevaluation of the crude systems of punishment insisted upon by the university as servant of the military-industrial complex, which mandates that all of our human products be labeled with phony precision as 3.8s or 2.6s, and therefore validated and justified. If we are only producing Foucault's "docile bodies" by virtue of our disciplinary approach, we are failing.

The collaborative possibilities in distance instruction provide their own incentive: it is inherently joyful to work as part of a productive team formed for the sole purpose of learning and developing skills. I can't imagine a more powerful motivation than to create a performance space—not as a system of control or surveillance, but a theatre of learning. The instructor foregoes Bentham's "sentiment of an invisible omniscience" as dishonest and unproductive, but serves as a model for community building, creative response, and exploration of the self.

I was, frankly, in spite of my email rationale, an unlikely member of this new team: the "odd white guy" as some of my team members joked—and an eighteenth-century British literature specialist, for heaven's sake! I had to guard against "phallic creep" (there are enough phallic creeps in the profession already). I had to serve quietly, to work behind the scenes, as one with an ill-defined role, to help the team function. I had to learn never to "speak for" but to listen and query, along with my students. As Linda Alcoff (1991) has written, "There is a strong, albeit contested, current within feminism which holds that speaking for others—even for other women—is arrogant, vain, unethical, and politically illegitimate"

(6). This admonition represents another complication for our assuming ethical authority: like the white Jewish woman specializing in African diaspora studies (who was, in fact, my "fem-tor" as she called herself when I was a new assistant professor); the British woman writing books about Latinx literature—the challenge of leading a learning community without coopting or affecting any kind of "inside understanding." Does one have to be queer-identified to specialize in LGBTQ studies? I would hope not, even though this path might be difficult for a "straight" person (such a loathsome term) to navigate. It might, in fact, be a path that leads to a more profound understanding of professional service and the kind of humility that underlies genuine professional authority.

The price of admission for this newly minted distance education-teaching multiculturalist was to serve as the area coordinator and student advisor, as well as formulating an introductory course for the concentration. For years, I had served on a large number of thesis committees for students writing about African American subjects and other ethnic American and world literature topics, so that experience proved helpful as someone who could at least minimally communicate among the various specializations.

The success our program has experienced gives enough leeway to imagine and construct the outlines of a future. That means dealing with the walls and boundaries that seem to come with the territory—faculty hiring lines, curricular development, program assessment—boxes within boxes. Our program developed not only as a site of resistance but as a place for students and working teachers to experiment with literatures from Africa, the Middle East, Asia, and elsewhere in a way that is appealingly accessible—while encouraging deeper and deeper immersion into the cultures, languages, histories, and theoretical understandings of peoples with whom they'd had no previous contact. Applying this approach, bell hooks (1990) addresses the white academic reader on behalf of "subalterns" in the conclusion to her paper "Marginality as a Site of Resistance": "This is an intervention. A message from that space in the margin that is a site of creativity and power, that inclusive space where we recover ourselves, where we meet in solidarity to erase the category colonized/colonizer. Marginality is the space [site] of resistance. Enter that space. Let us meet there. Enter that space. We greet you as liberators" (343).

We are moving away from the margins, but I think the idea of multiculturalism as a site of resistance needs to guide us as we imagine a future that is not simply a matter of reacting against some established canon or defining a "non-Western" space in the academy. Because of the nature of the traditional academy, some wall-building is unavoidable, an essential part of the business of creating a discipline. The act of choosing—selecting and rejecting—puts us at risk of recreating the mistakes that I think bound and undermined the study of literature as it existed in the academy for much of the twentieth century. We could monumentalize a list of books and authors (perhaps Gloria Anzaldúa's *Borderlands/ La Frontera*, Said's *Orientalism*, Friere's *Pedagogy of the Oppressed*, the writings of Spivak and Franz Fanon), create fixed comprehensive exams, rigidly define our new boundaries. Rather, I think we need to remember the lessons of our origins in imagining our own futures.

Our disciplinary roots are instructive as we plan for the future. A part of our birthright is the American Civil Rights movement and also the political critique associated with the formation of cultural studies—a pedagogy that grows out of our commitment to challenge oppression and racism and to see in the literature we study and write about the possibility for resistance and activism. Above all, we have to avoid becoming what Freire critiqued in his attack on the "banking concept of education." That is the problem with canons and disciplinary formation: they tend to lead to the paradigm Freire rejects. Yet again, "something there is that doesn't love a wall"—we survive by remaining flexible, fluid, undoctrinaire, passionate about learning and social justice and our commitments to diversity: a moveable feast.

This semester, students in my research methods class are interrogating the question "Is GLBTQ Literature Multicultural?" Within the past few years, the presence of GLBTQ students and faculty members has been acknowledged institutionally after a period of neglect and (mostly) quiet hostility. Our English department has never had a course in GLBTQ literature, nor a specialist in the area, although the course has been taught very sporadically as a special topics or honors course. For the Multicultural concentration, this historical neglect represents an opportunity, and we have essentially borrowed a specialist in queer theory to teach a special topics course for us. In my judgment, this should be a first step in our development of a GLBTQ course and component in our area, with a hiring line dedicated to this flourishing field.

It's this last step that is the tricky one: it's in our priorities and how we spend diminishing resources that really defines who we are. On what basis do we decide whether GLBTQ literature is rightfully a part of the so-called multicultural canon? The shared roots, to me, are obvious: a literature about identity and oppression, with its theoretical critique of the structures of power and oppression. Not all of our faculty members see it this way. Is queerness an ethnicity? Are GLBTQ people collectively a cultural group? I think that's an open question, one whose contested nature is yet another argument for the irresistibility of incorporating this literature as part of our mission. What we've seen, though, even in many of our campus-sponsored events celebrating and interrogating the idea of diversity, is that there is surprising resistance, even among members of our core MTL constituency, to the full embrace of GLBTQ studies as a civil rights movement and as a valued partner in our educational mission.

A Future to Perform

I claim no particular skill in clairvoyance: the flying cars I imagined as a child, the weekend getaways to Mars, the robots that could tell us all the mysteries of life and death—all have proven illusory in the future we inhabit, at least so far. Yet from the standpoint of technological change, the transformations wrought by the advent of the personal computer and of the internet have changed the profession of English to a degree none of the Nostradamuses musing in the 1970s and 1980s could have predicted. The best prognosticators imagine futures grounded in present realities, indicators of necessary change, and perhaps in the aspects of humanity (in this case the nature of learning and the inherent curiosity and ambition of the species) that remain stable over the eons.

This essay has argued that the kind of nationalism that has seemed inevitable over the past four centuries or so may, in fact, be as mutable as other organizing principles have been; the backlash against globalization and a new and virulent nationalism might actually be a sign that dramatic change is in the offing. Similarly, I find evidence that the nationalism that organized literary study has been challenged, if not yet overthrown, in English studies programs that are struggling to justify a literary study based on its Americanness or its Britishness, for example. The English language has been infused with a powerful new internationalism, witnessed in the Booker Prize nominees and other literary awards; the flourishing of fiction in translation and originally in English published in Africa, Asia, the Middle East—transnationally; the importance of migration as a central narrative concern; and all of the aspects that have marked "the Transnational Turn" in literary studies for the past decade. The virtual collapse of comparative literature as a discipline, chronicled by Gayatri Spivak and anticipated by Edward Said, provides an opening for an approach that is less Western European, less elitist, less costly in terms of the price of admission for specialists.

The so-called assault on the humanities is hardly new, although in an academy reconstructed around business models, declining enrollments and tightened budgets produce a downward spiral. Our response as professionals in English studies should be to insist upon our social relevance—not by lofty declamation but by redefining our mission as an ingredient in the struggle for social justice. The stories we tell and listen to and study are a powerful force for combating xenophobia and identity-based bigotry. Programs such as the one I've been fortunate enough to contribute to have worked as tools—albeit inefficient ones—for the painfully slow transformation of a historically impoverished and racially segregated region. But it is still, in terms of outreach, speed, and flexibility, an Underwood typewriter rather than a World Wide Web.

I caught a glimpse of that future in a seminar on Middle Eastern Literature in Spring 2011. My students and I were reading Alaa Al-Aswany's (2002) *The Yacoubian Building*, a remarkably prescient novel that anticipated the "Arab Spring" as it unfolded before our eyes in Cairo. Our class Skyped with the novelist Samia Serageldin, who was holed up in Tahrir Square and who was generous enough to turn her laptop to face the revolution happening outside the window of her flat. That is one future, and campuses all over the world are connecting via "global classrooms" to bring different geographically and ethnically diverse students together to share the stories their bards and troubadours create and transmit. The industrial classroom is a model of isolation and control, however much our annual teaching statements proclaim our belief in a "de-centered" classroom. The instrument of the global classroom and all its variations and offshoots offers a powerfully disruptive force for learning and for social change. Of course, this kind of liberatory potential threatens autocrats of both the political and academic variety, and the "failure" of the Arab Spring is, in my judgment, a temporary set-back and product of a justifiable fear that old sources of power are being undermined. The new contact zone is international, each classroom a single collective voice in a learning collaborative.

Those of us with skills and experience and credentials in critiquing language, culture, and identity—and a shared commitment to human liberation and social justice—can and must forge their own web. Many of us preach to our students that true education is autodidactic, and the tools already available for self-teaching are staggering, essentially infinite. Teams of us who are skilled at learning can facilitate the formation of other teams to form a chain connected spiritually and electronically. It strikes me as no insurmountable task to create a professional credentialing process that is not dependent on the validation of a single institution or even a single, circumscribed knowledge base. Medicine and law have done so to an extent, although they are brutally reliant on single standardized exams. As we form these connections, and the connections form connections, our world can start to change exponentially in ways I certainly can't imagine. I hope that each of us can sacrifice our personal authority and institutional loyalties in the service of remaining nimble enough to adjust to change: to respond to our students everywhere, to their cultures and histories, and to the exigencies of the moment. The international curriculum and educational delivery system that I imagine is phenomenally diverse and flexible, driven by our imaginations and by the needs of the present. The industrial brick-and-mortar structures replicating each other and representing a catastrophic drain on personal and public resources will go the way of gas-powered vehicles.

References

Al-Aswany, Alaa. 2002. *The Yacoubian Building.* Cairo: American University in Cairo Press.

Alcoff, Linda. 1991. "The Problem of Speaking for Others." *Cultural Critique* 20: 5–31.

Alsanea, Rajaa. 2007. *Girls of Riyadh.* New York: Penguin Press.

Anzaldúa, Gloria. 1987. *Borderlands/La Frontera: The New Mestiza.* San Francisco: Aunt Lute.

Bentham, Jeremy J. 1843. *The Works of Jeremy Bentham*, vol. 4. https://oll.libertyfund.org/title/bowring-the-works-of-jeremy-bentham-vol-4. Accessed 3 May 2021.

Bejerano, Arleen R. 2008. "Face-to-Face or Online Instruction? Face-to-Face Is Better." National Communication Association. https://www.natcom.org/communication-currents/face-face-or-online-instruction-face-face-better.

Dasenbrook, Reed. 1999. "Why Read Multicultural Literature? An Arnoldian Perspective." *College English* 61 (6): 691–701.

Fiedler, Leslie. 1999. "Come Back to the Raft Ag'in, Huck Honey." In *The New Fiedler Reader.* New York: Prometheus Books.

Foucault, Michel. 1975. *Discipline and Punish.* New York: Random House.

Freire, Paulo. 1970. *Pedagogy of the Oppressed*. New York: Continuum.
Frost, Robert. 1969. "The Gift Outright." In *The Poetry of Robert Frost*, edited by Edward Connery Lathem, 348. New York: Henry Holt and Company.
GoDistanceLearning.Com. "History of Distance Learning." Accessed 13 April 2019. http://www.godistancelearning.com/history-of-distance-learning.html.
Graff, Gerald. 1987. *Professing Literature: An Institutional History*. Chicago: University of Chicago Press.
hooks, bell. 1990. "Marginality as Site of Resistance." In *Out There: Marginalization and Contemporary Cultures*, edited by Russell Ferguson, Martha Gever, Trinh T. Minh-ha, and Cornel West. Cambridge, MA: MIT Press, 341–43.
Jay, Paul. 2010. *Global Matters: The Transnational Turn in Literary Studies*. New York: Cornell University Press.
Lauter, Paul, ed. 1989. *The Heath Anthology of American Literature*. New York: Cengage.
Martine, James J. 1973. *Fred Lewis Pattee and American Literature*. State College, PA: The Pennsylvania State University Press.
McComiskey, Bruce, ed. 2006. *English Studies. An Introduction to the Discipline*. Urbana, IL: NCTE.
Robinson, Lillian S. 1997. *In the Canon's Mouth: Dispatches from the Culture Wars*. Bloomington, IN: Indiana University Press.
Said, Edward. 1979. *Orientalism*. New York: Vintage.
Shafak, Elif. 2006. *The Bastard of Istanbul*. New York: Viking.
Spivak, Gayatri Chakravorty. 2003. *Death of a Discipline*. New York: Columbia University Press.
Stern, Barbara Slater. 2004. "A Comparison of Online and Face-To-Face Instruction in an Undergraduate Foundations of American Education Course." *CITE Journal* 4. https://www.citejournal.org/volume-4/issue-2–04/general/a-comparison-of-online-and-face-to-face-instruction-in-an-undergraduate-foundations-of-american-education-course/.
Watters, Audrey. 2015. "The Invented History of 'The Factory Model of Education.'" Accessed 29 November 2018. http://hackeducation.com/2015/04/25/factory-model.

16 Lessons from Journalism: Developing Online Programs for the Public Good

Erin A. Frost

"Teaching online is just teaching out of a box."
     When a full professor at my institution said this at a faculty meeting in 2017, I could hardly believe my ears. I looked around the room and saw a range of reactions on the faces of my colleagues. Our department has a robust online master's program and graduate certificate programs, so most faces showed annoyance, anger, shock, or dismay. A few people—exclusively those who've never taught online, like the speaker—were nodding.
     Online education is a broad concept. It can mean many things. It is possible, of course, that someone could teach an online class "out of a box"—in the very same way that a teacher who has laminated their lesson plans might teach "out of a box" in a face-to-face context. However, plug-and-play teaching is not actually correlated with the digitality of online education; it is correlated, rather, with a particular and uncritical orientation to pedagogy. The anecdote I share above demonstrates that many people—including seasoned instructors with ranks that ought to reflect some manner of pedagogical achievement—sometimes see online teaching as a product of technology and a poor facsimile of "real" teaching, a high-tech shadow version of the face-to-face classroom.
     In this chapter, I aim to confound the popular assumption that online teaching is solely a product of tools. This assumption undergirds many of the ways even proponents of online teaching talk about their work—just look at how often scholarship that is explicitly about teaching online is also focused on specific technologies. I suggest that online teachers must shift our thinking to be less tool-oriented and more overtly rhetorical in

our framing. Online teaching—like any teaching—is a product of an instructor's theoretical commitments and pedagogical orientations. As such, online teaching can be—should be, as I will argue—progressive. In fact, teaching online can be a fertile space for progressive and innovative pedagogies and practices. Online teaching can be feminist in nature. It can be pro-collaboration, pro-open-source, pro-hypertext—but it isn't by nature. Online platforms offer affordances that make re-examining our pedagogical orientations worthwhile, but they do not preclude the uptake of their offerings in masculinist, singular, paywalled, linear ways. Uncritical update of such platforms is easy to do, particularly in situations like many we have seen since the advent of COVID-19—in which teaching must be shifted from face-to-face to online, and in which such a transition must happen quickly. Online teaching is a proposition that, like any teaching, is laced with nuance and complexity and thus must be engaged with care.

In re-orienting our understandings of online teaching and particularly our understandings of teaching English studies online, this chapter draws on the recent history of the field of journalism to underscore the importance of a thoughtful approach to industry migrations to online spaces. Happily, teaching English studies online is more adaptable to revision after the initial digital transition than is journalism, which may prove important in the years to come as post-secondary institutions re-evaluate the materiality of education. I utilize the journalism industry as an instructive example for English programs seeking to develop online curricula because journalism and English studies, as fields, share commitments both to public education and to the public good. Like journalism, English studies stands to gain a lot from online engagement in terms of these commitments. However, it also risks eroding its own foundation—an experience US-based journalism is still recovering from—if online curricula are not developed thoughtfully.

Teaching English Studies Online, Social Justice, and the Public Good

One of the most important benefits of online education, for me, is its effect in expanding access. I work at a university whose regional focus includes a dedication to reaching and serving students from populations historically underrepresented in university settings; many of the students in our online master's program would not be able to pursue that education in a traditional, face-to-face context. Online curricula can support women (who are often primarily responsible for childcare, and thus may need flexible schedules), low-income students (who may not have the resources to live away from their families), rural and first-generation students (for whom cultural difference presents challenges and barriers in the university setting), students of color (for whom navigating predominantly white institutions may be overwhelming, dangerous, or impossible), and students who are fleeing environmental crises or find themselves in other "not normal" situations (Jung 2007). Many of these populations are particularly affected by global and national disasters, and thus large-scale events make the importance of online education to vulnerable populations even more acute. For example, our program developed in part out of temporary and urgent access problems; Hurricane Floyd created a push to move online when flooding rose to historic levels in 1999 and campus was closed (Frost 2018, 31). Creating meaningful access to education—working for social justice and the public good—is at the heart of what we do.

Social justice also is at the heart of English studies as a discipline. English studies (as understood in US-based contexts) is the coordinated study of English literature, composition, and sociolinguistics.[1] Illinois State University (2019) was the first in the nation to offer a doctoral program in English studies, which they currently describe as follows:

> In English studies, multiple and interdisciplinary perspectives are used to examine and produce texts for audiences communicating in English: How do cultures shape language and how does language shape culture? How do intersections of cultures affect communication across borders? What forms can we create to connect and enter into dialogue with each other?
>
> Children's Literature, Creative Writing, English Education, Linguistics, Literary and Cultural Studies, Rhetoric and Writing (including New Media Studies, Professional Writing and Rhetorics, Rhetoric and Composition, and Teaching Writing), and TESOL offer our community of students and researchers the means of examining how we teach, learn, and understand

---

1. It is worth noting that this configuration of English studies is not entirely stable. For example, Ohio University defines English studies as being comprised of literary history, creative writing, and rhetoric and composition (Ohio University 2018).

ourselves and others through the stories we tell and the ways in which we tell them.

The focus of English studies on issues of culture requires that its students recognize and analyze issues of access, (in)justice, and ethics. This turn in the field's understanding of its role is relatively recent; as Haas notes in her 2012 article "Race, Rhetoric, and Technology," her teaching of a course on technology in English studies would have been enriched by scholarship that emerged in the time between the 2009 course and the article's publication. Today, the connection of English studies—and perhaps especially the constituent disciplines of composition and technical communication, with their attendant more intense foci on online teaching—with culture and with social justice has been well established (Banks 200; Banks and Eble 2007; Bowdon 2004; Colton and Holmes 2018; Haas and Eble 2018; Jones 2016; Jones, Moore, and Walton 2016; Katz 1992; Savage and Mattson 2011; Savage and Matveeva 2011; Williams 2010), particularly since the cultural turn in technical communication (Scott, Longo, and Wills 2006). While some scholars have paid attention to the importance of cultural approaches to English studies specific to online teaching (as one example, Cargile Cook and Grant-Davie's 2013 collection addresses the significance of institutional culture in being responsive to distance education needs), English studies needs more research in this area. In short, scholar-teachers of English studies are and should be especially concerned with social justice and the public good because of the field's focus on cultural issues.

JOURNALISM, CAPITALISM, AND ACCESS

Like English studies,[2] journalism—and here I am focused on print journalism—is an enterprise aimed at public education. Journalism is an institution that has been especially important to the political development of the US, which is perhaps unsurprising given the timelines of the country's development and the uptake of mass-printing technologies in the West. Journalists have been depicted as both objects of ire (Grynbaum 2017) and cultural heroes (Orlando 2018), and the role of the journalism industry as a government watchdog has been critical. A

---

2. And, ideally, public education writ large—though this cannot be assumed based on current national conversations about the role of education and an informed citizenry, and I do not have the space to take up that issue in this chapter.

major difference between journalism and English studies, however, is the location of English studies programs mostly in public educational institutions, while journalism is by nature a privately-owned, commercially funded enterprise.

With the commercialization of the internet in the mid-1990s came a new medium for disseminating reporting work. Journalists—whose allegiance is to the public good—began to put content online. As a means of protecting the perceived objectivity of the journalistic enterprise, newspapers are structured so that the newsroom (where reporters work) is separate from the advertising department. Due in part to this separation, journalists largely failed to recognize the effects their well-intentioned rush to offer open-access content would have on their own support systems. To more fully explain, journalism has historically relied on advertising revenue—not subscription revenue—for its support.[3] Advertising revenue functions differently in digital versus print media. Thus, a simple conversion of subscriptions from print to online—which many newspapers attempted to do retroactively, almost always with a significant decline in readership as a consequence—actually results in a significant net loss for newspapers. As an example, while I was working at a small daily newspaper in Lincoln, Illinois, in 2008, an advertising executive told me that she was able to sell an online advertisement for only about 15 percent of the price of a similar print advertisement. Thus, the newspaper would need to multiply its readership and/or advertisers significantly and affect new and more persuasive arguments with advertisers to make up the difference.

As members of the journalism industry learned, the migration to online platforms is more than a simple implementation of a new tool, a fitting of existing content into a new "box." The critical point here is

---

3. Income from subscriptions is important but is a relatively small piece of a newspaper's financial pie. Lost subscription revenue was not nearly so important a factor in the history of digital journalism as was developing new models for monetizing the advertisements that accompany reporting. Although this chapter does not focus on literal capital, this reality suggests that universities would do well to consider how their funding models work across face-to-face and digital contexts. While newspapers have historically relied on readership as social capital to trade with advertisers, public education relies on enrollment—often colloquially referred to as "butts in seats," a metaphor predicated on face-to-face engagement—to generate monetary capital beyond that provided by the tax base. The ways that enrollments translate to budgeting are—and should be—a subject of much concern for those who administer online programs.

that journalism, as an industry, rushed into the digital realm because of a perception that the internet was a useful tool for dissemination of information while failing to realize that this new medium also required structural differences in content development and deployment. The journalism industry, by and large, has thus had to do significant work in retrofitting its models for engagement, and it has been plagued by the drawbacks of retrofitting as a way of doing business: A "retrofit does not necessarily make the product function, does not necessarily fix a faulty product, but it acts as a sort of correction" (Dolmage 2008, 20). While the retrofit is one way to think of transitioning to online teaching—and transitioning face-to-face courses to online delivery systems is a practical inevitability—I take the position that we should treat online teaching as a new venture entirely. By imagining online teaching as the new modality it is, and by paying critical attention to the relationships of the tools we use to our theoretical commitments, we can ensure that transitions to English studies online curricula are responsible, functional, and true to the values of our discipline.

THEORETICAL ORIENTATIONS/PEDAGOGICAL APPLICATIONS

Having established that "migrating" a face-to-face course or curriculum to an online space is more than a re-structuring—it is a fundamental re-imagining of that course, its content, and associated pedagogy—and that social justice orientations are a necessary part of this pedagogical labor, I now offer ideas for doing the work of this cognitive transition. As I have asserted both implicitly and explicitly throughout this chapter, I draw on decolonial, cyberfeminist, and queer frameworks to do so. In other words, this section details ways of *doing* online teaching in English studies. More specifically, I suggest that progressive English studies online pedagogues might intervene in current understandings toward more innovative and socially just approaches to online teaching by: (1) conceptualizing virtual spaces as real; (2) de-centering authority; and (3) orienting away from tools and toward experiences.

CONCEPTUALIZING VIRTUAL SPACES AS REAL

An initial method for changing the ways we talk and think about online teaching is by purposefully conceptualizing virtual spaces as real. Virtual spaces are not artificial. They are complex and nuanced; they have material effects (Dibbell 1993). The ability to "live" in virtual spaces has given some users a sense of having left their bodies behind, a pretension to a modern Cartesian split. Cyberfeminist scholars have pointed out that this is a false perception. N. Katherine Hayles (1999) distinguishes between the body and embodiment as a way of demonstrating that while one may be able to enter a digital world in which one's body is not apparent to other users, markers of the experiences that body has had as it has moved through the world remain. In other words, we can never fully separate information from materiality (or form from content). In the context of online teaching, this reminds us that students come to the virtual classroom embodied (in bodies). They manipulate technologies with their bodies so as to interact with the instructor and their peers, and the communication they send through the screen is a result of their experiences of the world as mediated through their bodies. Those bodies are real, even if they are not apparent in online spaces. Those online spaces, in turn, have material effects on students' (and teachers') bodies.

I am just finishing teaching an online course, Public Interest Writing. The last book I assigned in the course was Patricia Williams's (1992) *The Alchemy of Race and Rights*.[4] I gave a great deal of thought to whether I would assign this text and how to approach it. The subject matter is racism and the law, and I knew it would be a difficult read intellectually and affectively. I elected to take the risk, to assign the book, believing that if it affected the worldview of even one student as it had affected mine, it would be worth it. I didn't fully consider, however, the visceral way in which this book might read for students of color. Williams opens the book by talking about having to review historical legal documents setting out the value of slaves, and one student immediately responded that she hadn't been emotionally prepared to read about slavery in a public interest writing class. Her response reminded me of the material ways—from something as minute and essential as heart rate to something as far-reaching and general as the ways students might raise their children—that online teaching choices affect students.

All of the above, however, presupposes that "real" means "embodied." While considering the material effects of online work is important, I resist the notion that material effect is the only measure by which we should consider realness. As an example of other measures we might use, I offer a course I taught several semesters ago on Writing Public Science. After initial resistance to using Twitter as a means of sharing ex-

---

4. It is worth noting that I first encountered this text as a student in the course described in the article by Angela M. Haas cited earlier in this chapter.

amples of science and scientific writing, students eventually used Twitter to form a community whose interactions continued after the class ended, though most of the students have never met outside of class—and likely will not. Additionally, after I created mentoring pairs between graduate Writing Public Science students and undergraduate Scientific Writing students, some co-mentors maintained relationships after the class; one pair, both African-American women in the sciences, talked regularly via phone after the semester ended. We sometimes think of digital spaces—and perhaps especially digital classrooms—as important only when they affect the material world. We think of them also as constrained by time and space. However, online teaching creates opportunities to transcend these constraints. Incorporating media that support relationship-building is just one way of moving students toward understanding their digital work as impactful and thus taking advantage of the rich multidimensionality (and materiality) of online teaching and learning.

DE-CENTERING AUTHORITY

Conventional classrooms have a lectern near the front. Upon entering the space, it is clear where attention is meant to be focused. Most classrooms are physical instantiations of what Freire (1972) called the banking model of education, where a "sage on a stage" imparts knowledge to uneducated masses of students. Despite what we might like to think about the networked, democratizing nature of digital spaces, online classrooms often mimic this structure. They mimic practices that "are more about our need to feel knowledgeable . . . than about our helping students to understand" (Spangler 2009, 130). For example, when I enter a Blackboard discussion board, every entry I write is marked with a star, which seems to indicate that my contributions are somehow more important than others.

In both online and face-to-face classrooms, I work to de-center[5] my authority as instructor. I utilize an apparent feminist pedagogy to do so, which means I begin by identifying myself as a feminist and asking students to resist essentializing language, to treat all identities as valid,

---

5. While I work to de-center my authority, I do not completely destabilize or neutralize it for two reasons. First, to suggest that this is a sought-after approach is hugely problematic for women and POC instructors, whose authority is always already under siege. Second, I am aware that an abdication of power in a classroom setting can never be fully accomplished and to believe that it could would be to fall victim to uncritical notions of how power works.

and to actively advocate for social justice. I also ask them to consider making their own theoretical orientations apparent, to treat others with complementary approaches as allies regardless of identity, and to critique rhetorics of efficiency (Frost 2015). While I give students examples of what such practices might look like, I do not prescribe how they go about their learning. De-centering my authority by making my biases apparent helps students to understand that bias and expertise are related concepts and that their own biases and experiences, with appropriate reflection, are actually strengths they can speak from.

De-centering the authority of the instructor gives students room to wander, and this is a concept that is familiar to students who operate in digital spaces. Recent gaming platforms operate without the scaffolding and tutorials that were characteristic of games in times past; risk and failure are part of the fun (McGonigal 2011). Rather, players enter a new space alongside more experienced players and must make their way along, figuring things out as they go (reminiscent of MakerSpace approaches to education). In this way, de-centering the teacher's authority in online teaching can allow students to recognize an invitation to wander, to make their own way into a course and find ways to make unique contributions that would not be possible in face-to-face settings. As an example, I recently asked students in an online scientific writing course to incorporate credible outside sources into their discussion posts. One woman wrote about climate change and pulled in an article claiming that one hundred companies were responsible for more than 70 percent of global emissions, prompting a lively discussion among students that did not require or involve my direct guidance. In fact, I often take a backseat in virtual spaces, lurking in order to let students interact with one another and just occasionally intervening when necessary or drawing together relevant threads of conversation after a discussion has reached an organic stopping point.

Orienting Away from Tools and Toward Experiences

To begin thinking about orienting ourselves away from tools and toward experiences, an example from a traditional teaching context may be of use. In "Stop Reading Shakespeare!," Spangler (2009) encourages literature instructors to draw on students' tacit knowledge of the drama as a way to meet them where they are: "If Shakespeare's plays were shown instead of read, teachers could capitalize on students' primary discourse and help them consciously articulate that tacit knowledge, collaborating with students instead of working against them" (131). In making this argument, Spangler also points out that most modern students encounter Shakespeare through assigned reading—which is not how Shakespeare's works were intended to be experienced; Shakespeare was a playwright and his plays were meant to be acted out before an audience. This is a case of professionals choosing a tool—in this case, the book—because it was there (and perhaps because it was easy), rather than because it was the most useful or meaningful medium available. By re-orienting ourselves to the student experience, as Spangler does, we can see a new way of teaching that is more useful, useable, and productive—and this re-orientation is not even, in fact, that radical.

Another method of re-orienting ourselves away from tools and toward experiences is by thinking about what is unfamiliar to students, as Cox (2018) describes in his explanation of queering online teaching and learning. He used some familiar elements/tools of online courses (course readings, online discussion boards, weekly group leaders for reading discussions), but he also used unfamiliar elements (multi-user video/audio chat rooms, nontraditional writing assignments, guest participants) as a way of pointing out that the tools we first think of are not the only ones available. Further, Cox created infrastructure that made tools into experiences. He encouraged students to "queer/disrupt ideas of online discussion board space. Examples included responses that often ranted, felt comfortable showing anger and frustration, and showed emotional vulnerability and discomfort with difficult topics and experiences and that often-used video recorded responses between one another" (295). Cox's goal of "disrupting otherwise often fairly stagnant/conservative online course structures" (301) was also achieved in part by capitalizing on the fact that some of the students in the class had ready access to campus even though the class ran as a distance education course, so he was able to organize face-to-face interactions and hybrid small-group work—breaking down the boundaries between what is "online" and what is "face-to-face."

Orienting toward students' experiences means using a variety of tools and doing so with explicitly rhetorical goals. It also means orienting explicitly toward positions of both comfort and discomfort, treading a line that encourages students to take risks while letting them stay grounded enough that they remain invested in the course. I often engage in some of this pushing-pulling, comfort-discomfort work by requiring a variety of media. Years ago, I held office hours in Second Life because that was familiar to some students (though it stretched my own comfort zone); I also required at least one office hours meeting to happen over the phone, which was a decidedly less comfortable medium for students. By examining how our interactions differed in these different platforms, students could begin to understand the rhetoricity of tools and the importance of understanding tools as formative of experiences—but they also recognized their own need to adapt, and the importance of practicing with a tool so that it could yield the experience they desired.

Productive Pathways

Online programs, and particularly those in English studies, are positioned to support social justice pedagogies. They are positioned to increase access to information and to sponsor collaborative and multimodal learning. They are positioned to emphasize their own realness, de-center authority, and orient students toward experience. However, online tools do not necessarily predispose pedagogues to incorporate theories that support these concepts into their teaching. We cannot allow ourselves to believe that tools are all we need; we must constantly and recursively question our own use of these tools. Kerschbaum (Yergeau et al. 2013) warns that "For educators, it is ethically questionable to practice pedagogies and construct spaces that categorically exclude entire classes of people." Kerschbaum points to disability studies as a generative theoretical orientation for building inclusive spaces, and she emphasizes the importance of proactive approaches. Since "by the time a user has complained about a lack of accessibility, the moment of communication has often passed," we know that retrofitting online course design is not an ideal option; this concern also points to the fact that a user without access may lack the opportunity to complain/engage at all.

If we accept the premise that English studies must embrace social justice, then moving courses and programs online is one way of making that commitment broader and more apparent. If the purpose of education is to create situations where students can grow and learn so as to have more options for bettering their lives—the public good, as with journalism—then the importance of proactively developing responsible models for online education is a foregone conclusion. This chapter has sought to aid in that project by offering specific strategies to help English studies scholar-teachers as they work to be careful, critical, and reflective in imagining a more carefully designed digital and connected future for English studies online.

REFERENCES

Banks, Adam. 2006. *Race, Rhetoric, And Technology: Searching for Higher Ground*. Mahwah, NJ: Erlbaum.
Banks, William P., and Michelle F. Eble. 2007. "Digital Spaces, Online Environments, and Human Participant Research: Interfacing with Institutional Review Boards." In *Digital Writing Research: Technologies, Methodologies, and Ethical Issues*, edited by Dànielle DeVoss and Heidi McKee, 27–47. Cresskill, NJ: Hampton Press.
Bowdon, Melody. 2004. "Technical Communication and the Role of the Public Intellectual: A Community HIV-Prevention Case Study." *Technical Communication Quarterly* 13 (3): 325–40.
Cargile Cook, Kelli and Keith Grant-Davie. Eds. 2013. *Online Education 2.0: Evolving, Adapting, and Reinventing Online Technical Communication*. New York: Routledge.
Colton, Jared S., and Steve Holmes. 2018. "A Social Justice Theory of Active Equality for Technical Communication." *Journal of Technical Writing and Communication* 48 (1): 4–30.
Cox, Matthew B. 2018. "Shifting Grounds as the New Status Quo: Examining Queer Theoretical Approaches to Diversity and Taxonomy in the Technical Communication Classroom." In *Key Theoretical Frameworks: Teaching Technical Communication in The Twenty-First Century*, edited by Angela M. Haas and Michelle F. Eble, 287–303. Logan: Utah State University Press.
Dibbell, Julian. 1993. "A Rape in Cyberspace: How an Evil Clown, a Haitian Trickster Spirit, Two Wizards, and a Cast of Dozens Turned a Database into a Society." *The Village Voice*, December 23, 1993. http://www.juliandibbell.com/texts/bungle_vv.html.
Dolmage, Jay. 2008. "Mapping Composition: Inviting Disability in the Front Door." In *Disability and the Teaching of Writing: A Critical Sourcebook*, edited by Cynthia Lewiecki-Wilson and Brenda Jo Brueggemann, 14–27. Boston, MA: Bedford/St. Martin's.
Freire, Paulo. 1972. *Pedagogy of the Oppressed*. New York: Herder and Herder.
Frost, Erin A. 2015. "Apparent Feminist Pedagogies: Embodying Feminist Pedagogical Practices at East Carolina University." *Programmatic Perspectives* 7 (2): 251–76.
Frost, Erin A. 2018. "Apparent Feminism and Risk Communication: Hazard, Outrage, Environment, and Embodiment." In *Key Theoretical Frameworks: Teaching Technical Communication in the Twenty-First Century*, edited by Angela M. Haas and Michelle F. Eble, 23–45. Logan: Utah State University Press.

Grynbaum, Michale M. 2017. "Trump Calls the News Media the 'Enemy of the American People.'" *The New York Times*, February 17, 2017. https://www.nytimes.com/2017/02/17/business/trump-calls-the-news-media-the-enemy-of-the-people.html.

Haas, Angela M. 2012. "Race, Rhetoric, and Technology." *Journal of Business and Technical Communication* 26 (3): 277–310.

Haas, Angela M., and Michelle F. Eble. Eds. 2018. *Key Theoretical Frameworks: Teaching Technical Communication in the Twenty-First Century*. Logan: Utah State University Press.

Hayles, N. Katherine. 1999. *How We Became Posthuman: Virtual Bodies in Cybernetics, Literature, and Informatics*. Chicago, IL: University of Chicago Press.

Illinois State University. 2019. "English Studies Doctorate." https://illinoisstate.edu/academics/english-studies-doctorate/.

Jones, Natasha N. 2016. "The Technical Communicator as Advocate: Integrating a Social Justice Approach in Technical Communication." *Journal of Technical Writing and Communication* 46 (3): 342–61.

Jones, Natasha, Kristin Moore, and Rebecca Walton. 2016. "Disrupting the Past to Disrupt the Future: An Antenarrative of Technical Communication." *Technical Communication Quarterly* 25 (4): 211–29.

Jung, Julie. 2007. "Textual Mainstreaming and Rhetorics of Accommodation." *Rhetoric Review* 26 (2): 160–78.

Katz, Steven B. 1992. "The Ethic of Expediency: Classical Rhetoric, Technology, and the Holocaust." *College English* 54: 225–75.

McGonigal, Jane. 2011. *Reality is Broken: Why Games Make Us Better and How They Can Change the World*. New York: Penguin.

Ohio University. 2018. "English Ph.D." https://www.ohio.edu/cas/english/grad/english-phd/index.cfm.

Orlando, Jordan. 2018. "William Goldman Turned Reporters into Heroes in 'All the President's Men.'" *The New Yorker*, November 27, 2018. https://www.newyorker.com/culture/cultural-comment/william-goldman-turned-reporters-into-heroes-in-all-the-presidents-men.

Savage, Gerald, and Kyle Mattson. 2011. "Perspectives on Diversity in Technical Communication Programs." *Programmatic Perspectives* 3: 5–57.

Savage, Gerald, and Natalia Matveeva. 2011. "Seeking Inter-Racial Collaborations in Program Design: A Report on a Study of Technical and Scientific Communication Programs in Historically Black Colleges and Universities (HBCUs) and Tribal Colleges and Universities (TCUs) in the United States." *Programmatic Perspectives* 3: 58–85.

Scott, J. Blake, Bernadette Longo, and Katherine Wills, eds. 2006. *Critical Power Tools: Technical Communication and Cultural Studies*. New York, NY: SUNY Press.

Spangler, Susan. 2009. "Stop Reading Shakespeare!" *English Journal* 99 (1): 130–32.
Williams, Miriam F. 2010. *From Black Codes to Recodification: Removing the Veil from Regulatory Writing.* Amityville, NY: Baywood.
Williams, Patricia J. 1992. *The Alchemy of Race and Rights.* Cambridge: Harvard UP.
Yergeau, Melanie, Elizabeth Brewer, Stephanie Kerschbaum, Sushil K. Oswal, Margaret Price, Cynthia L. Selfe, Michael J. Salvo, and Franny Howes. 2013. "Multimodality in Motion: Disability and Kairotic Spaces." *Kairos: A Journal of Rhetoric, Technology, and Pedagogy* 18 (1). http://kairos.technorhetoric.net/18.1/coverweb/yergeau-et-al/pages/access.html.

Contributors

Joanne Addison is Professor of English at the University of Colorado Denver. At the heart of her work is a desire to empower people through increased access to written literacy. Her most recent co-authored book, *Writing and School Reform*, focuses on the barriers to accessing written literacy in the articulation from high school to college. She is currently working in the areas of online education and critical media literacy in an effort to expand our theoretical and pedagogical responses to the current challenges and opportunities of mass digital writing.

William P. Banks is Professor of Rhetoric, Writing, and Professional Communication at East Carolina University. In addition to directing the University Writing Program and the Tar River Writing Project, Will teaches courses in writing, research, pedagogy, and LGBTQ and young adult literatures. His essays on digital rhetorics, queer rhetorics, pedagogy, and writing program administration have appeared in several recent books, as well as in *College Composition & Communication*, *College English*, and *Computers & Composition*. He has edited multiple recent collections of scholarship, including *Re/Orienting Writing Studies: Queer Methods, Queer Projects*, and *Reclaiming Accountability: Improving Writing Programs through Accreditation and Large-Scale Assessments*.

Lisa Beckelhimer has taught at the University of Cincinnati since 1998, online since 2007, and in hybrid formats recently. She teaches primarily composition, but in her capacity as Director of Undergraduate Studies interacts with faculty and curricula in all areas of English studies. Her first task upon becoming Director was to revise the core five courses required of all English majors. In addition to a white paper with co-authors Ris and Griegel-McCord, Lisa has published articles and book chapters relating to online pedagogy and utilizing technology in the teaching of writing. You can contact Lisa at lisa.beckelhimer@uc.edu.

Dev K. Bose, PhD (he/him) is Assistant Professor of English at the University of Arizona, affiliating as Assistant Director in Writing Program, faculty in Rhetoric, Composition, and the Teaching of English, Faculty Fellow for Disability Cultural Center, and Co-Chair for Disability Studies Initiative. His research focuses on composition and professional writing, especially rhetorical privilege and access pertaining to technology and invisible disabilities. His work has appeared in *Disability Studies Quarterly, Deaf Studies Encyclopedia, Intermezzo, Enculturation, Pedagogue, Technoculture, Currents in Teaching and Learning, Journal of Business and Technical Communication*, and *Chronicle of Higher Education*. He is currently editing a second edition of *Disability and the Teaching of Writing: A Critical Sourcebook* (originally published in 2007 by Bedford/ St. Martin's).

Amy Cicchino is Associate Director for University Writing at Auburn University. She received her PhD from Florida State University in 2019. Her research, which spans writing program administration, digital multimodal pedagogy, and curriculum development, has appeared in *Research in Online Literacy Education (ROLE), WPA: Writing Program Administration,* and *ePortfolio as Curriculum* (2019).

Erin A. Frost is a technical communication, rhetoric, and composition specialist. Her employment history as an investigative journalist informs her work, and her scholarly interests center on issues of gender and feminism in technical communication, most often as they manifest in rhetorics of health and medicine, environmental rhetorics, and risk communication. She also engages in the scholarship of teaching and learning. Her work has appeared in *Computers and Composition, Journal of Business and Technical Communication, Technical Communication Quarterly, Programmatic Perspectives,* and *Peitho: Journal of the Coalition of Feminist Scholars in the History of Rhetoric & Composition*.

Michele Griegel-McCord is currently the Coordinator of Intermediate Composition for the University of Cincinnati's English Composition Program and serves as Coordinator of Online Instruction for the English department. Over ten years of experience teaching in online and hybrid environments has helped her develop a broad view of the complex nature of collegiate-level online instruction and administration. Her professional work and pedagogical interests address online writing instruction, multimodal composing practices, pedagogical impacts of new technologies, and popular culture rhetorics. You can contact Michele at griegeml@uc.edu.

John C. Havard is Associate Professor and Department Chair of English and Philosophy at Auburn University at Montgomery. His scholarship pertains to transatlantic and hemispheric conceptualizations of early American literature. His book, *Hispanicism and Early US Literature:*

Spain, Mexico, Cuba, and the Origins of US National Identity, was published in 2018 by the University of Alabama Press.

Marcela Hebbard is Lecturer in the Department of Writing and Language Studies at the University of Texas Rio Grande Valley where she teaches first-year composition, linguistic and teacher preparedness courses. Her research interests include online writing pedagogy, language and identity, first-year writing, translingual and transnational writing, writing across the curriculum, second language writing and teacher preparedness. She has published articles in *Across the Disciplines* and chapters in books. A recent collaborative chapter appears in the edited collection *Latinx identities and Literacy Practices at Hispanic-Serving Institutions* (SUNY Press, 2019).

Stephanie Hedge is Assistant Professor of English and the Writing Program Administrator at the University of Illinois Springfield. Her research includes digital literacies and practices, digital identities, game studies, writing program administration work, and digital pedagogies.

Ashley J. Holmes is Associate Professor of English and Director of Writing Across the Curriculum at Georgia State University in Atlanta. Her book *Public Pedagogy in Composition Studies* was published with the Conference on College Composition and Communication's Studies in Writing and Rhetoric series in 2016. Holmes has published articles in *Community Literacy Journal, Reflections, Kairos,* and *English Journal,* and she has chapters in the edited collections *Mobile Technology and the Writing Classroom* and *Overcoming Writer's Block*. She currently serves as co-editor for the Program Profiles section of *Composition Forum* and was awarded a university-level Instructional Effectiveness teaching award in 2019.

George H. Jensen is Professor of Rhetoric and Writing at the University of Arkansas—Little Rock where he teaches rhetorical theory and creative nonfiction. His books include *Personality and the Teaching of Composition* (with John K. DiTiberio, 1989), *Storytelling in Alcoholics Anonymous: A Rhetorical Analysis* (2000), and *Identities Across Texts* (2002). In addition to these scholarly books, he published *Some of the Words Are Theirs: A Memoir of an Alcoholic Family* with Moon City Press in 2009. He is currently publishing a series of essays on The Federalist Papers on his blog, *Democratic Vistas* (www.democraticvistas.com), and *Homo Academicus*, a serial novel about self-absorbed professors (www.homoacademicus.us).

Karen Kuralt is Associate Dean of the Graduate School at the University of Arkansas at Little Rock. She was the MA program coordinator in the Department of Rhetoric and Writing for twelve years. She teaches graduate and undergraduate courses in business and technical writing both on campus and online. A winner of the College of Social Sciences and Communication Faculty Excellence Award for Public Service, Kuralt has worked as a science editor and workplace writing trainer with a variety of organizations including the National Center for Toxicological Research (NCTR), the Arkansas Department of Human Services, the Arkansas Department of Environmental Quality (ADEQ), and the University of Arkansas Cooperative Extension Service. She is a member of the board of directors at Wildwood Park for the Arts in Little Rock and serves as the park's publicity coordinator.

Lilian Mina is Assistant Professor and the Director of Composition at Auburn University at Montgomery. She researches digital rhetoric with focus on multimodal composing and writing teachers' use of digital technologies. Her research in multilingual composition is centered around multilingual writers' use of digital technologies and examining their (digital) writing experiences. She is also interested in WPA scholarship, especially (technology) professional development of writing teachers, program assessment, and curriculum development. Her work has appeared in multiple journals and edited collections.

Catrina Mitchum is Lecturer in the Department of English at the University of Arizona. Her research interests are in retention in online writing courses, predesigned online courses, instructor presence in online courses, and online instructor preparedness. She has scholarly work published in *The Journal of Teaching and Learning with Technology*, *MediaCommons*, and *Enculturation*. She teaches first year writing and professional and technical writing courses online.

Janine Morris is Assistant Professor in the Department of Writing and Communication at Nova Southeastern University, where she is also a faculty coordinator at the NSU Writing and Communication Center. Her current research focuses on the affective dimensions of writing center work and on student experiences in online writing classes. Her other research on editorial work, reading, digital composing, and multimodal literacies appears in *College English*, *CEA Critic*, *Pedagogy*, and *Computers and Composition*.

Michael Neal is an associate professor of English at Florida State University, where he serves as the Director of the Graduate Program in Rhetoric and Composition. His research explores intersections between composition, digital technologies, and writing assessment, and he is the author of *Writing Assessment and the Revolution in Digital Texts and Technologies* (Teachers College Press, 2011). He teaches classes in digital composition and multimedia editing in the Editing, Writing, and Media major in English as well as graduate courses in composition and research methods at Florida State.

Cynthia Nitz Ris teaches primarily in the field of composition and has been teaching online since 2008. Her service work includes a wide variety of university-level committees, including work to promote shared governance through the faculty union and as Chair of Faculty Senate. Cynthia's scholarship and coursework are in the areas of first-year experience, online education, legal rhetoric, and the rhetoric of civil discourse. Conference presentations include best practices in online teaching and the use of legal issues and popular culture in composition pedagogy to foster understanding and analysis of complex civic issues.

Rochelle (Shelley) Rodrigo is the Senior Director of the Writing Program; Associate Professor in the Rhetoric, Composition, and the Teaching of English (RCTE); and Associate Writing Specialist (Continuing Status) in the Department of English at the University of Arizona. She researches how "newer" technologies better facilitate communicative interactions, specifically teaching and learning. As well as co-authoring three editions of *The Wadsworth/Cengage Guide to Research*, Shelley also co-edited *Rhetorically Rethinking Usability* (Hampton Press). Her scholarly work has appeared in *Computers and Composition, C&C Online, Technical Communication Quarterly, Teaching English in the Two-Year College, EDUCAUSE Quarterly, Journal of Interactive Technology & Pedagogy, Enculturation*, and various edited collections.

Cecilia D. Shelton is a technical and professional communication scholar whose work is situated at the intersections of digital and cultural rhetorics. She is currently Assistant Professor of English at the University of Maryland. Drawing on Black feminist theory and praxis, her research prioritizes the perspectives, goals, and experiences of Black people (and other communities structured into the margins) as a way to insist on more equitable solutions to contemporary social, political, and organizational problems. Her work is published in *Technical Communication Quarterly*, *The Journal of Multimodal Rhetorics*, and *Praxis: A Writing Center Journal* among other places. Her current project argues that the Black activist tradition is a kind of technical communication and offers a methodology that enables a cultural rhetorical framing of technical and professional communication.

Heidi Skurat Harris is Associate Professor of Rhetoric and Writing at the University of Arkansas—Little Rock where she coordinates the Graduate Certificate in Online Writing Instruction and is the advisor for the online BA in professional and technical writing. She is the lead editor of the *Bedford Bibliography of Research in Online Writing Instruction*, and her publications on online writing instruction have appeared in *Comp Studies*, *Technical Communication Quarterly*, *Computers and Composition*, *Communication Design Quarterly*, and the collections *Applied Pedagogies: Strategies for Online Writing Instruction* and *Weathering the Storm: Independent Writing Programs in the Age of Fiscal Austerity*.

Susan Spangler has taught online for the last decade at the State University of New York at Fredonia and has earned a certificate in instructional design from the Online Learning Consortium. Throughout her career, Susan has taught at the secondary level and in higher education, and she served as a technology liaison for the Illinois State Writing Project, a local chapter of the National Writing Project. She has developed numerous courses for the English department at Fredonia in every area of English studies, including writing, language, teacher education, and literature. Susan currently serves on the Committee of Online Learning at Fredonia as well as the United University Professionals Online Education Advisory Committee. She reviews manuscripts for *English Journal* and teacher-designed lesson plans for NCTE's ReadWriteThink website.

Katelyn Stark is a PhD Candidate at Florida State University, where she teaches upper-level writing and editing classes in the Editing, Writing, and Media major and serves as the Assistant Director to the College Composition Program. Her research investigates writing knowledge transfer, graduate TA preparation, and writing across the curriculum.

Eric Sterling earned his PhD in English from Indiana University in 1992. He is Professor of English at Auburn University at Montgomery, where he has taught for twenty-five years. He serves as director of the

Master of Liberal Arts program, the only interdisciplinary graduate program in Alabama.

Richard C. Taylor is the author of *Goldsmith as Journalist* (1993) and co-author of *New Century Literature* (2016), along with essays and reviews on British culture and multi-ethnic literatures. He has served as coordinator and advisor for the Multicultural and Transnational Literatures concentration in the English Department at East Carolina University, and in 2017 was selected as UNC Board of Governors Distinguished Professor for Teaching.

Index

ableism, 228, 260
Acapella, 139
accessibility, 5, 15, 17, 32, 34, 51, 62, 79, 87, 91, 100, 144, 146–148, 151–152, 155,–160, 185, 189–190, 198, 228–229, 248, 258–261, 263, 266–273, 275–276, 278, 284, 298, 314
accessible courses, 17, 272
Acrobat, 269
ADA compliance, 100, 228
adjunct faculty: see faculty: adjunct
administrators, 1–2, 6, 12–13, 15, 17, 25, 35–37, 50–53, 60–61, 62, 75–79, 86, 145, 160, 226, 234, 239–240, 248–249, 259–261, 263, 268, 272, 274–76
adult learning theory, 33
Agarwal, Nina, 95, 104
Al-Aswany, Alaa, 301–302
Alcoff, Linda, 297, 302
American Disability Act, 73
American Sign Language (ASL), 260
Arab Spring, 301
architecture, 261
assessment, 5, 13, 24, 26, 30, 33, 35, 38, 43, 64, 68, 75, 114, 124, 164, 178, 207, 217–218, 225, 227, 258, 265, 269, 271, 274–275, 277, 285, 298
assignment sheets, 15, 91, 113, 116–118, 123–124, 143–144, 146–150, 152–153, 155–160, 186, 189, 225, 276
assistive technologes, 261–262
Association of Departments of English (ADE), 42, 44, 57, 142, 143, 148, 161
asynchronous online discussion, 131
Atkins, Anthony, 110, 126
at-risk students, 62, 64, 66
Auburn University at Montgomery (AUM), 13, 60–65, 67, 70, 74, 76,–78, 81, 88
audio, 29, 68–69, 103, 147–149, 160, 179, 239, 242, 247, 265–266, 313
authenticity, 74, 84
author interviews, 44
auto-captioning, 152–153

Baker-Bell, April, 11, 22
Bakhtin, Mikhail, 96
Barber, John, 66, 68, 81, 86–87, 91–92, 94–96, 101, 104
Battershill, Claire, 158, 161
Bawarshi, Anis, 144
Black Lives Matter, 282
Black students, 11
Blackboard, 30, 62, 67, 71–75, 79, 88, 96, 102, 105–106, 112, 115, 119, 131, 311
Blackboard Collaborate, 73, 75
Blair, Kristine L., 44, 57, 111, 126, 194

327

328 Index

Blakeslee, Sarah, 89–90, 104
Blogger, 116, 214
blogging assignments, 148–150, 152, 154–155, 157–158
blogs, 44, 101, 106, 108–109, 131, 140–141, 143, 146, 149–150, 163–164, 188, 190, 214–216, 255
Bowling Green State University, 111
Brescoll, Victoria, 206, 219
Breuch, Lee-Ann Kastman, 67, 69, 82
Brown, Jr., Michael, 282, 290
budgets, 41, 301
Burns, Hugh, 4, 59, 247, 250
Bush, Jeb, 20
Butler, Janine, 153, 161

Canva, 28
Canvas, 116, 131–132, 138, 188
career advancement, 272
Cazden, Courtney, 140, 191, 199, 203, 219
CCCC: see Conference on College Composition and Communication
Center for Applied Special Technology (CAST), 161, 259, 261–269, 279–280
certificate programs in online writing instruction, 304
chatrooms, 294–295
Christensen, Ward, 130
chunking, 87, 149, 154, 155–157, 159–160, 162
citation practices, 86, 148
Civil Rights Movement, 292
Clark, Cynthia, 63
Clark, J. Elizabeth, 109
class discussion, 15–16, 68, 73, 115, 132, 134, 183, 190–193, 201–203, 205–208, 210, 213, 217–219, 228, 239
classrooms: flipped, 52, 73

closed captioning, 73, 189, 261
Collaborate Ultra, 79–80
collaborative learning, 133, 283
collaborative spaces, 14
College Composition and Communication (journal), 82, 104–105, 127, 162, 171, 174, 181, 183, 251, 253, 255, 281
community building, 30, 297
community colleges, 1, 3, 226
community of practice (CoP), 41, 50–51, 56
compensation, 5
composing practices, 8, 84, 121, 267
composition courses, 65–66, 77–79, 81, 84–86, 102, 125, 184
Computers and Composition (journal), 4, 23, 39, 126, 171, 174, 180, 181, 199, 200, 250, 253, 255, 278
Computers and Composition Online (journal), 171, 174
computers and writing, 3, 18
Computers and Writing (conference), 4, 180
Conference on College Composition and Communication (CCCC), 4, 6, 22, 24, 32–33, 35, 39, 65–67, 70, 82, 97, 170, 175–176, 181, 254
contact zones, 95, 286
contingent faculty: see faculty: contingent
Cooke, Sam, 293
Course Management System (CMS), 115, 150, 152–157, 164–165, 255
courses: asynchronous, 2, 9, 28, 71, 74, 79, 91–92, 120, 130–131, 141, 194, 227, 239, 270, 286; predesigned (PDCs), 17, 259, 271–278; synchronous, 15, 29,

33, 36–38, 73, 79, 91–92, 103, 129, 130, 132, 134, 137, 139–141, 194, 195, 197, 201, 227, 238, 247, 249
COVID-19, 18–19, 60, 75, 78, 89, 129, 143, 145, 160, 182, 185, 198, 217–218, 270, 305
Crafting Digital Writing (Hicks and Lehman), 7, 22
CRAP (contrast, repetition, alignment, proximity), 229
CRAPP test (currency, relevance, authority, accuracy, and purpose), 89–90, 104
creative writing, 9, 42, 45, 106, 119, 146, 234, 243, 306
Crello, 28
cultural studies, 292, 299
culturally sustaining pedagogy, 237
Cuomo, Andrew, 20

D, F, or Withdrawal (DFW) rates, 62, 63, 64, 76, 77, 78, 80
D2L, 96, 131, 164
Daniels, Harvey, 133, 141
de-centering (teacher's authority), 309, 312
decolonialism, 17, 309
democratization, 1
Department of Education (US), 171–173, 176–177, 256
DePew, Kevin Eric, 6, 22, 68, 82–83, 105, 254
Dewey, John, 170
DFW: see D, F, or Withdrawal (DFW) rates
digital archives, 44
digital humanities, 8, 110, 158
digital literacy, 3, 44, 107, 109–110, 113–114, 120–121, 123
digital platforms, 1, 15, 191, 229
digital stories, 143, 158

digital tools, 4, 10, 44, 131, 134–135, 143, 224, 227
Digital Writing Workshop, The, (Hicks), 7, 22
disability services, 100
disciplinary practices, 48–49, 51, 55, 110–111, 128, 168, 213, 223–224, 274, 288, 291, 293, 297, 299
discussion, 15–16, 68, 73, 115, 132, 134, 183, 190–193, 201–203, 205–208, 210, 213, 217–219, 228, 239; face-to-face, 202, 205, 213; online, 31, 71, 74, 130, 190–91, 202–203, 205, 213, 215–216, 218–219, 239, 313
discussion boards, 33, 38, 44–45, 52, 73–74, 108, 130–131, 137, 140, 183, 186, 190–192, 198, 239, 241, 245
distance education, 18, 71, 171, 283–289, 291, 294–298, 307, 313
document design, 26, 28, 225
Dolmage, Jay, 121, 147, 161, 258, 260, 278–279, 281, 309, 315
Drupal, 131

East Carolina University, 128, 315
emergent technologies, 106, 107, 109, 110, 115, 118, 121
engagement, 2, 9–10, 15, 19, 38, 41, 51–54, 69, 73–74, 77, 93, 95, 113, 115, 124, 135, 137, 147, 158, 183, 186–187, 194, 202, 213, 222–223, 233, 242, 246–247, 259, 261–262, 265, 270, 273, 285, 293, 294, 297, 305, 308–309; emotional, 95
English departments, 8, 12, 43, 44, 46, 142–143, 158–159, 248, 273, 278, 284
English majors, 42–43, 143, 148, 158

enrollment, 27, 30, 41, 55, 61, 66, 70–71, 236, 289, 308
eportfolios, 108, 115, 123, 185, 195
equity, 16–17, 230, 250
ethics, 16–17, 258–259, 263, 298, 307
evaluation, 5, 10, 68, 133, 152, 179, 191, 201, 207, 217
extroverts, 206
Eyman, Douglas, 147, 161

F2F (face-to-face teaching), 1, 19, 36, 37, 38, 68, 76, 91, 108, 112, 120, 124, 132, 134–135, 137–139, 150, 157–159, 183, 185–194, 196–199, 208, 213, 217–219, 232–233, 237–238, 245–246, 248, 286, 289, 296
Facebook, 31, 96, 105, 115–116
faculty: adjuncts, 36–37, 46–47, 49, 50, 78, 79, 111, 270–274, 278; contingent, 17, 46–67, 68, 69, 234, 259, 272–273
faculty buy-in, 35–36, 37, 112
faculty governance, 53
Fanon, Franz, 299
feminism, 17, 305, 311
Fetzner, Marie, 63, 82
first-year composition, 14, 60, 62, 65, 78, 111, 125, 258, 260
first-year composition (FYC), 65, 80, 258, 260
Fleckenstein, Kristie, 108, 126
Flickr, 44
Flipgrid, 74, 82
flipped classrooms, 52, 73
Flynn, Ellen, 64, 82
focus groups, 25, 35
Foundational Practices of Online Writing Instruction (Hewett and DePew), 6, 22, 82–83, 105, 252, 254, 281

From Texting to Teaching (Hyler and Hicks), 7, 23
Frost, Robert, 292, 303

Gates, Bill, 20
Gates, Melinda, 20
gender, 8, 205, 216–217, 238, 272, 296
general education, 42, 125, 270, 276–277, 284
Georgia Perimeter College, 145
Georgia State University, 145
GLBTQ studies, 299–300
Google Apps, 29, 30
Google Docs, 10, 69, 108, 186, 192, 195, 198
Google Drive, 163, 265
Google Meets, 138
Gos, Michael, 64, 69, 82
grading, 73, 114, 124, 164, 207, 250, 264, 288
graduate certificate program in online writing instruction, 24, 32, 34, 38
graduate students, 25, 30, 37–38, 46–47, 49–50, 72, 79, 106, 107, 110, 132, 136–138, 140, 185–186, 272
graduate teaching assistants (GTAs), 36–67, 68–69, 185, 278
graduation rates, 55, 63, 289
grammar checkers, 11
Grant, Cary, 296
graphic literature, 15, 208–212
Greer, Jane, 32–34, 38, 39
Griffin, June, 66, 82
Grouling, Jennifer, 144, 161
GTAs: see graduate teaching assistants (GTAs)

Haley-Mize, Shannon, 154, 156–157, 161

Hangouts (Google), 134–141, 195–196
Harman, Kristyn E., 183, 199
Hawisher, Gail, 3, 4, 22, 110, 127
Hayes, John R., 169, 251
Herman, Peter, 20–21
Hesse, Douglas, 168, 181, 273, 279
Hewett, Beth L., 6, 22, 29, 39, 82–83, 100, 105, 127, 183, 199, 244, 252, 254, 281
Hicks, Troy, 7, 22, 23, 59
higher education, 1, 3–4, 8, 10, 18–19, 20, 56, 80, 111, 125–126, 175, 204, 222–223, 234, 288, 290
Hillocks, Jr., George, 16, 168–170, 175–181
Hispanic students, 233, 236
holistic feedback, 91
homophobia, 228, 291
hooks, bell, 298, 303
Howard, K. Shannon, 74
humanities, 2, 8, 12, 18, 41, 54, 182–183, 301
hybrid model, 4, 6–7, 9, 12, 15, 36, 42, 44, 46–49, 80, 142–146, 150, 154, 157, 159–160, 172–173, 183, 185, 199, 260, 270, 274, 313
hyflex model, 35–36
Hyptothes.is, 269

iCollege, 150, 152
identity, 14, 18, 108, 113, 120–122, 185, 205, 216, 223, 226–227, 230, 237–239, 249, 260, 287–288, 291, 293–294, 296, 300–301, 311, 312; disciplinary, 48–49
inclusion, 16, 169, 230, 239, 250, 272, 275, 291
infographics, 143, 146
insecurities, 240–241, 249
institutional pressure, 46
institutional support, 245–247
instructor: roles, 111
interactivity, 15, 31–32, 74, 84, 151–152, 157, 158, 160, 185
introverts, 141, 206, 218
Iowa Writers Workshop, 9
iPads, 144, 161
IRE (intiate, respond, evaluate), 191, 203–205, 208, 218
iterative design, 33–34, 38

Jay, Paul, 291
journalism, 17, 26, 146, 305, 307–309, 314
journalists, 19, 308

K–12 schools, 3, 6–7, 132, 139, 234
Kairos (journal), 126, 147, 161–162, 171, 174, 281, 317
Kaltura, 153
Kershbaum, Stephanie, 151–152, 155
Kiefer, Kate, 183, 196, 199
Kindle, 264

labor, 17, 20, 46, 153, 157–158, 175, 189, 224–225, 228, 246, 250, 258–259, 263, 265, 270–273, 276, 278, 295, 309
Lanham, Richard, 4
Latinx literature, 298
Lauter, Paul, 291, 303
learning centers, 84–86, 90–91, 93, 94, 99, 101–103
learning disabled (LD) writers, 260
learning management system (LMS), 10, 19, 30, 37–38, 49, 52, 54, 62, 68–69, 72, 84, 86, 88, 92–93, 95–97, 99–100, 103, 108, 115–116, 118, 123, 131, 138, 167, 180, 182, 188, 190, 197, 242–243, 245–247, 266, 268, 276
Leave It to Beaver, 204

lesson plans, 119, 282, 304
LGBTQ studies, 298
LGBTQ-themed courses, 137, 298
liberal arts education, 12
librarians, 14, 85, 88, 89–90, 94, 101, 103, 257, 265
libraries, 1, 84–86, 88, 89–91, 93–95, 99–103, 106, 136, 189, 196, 245, 247, 252, 280–281
library guides (LibGuides), 88–90, 94
linguistic background, 234–236, 238–239, 244, 249, 260
literacy, 4, 14, 66, 90, 99, 109, 121–122, 142, 161, 174; critical, 109; digital, 3, 44, 107, 109–110, 113–114, 120–121, 123
literary theory, 44
literature circles, 129–130, 132–135, 239
literature courses, 44, 76–78, 129, 132
LMS: see learning management system

Manjoo, Farhhad, 149, 162
mapping applications, 269
marginalization, 288
McLuhan, Marshall, 108, 127
mental health, 40
Mick, Connie Snyder, 73, 82, 91–92, 100, 105
Microsoft Word, 143–144, 148, 150, 162
Middlebrook, Geoffrey, 82, 91–92, 100, 105
migration (of courses online), 67, 198, 293, 300, 308
millennials, 72
Miller, Susan Kay, 171
Minter, Deborah, 66, 67, 68, 82, 83
modeling, 14, 33, 57, 86, 139, 149, 152, 158, 221

modes of instruction, 168, 170, 172, 176–180, 227
monolingualism, 236–238
MOOCs, 41, 109, 173
Moodle, 115
Moran, Charles, 4, 22, 149, 162
motivation, 194, 241–242, 263, 265, 297
multiculturalism, 136, 289–290, 300
multiethnic literatures, 18, 283, 288–289, 291–292, 294
multilingual students, 66, 234, 237
multimedia, 29, 69, 160, 240, 261, 267
multimodality, 15, 147–148, 151–153, 156–158, 160

National Center of Education Statistics, 41
National Writing Project, 7, 139
neoliberalism, 20
Netflix Party, 139
New London Group, 143, 148, 162
North Carolina Virtual Public School, 7

office hours, 69, 75, 225, 314
online degree programs, 12–13, 18, 24–25, 27, 30, 36, 38, 145, 308
online pedagogy, 2, 9, 63, 112–113, 130, 185, 187, 221
online programming, 13–14, 55, 60–62
online writing course (OWC), 69
online writing instruction, 3–6, 12, 16, 22, 24, 32–34, 37, 65–68, 70, 74, 82–83, 93, 105, 108, 167, 170–173, 175–176, 181, 183–187, 189, 194, 232, 254, 281
online writing tutoring (OWT), 91–93

outcomes: learning, 31, 35, 42, 49, 56, 80, 122, 171, 208, 224, 232, 275, 277
OWI principles, 5–6, 32, 66–68, 170, 175, 186–187

Padlet, 69
pandemic (influence on teaching), 18–20, 37–38, 40, 42, 44, 46–50, 52, 54, 75, 93, 102–103, 107, 125–126, 130, 132, 138, 145, 160, 182, 185, 217–218, 223, 270, 278
panopticon, 287, 294
pedagogy, 7, 9, 11, 14, 50, 52, 60, 62, 65, 79, 91, 106–119, 123, 125, 128, 182–183, 187, 191, 198, 216, 221, 224, 259, 273, 283, 299, 304, 309, 311; critical, 8; digital, 3, 5, 7–12, 16, 48, 67–68, 85, 106–108, 112–114, 116–120, 123, 125–126, 133, 160, 175, 183, 185, 187, 192, 198–199, 222, 232–234, 236–237, 248–249, 270, 272, 274, 276, 287, 305, 314; in-person, 2, 19, 20, 44, 48, 88, 128, 130, 135, 137–138, 160, 172; online, 2, 9, 63, 112–113, 130, 185, 187, 221
peer review, 2, 9, 38, 69, 87–88, 124, 132, 139, 163–164, 169, 174, 177, 185, 264–265, 276
philosophy courses, 62–63, 67, 70, 76, 78–80, 114, 115, 119–120, 122–123, 178, 195
plagiarism, 11, 86
podcasts, 157, 160
poetry, 137, 159, 285, 291, 293–294
polls, 73
portfolios, 26, 30, 38, 114, 123–125, 242
PowerNotes, 264, 269

PowerPoint, 59, 69, 80, 94, 103, 128, 286
predesigned courses, 17, 258, 271, 273, 275–278
presentations: video, 75, 97
Prezi, 116
print media, 308
professional development, 5–6, 13, 41, 46–47, 49–50, 52–53, 55–56, 60–61, 65, 68, 70, 74, 76–78, 85, 101, 102, 128, 144, 179, 199, 258, 271, 273
professional identity, 286
professional writing, 25, 42, 267
public writing spaces, 95, 97, 99
Pullman, George, 99, 105
Purves, Alan C., 169

queer frameworks, 17, 136–137, 298–299, 309, 313
queer theory, 137, 299
QuickTime, 152
quizzes, 11, 52, 154, 227

race, 8, 205
racist language practices, 11
rapport, 34, 50, 79, 187, 194
Read the World: Rethinking Literacy for Empathy and Action in a Digital World (Ziemke and Muhtaris), 7, 23
reading, 7–9, 19, 28, 29, 41, 44, 64, 66, 73, 87, 102, 106, 109, 113, 132–136, 142–143, 149–150, 155, 159, 162, 174, 186, 190–194, 201, 209–214, 224, 227, 239, 263–264, 286, 301, 313; digital, 44, 57
Reading Workshop 2.0 (Serafini), 7, 23
Reiff, Mary Jo, 144
retention, 34, 38, 60, 61–64, 74, 76–78, 85, 103–104, 171, 187,

234, 243–245, 247, 249, 258, 263, 273
rhetoric, 15, 26, 37, 87, 99, 143, 146, 159, 204, 214–215, 273–274, 306
rhetorical awareness, 43, 239
rhetorical situations, 43, 153
Ross, Shawna, 158, 161
rubrics, 87, 155, 179, 210–211, 218, 265–266, 275–276

SafeAssign, 11
scaffolding, 68, 137, 192, 239, 244, 264, 272, 274, 312
Scholarship of Teaching and Learning (SoTL), 10, 253
Second Life, 109, 314
Selber, Stuart, 109, 127, 143, 162
Selfe, Cynthia, 3, 4, 22–23, 96–97, 99, 101, 104–105, 109–110, 127, 143, 152, 162, 317
Serageldin, Samia, 301
sexuality, 8
Shakespeare, William, 2, 276, 285, 291, 312–313, 317
Skurat Harris, Heidi, 12, 24, 26, 32–34, 38–39
Skype, 75, 192, 196
Slack, 69, 106, 116, 120
slavery, 310
SLOs: see student learning outcomes
smartphones, 72
Snart, Jason, 95, 105
social interaction, 47, 194
social justice, 16–18, 221, 226, 230, 288, 299, 301, 306–307, 309, 312, 314
social justice pedagogies, 314
social media, 44, 68, 95–96, 101, 163
SoTL: see Scholarship of Teaching and Learning

Spivak, Gayatri, 299, 301, 303
stakeholders, 49–50, 118, 226–227, 248, 259–260, 273, 275
Stern, Barbara Slater, 285, 303
stipends, 71
Stotsky, Sandra, 169
Strudler, Neal, 63–64, 82
student backgrounds, 17, 233–234
student conferences, 69, 93
student learning outcomes (SLOs), 31, 35, 42, 49, 56, 80, 122, 171, 208, 224, 232, 275, 277
student preparedness, 78
student-centered classes, 84
students: at-risk, 62, 64, 66; background, 17, 232–234; graduate, 25, 30, 37–38, 46–47, 49–50, 72, 79, 106–107, 110, 132, 136–138, 140, 185–186, 272; nontraditional, 35, 61, 69–70, 72, 77, 261, 313; of color, 306, 310; working-class, 69, 237
Suess, Randy, 130
support services, 51, 54, 245, 247
syllabi, 16, 75, 94, 113–114, 123–124, 147, 156–158, 185, 221–230, 245, 272, 275, 282

TA training, 110–111
Tannen, Deborah, 206, 220
Taparia, Hans, 19–21
teaching: during the pandemic, 18–19, 60, 75, 78, 89, 129, 143, 145, 160, 182, 185, 198, 217–218, 270, 305; ethical, 16, 259, 263, 298; reflective, 177, 180, 199
teaching online, 8, 14–15, 21, 28, 36, 47, 49, 51, 56, 60, 67–68, 78, 79, 107, 108, 111–112, 114, 116, 120, 128–129, 144, 148, 160, 197, 199, 201, 216, 232, 239, 249, 258–259, 271, 304–305

teaching philosophy, 107–108, 115, 118, 120, 123, 195
technical and professional communication, 221–222, 225
technical writing, 12, 24–27, 39, 42, 44–45, 151, 171, 267, 270
TED Talks, 157, 284
testing, 11, 14, 33, 128, 171, 180, 182, 197, 202, 267, 295
threaded discussion, 131, 190
time management, 51, 64, 243–244
transfer (of skills), 41, 43
transnationalism, 290
TurnItIn, 11
tutor training, 85
tutoring, 91–92, 125, 247, 260
Twitter, 109, 116, 310–311

ubiquitous computing, 1
UDL: see Universal Design for Learning (UDL)
universal design (UD), 17
Universal Design for Learning (UDL), 144, 146–147, 157–158, 258–259, 261–273, 277, 280
University of Arkansas at Little Rock (UALR), 12, 24–25, 27, 29–30, 39
University of Illinois Springfield, 14, 106
University of Phoenix, 10
Usenet, 131

Vectr, 28
video conferencing, 28, 49, 69, 73, 138–139, 196
video lectures, 44, 69, 186

video technologies, 29, 69
videoconferencing, 74
Voice over Internet Protocol (VOIP), 29
VoiceThread, 266

Walden University, 10
Walters, Shannon, 147, 151, 155–156, 162
Warnock, Scott, 6, 22, 67, 69, 77, 83, 108, 127, 172, 181, 188, 232, 234, 239, 244, 246, 252, 256
Watters, Audrey, 295, 303
Web 2.0, 109, 278
Weebly, 96–97, 99
West-Puckett, Stephanie, 139
wikis, 109, 131, 140
Williams, Patricia, 63, 81, 190, 200, 229, 231, 307, 310, 317
Wix, 96–97, 99, 196
WordPress, 131, 149, 162
workshopping, 16, 119, 194–198
World Wide Web, 4, 131, 280, 301
writing instruction: online, 3, 12, 16, 24, 32, 93, 108, 167, 170–173, 175, 176, 183, 185, 232
writing program administrators (WPAs), 5, 65, 68, 174, 181, 269, 279

Yancey, Kathleen Blake, 97, 101, 105, 269, 280,
YouTube, 28, 44, 97, 116, 134, 138, 152–153, 155

Zoom, 29, 36, 45, 75, 79, 80, 102–103, 186, 196

www.ingramcontent.com/pod-product-compliance
Lightning Source LLC
Chambersburg PA
CBHW031434230426
43668CB00007B/526